SHUNGA + BIJINGA = EROTICA

First published in the United Kingdom in 2018 by Kahboom Ltd.

office@kahboom.com

ISBN: 978-0-9576275-5-0

Printed by Kopa in Lithuania

SHUNGA + BIJINGA = EROTICA

FROM THE
COLLECTION OF
BOB BENTLEY

Kahboom

Notes for the reader

HISTORICAL PERIODS

Edo:	1615 - 1858	**Showa:**	1926 - 1989
Mejji:	1858 - 1912	**Heisei;**	1989 - present
Taisho:	1912 - 1926		

COLOUR IMAGES

All colour images are woodblock prints from the collection - unless otherwise stated.

Woodblock: made of cherry wood for duplicating images - one for each colour/component.
Originals: a term for prints made at the time of creation - sometimes 'first strike' prints.
Re-prints: subsequent printings from after the creation date, usually from new blocks.
Bokashi shading: a gradation technique commonly used for depicting sky and/or sea.
Mica: a crystalline mineral with a metallic appearance used for backgrounds and highlights - and sometimes random effects.
Sumi drawing: original image on thin paper for pasting onto woodblocks for carving.

BLACK & WHITE IMAGES

The black & white images are not in the collection. They are used for reference to help the reader understand context. Artists are not in the content listing.

TITLES & TEXT

Every featured artist is in **Bold**
The series titles and/or book names and authors are in *italics*.
Known titles for individual works are in *'italics and have single quote marks'*
Quotes of dialogue taken from the print texts in are in 'regular with single quote marks'
Spelling of names is simplified so **Eishōsai Chōki** is written as **Eishosai Choki.**

PRINT SIZES

The most common print sizes for Japanese prints are *Oban*, *Chuban* and *Aiban,* although there are many others. Dealers often refer to their print sizes using these names instead of precise measurements.

Format	Size in inches	Size in cm
Aiban	9 x 13	22.5 x 34.5
Chuban	7.5 x 10	19 x 25.5
Oban	10 x 15	25.4 x 38

Most portrait shaped prints in this book are Oban.
Triptychs are usually three Oban sized sheets in a row.
Diptychs are usually two Oban sized sheets next to each other.
Sometimes there are vertical diptychs, one sheet above the other.
The books here have closed sizes of:

6 x 8.77	15.5 x 22.5
4.75 x 7.20	182 x 120

EXTRAS & RUMINATIONS

These are on a coloured background at the end of each chapter.
This is an opportunity to show images and discuss issues that don't easily fit within the timeline.

CONTENTS

DOES NOT INCLUDE OTHER ARTISTS REFERRED TO AND UNKNOWN ARTISTS

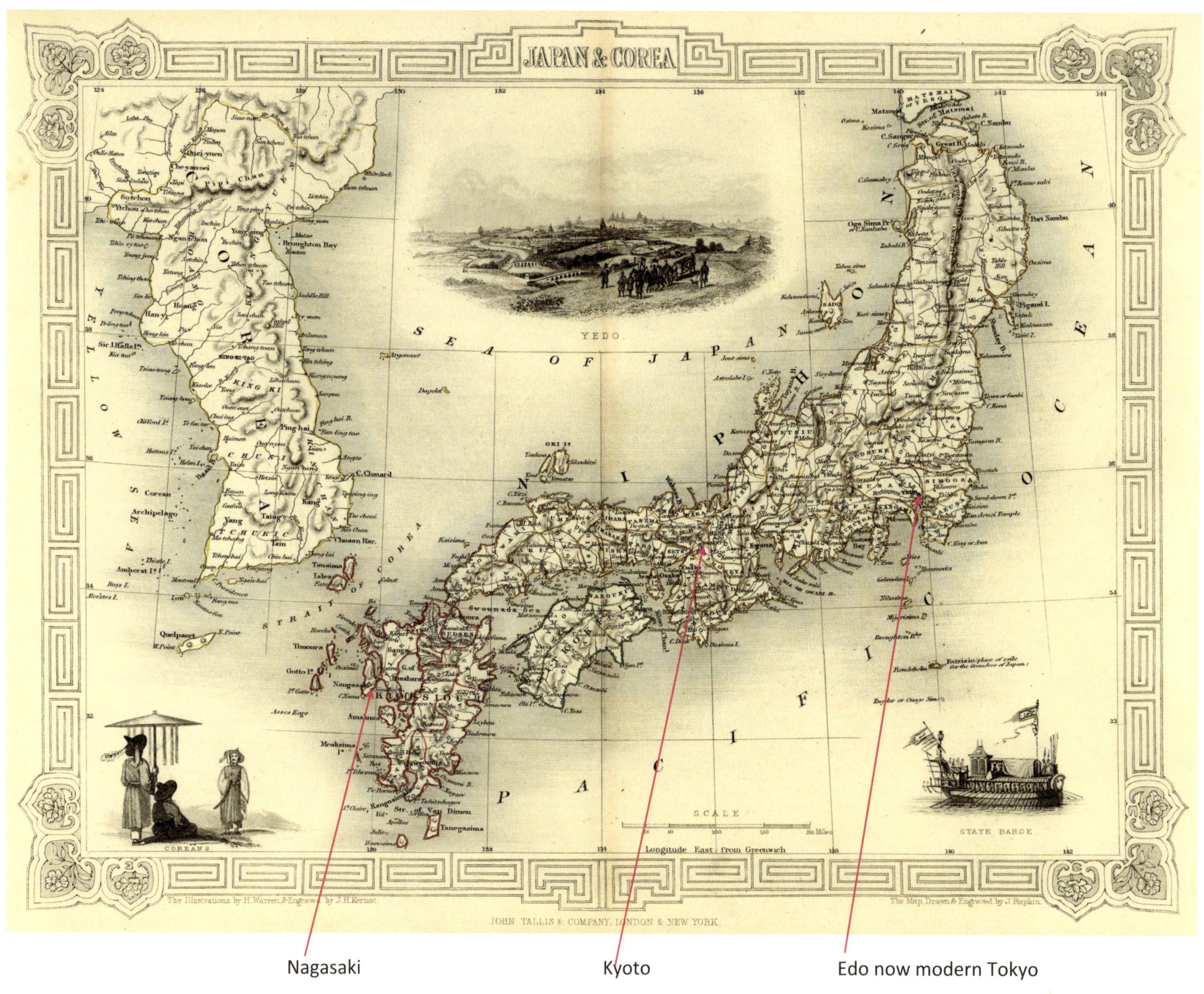
JAPAN & COREA
YEDO.
SEA OF JAPAN
PACIFIC OCEAN
COREANS.
STATE BARGE.
SCALE
Longitude East from Greenwich
The Illustrations by H. Warren & Engraved by J.H. Kernot.
The Map Drawn & Engraved by J. Rapkin.
JOHN TALLIS & COMPANY, LONDON & NEW YORK.
Nagasaki
Kyoto
Edo now modern Tokyo

Introduction

WHAT THIS BOOK IS ABOUT

This book is about the shunga and bijin-ga in Japanese art. The genres are inextricably linked, with artists moving effortlessly between both, together creating the erotic landscape of a unique culture. The translation of shunga is 'spring pictures' but means 'erotic art'. The translation of bijin-ga is 'pictures of beautiful people' meaning women, commonly referred to as 'beauties'.

The setting for the book is Japan, based on a period when the country was isolated from the rest of the world - through to a time in the late 1800's when the beauty of its art and style exploded into the western imagination. Up until then for almost three hundred years the pursuit of pleasure was the principal ambition in a society that had all but eliminated war and conflict. The images describe a fascinating life-style, with pictures of 'The Floating World' (ukiyo-e) and then on to less idealistic times. Eventually the rise of nationalism put paid to this way of life - leading to the disaster of the 2nd World War. The pictures tell the story of people who lived out their lives in a Japan that no longer exists - and into a new modern age.

PERSONAL INTRODUCTION BY BOB BENTLEY

I became interested in this art through making a programme in a series for British television (BBC) called *The Private Life of a Masterpiece*. It was about Hokusai's *'The Great Wave'*, a modest woodblock print that has become the best known image in Japanese art. Hokusai's shunga and bijin-ga intrigued, as well as other subjects, and gradually I started to acquire a few prints. After becoming more and more drawn in over a 12 year period, the collection has expanded considerably.

This book is just about the shunga and bijin-ga in my collection. There is a very definite link between them, as both are erotic in nature, the shunga explicitly about sex and the bijin-ga about beautiful women, many of them courtesans or women seen as subjects of sexual desire. But of course there is a lot more to it than that.

However, this is not an academic book, but more a personal journey of discovery by an accidental collector. I hope to inform, entertain and perhaps inspire like-minded fellow travellers who are embarking on similar explorations.

I have acquired a few rare and valuable original prints, as well as a larger number of inexpensive ones, including reprints, some of which are almost as wonderful.

This territory is a minefield, but nonetheless wonderful to explore. Some people collect for financial reasons, trading at the top end, where a very rare print might cost thousands of dollars at auctions making them too valuable to put on show. An old reprint, made exactly the same way and similarly aged can be extraordinarily inexpensive - often for much less than $100 - suitable to adorn a living room, bedroom or anywhere else.

This is the most wonderful art that almost anyone can acquire - at one level or another. As prints there may be several of the same image, but no two are identical. That is part of the appeal, along with not knowing how many impressions exist, with so many destroyed in fires, wars and earthquakes, etc.

So, in buying prudently, it is possible to enjoy originals by the greatest artists, to hang alongside affordable and beautifully crafted reprints.

I collect all types of print, principally woodblocks, with the occasional etching or lithograph (but no modern reproductions). My preference is artwork with history, enjoying the idea of being a temporary custodian of a print that could have had a dozen or more owners over the past few hundred years - or maybe just a couple of decades. I like the print with patina and well thumbed corners, evidence that many admirers have inspected it or turned the page.

Chapter 1

THE GOLDEN AGE

the late 1600's to the beginning of the 1800's

WE BEGIN THIS JOURNEY through the long history of shunga and bijin-ga with the prints in my collection that belong to the early period of Japanese woodblock printing - the late 1600's and the 1700's, long before full colour printing was possible.

Sugimura JIHEI (active c.1681-1698)

I'm including this old reprint because it is an example of 17th century shunga in black & white - although some editions were hand coloured. This is the cover picture of a series of twelve dated mid 1680's by **Jihei**, considered one of the founders of the ukiyo-e with the depiction of locations and setting expressing the 'floating world' of pleasure. The elaborately decorated kimonos have led some to wonder if **Jihei** had at one point studied textile design.

In the image we see a slightly older woman wanting to make a threesome with a young couple. Sex was often conducted in view of other people and voyeurism is a common theme which we will see again - and again!

Okumura MASANAOBU (1686-1764)

This is *'A Beauty after a Bath and Cockeral'* (c.1730) with a hen partly obscured. The cockerel has special iconographic meaning in Japanese mythology and the inscription reads 'Covered in sweat, a hen and her jealous spouse'. The 'beauty' has just had a bath and stepped onto her verandah with a yukata loosely draped around her - to be confronted by the birds.

Masanobu was a hugely significant artist in the early to mid 18th century and is particularly admired for for his bijin-ga.

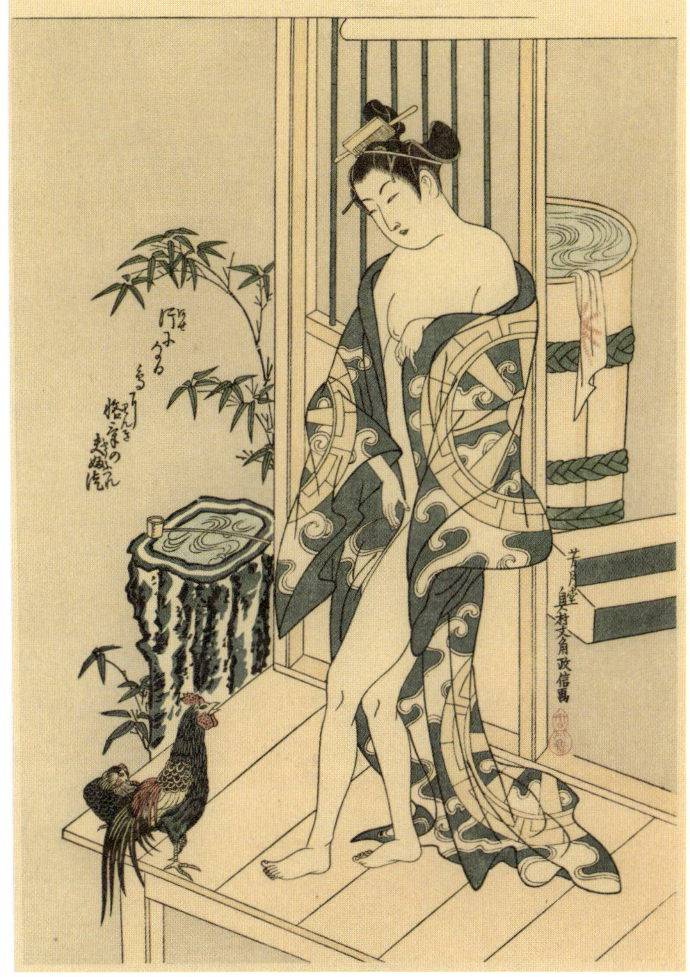

Unknown Artist (c.1790)

This pair of original prints (c.1790) are from the same story book. Peeking through or around walls and listening for tell tales sounds has been a dubious pass-time over the ages, everywhere!

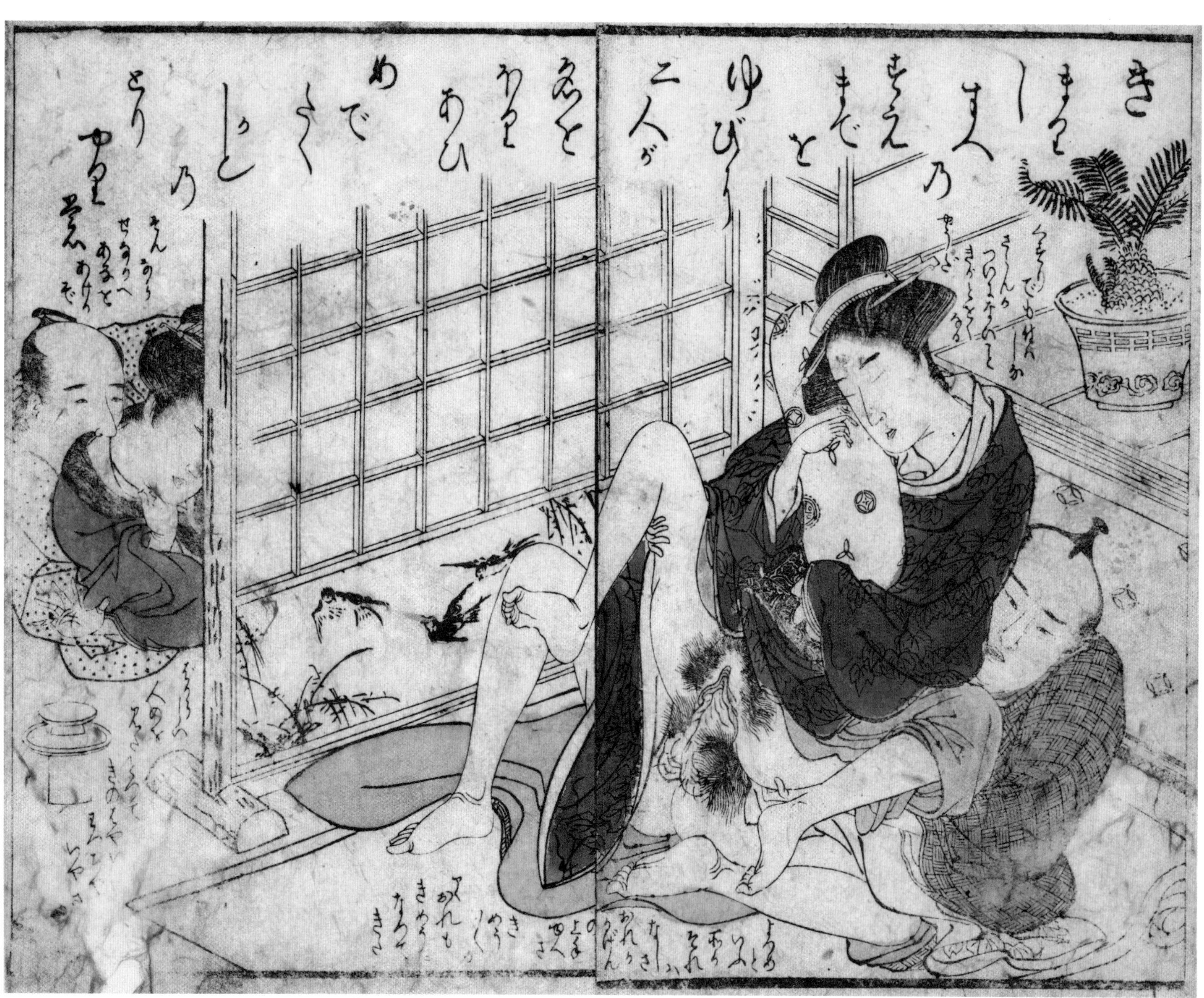

In shunga young children often appear, but not as participants. They just happen to be around or in the way when the adults are getting intimate. Here, the pointing child seems to be noticing somewhat inconvenient and unwanted attention.

With these prints there is an attempt to hand colour, although the pigment has lost it's vibrancy. It looks inept, so perhaps it was done at a later date.

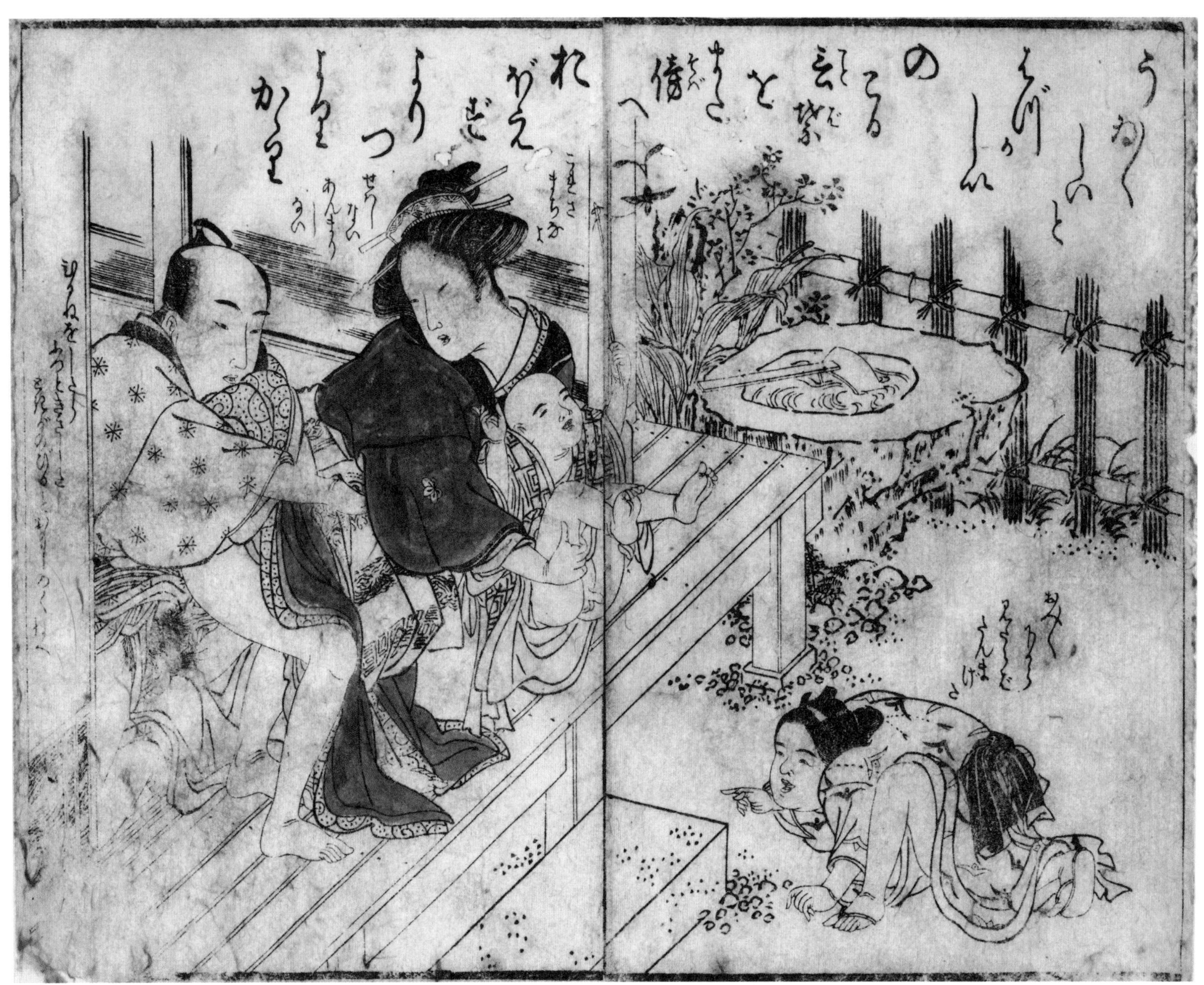

Takahara SHUNCHOSAI (1772-1801)

One could speculate that the same applies here, as the hand applied paint doesn't seem to match properly. Most likely it is a 'doodle' colouring in by a previous owner. Whatever the case this is a part of its history - which remains a wonderful double page.

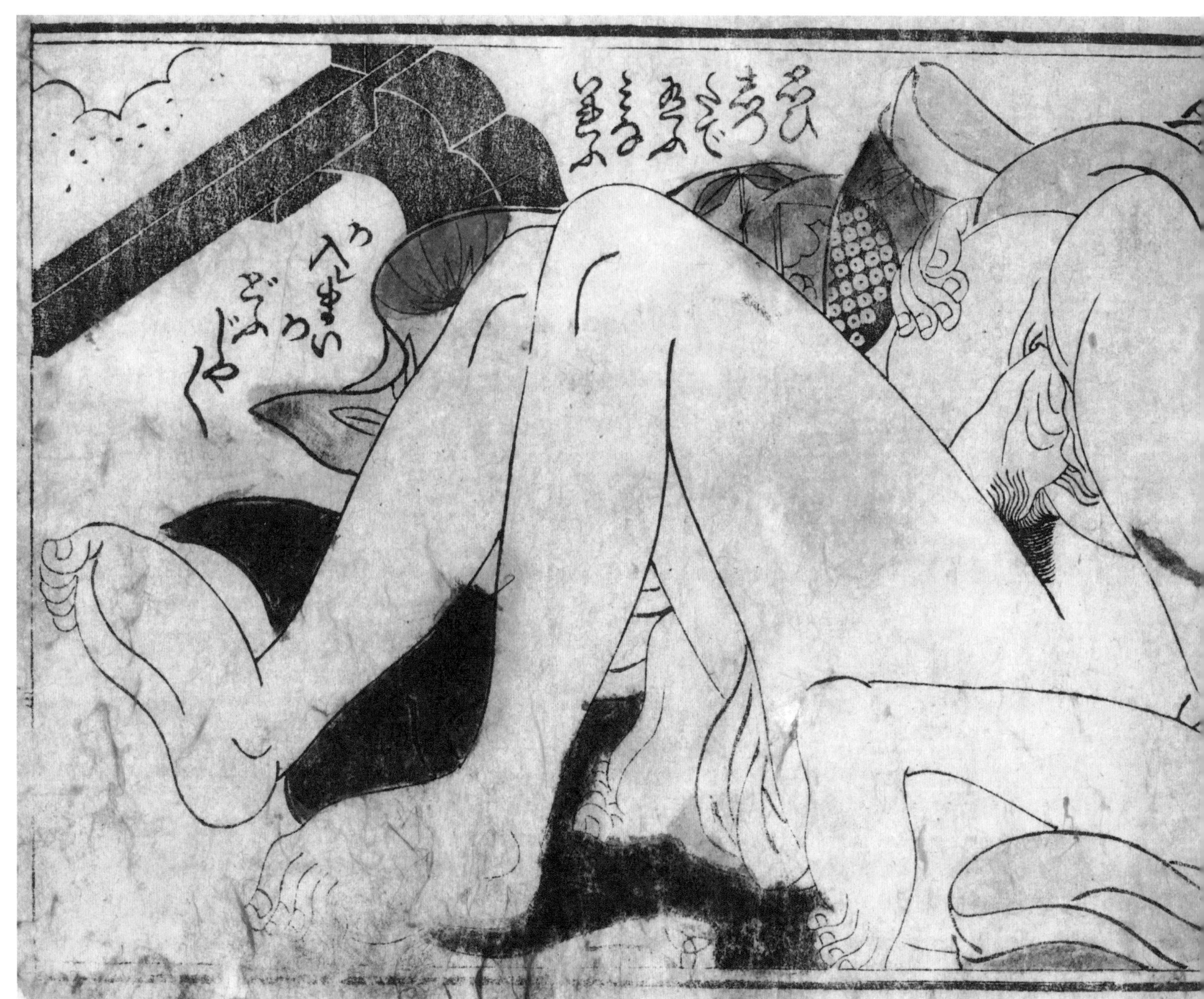

Shunchosai was known mostly for landscapes so it is rare to come across such a shunga. I find this print extraordinarily modern and could have been created by Picasso, who was known to be an enthusiastic collector of shunga.

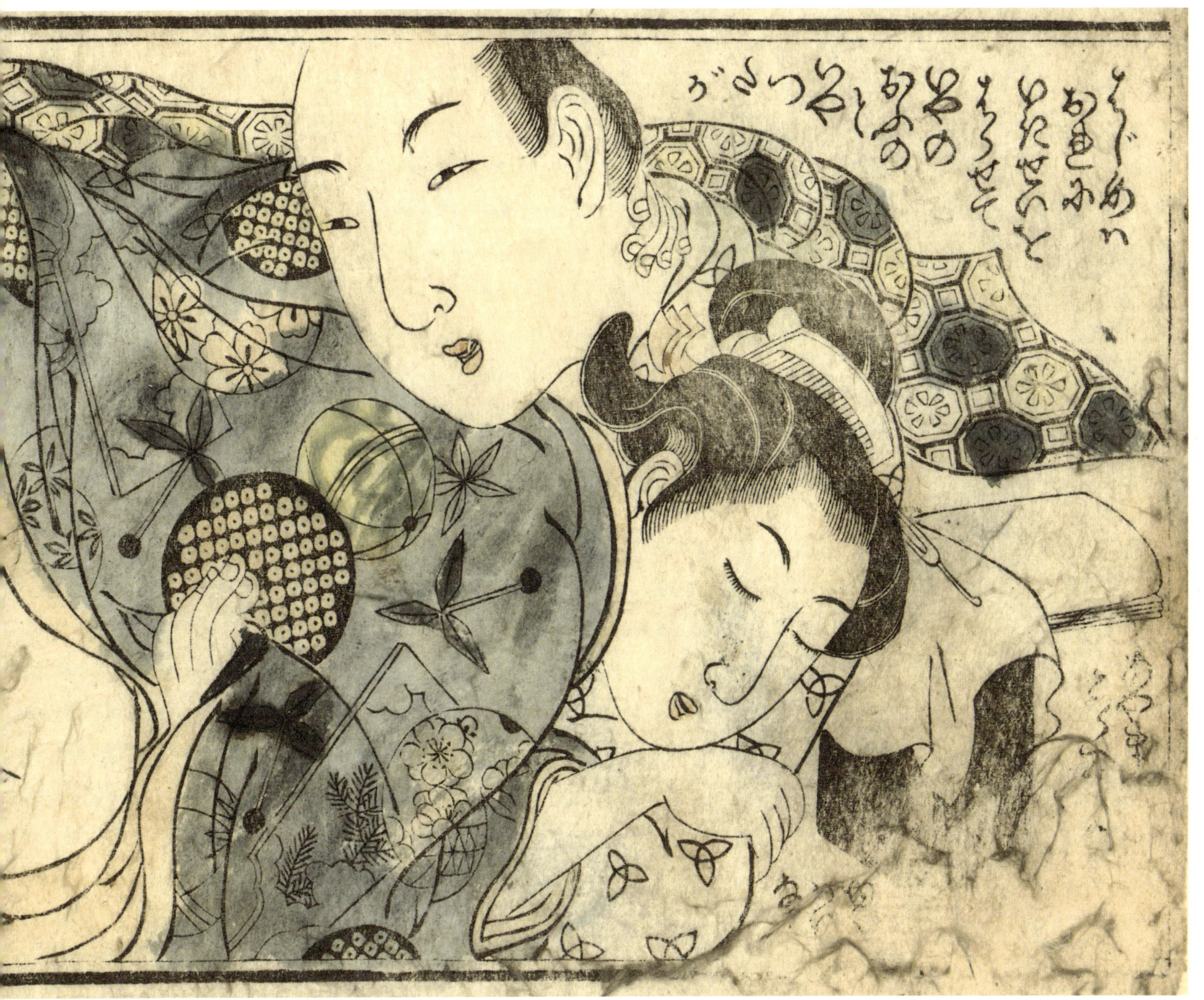

Katsukawa SHUNCHO (active 1780-1795)

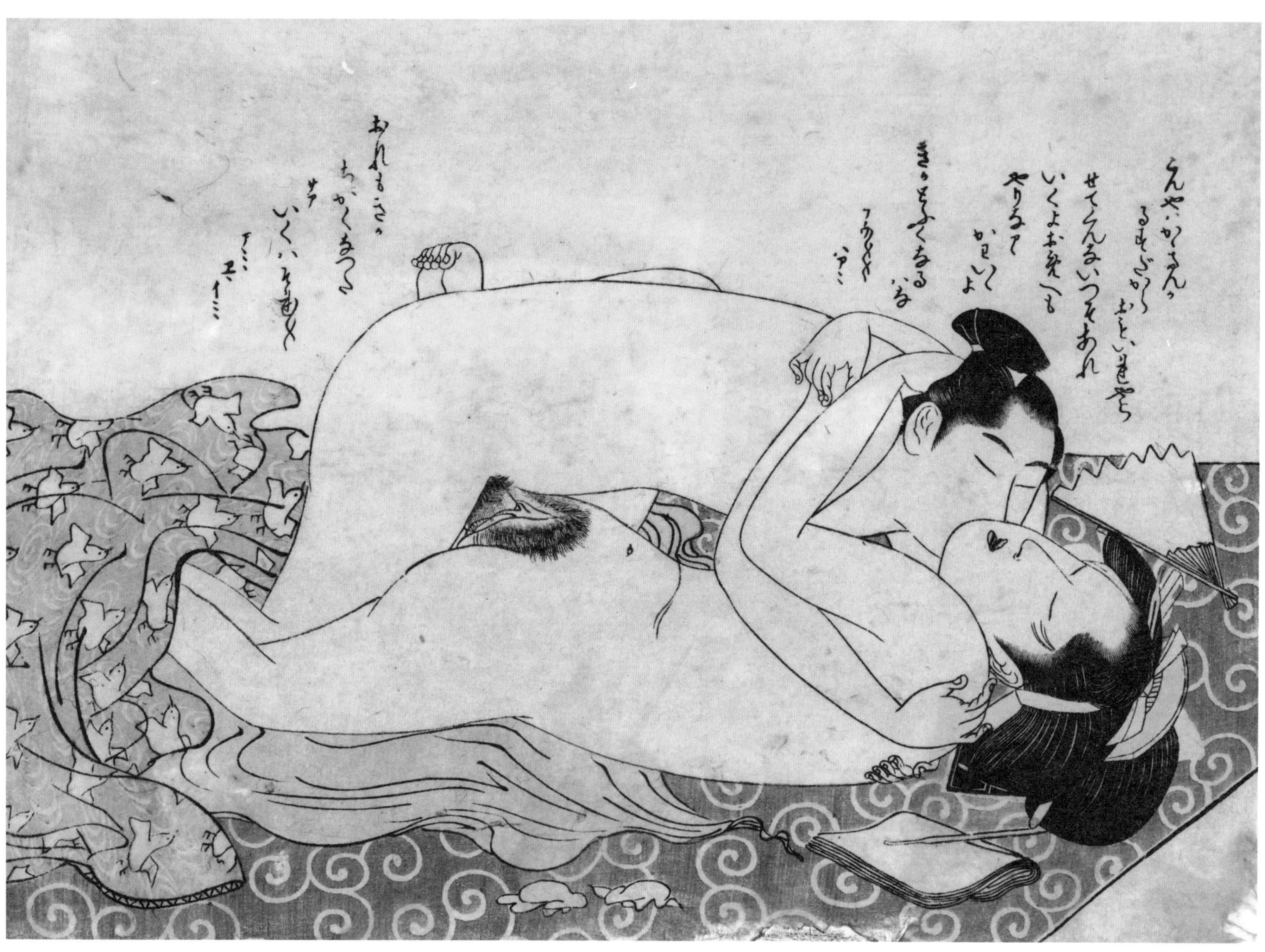

Others active in the 2nd half of the 18th century include **Shuncho**, who shows tender simplicity in this image of a couple, even though described as a courtesan and client (c.1786).

Many Japanese artists at this time had real difficulty drawing naked bodies so elaborate use of dress and drapes made up for it. In this charming image by **Shuncho** we see a number of 'beauties' hanging around chatting - with a cat on a lead.

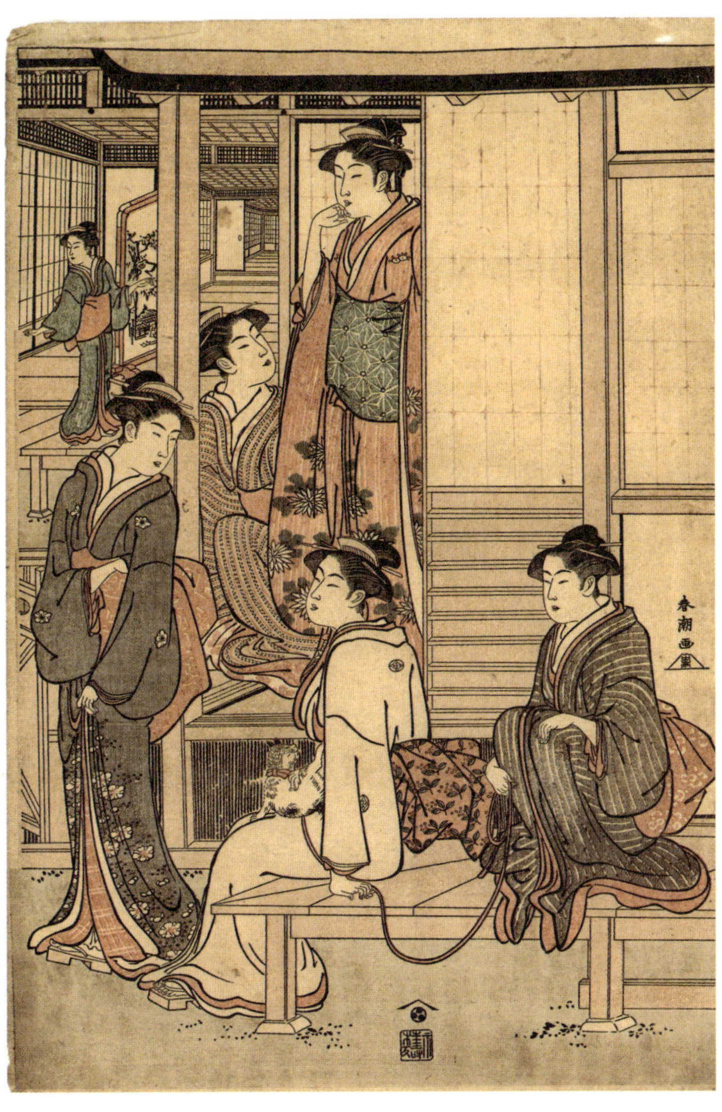

Suzuki HARUNOBU (c.1725-1770)

Here is an attempt at a full nude by **Harunobu**, although this reprint has been self censored, with genitalia omitted. It is in a sub-genre of shunga known as risque (abuna-e), half way between the full-on erotic and non explicit. I love the frog gazing up at the woman (c.1765-70).

The nude in Japanese art contrasts with the European experience which has at it's basis the traditions of realistic nakedness in Greek and Roman art - the Renaissance representing the high point of western sophistication.

Drawing from life was unheard of in Japan so the nude figures have a naive, somewhat 'primitive' quality. **Harunobu'**s young women, clothed or unclothed are often very slender - some say just like children. It is this that epitomizes **Harunobu'**s personal style as the celebrated authority, Richard Lane, describes: '**Harunobu**'s special province, one in which he surpassed all other Japanese artists - eternal girlhood in unusual and poetic settings'.

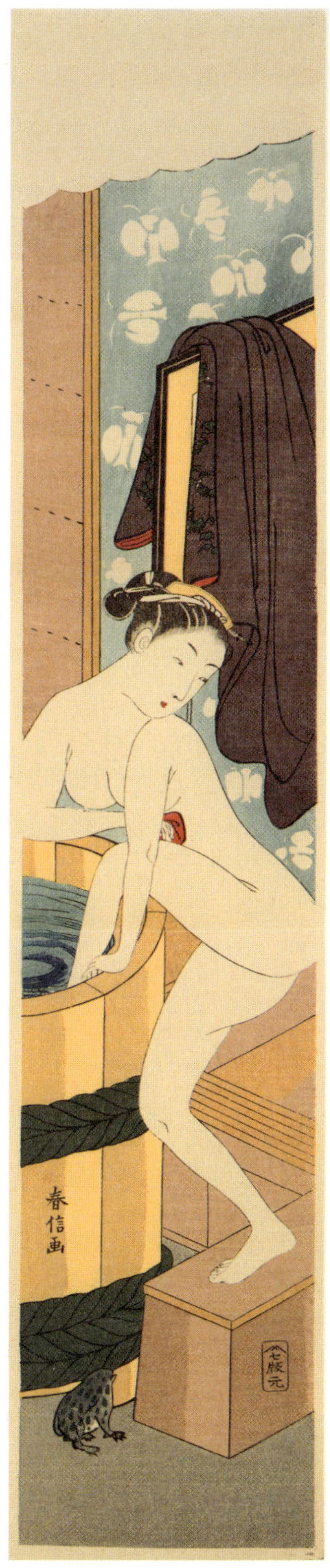

Original shunga by **Harunobu** are rare, like this of a man being shared by two women - although on this occasion the one on the right is not so slim (c.1765-70). In many of the late 18th century prints there is, what appears to be, the representation of clouds or mist. This is a nod towards an old Japanese aesthetic - perhaps to give gravitas or more likely to venerate tradition.

Around this time **Harunobu** devised multicolour woodblock printing, known as 'brocade', a technique that gradually all artists adopted. He became immensely popular with examples we can see here. Unfortunately he struggled with the demands of so much work, and the stress combined with a drink problem led to an early death - at only 46.

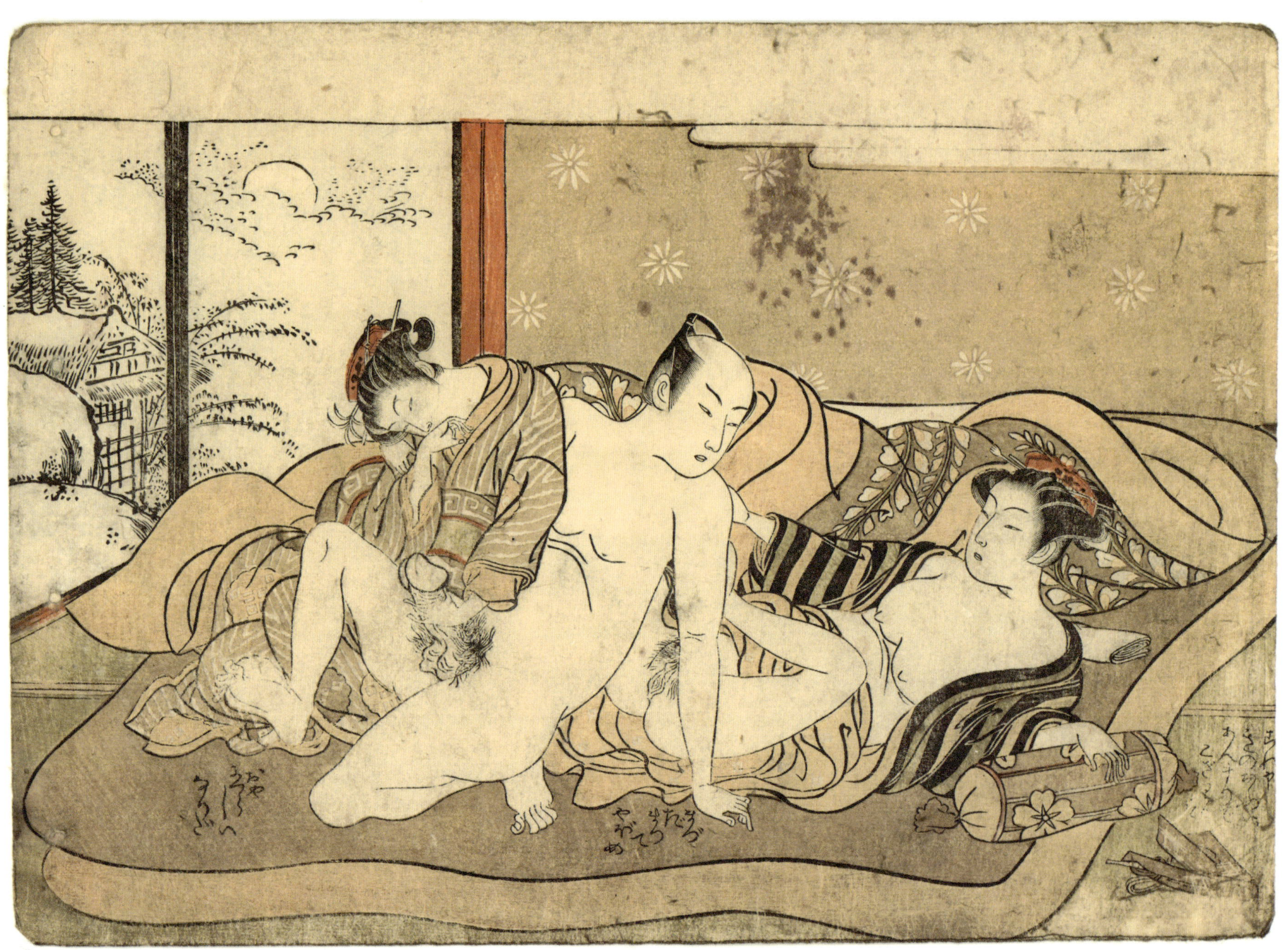

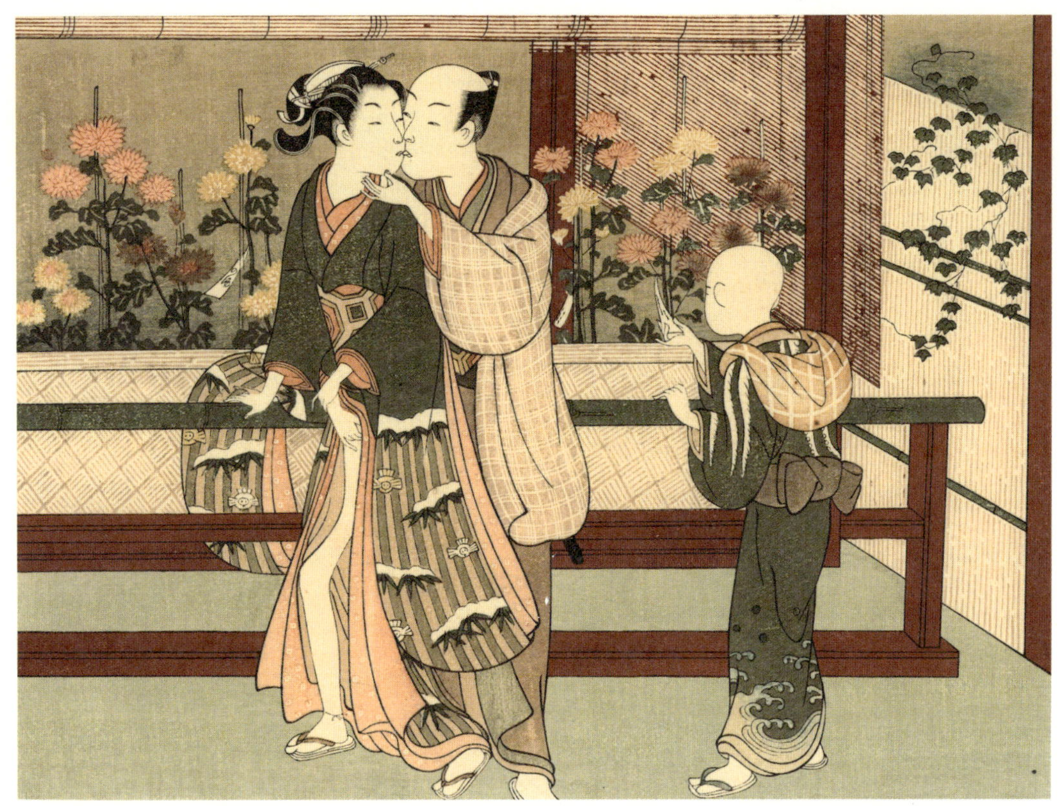

But no clouds or mist here. There are many reprints of **Harunobu**'s shunga and an example is this fine old Meiji version of a couple engaging in digital pleasure, at a chrysanthemum exhibition - accompanied by a child. (c.1765-70)

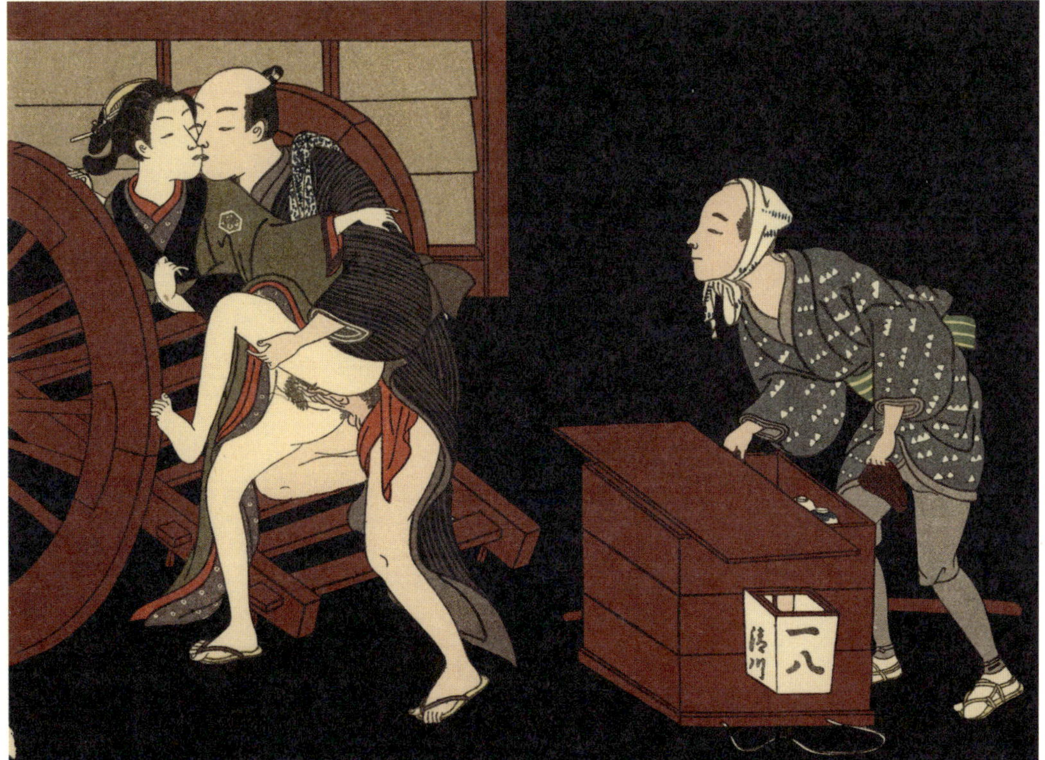

Depiction of more extreme outdoor activities show a sense of humour that appealed to the collectors at the time, as they do now.

This reprint is titled: *'A couple making love are discovered by a noodle vendor in the night'* (c.1766)

The shunga are attention grabbing, but **Harunobu**'s bijin-ga have always been popular. Inexpensive reprints are easily available - like this lovely picture of a 'beauty' lighting a lamp.

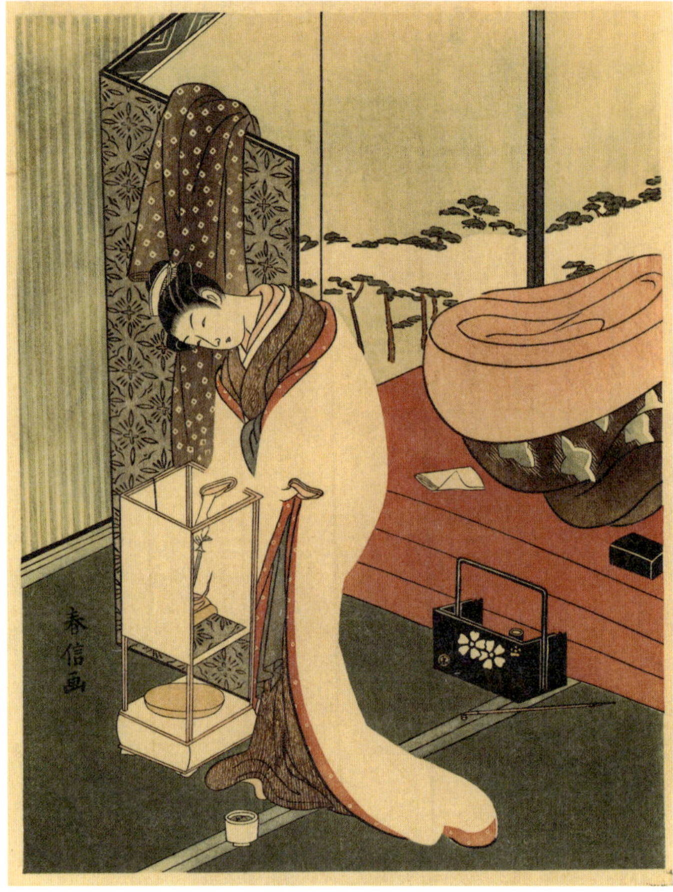

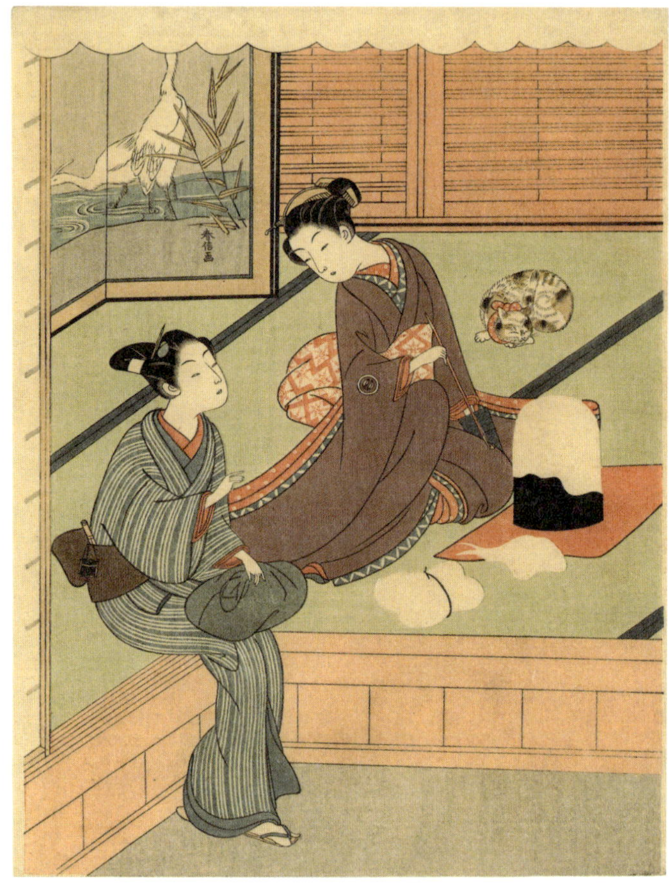

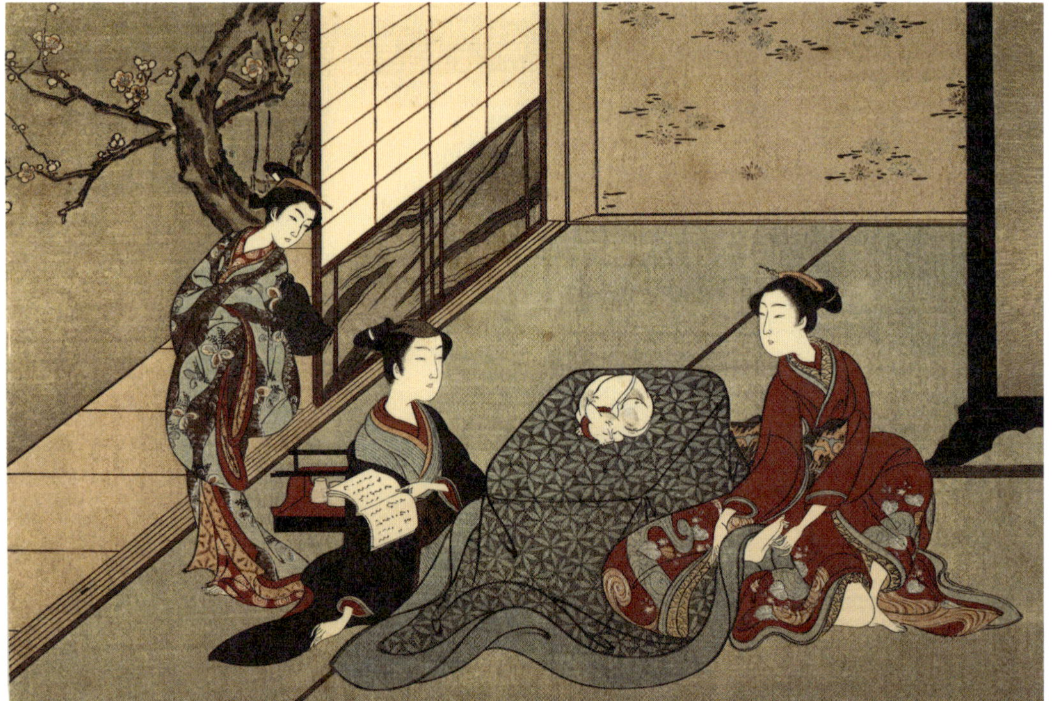

This is an interesting image of a woman stretching silk (or cotton), watched by a young man - which has sexual undercurrents not instantly obvious. It was generally known that most women working in 'floss stretching shops' were illegal, unlicensed prostitutes. **Haranobu** would have been fully aware of this, adding an erotic charge to an otherwise innocent encounter. He has signed his name on the screen behind the couple.

He also loved cats - which appear in two of these images, and is the centre of attention in this one.

Harunobu was obsessed with waitress Osen, who he depicted countless times at her tea stand outside the Kasamori shrine (see the red pillars). In the 1st print she is canoodling with a fan seller, in the 2nd fixing the hair of a young man playing a shamisan, in the 3rd serving tea to a young samurai and in the 4th eloping with her lover.

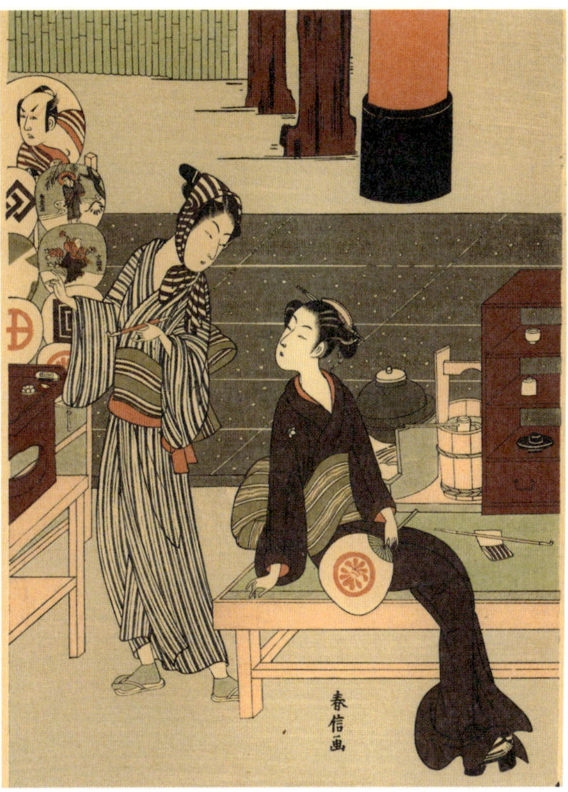

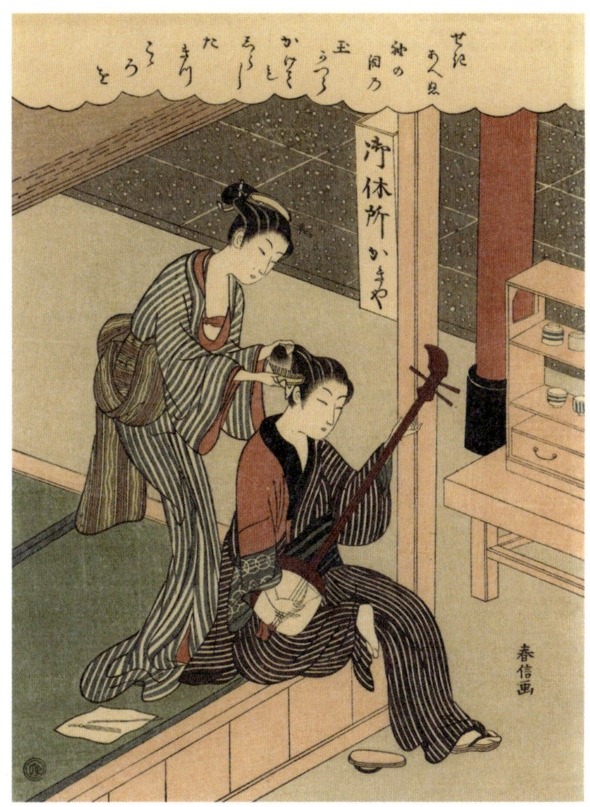

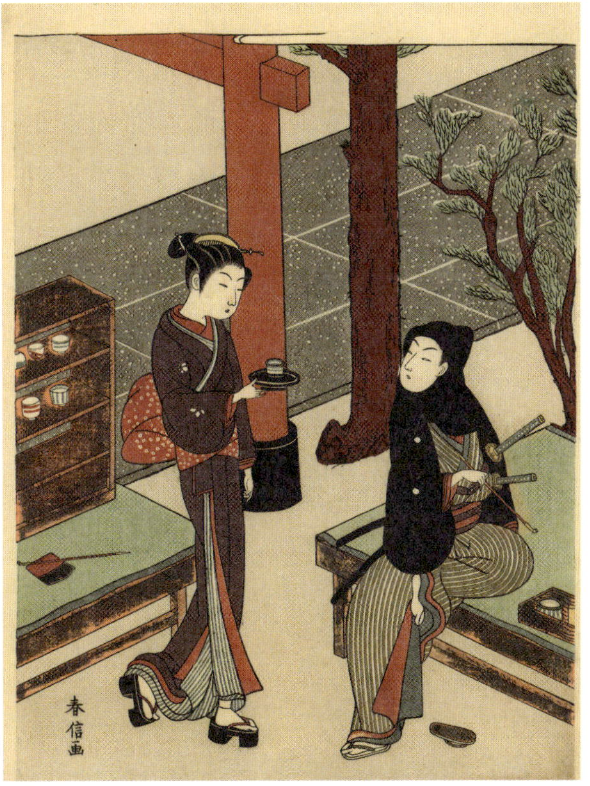

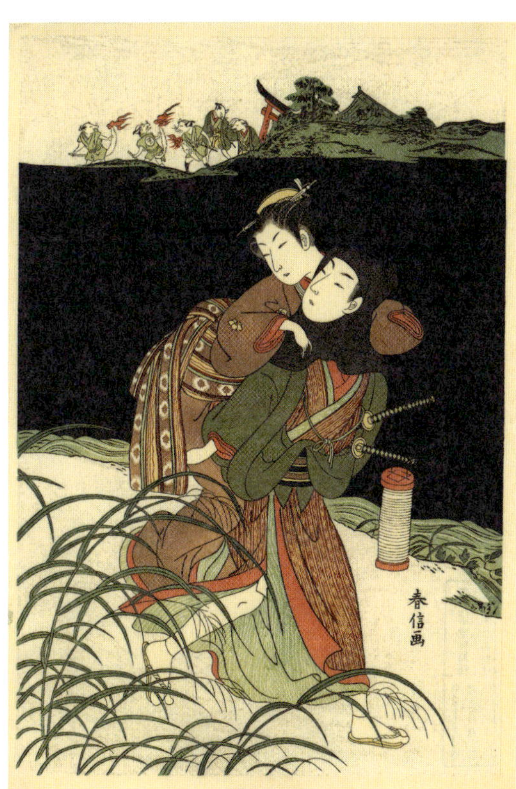

Ippitsusai BUNCHO (1765-1792)

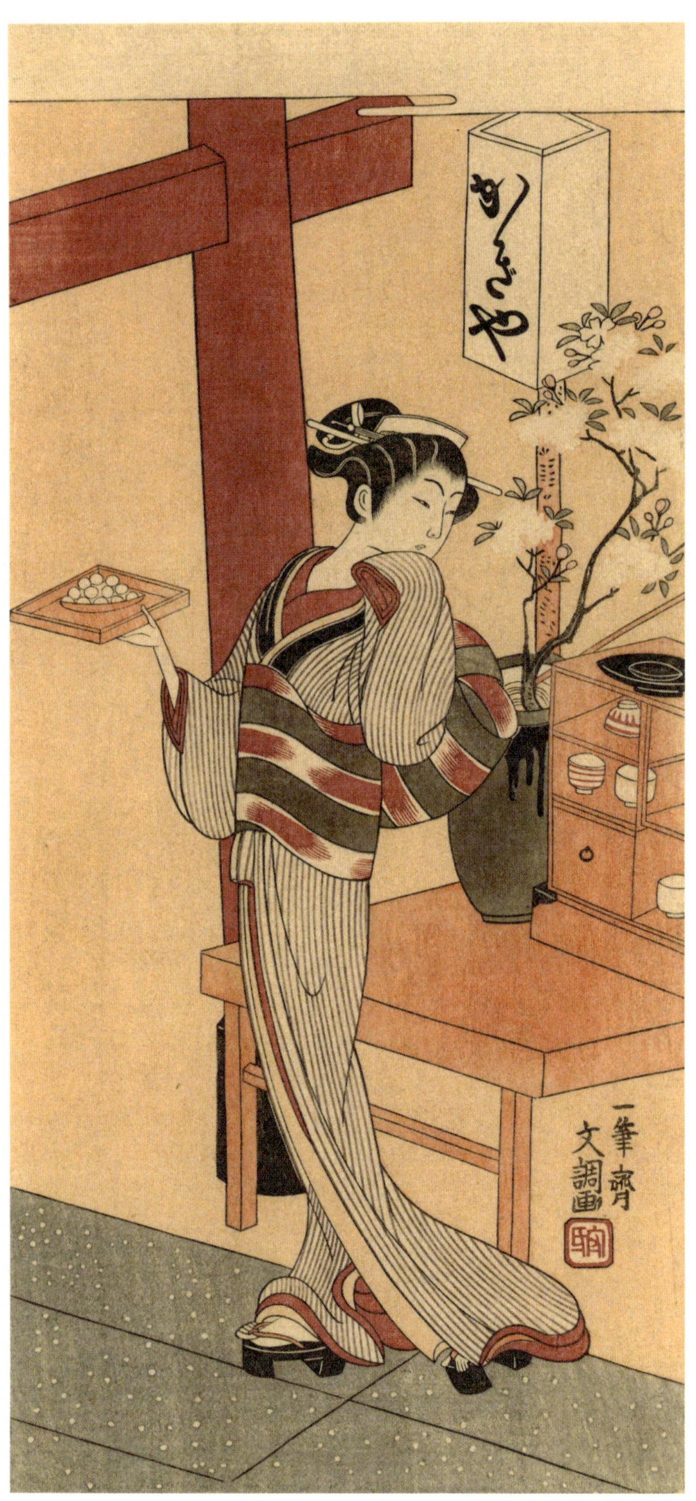

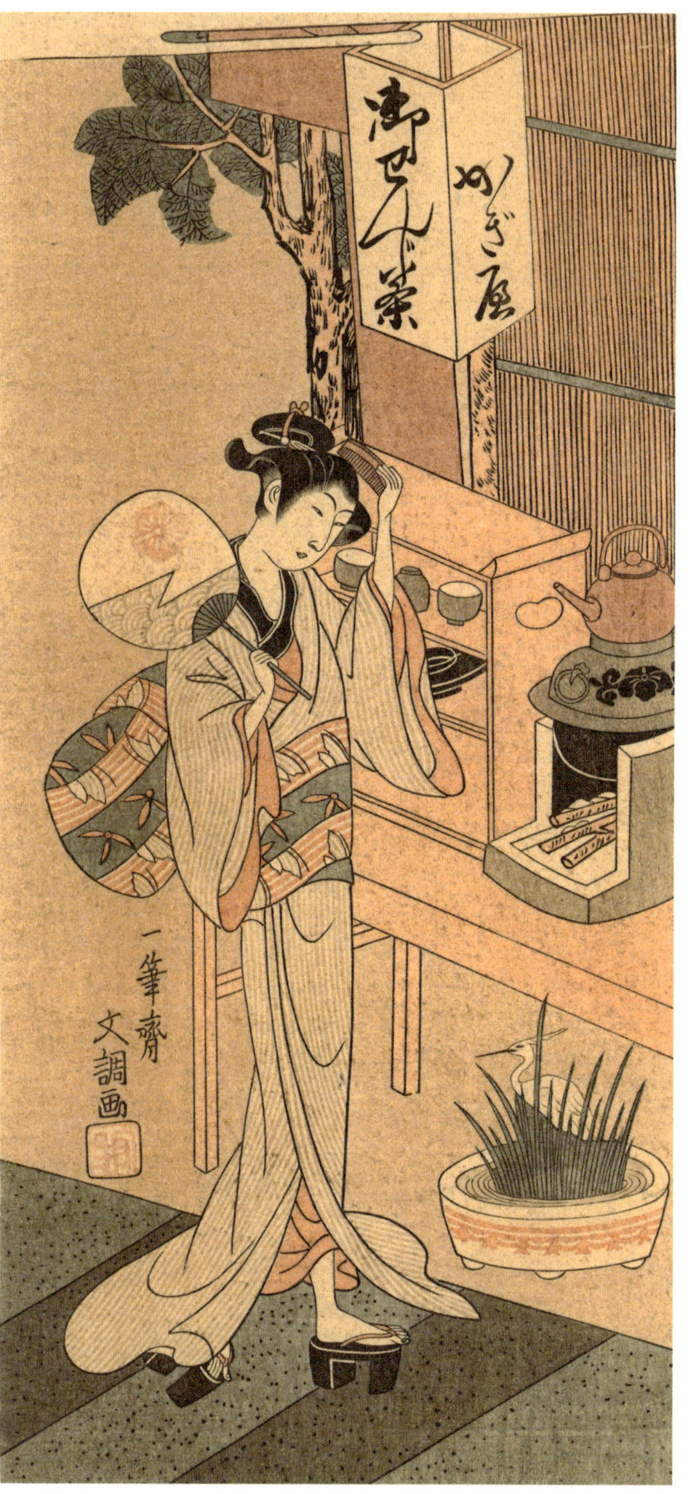

Active at much the same time, **Buncho** shared **Harunobu**'s passion for young waitresses, as is evident in these two lovely reprints. The image on the left is of the same waitress Osen. She is at her stall by the Kasamori shrine in Edo with an offering of cakes. Behind are tea utensils, cherry blossoms and the shop sign.

In the second image the waitress holds a fan, a fashionable must have for every young woman. Underneath the tea stand is a crane, hiding behind a plant in a pot - nice touch!

The waitresses might have admired Kabuki actor Yamashita Kyonosuke, seen here in an original sheet from a picture book of stage fans. He was the equivalent of a young pop idol, and going by his hair style was probably a wakashu (see p 27).

The figure in the image on the right is also of a young man - a Kabuki portrait of Segawa Kikunoju II as the 'beauty' Ohatsu.

I love the elegance of the figure and dramatic setting - with the grain sheaf, autumn flowers and night sky.

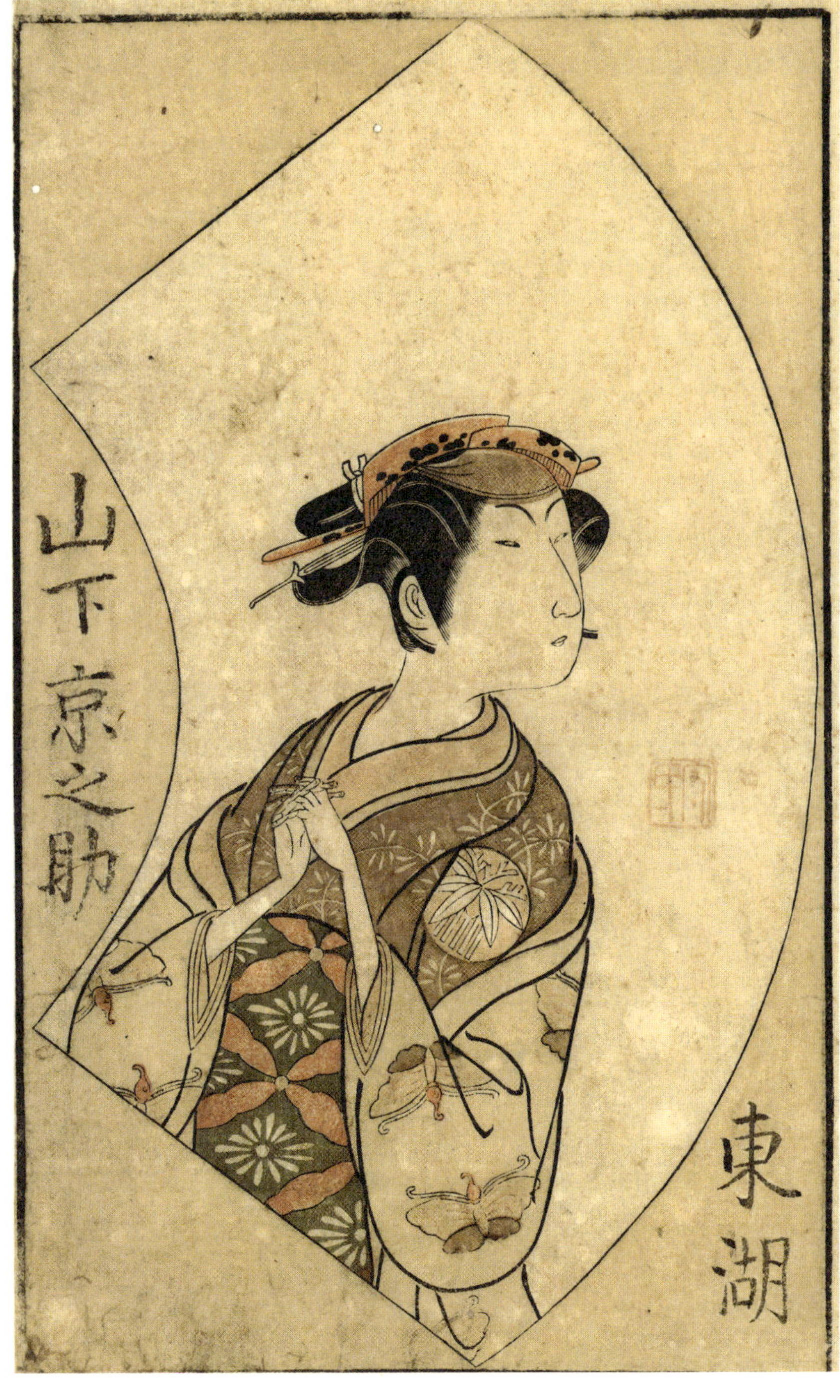

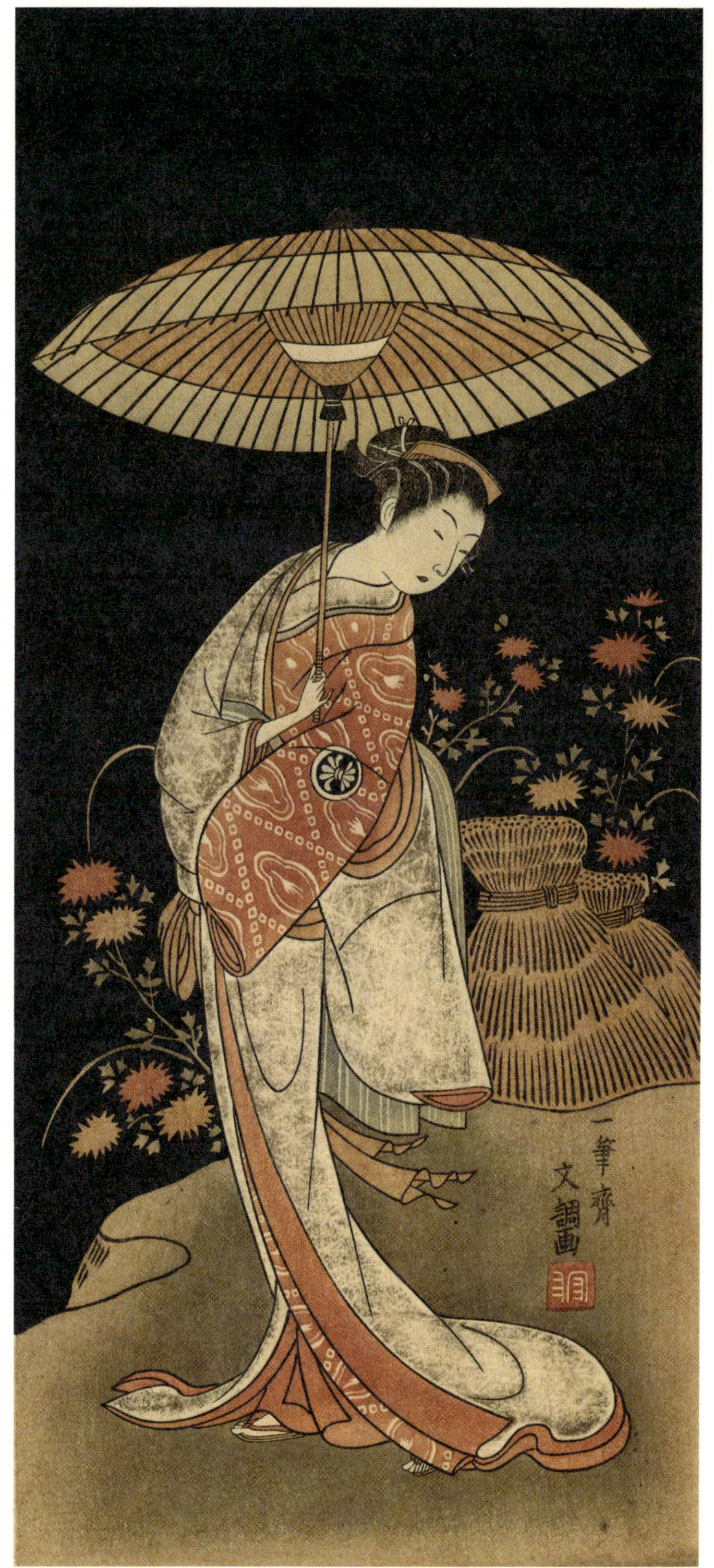

Isoda KORYUSAI (1735-1790)

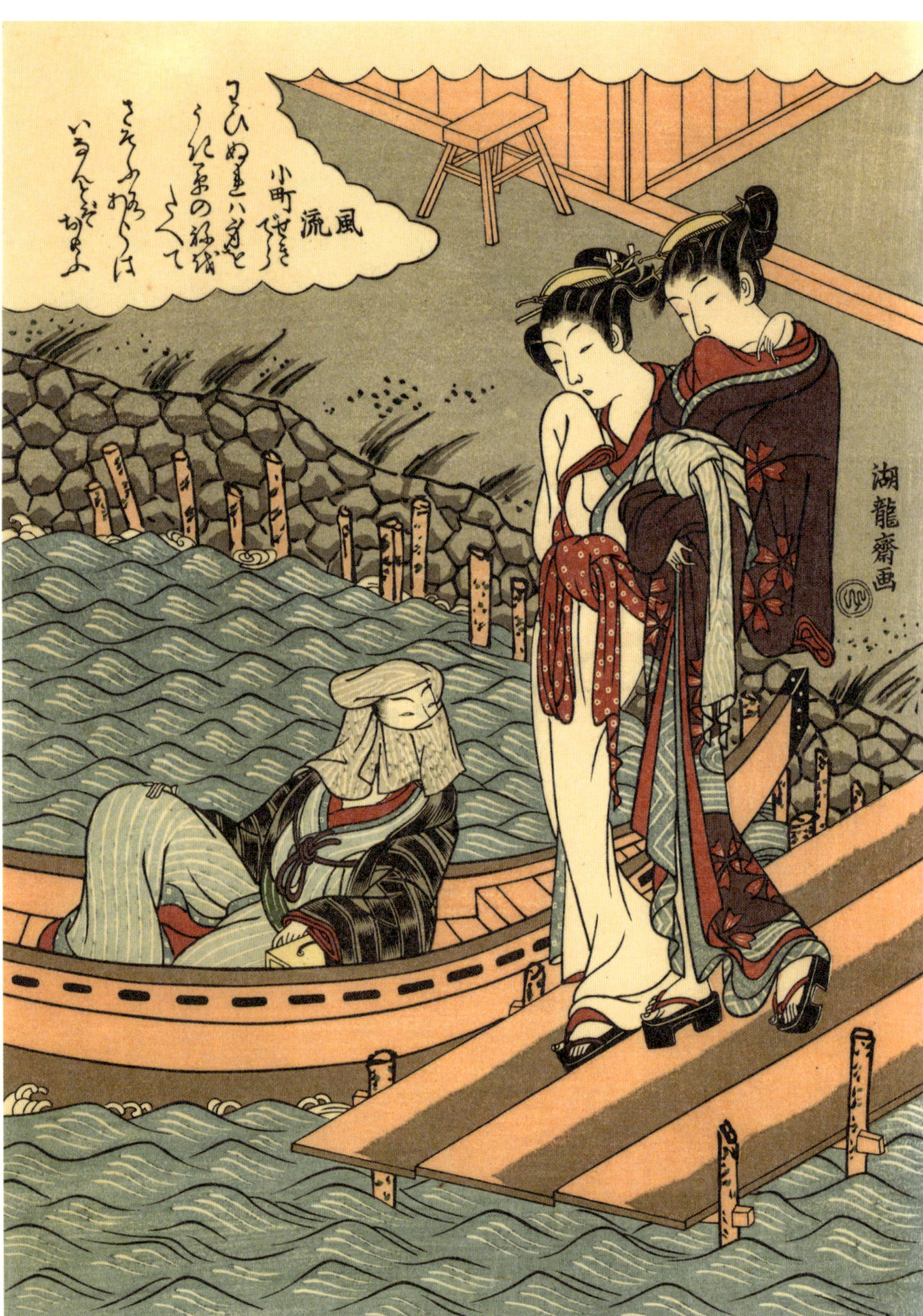

A former samurai **Koryusai** moved down from his high status to the inferior role of an artist.

He was a pupil of **Horunobu** and worked in his mentor's dreamlike style. He has been criticised for deriving his work too directly from his master but nonetheless created wonderful scenes of women in various situations - often erotic.

In this reprint we see two innocent young 'beauties' about to embark on a small boat. The boatman eyes them lasciviously, so one fears for their safety. I love the choppy water, which seems to be apt...

Suzuki HARUSHIGE (1747-1818)

Another notable artist of the period was **Harushige** who later became **Shiba Kokan** - introducing ideas on perspective. He was a student of **Harunobu** and after his death it was found that **Harushige** was forging his signature - to pass off some of his work as that of the great master.

Here in his original style we have a reprint of a young man visiting a courtesan while her attendant sleeps.

Then we have the popular pass-time of spying on young women, here through the damaged paper wall of *'The tea house at Fukagawa'*. Two 'beauties' are about to attend a party on a veranda where a number of men are waiting.

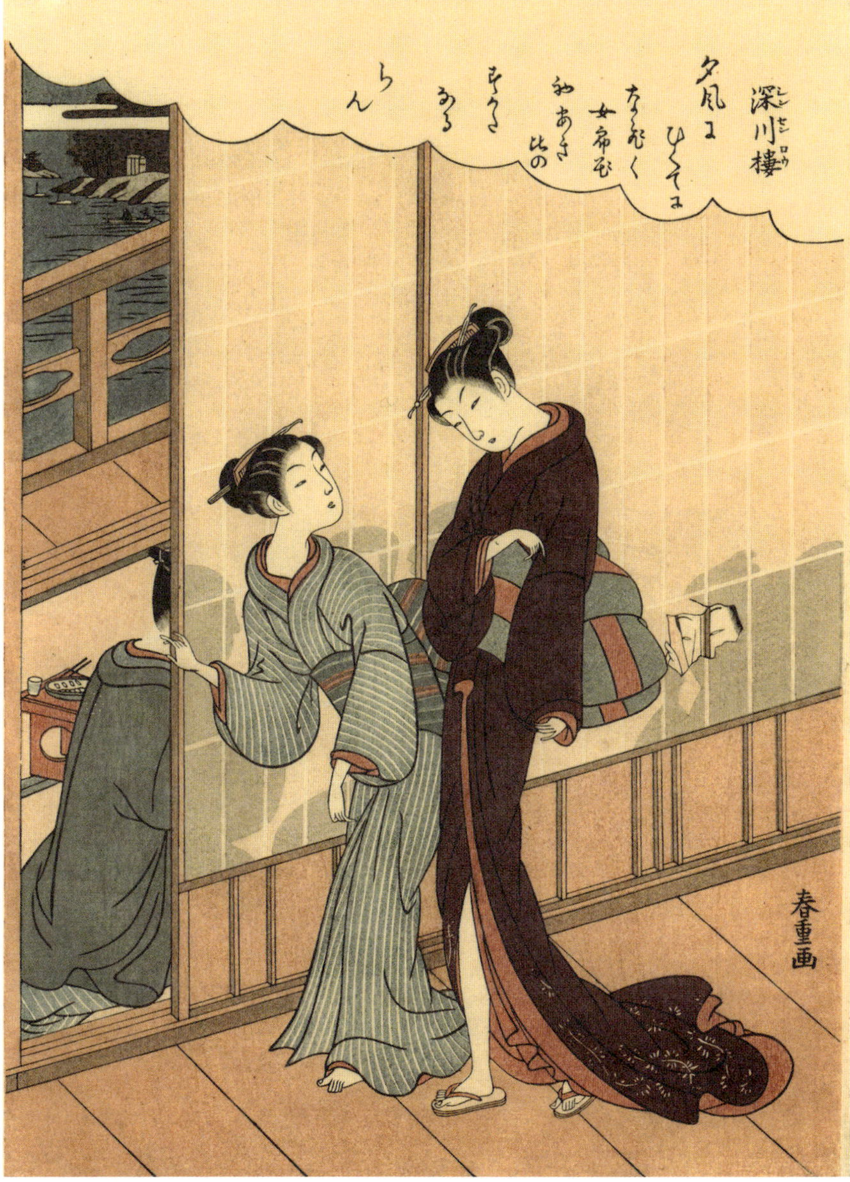

Torii KIYONAGA (1752-1815)

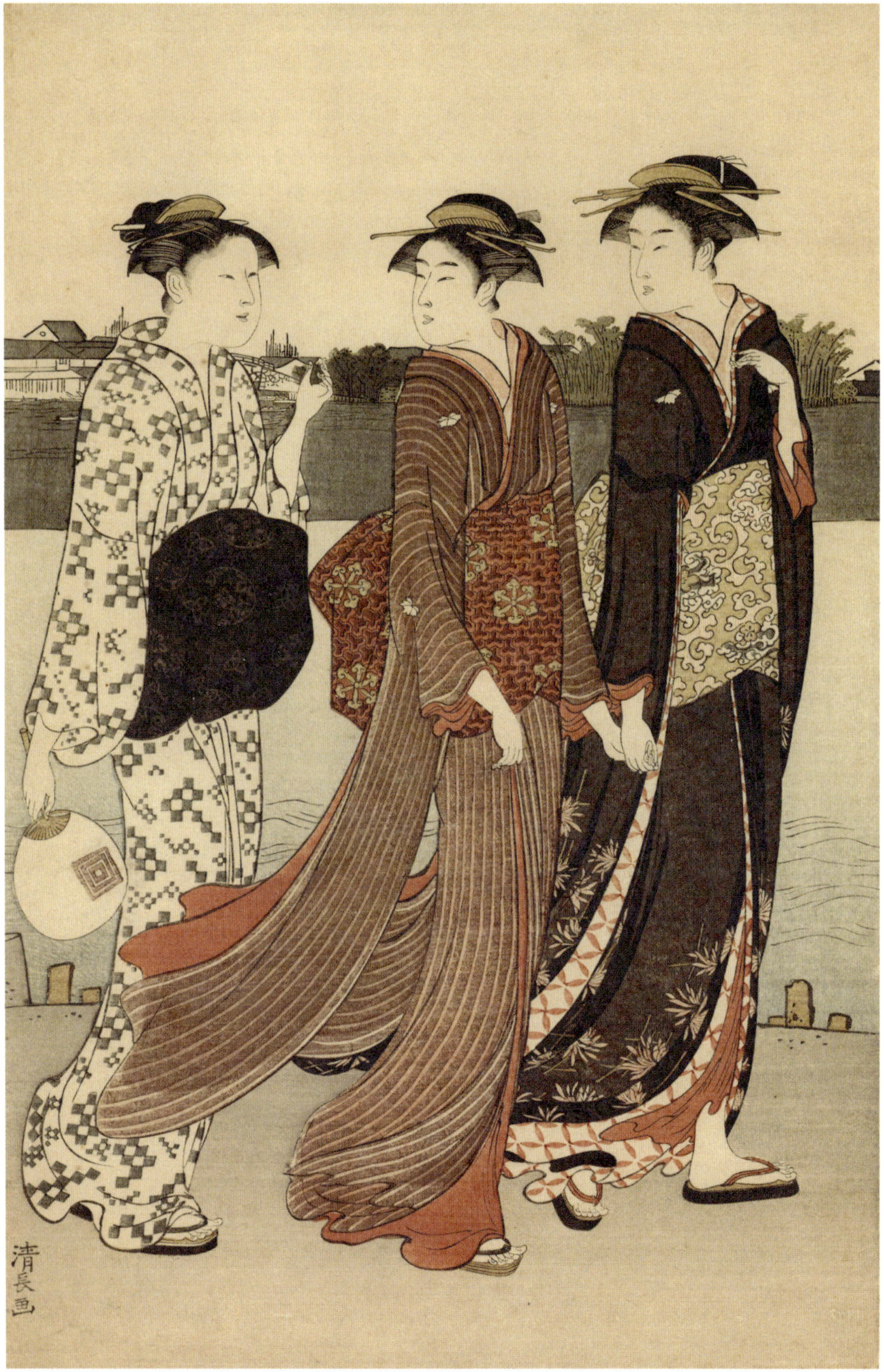

The artist **Kiyonaga** has a very distinctive style. I love how he uses cotton fabric that had just come into fashion to create elegant, feminine, flowing lines. This reprint is the right side of a diptych which we can see below. It is quite common for single prints to become detached from diptychs or triptychs and unbalanced compositions can be a give away. If in doubt research on-line before buying as often sellers won't provide this information - because a stray single sheet can be less collectable, and less valuable! In this case the price reflected it's lonely status, but I find the composition works anyway.

'Evening breeze on the banks of the Sumida River' c.1781-89

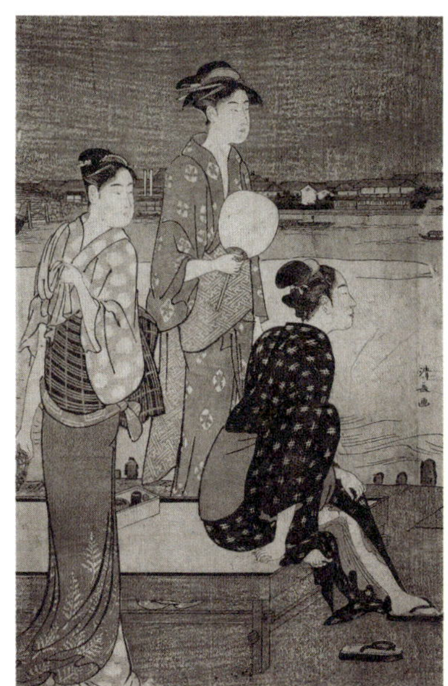

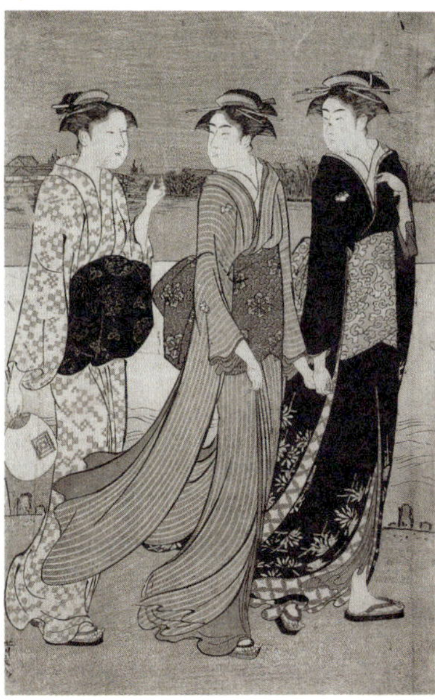

Kitagawa UTAMARO (1753-1806)

Little is known of **Utamaro**'s life and there is debate about whether he had a wife and children. There is no doubt that he had a passion for women. His work began to appear in the 1770's, and he rose to prominence in the early 1790's with his portraits of 'beauties' - like this reprint here of two women out on a stroll sharing an umbrella.

He produced over 2,000 known prints in his working career, including over 120 bijin-ga print series. He was one of the few ukiyo-e artists to achieve fame throughout Japan in his lifetime.

As with all his contemporaries **Utamaro** had to be careful about revealing himself as an erotic artist as the legality of the work often changed and censors could dish out sever punishments. As a result most shunga was unsigned. There is though enough that is attributed to **Utamaro** to give him the reputation of being one of the finest artists in the genre.

In 1804 he was arrested and manacled for fifty days for making illegal prints depicting the 16th-century military ruler Toyotomi Hideyoshi - and died two years later.

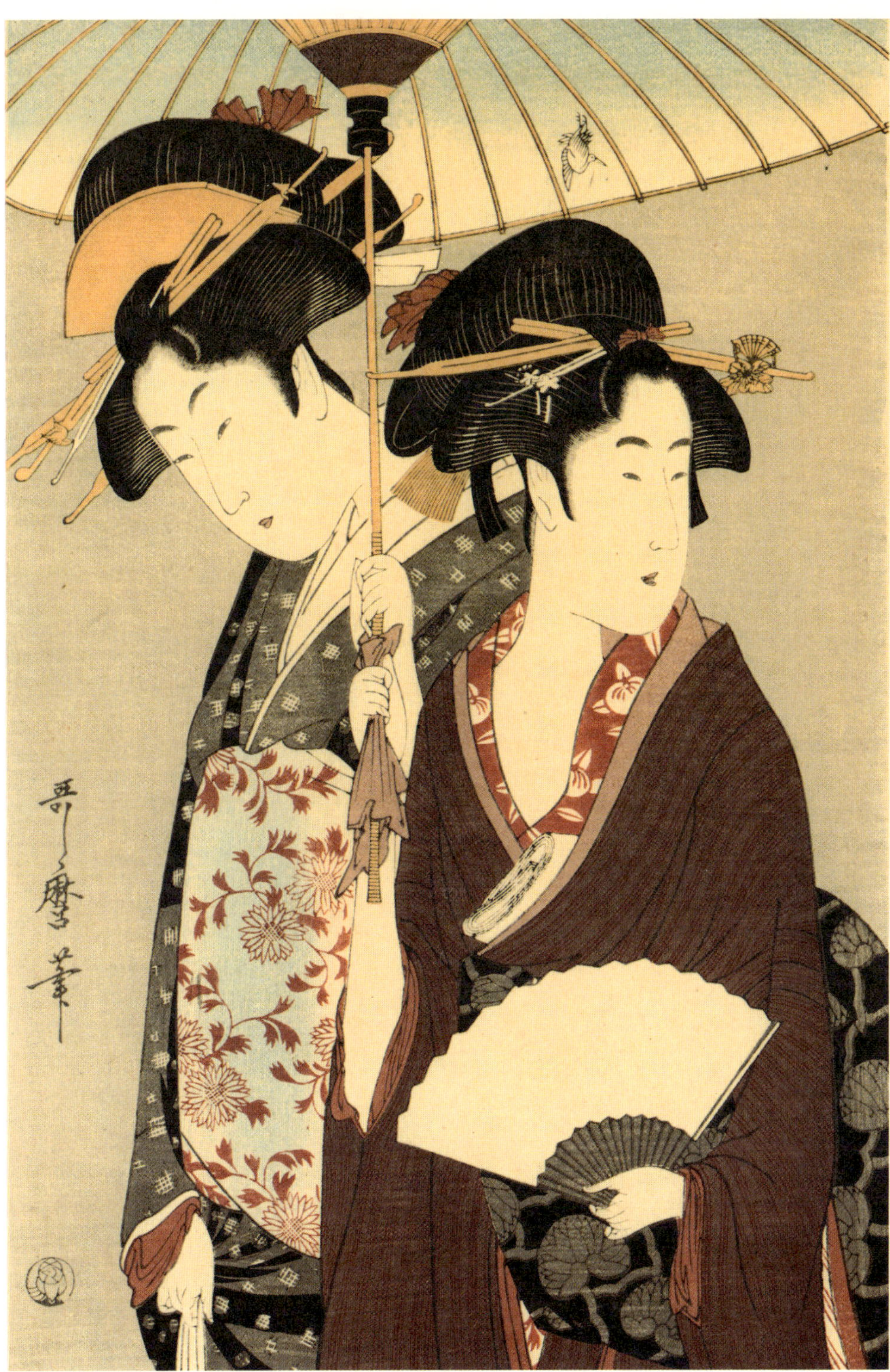

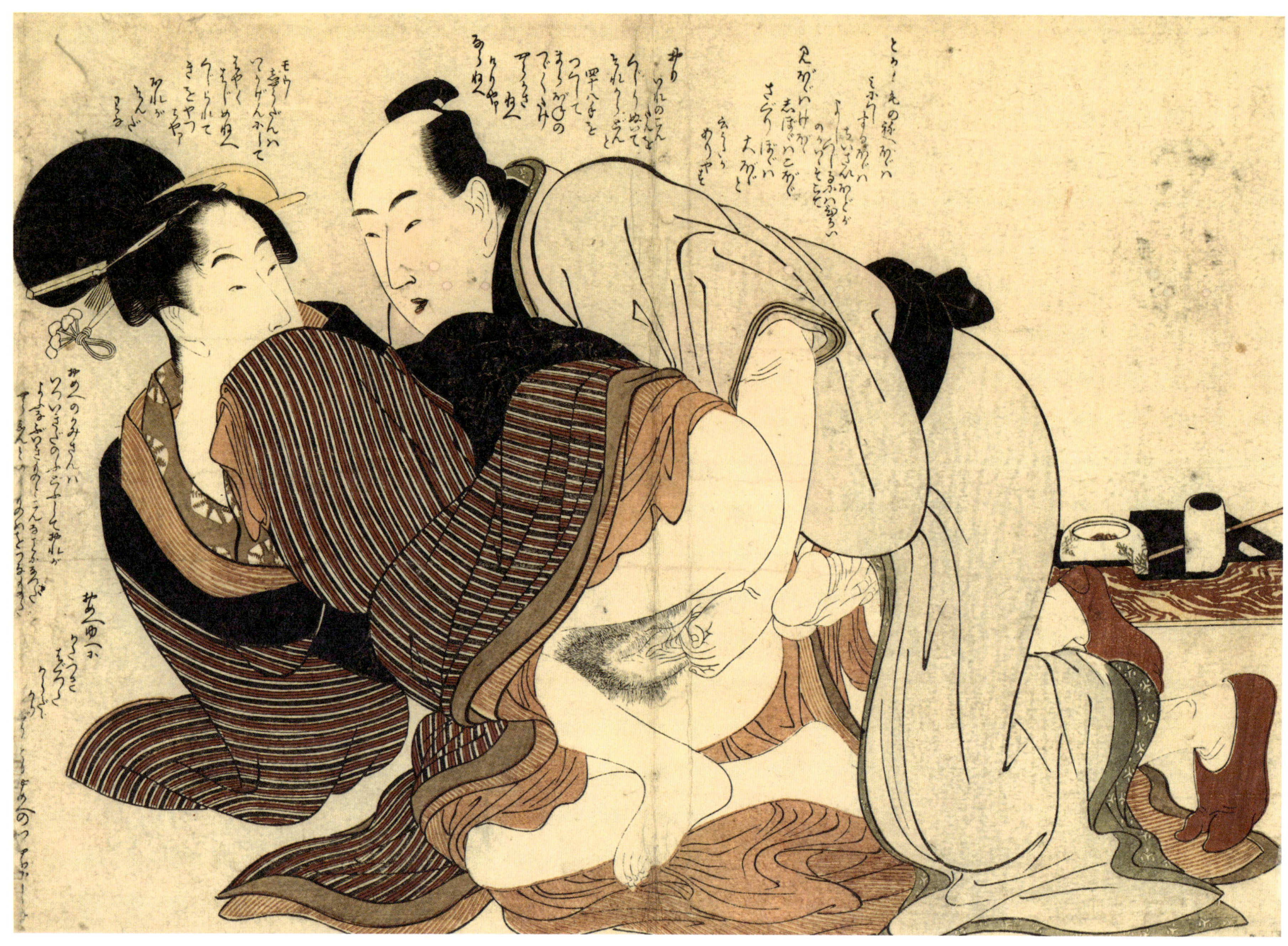

This original shunga by **Utamaro** is from a famous series of twelve named *Prelude to Desire* (1799) and the text tells that she is a widow and he a married man. There is some mention of her 'pussy' but she wants him to 'get started quickly', wondering what attracts him as he has a fashionable wife at home - although she is wearing the latest style striped robe.

Prints like this tell us a lot about the sexual attitudes in Japanese society at the time.

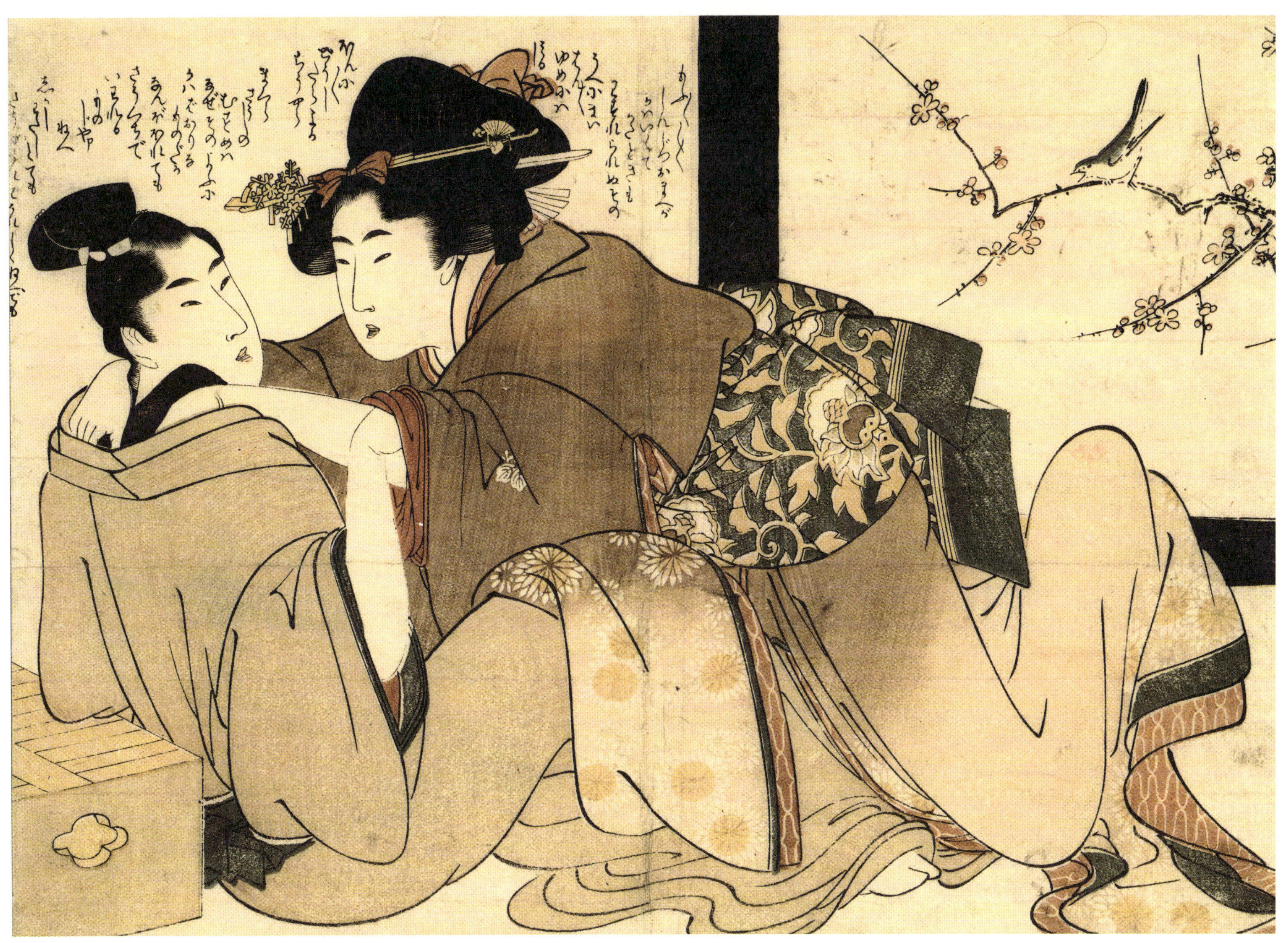

There is even more encoded in this **Utamaro** attributed original of a woman making advances to a younger man - a wakashu. As we have already seen they were actors who played both young men and young women in the Kabuki theatre - when it was all male performance art. They are sometimes described as 'the third sex'.

It was quite usual for them to be targeted by older men - often priests! This is different in that the advances come from an older woman, described in the text as 'lustful', and the wakashu is the reluctant focus of her attention.

There is a long history of cross dressing with tradition going back centuries, when Kabuki actors were women. Because of unruly audience behaviour the authorities stepped in so men and boys were given all of the roles. This then became the norm.

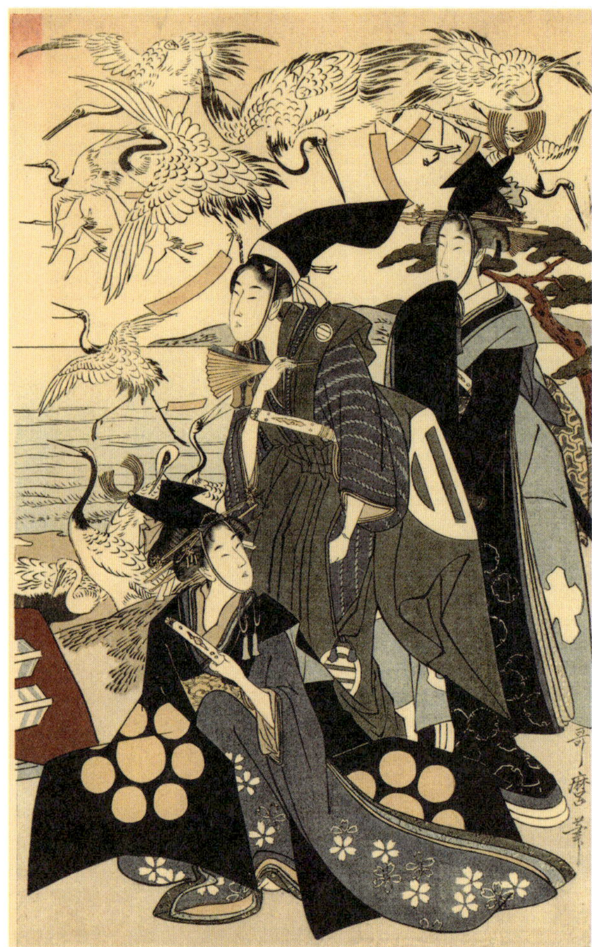

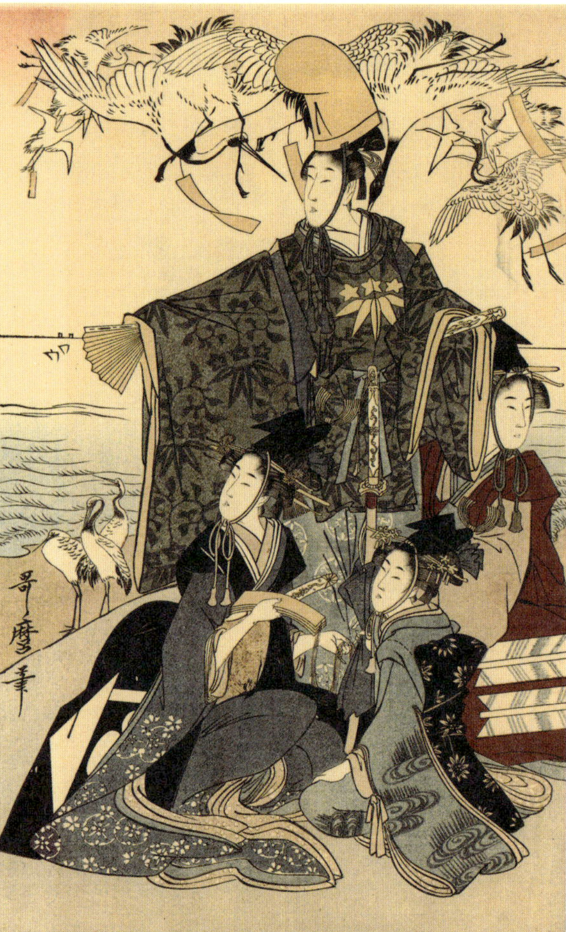

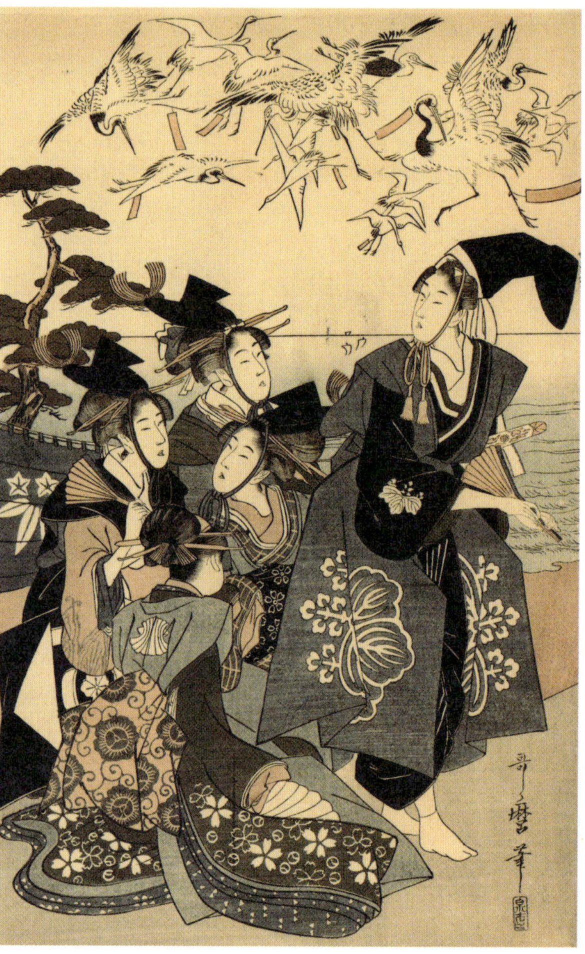

This triptych reprint is titled: *'Parody of the Story of Yoritomo releasing Cranes at Yuigahama'* (1805), and in it we see women dressed as noblemen, with tall court caps and swords. At the centre is Yoritomo and around her 'beauties' are folding poem slips to be attached to the cranes who fly off with them.

Narratives were important to the public who had a passion for prints, and it wasn't just the theatre that provided the drama.

These black & white originals (here and overpage) come from a series in a book of twelve - *On the road: Love songs for the Thick-necked Shamisen* (1802).

Each print documents a true story of star-crossed lovers, made famous in bunraku (puppet) plays - for committing double suicide.

The series became so popular that subsequent editions were printed in colour - to keep up with the demands of fashion.

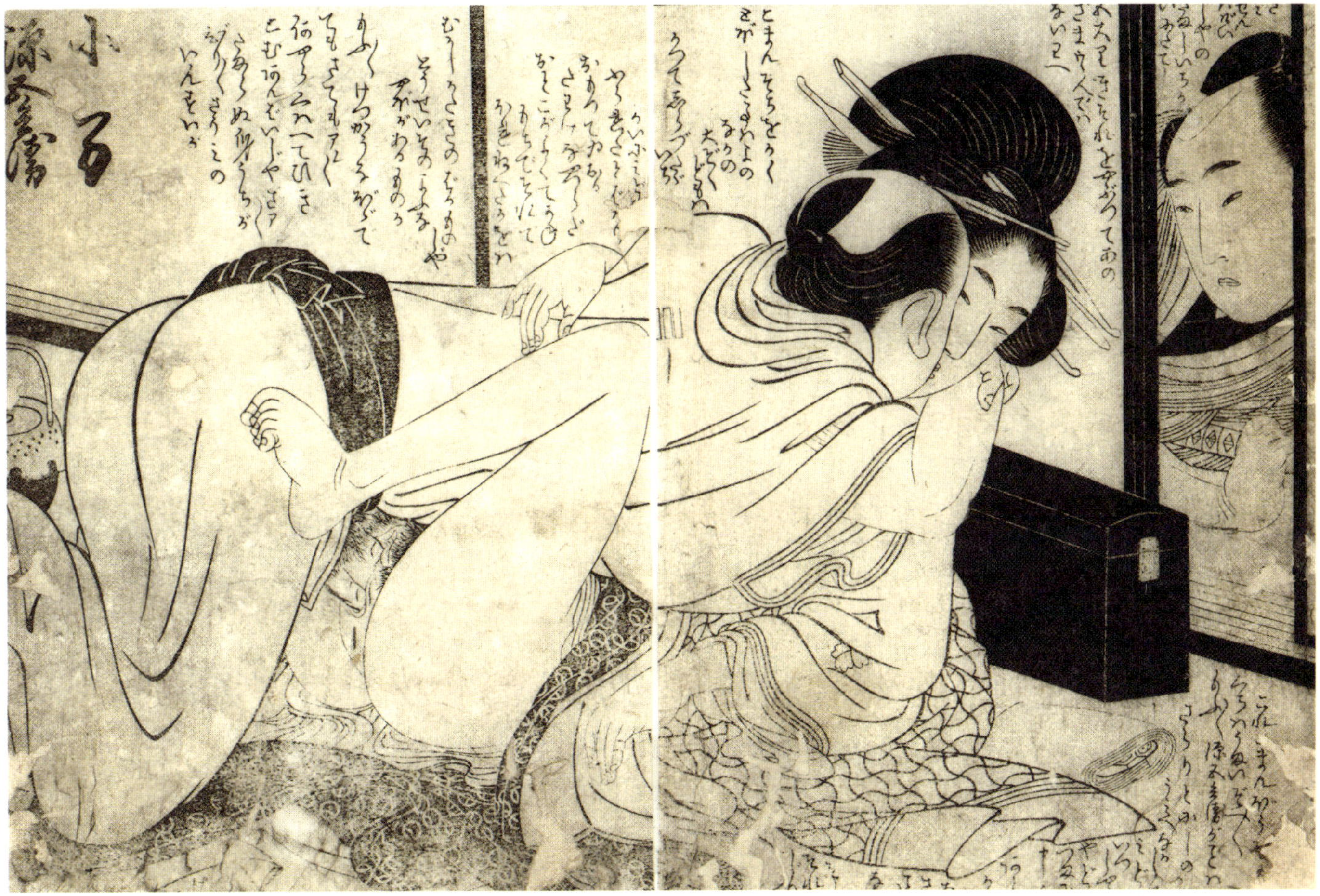

We see the female puppeteers in action. These images would have been on the frontispiece - to reinforce the idea that in the prints are depictions of popular bunraku characters.

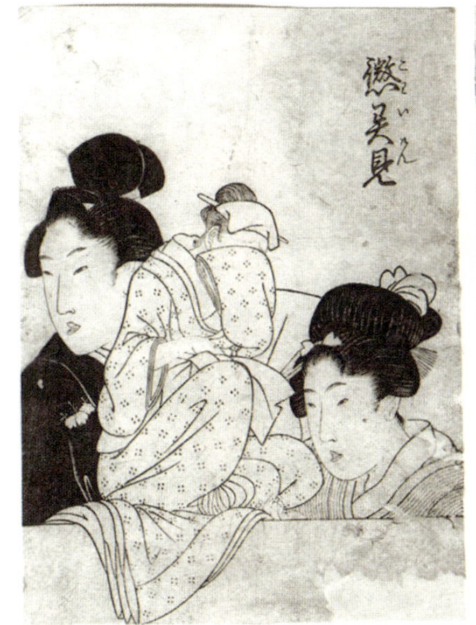

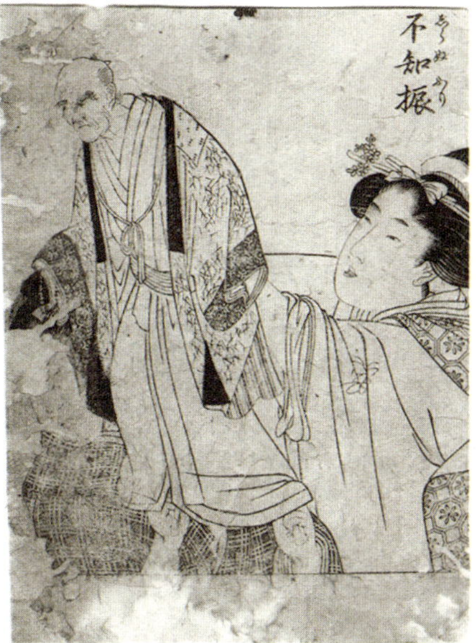

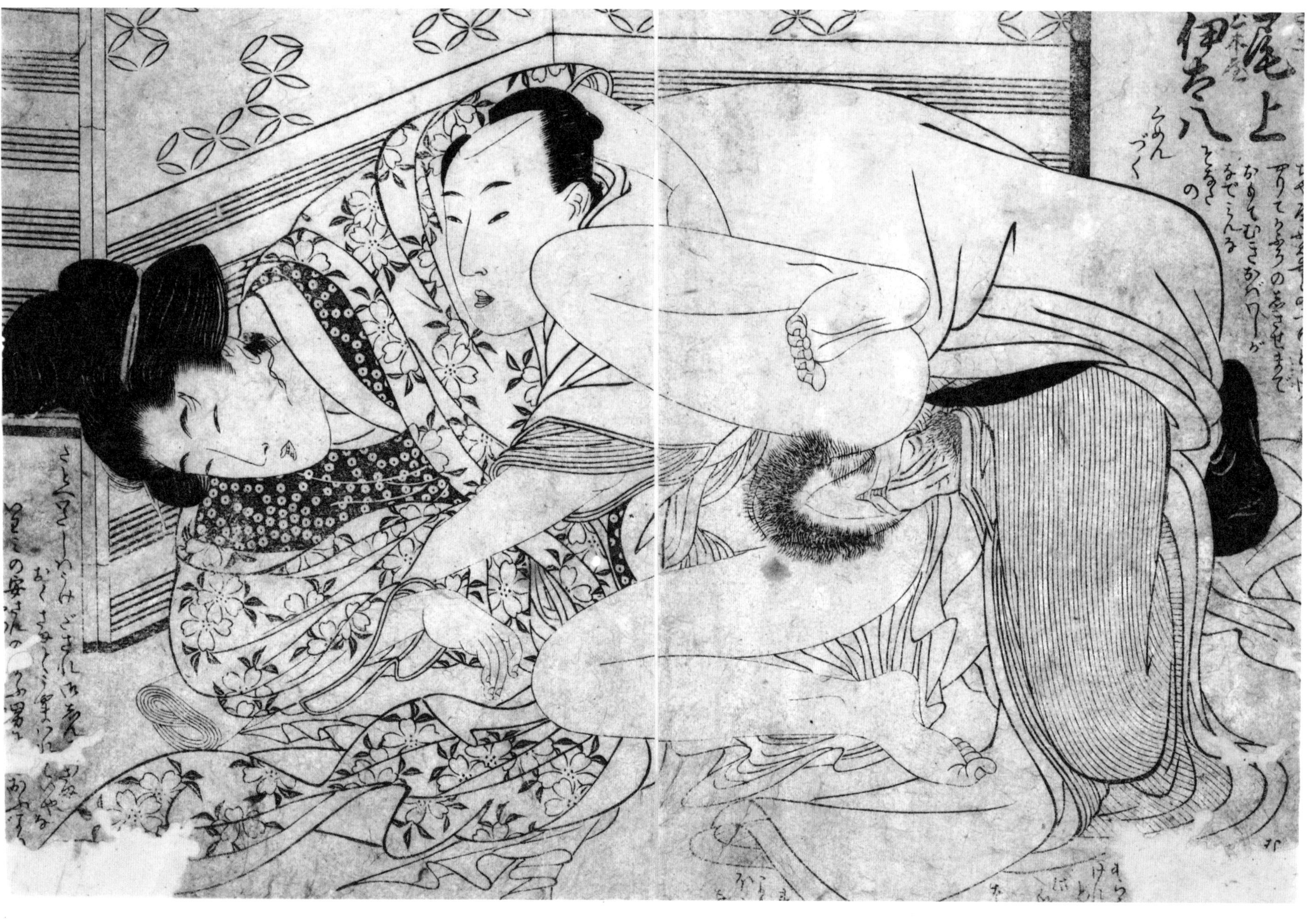

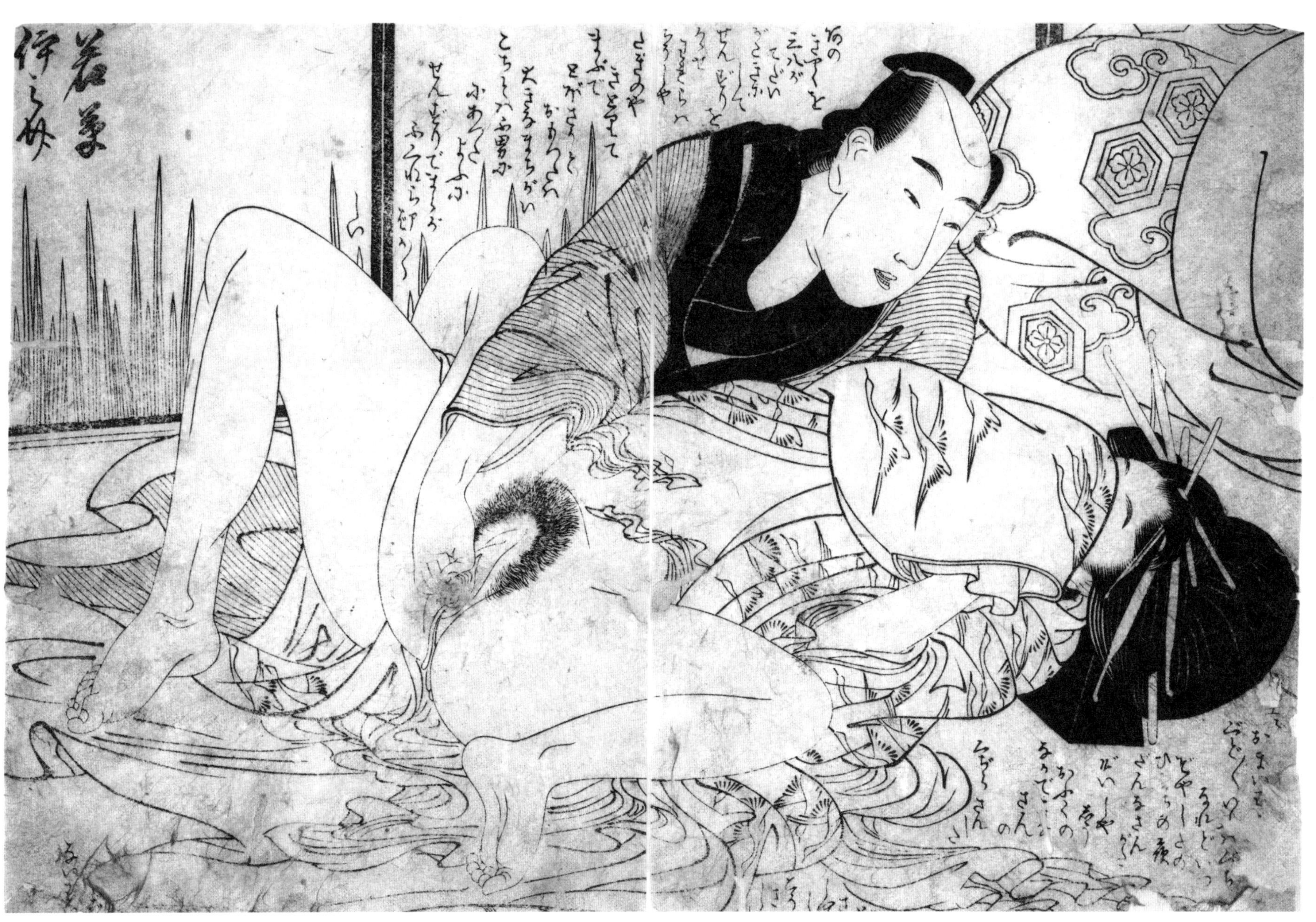

Utamaro is considered to be one of the greatest Japanese artists of all time and in discussing his shunga one has to mention in passing this rare and most famous image from the series *Poem of the Pillow (1788)*. It is not explicit but it has an unsurpassed eroticism - in particular in the man's almost obscured gaze and the woman's sensual demeanour.

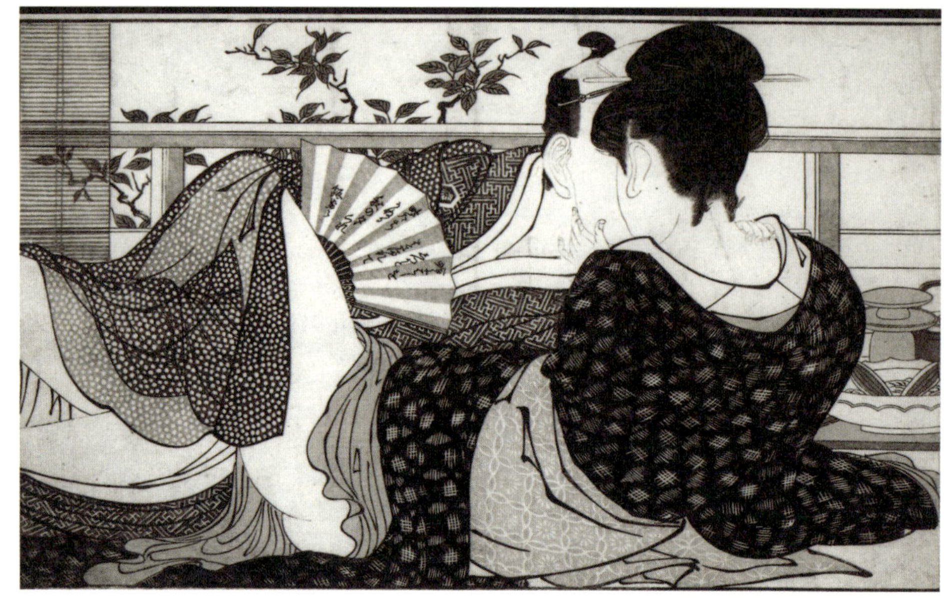

The women in **Utamaro**'s prints mostly appear tall and slim, the Japanese female physiognomy not quite measuring up to his fantasy. They look very much like the western ideal of the fashion model, which perhaps accounts for their continuing popularity. See here the lovely reprint: *'Women Overnight Guests'.* (C.1794-95)

This is a particularly wonderful expression of female intimacy, showing the gentle relationship between host, guests and servants.

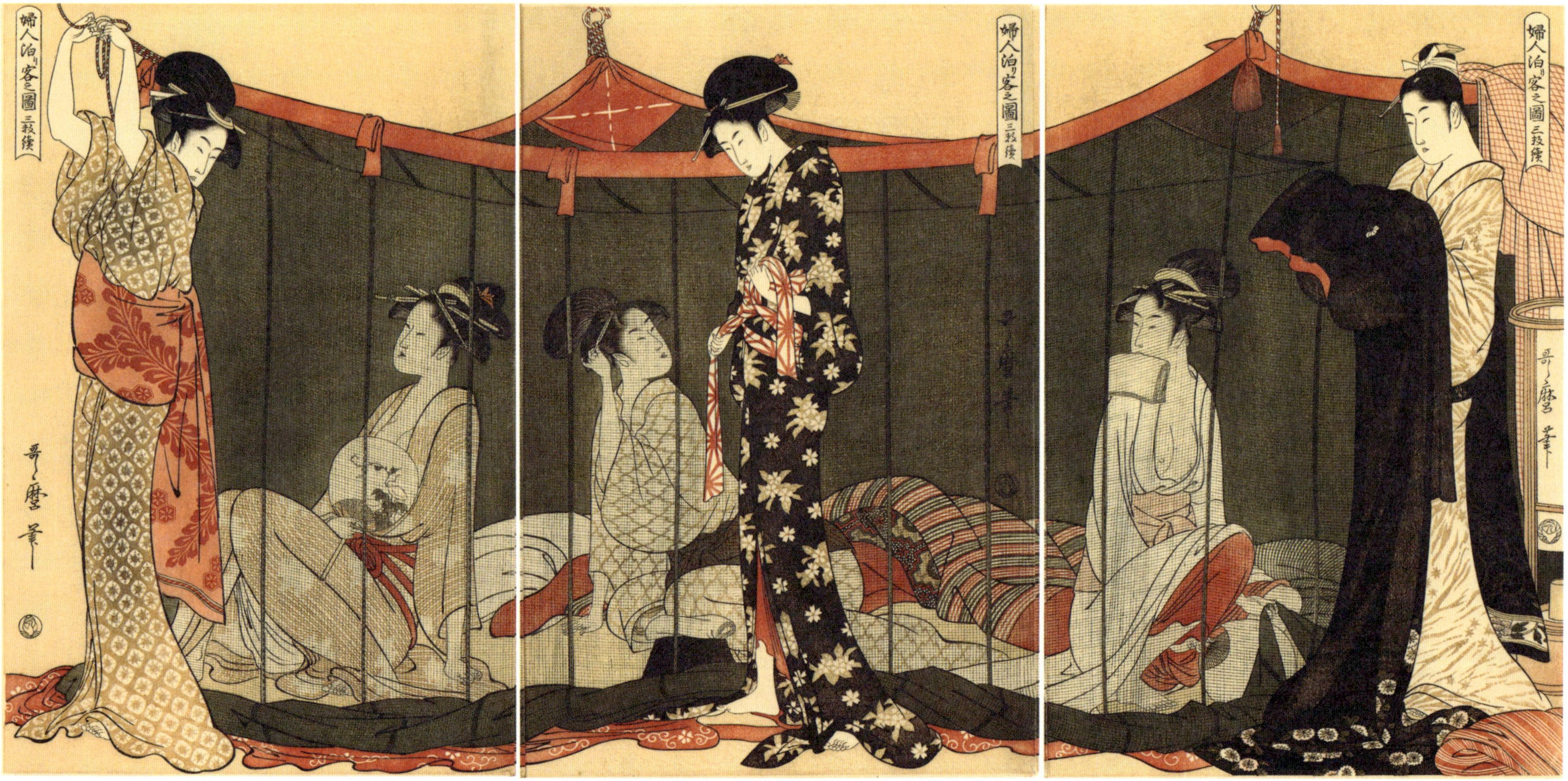

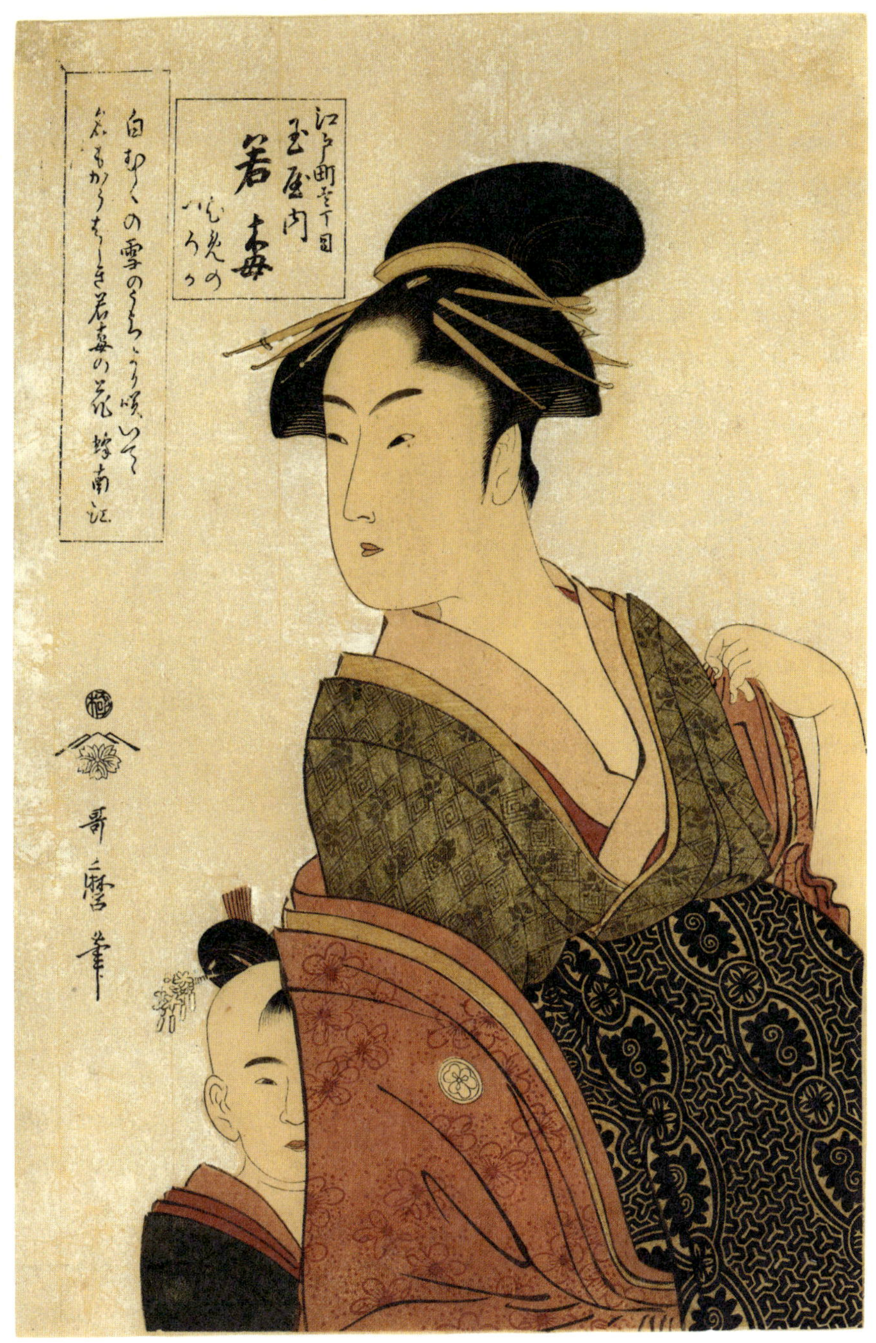

Often the bijin-ga are portraits of particular courtesans. Some of these images could be considered as advertising posters, perhaps in a similar way the internet promotes 'escorts'. Many of the women in these reprints were 'beauties' whose fame has transcended the time they were depicted. This is courtesan Wakaume with one of her kamuro (child apprentices) - from the series *Eight Famous Views of Women.*

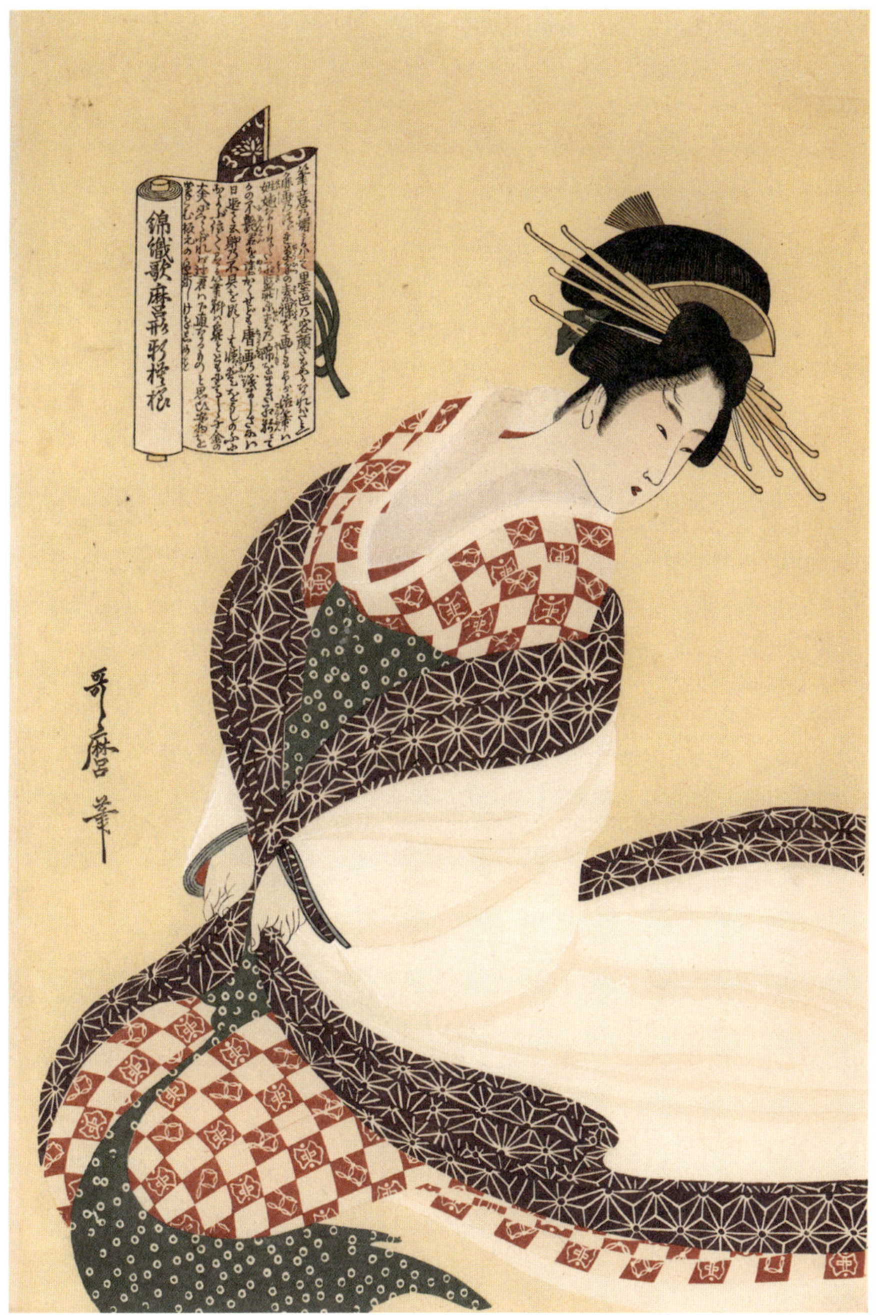

Then we have, most importantly, the fashions - as it was the courtesans who were the arbiters of taste and style. They most often created their own outfits from sumptuous bought-in fabrics, some of which came through the port of Nagasaki, the only link to the outside world. The significance of the clothes is made clear by the title of the print *'The White Surcoat'* (c.1795)

It is obvious that **Utamaro** was drawn to the emotional lives of women and liked to picture them in a variety of situations - experiencing love and loss - and sometimes getting drunk.

They were not always courtesans or entertainers, but ordinary women, as we can see in these three lovely images. The two on the left are from the series *Anthology of Poems, The Love Section* (1793)

The first is *'Love That Meets Each Night'*. A young woman holds a letter, perhaps from a lover, her expression innocent and optimistic.

The second, '*Reflective Love*', is of an older married woman, who appears rather embittered as she remembers something we can only guess at.

The third, from the series *A Parent's Moralising Spectacles* is called *'Vulgarly Called the Wanton' (*1802). The eyeglasses and the glass from which the woman drinks sake were both exotic imports brought to Japan by Dutch traders. The inscription describes her as someone who is completely without propriety, taking delight in flaunting her lack of self-restraint. An oddly moralistic message, this was supposed to encourage people to see how their debauched actions might be perceived by others.

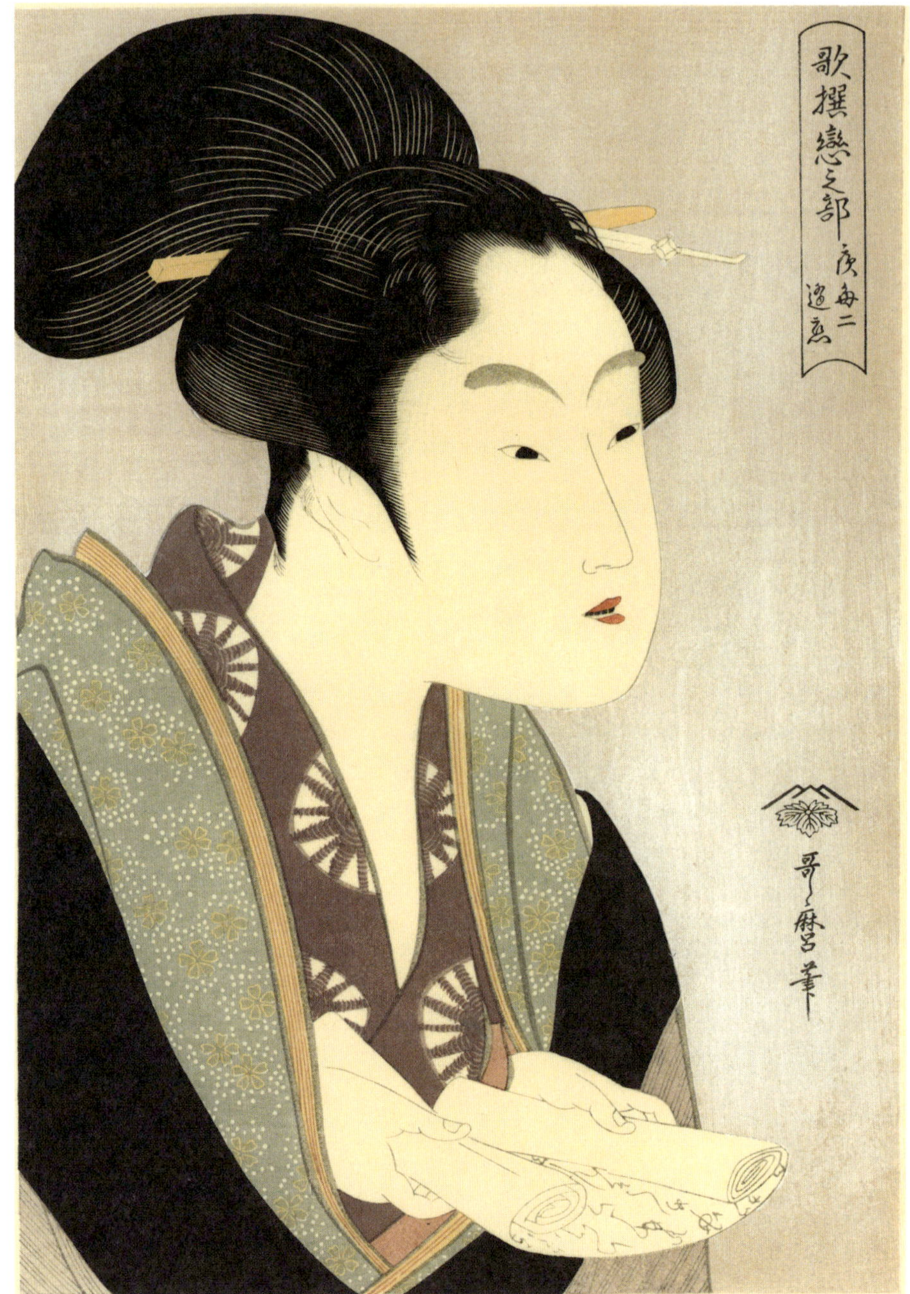

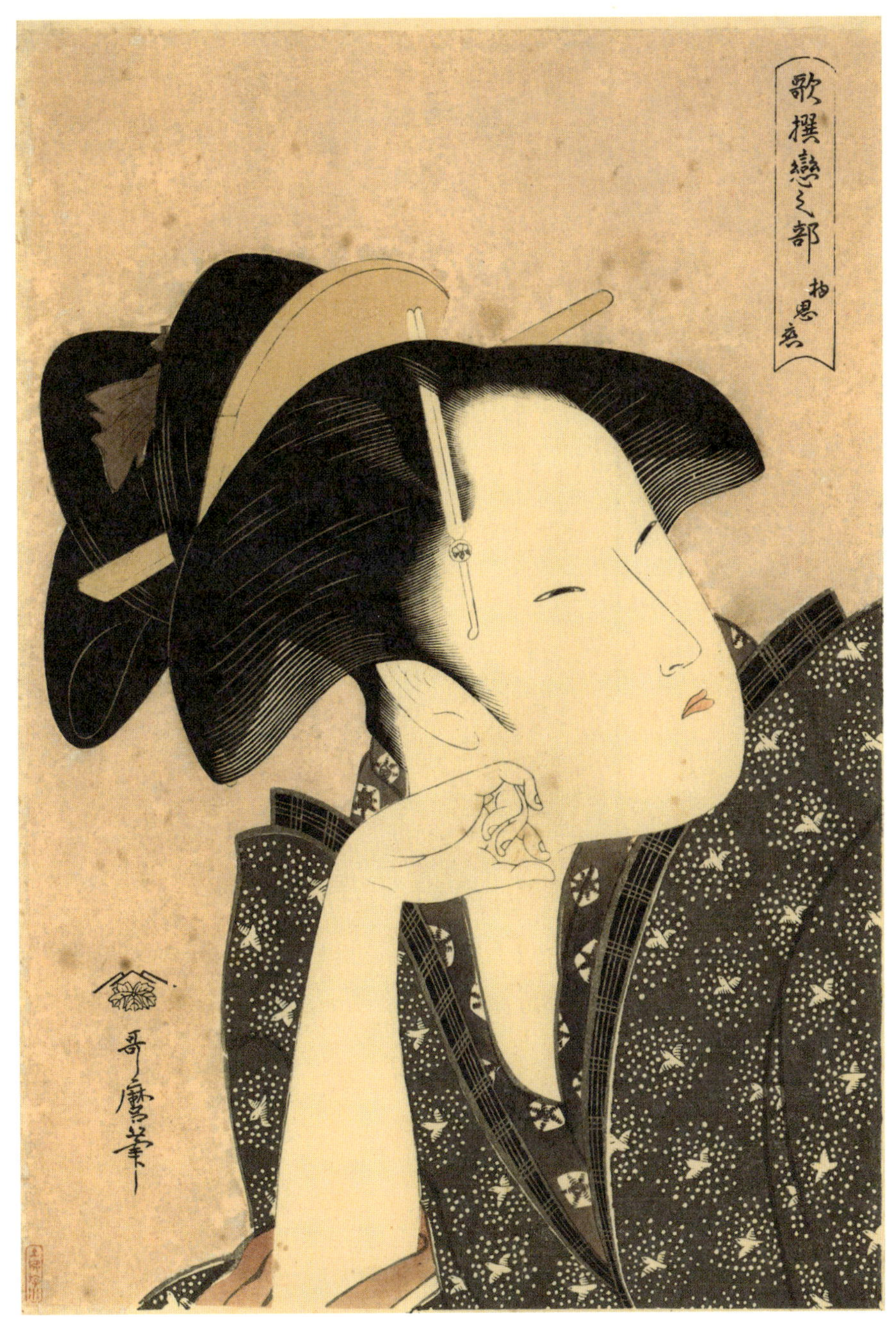

歌撰戀之部
物思恋
哥麿筆

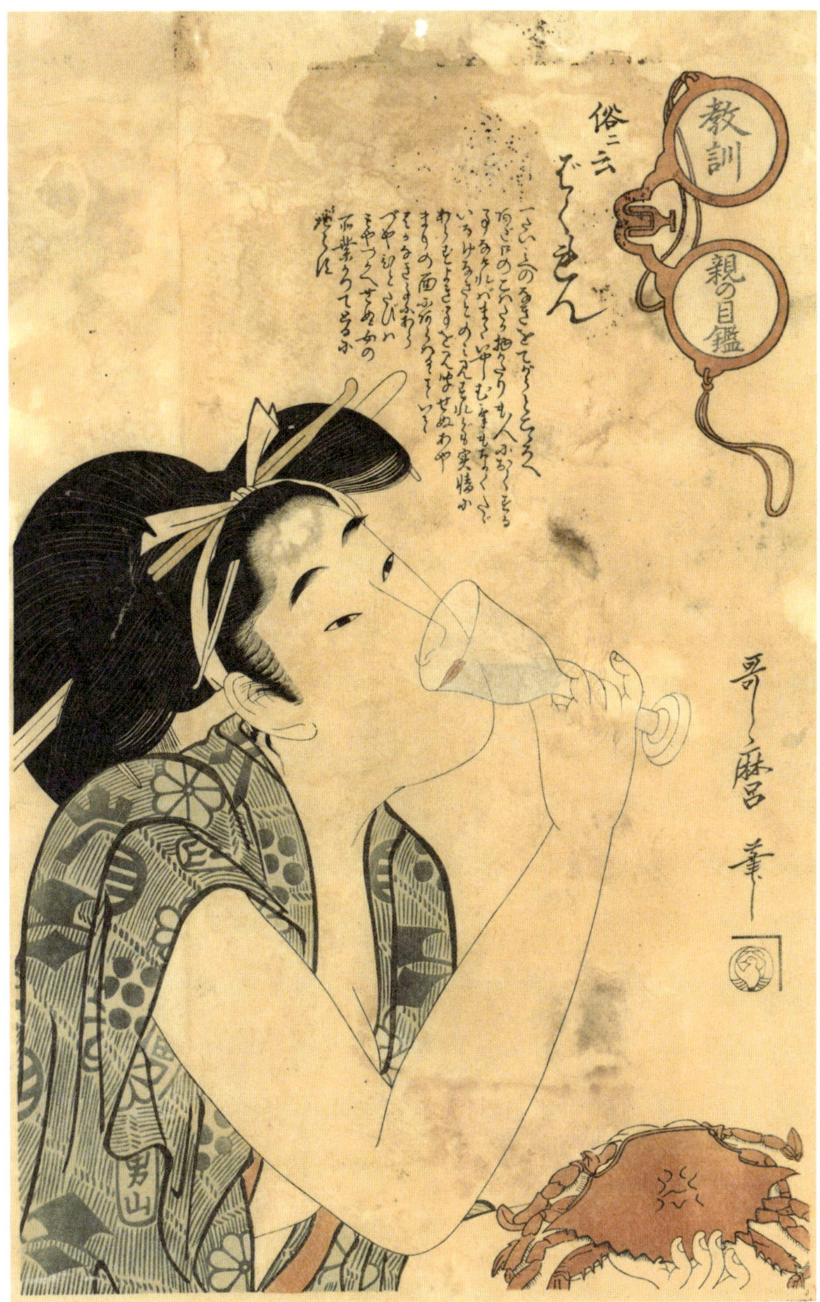

教訓
親の目鑑
俗ニ云
ばくれん
哥麿筆

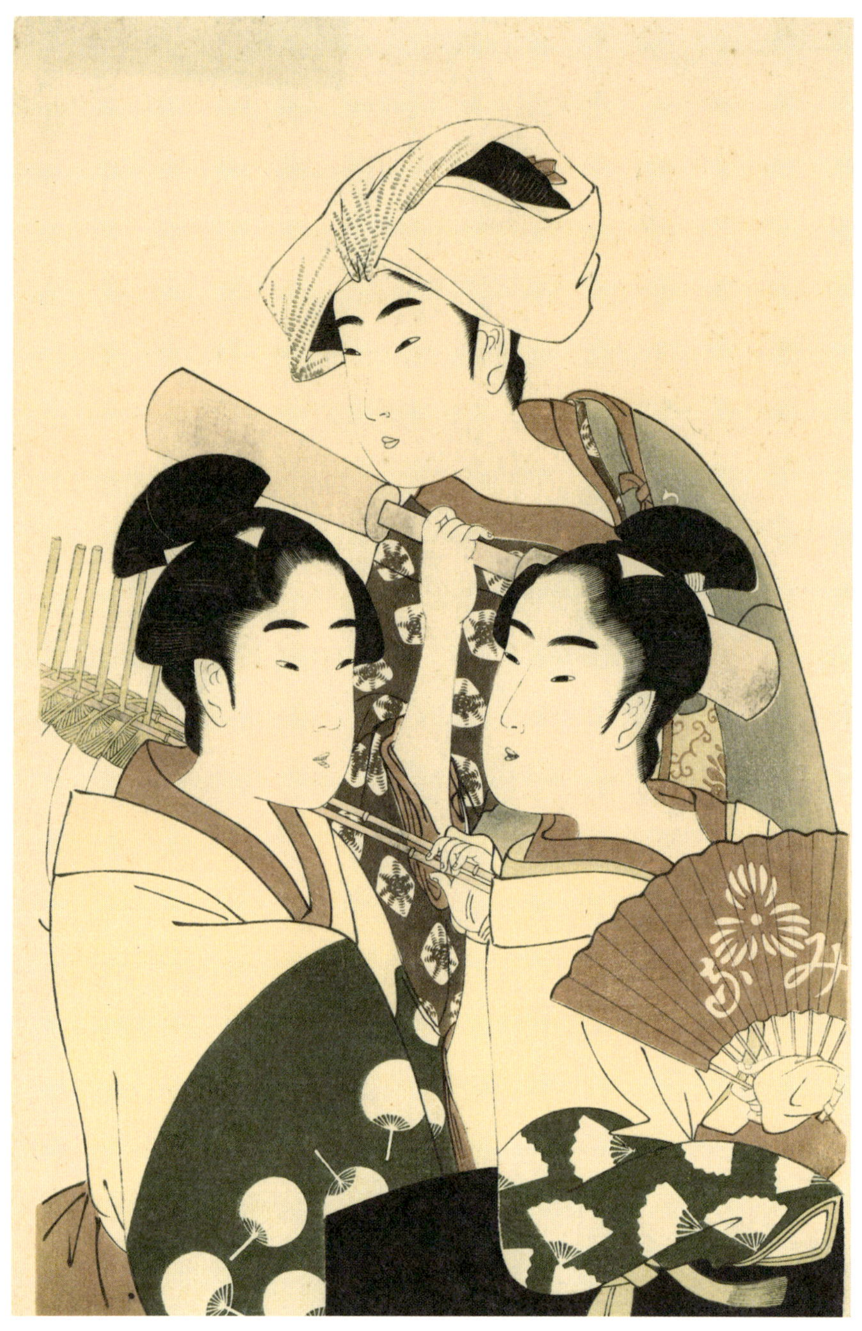

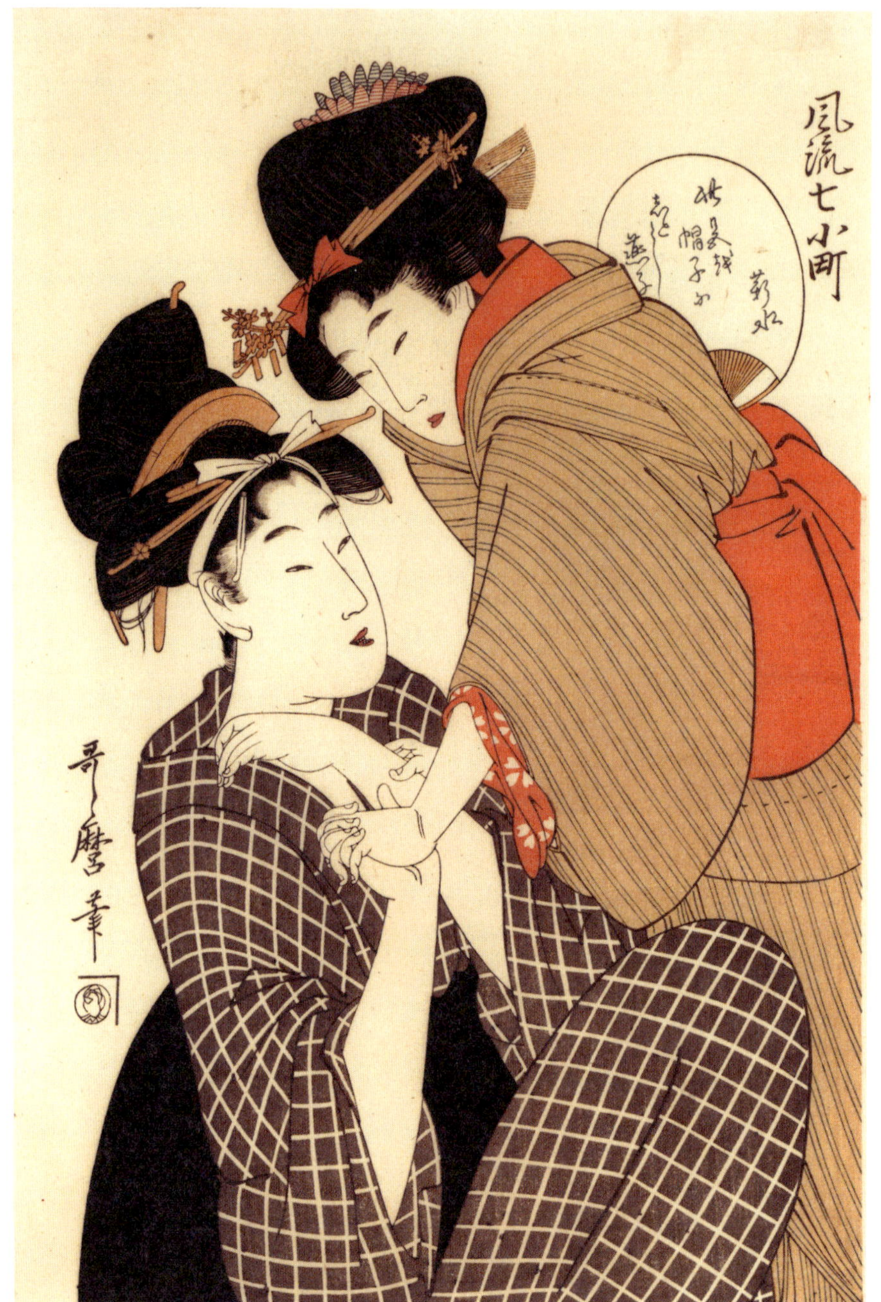

Utamaro documented women's lives so we see them at work,

- play

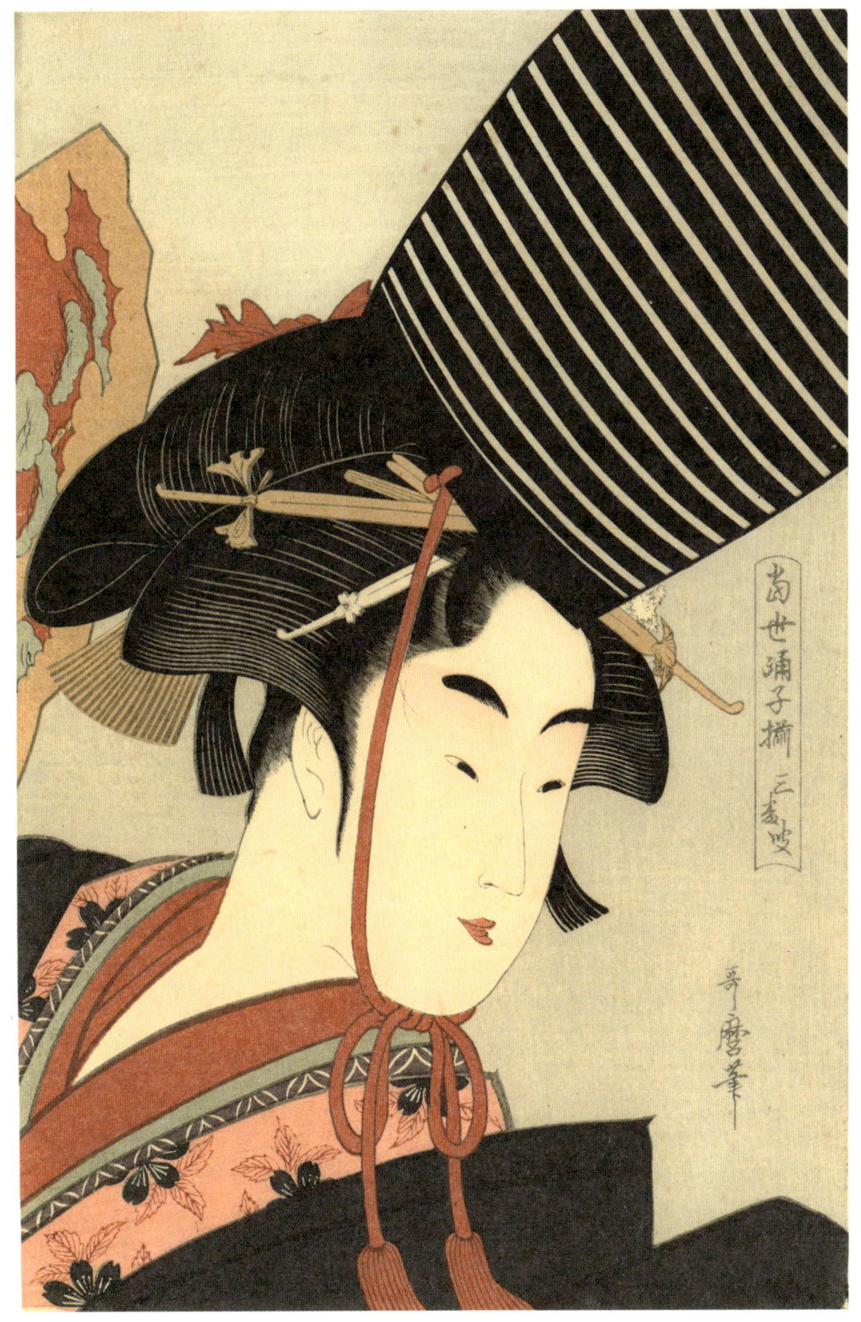

- dressed for dancing

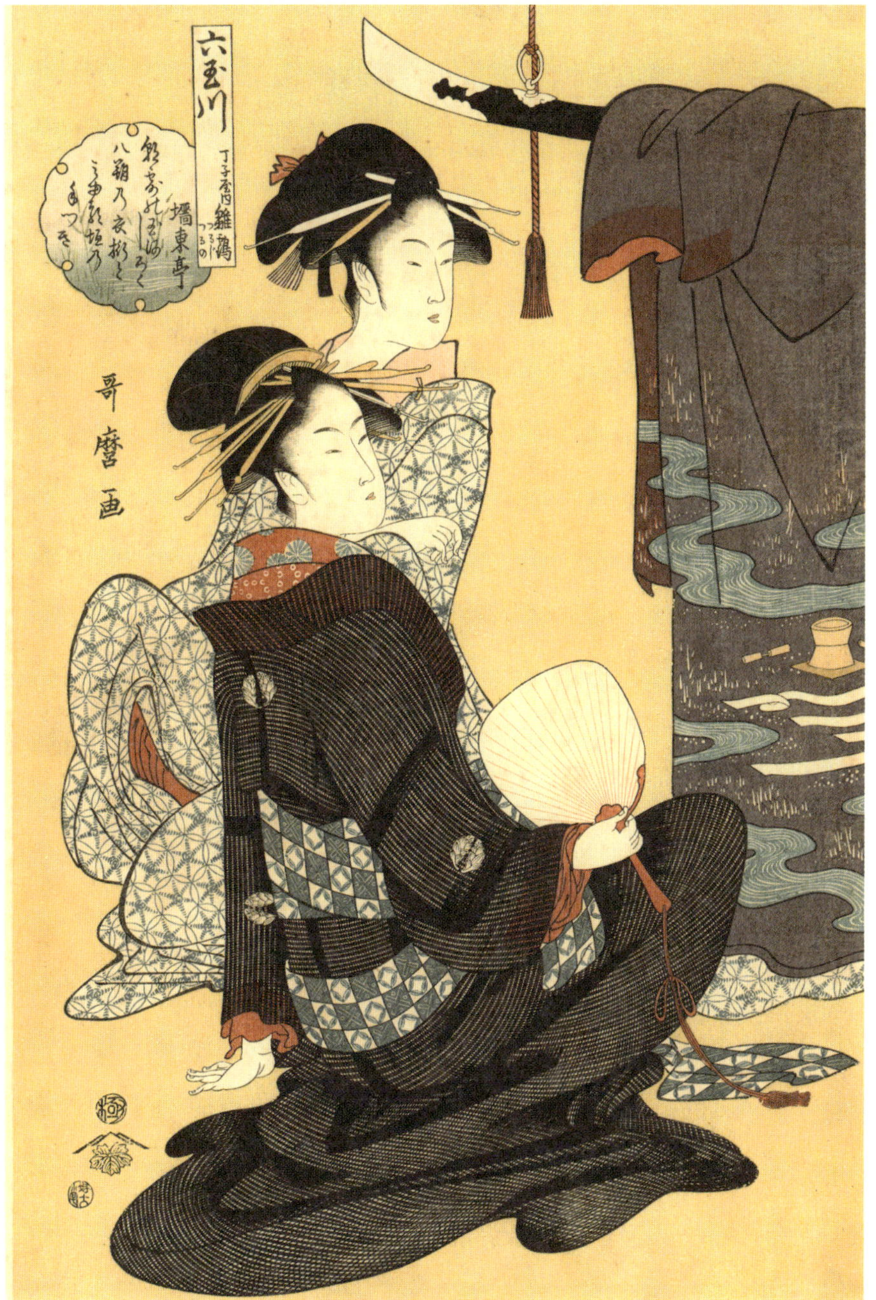

- talking kimonos

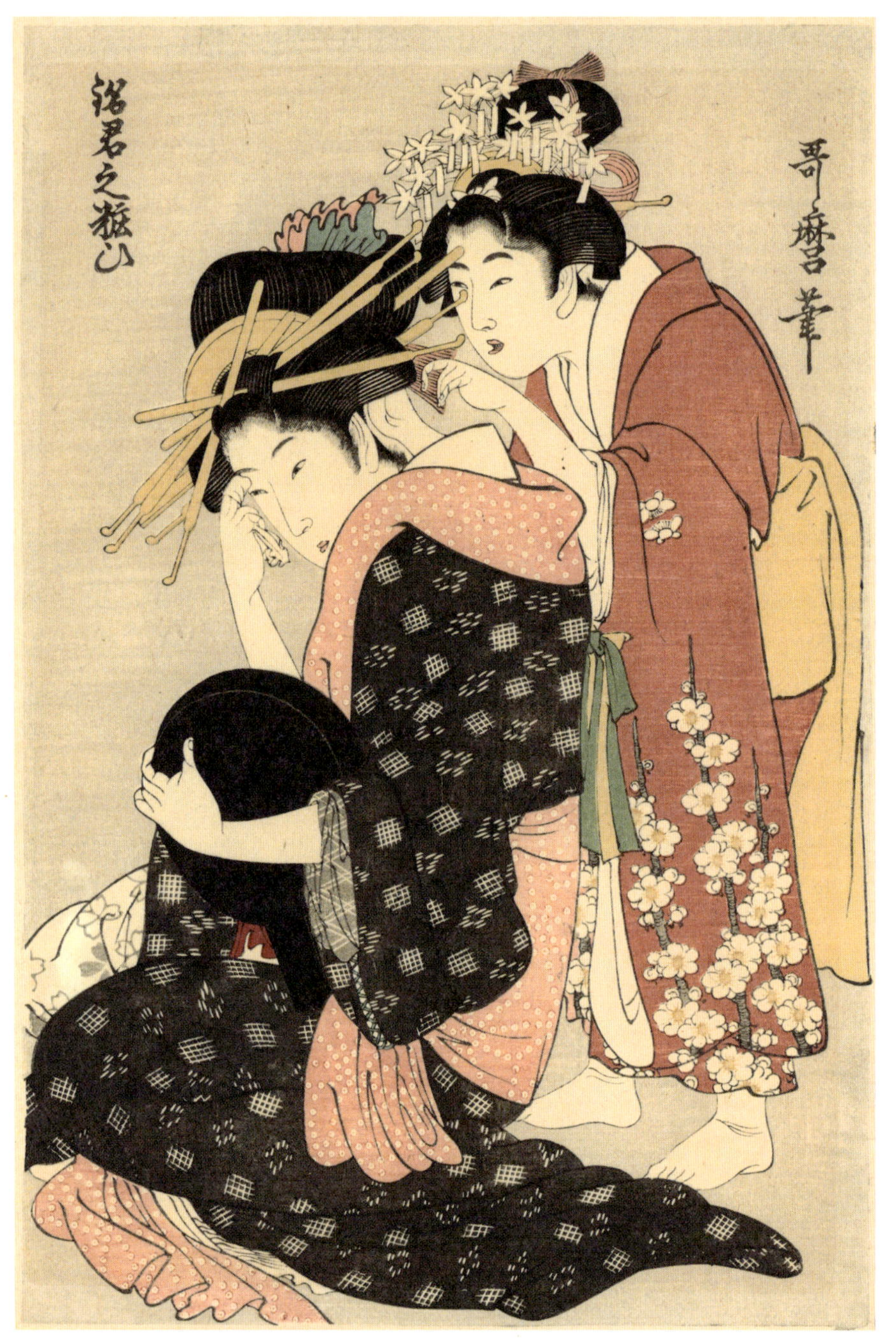

- attending to hair and make up

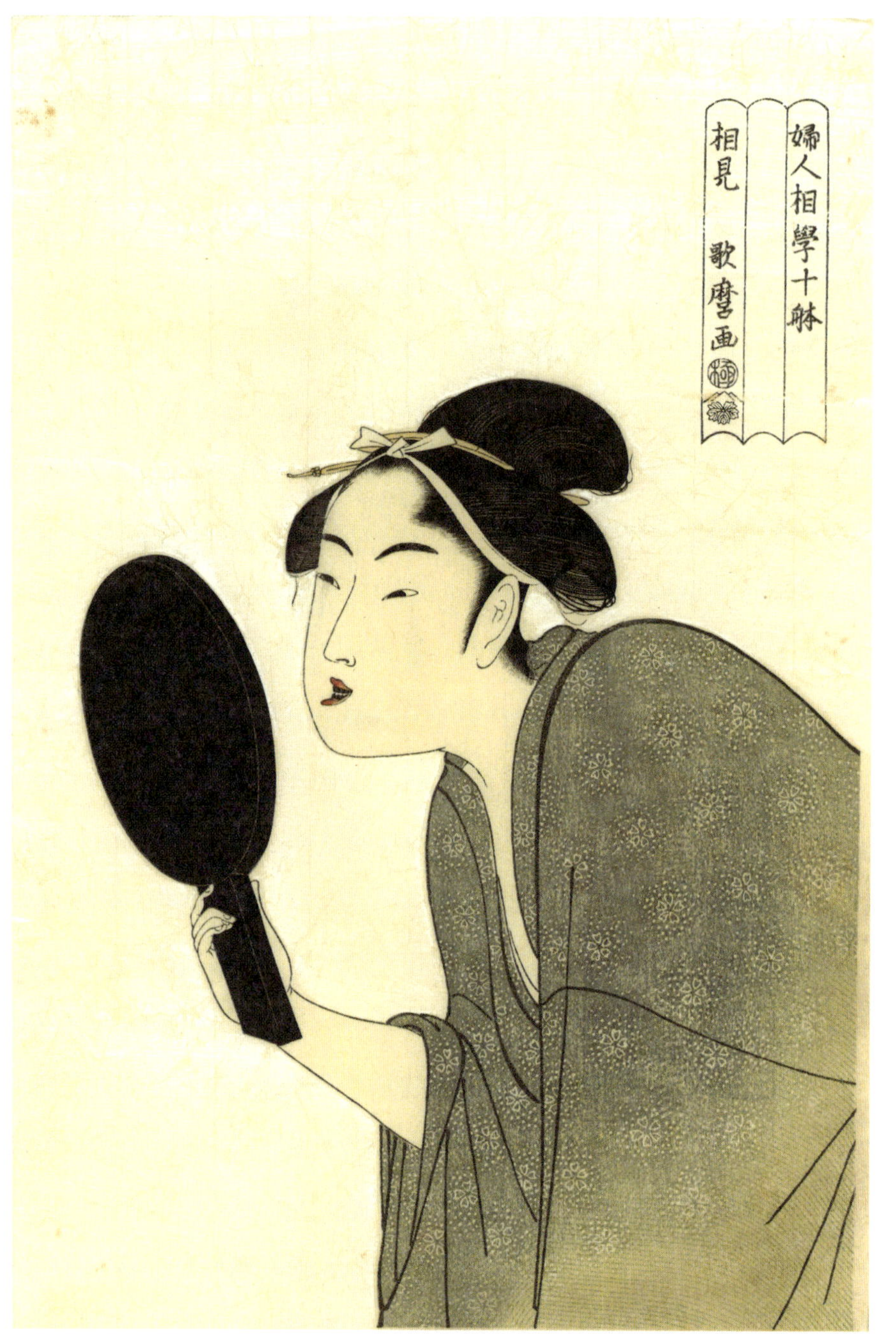

- and teeth.

This is '*The Interesting Type*' from the series *Ten Classes of Women's Physiognomy* (1792-93). It shows the practice of teeth blackening, ohaguro, popular in the Edo period. Black teeth signified a woman's sexual maturity - but also covered up the need for dentistry! The practice was banned in 1870.

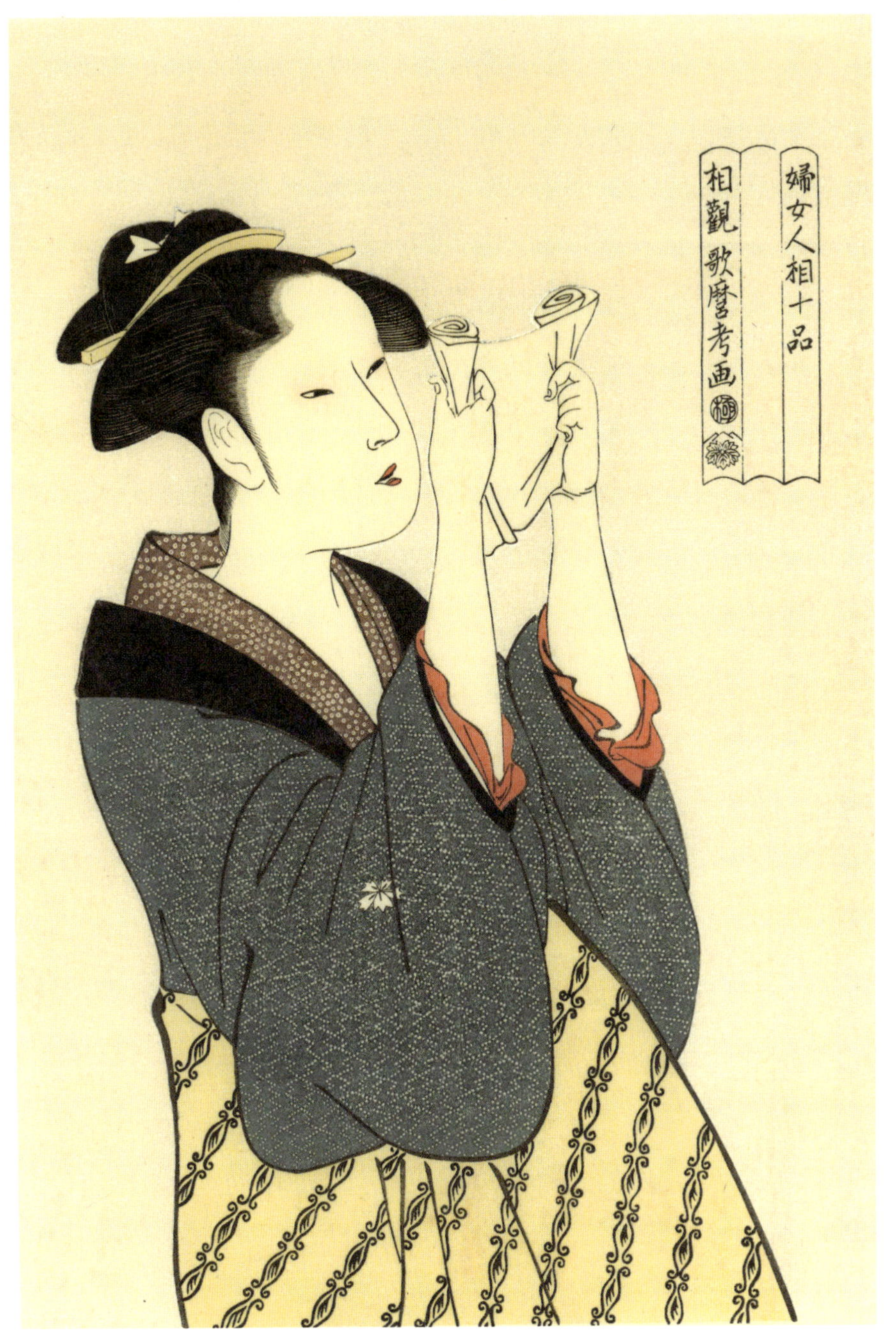

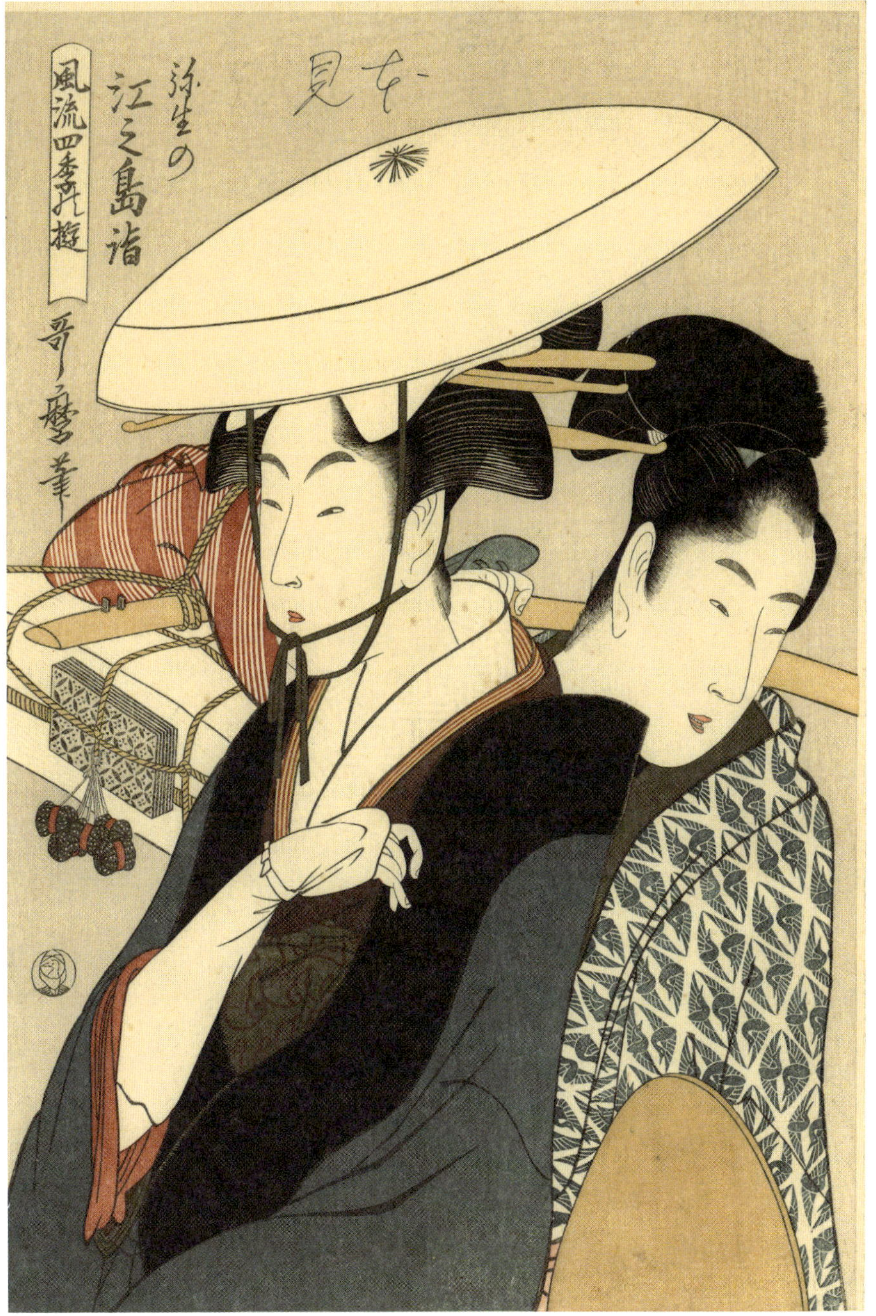

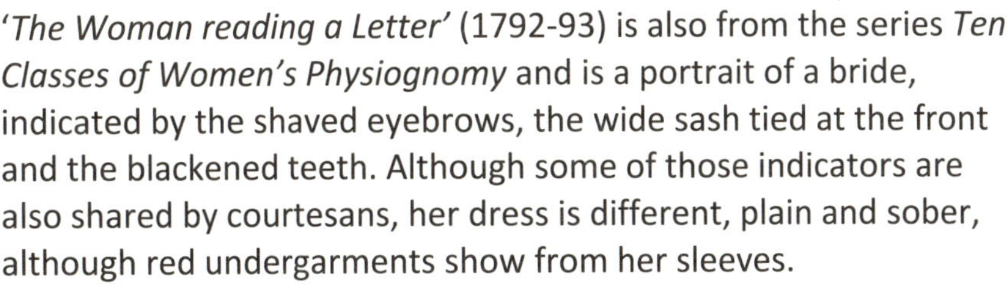
'*The Woman reading a Letter*' (1792-93) is also from the series *Ten Classes of Women's Physiognomy* and is a portrait of a bride, indicated by the shaved eyebrows, the wide sash tied at the front and the blackened teeth. Although some of those indicators are also shared by courtesans, her dress is different, plain and sober, although red undergarments show from her sleeves.

Utamaro was fascinated by high born women, like this mistress and male servant on the way to a shrine at Enoshima, near modern day Tokyo. It's title is *'Pilgrimage to Enoshima in the Third Month'* from the series *Elegant Pastimes in the Four Seasons.*

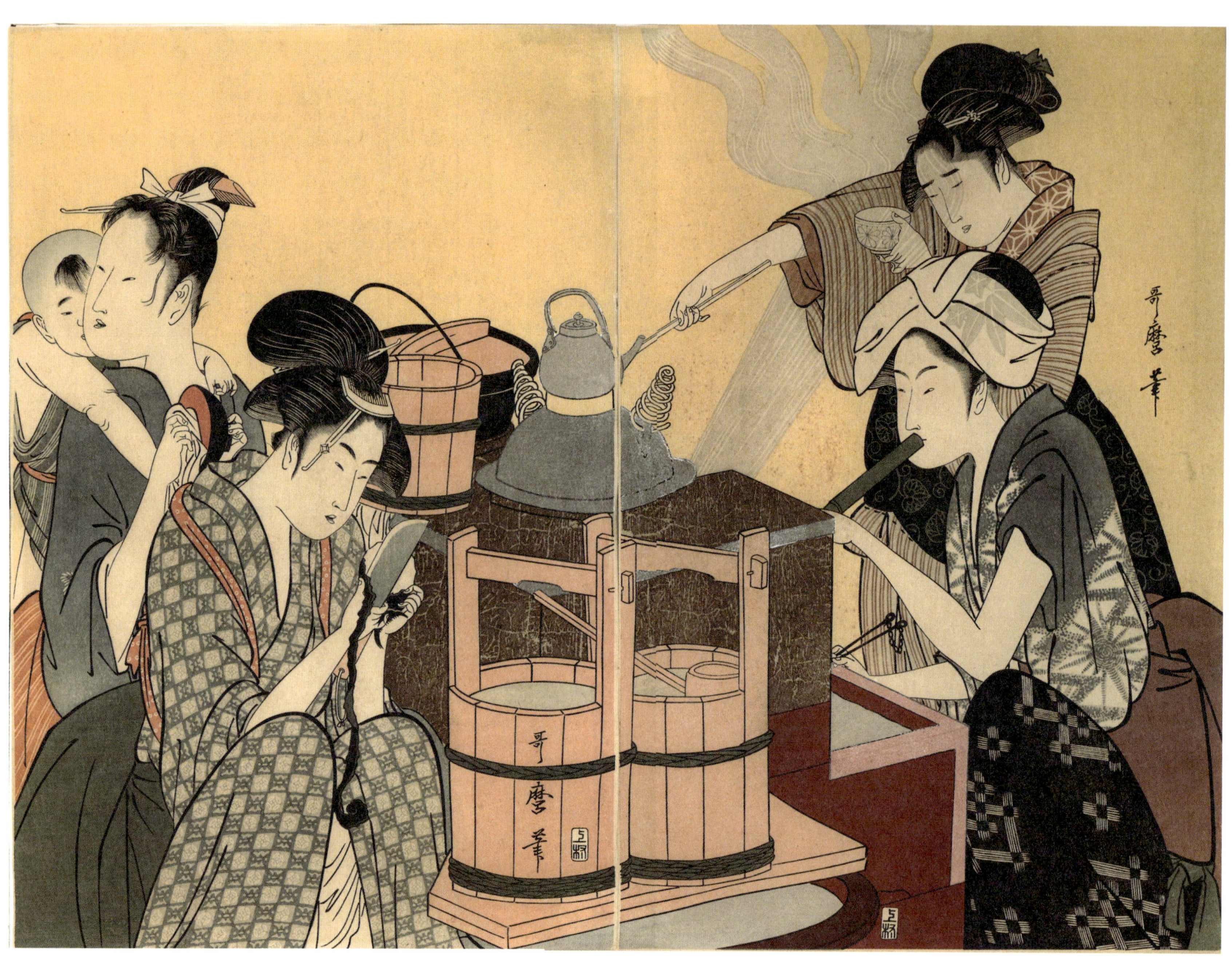

Utamaro also had a soft spot for women going about domestic activities. As we can see *'In the Kitchen'* (c.1794-95)

This is very different from the previous **Utamaro** images of women, which were very much 'types' depicted for the interest of men. Here he shows us the unglamorous world of women's work, showing informal female companionship.

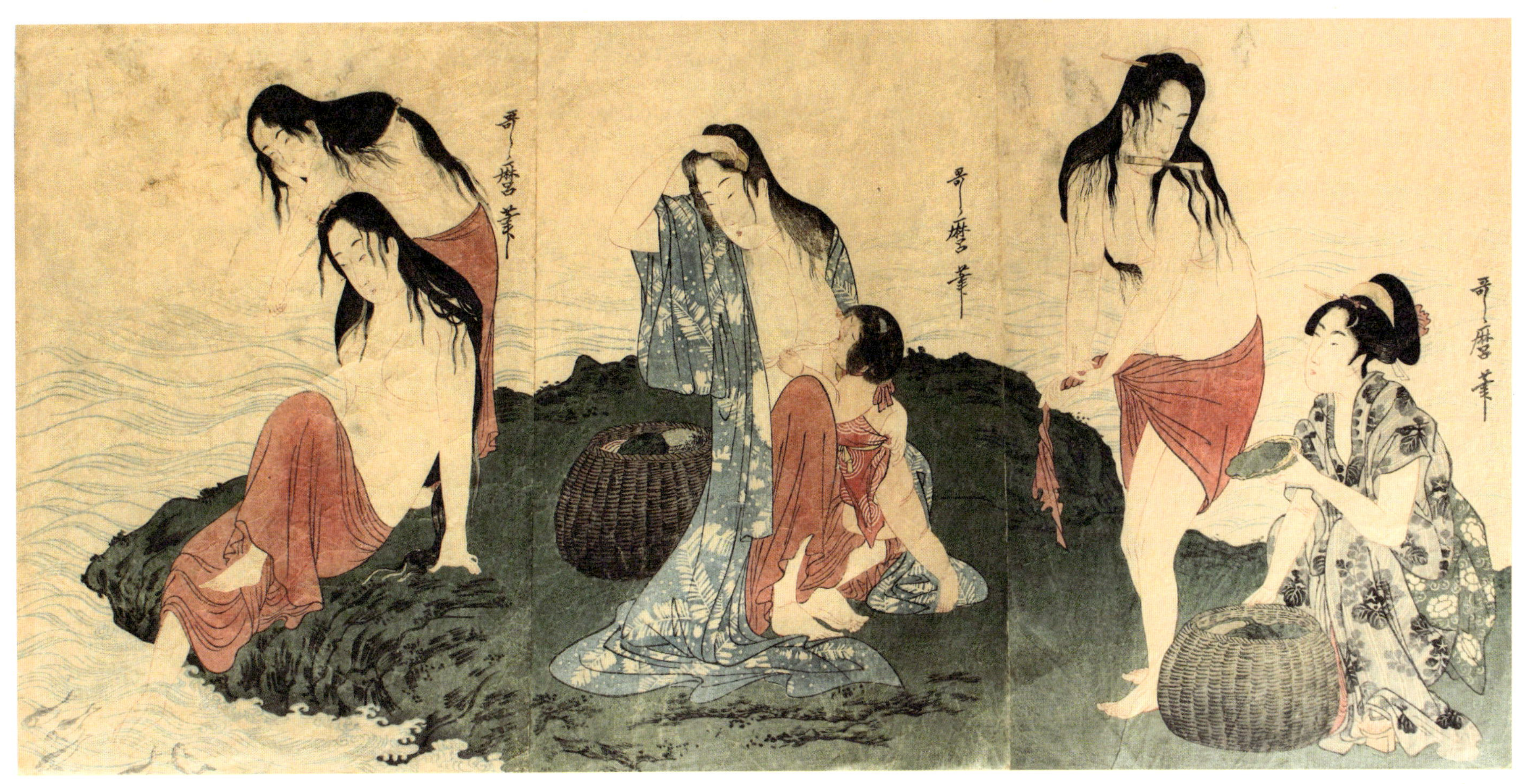

Then there is **Utamaro'**s fascination with the most physical and dangerous women's work - like in this *'Awabi Divers Triptych'* (1797). These are women who dive for abalone, here selling to a townswoman. It's a common enough subject but in this version **Utamaro** makes the women heroic goddesses and the mother and son in the centre almost a madonna and child - at least to western eyes. Good to conclude this section with an undisputed masterpiece.

Utamaro's contemporaries may have been somewhat overshadowed by him but many created fine bijin-ga, as we can see in the following reprints.

Ichirakutei EISUI (active 1790 to 1823)

Below we have a wonderful portrait by **Eisui** of the celebrated courtesan Hanaogi with a translucent fan, from her establishment the Ogi House.

Chobunsai EISHI (1756 to 1829)

To the right we have Ohane & Ofuku with musical instruments in *Selected Geisha of the Yoshiwara*. **Eishi** was born into a wealthy samurai family and left privilege to become an artist. This is the left panel of a triptych - see below.

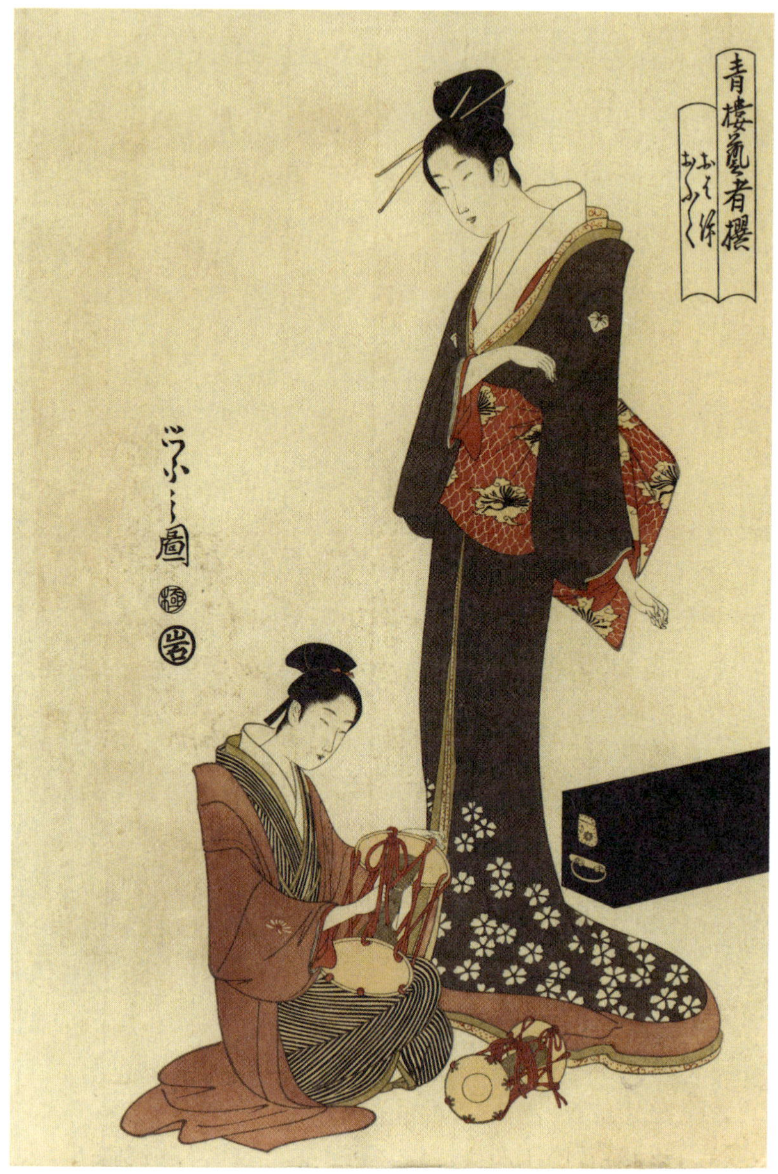

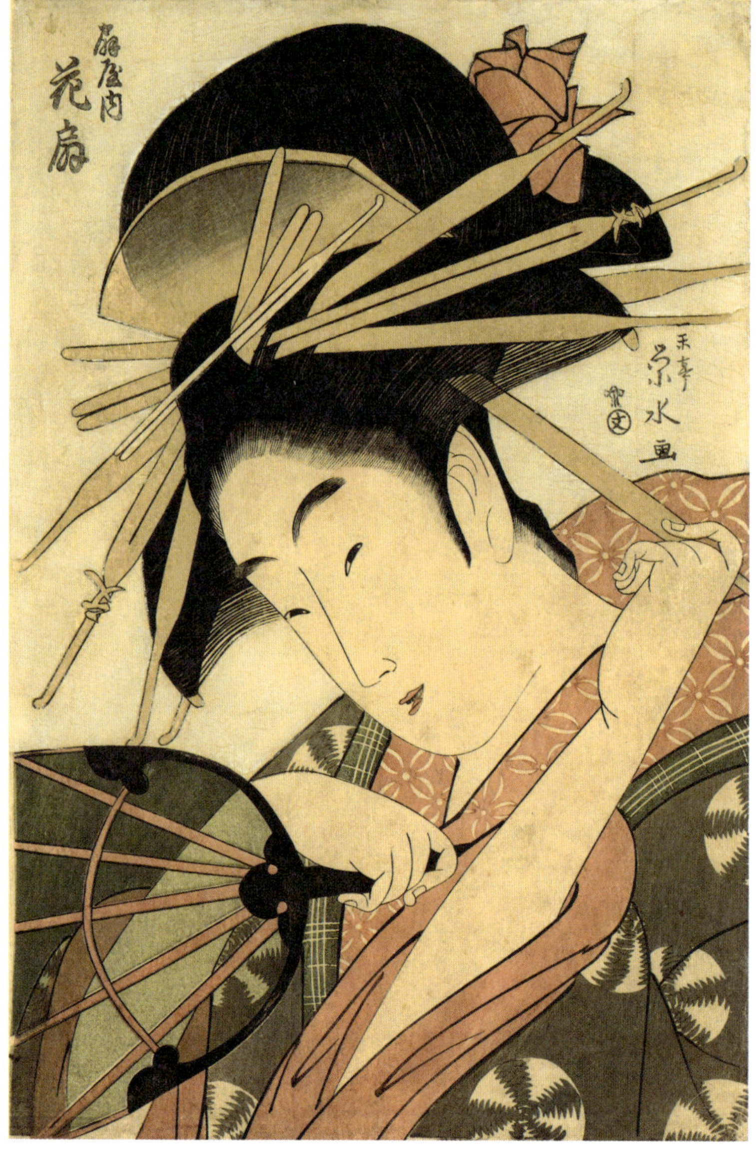

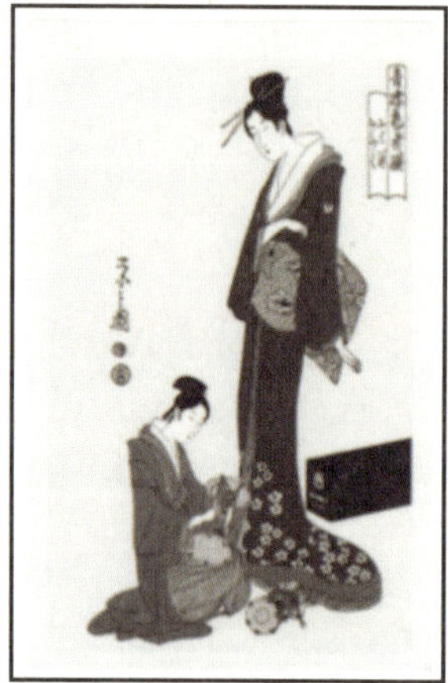

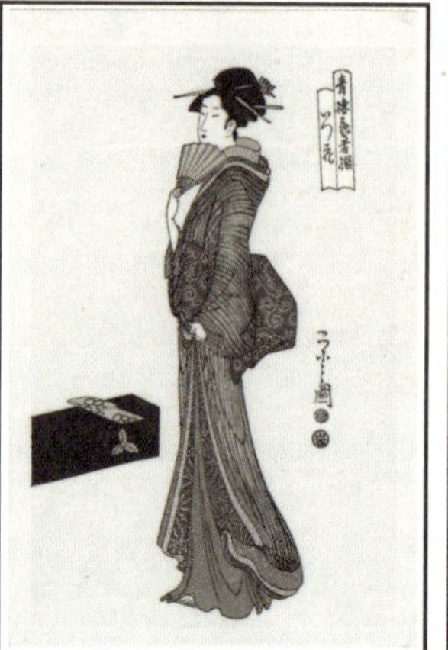

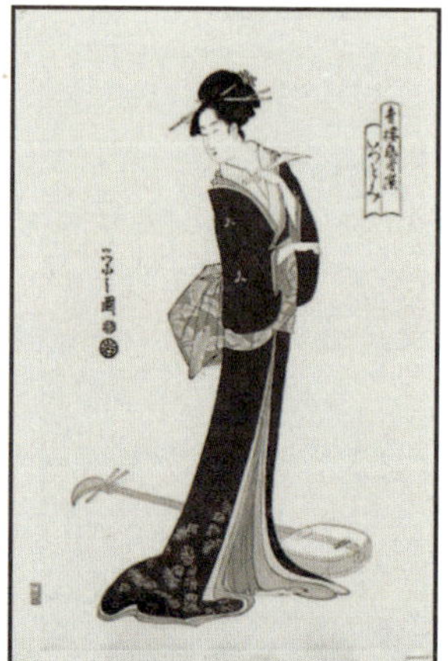

Eishosai CHOKI (active 1786-1808)

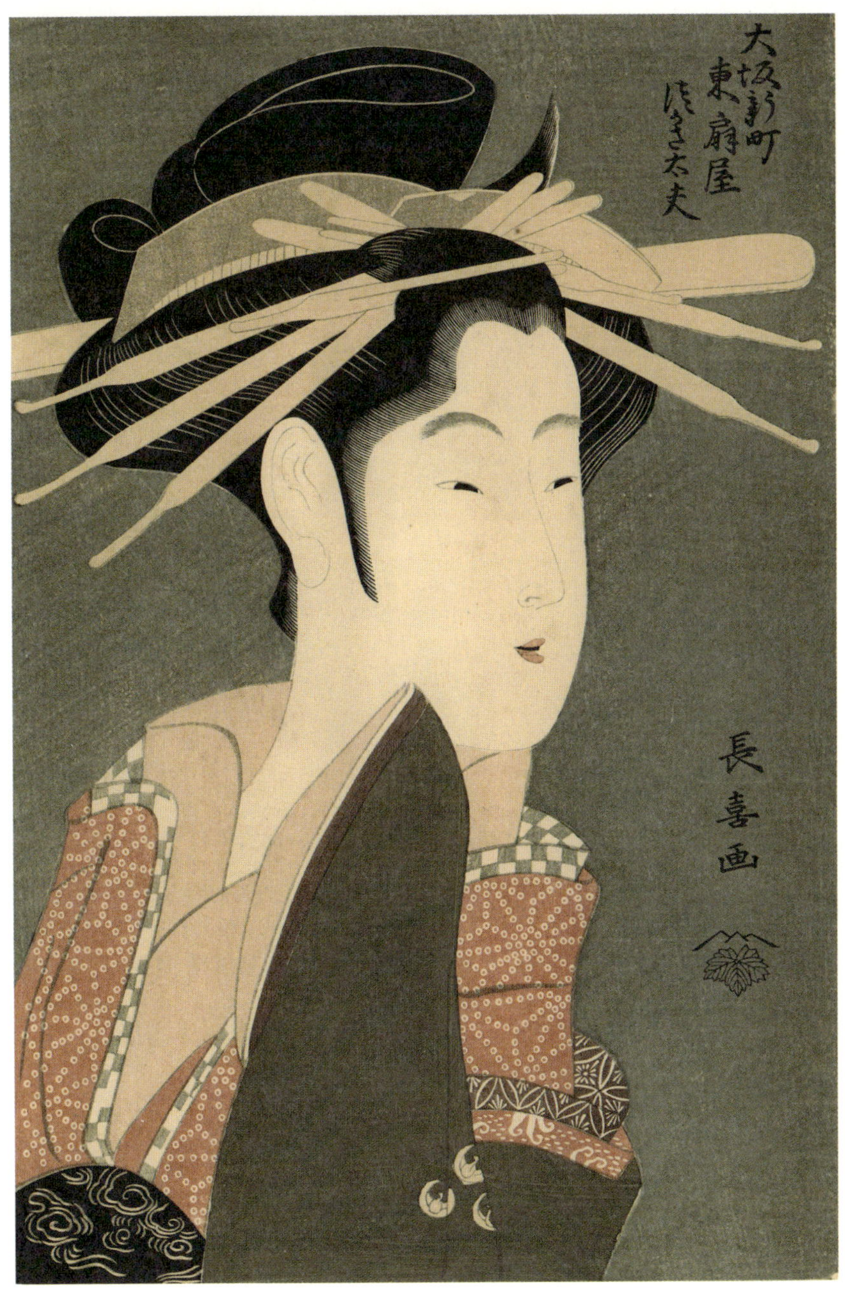

This lovely **Choki** image is of Tsukasa-dayu, from the Shinmachi 'pleasure district' in Osaka.

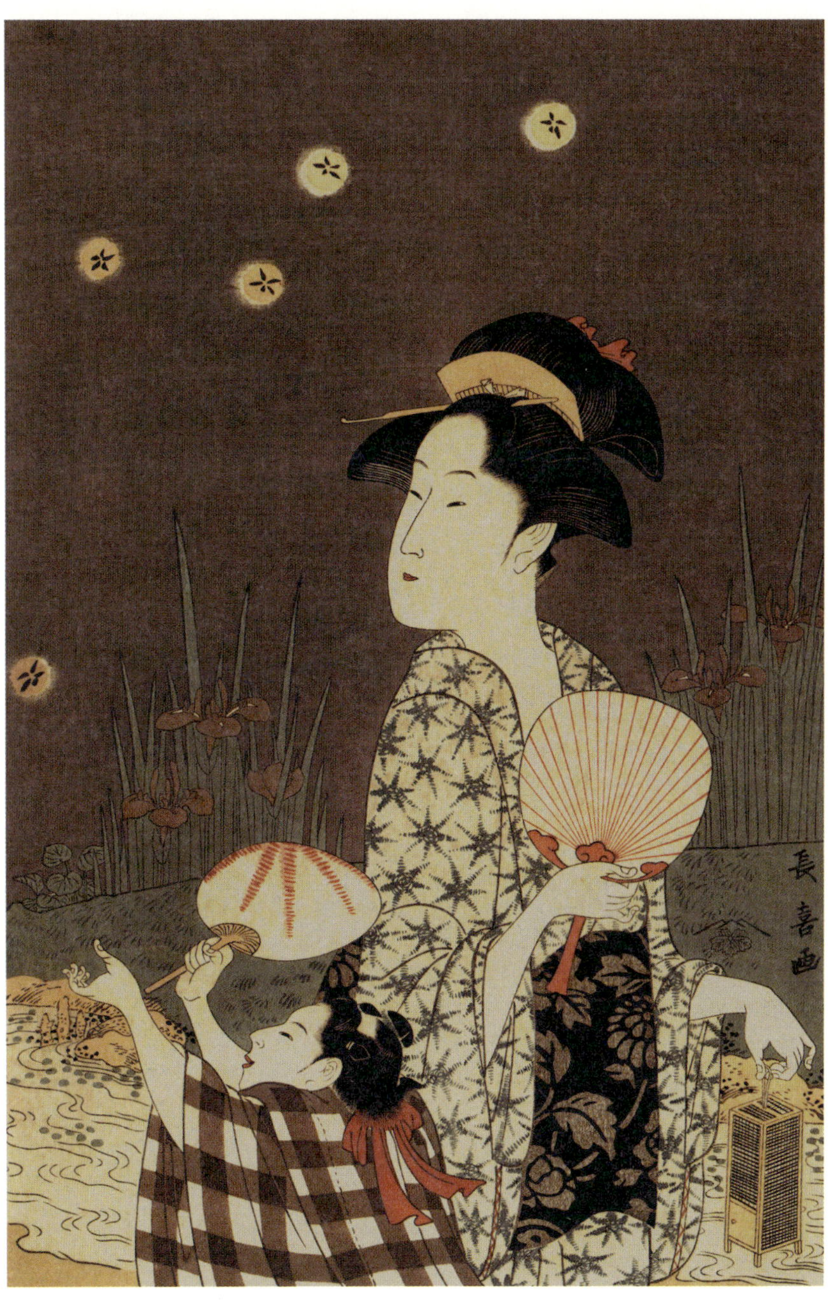

He didn't only make pictures of courtesans, as indicated by this masterwork of a *'Woman and Child Catching Fireflies'* (c.1795).

EXTRAS & RUMINATIONS AFTER CHAPTER ONE

Some say that the death of **Utamaro** in 1806 ended the greatest period of woodblock prints in Japanese art. I disagree but it is worth reading the evaluation of *'Woman seated on the Edge of a Veranda'* by the author A. Davison Ficke in his 1915 book *Chats on Japanese Prints.*

290 CHATS ON JAPANESE PRINTS

hyper-æsthetic tension of the hour. Toward the end of the decade his peculiarities grew even more marked. The necks of his figures became incredibly slender; the bodies took on unnatural length; a snaky languor pervaded them. One print, his famous "Woman Seated on the Edge of a Veranda," reproduced in Plate 40, may serve as representative of them all. The drawing of the draperies and of the figure beneath them is studied with extraordinary fidelity; in fact, so human and real a figure is hardly to be found in the work of any preceding artist. But on the other hand, Utamaro has used his keen realistic power merely as a scaffolding, and has proceeded to build up on it a work that goes over almost into the region of symbolism. In the slender delicacy of this figure, the splendid black of her elaborate coiffure, the drooping fragility of her body, the sensuous grace and refinement, the languor and exhaustion—in all these speak the super-sensible gropings and hungers of Utamaro himself. Out of a living woman he created his disturbing symbol of the impossible desires that are no less subtle or painful because they are born of the flesh. With nerves keyed beyond the healthy pitch, he dreamed this melody whose strange minor chords alone could stir the satiated spirit. He caught and idealized the lines and colours of mortal weariness.

"Woman," says Von Seidlitz, "had always played a prominent part in the popular art of the country, but now Utamaro placed one type of the sex in the absolute centre of all attention—the type, namely, of the courtesan initiated into all the refinements of

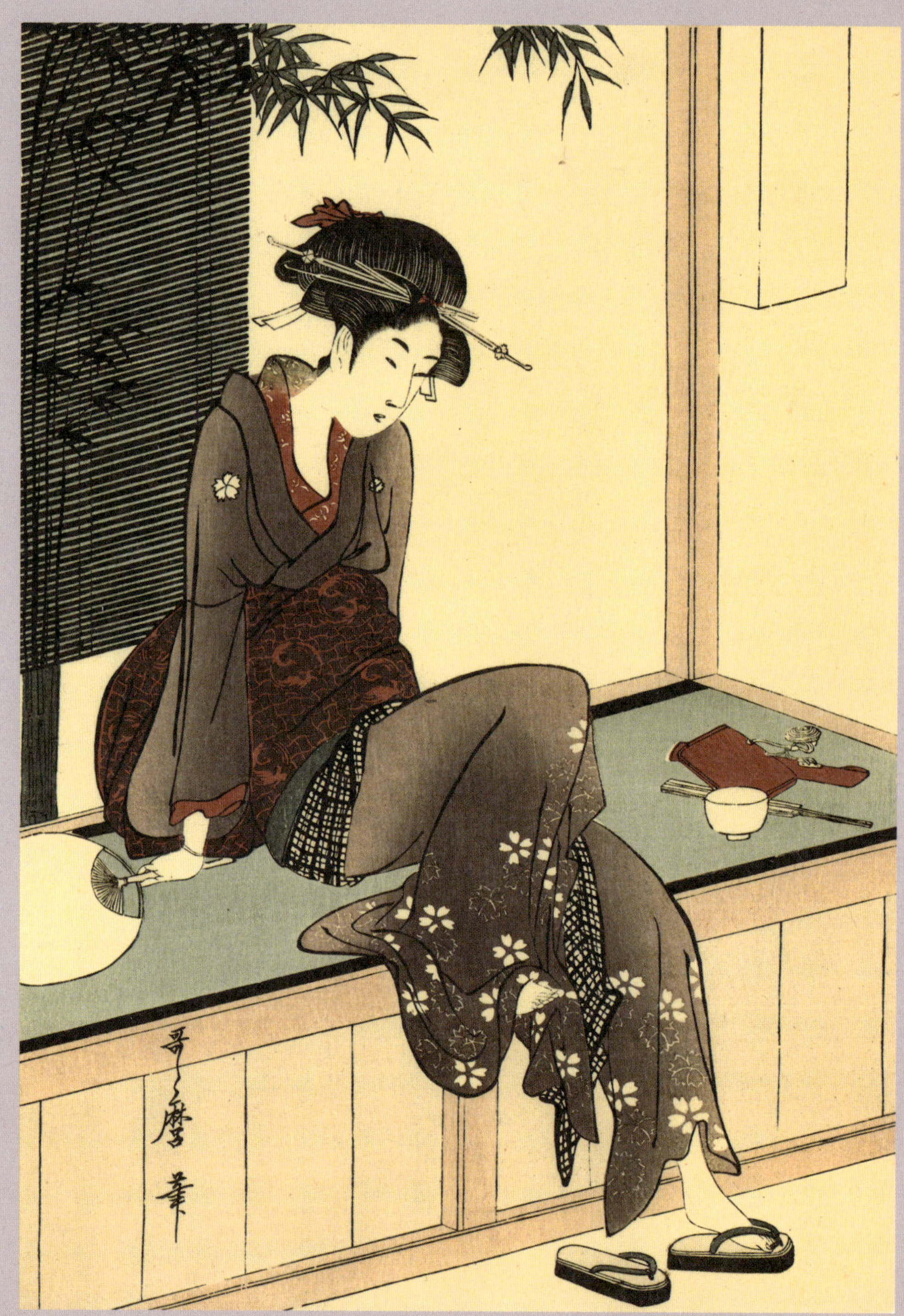

We shouldn't forget the influential and mysterious **Toshusai SHARAKU** who was active for only ten months in 1794-95. This Kabuki portrait is rare and much desired. One that I know of was recently on sale at a top London art gallery for £69,000 - but mine is a lowly reprint.

The portrait is of admired male actor Matsumoto Yonesaburo in the role of Shinobu. She became a courtesan in order to trap and wreak vengeance on her father's murderers. The play was performed in June 1794.

Sharaku was not valued in his own time, particularly by the people of Edo who found his work unattractive. He was though respected by other artists and his unique style permeates subsequent ukiyo-e. Also in the book *Chats on Japanese Prints.* A. Davison Ficke wrote 'Sharaku stands on the highest level of genius, in a greatness unique, sublime, and appalling.'

The second portrait is of the actor Hanshiro IV as Shigenoi, also in a Kabuki play. The poor condition makes it look like an original, but actually it cost all of $52 - so I think we can safely say it is not!

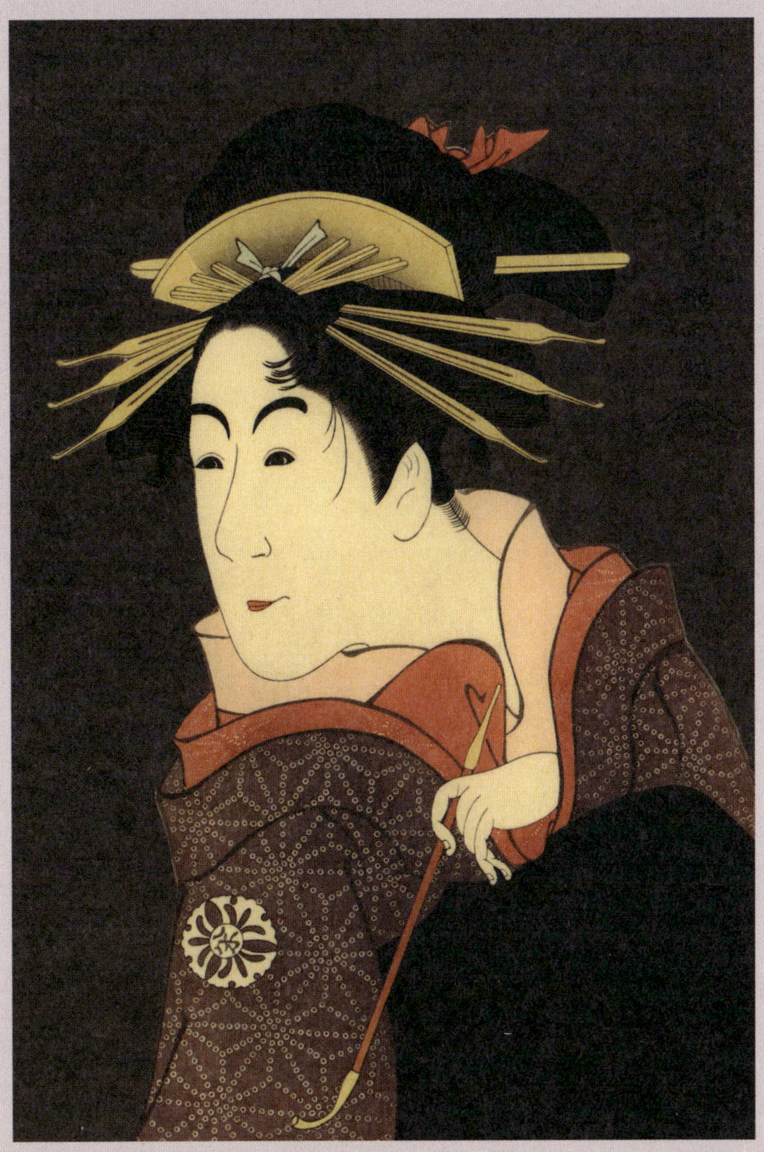

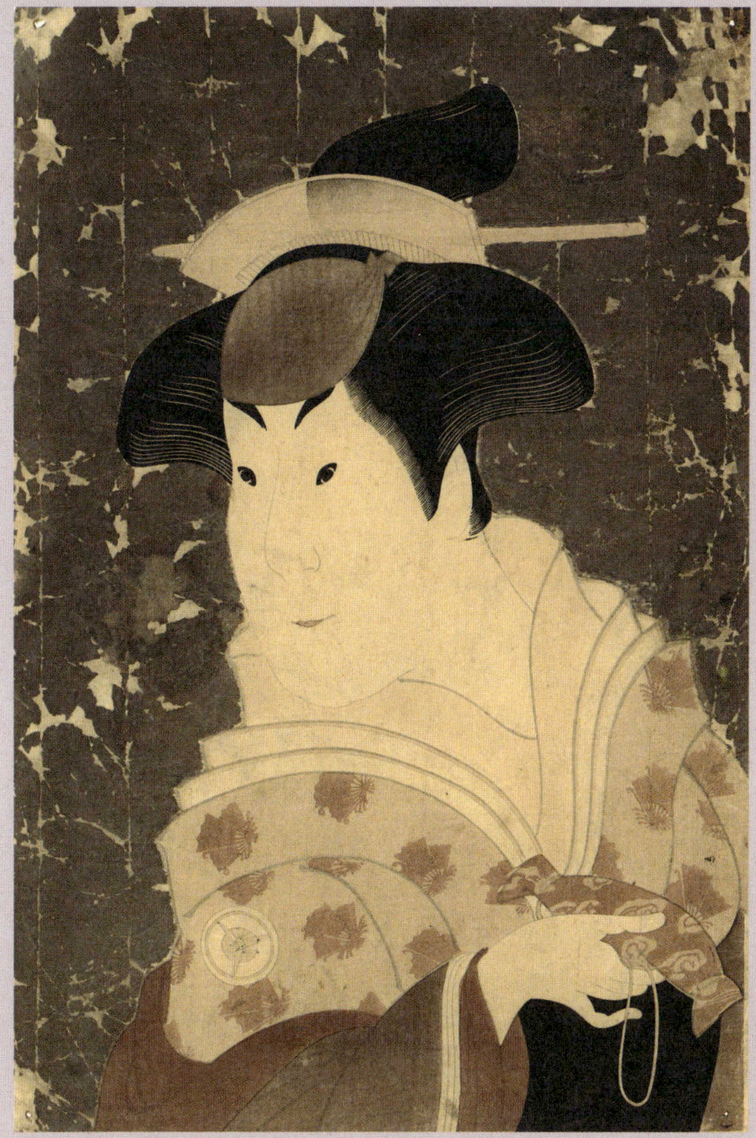

The popularity and high prices of bijin-ga and shunga have meant there have been many reprint editions, some of which are (or appear) old and could be mistaken for originals.

Most dealers are honest, but some do try it on, so there are a few basic things than can be done to avoid the simplest traps - online as well as in an art shop. Insist on seeing the back to look at the ink 'bleed-through'. Take account of the quality of paper, which is normally thin with an old print. Reputable on-line sellers will show the reverse on their websites.

This **Utamaro** has excellent bleed-through and the losses and stains at the bottom corners show it has received much attention over the years.

It is though an old reprint, that could be passed off as authentic - but the colours are a give away. In particular the red dye used for a first strike print would probably have faded more over time.

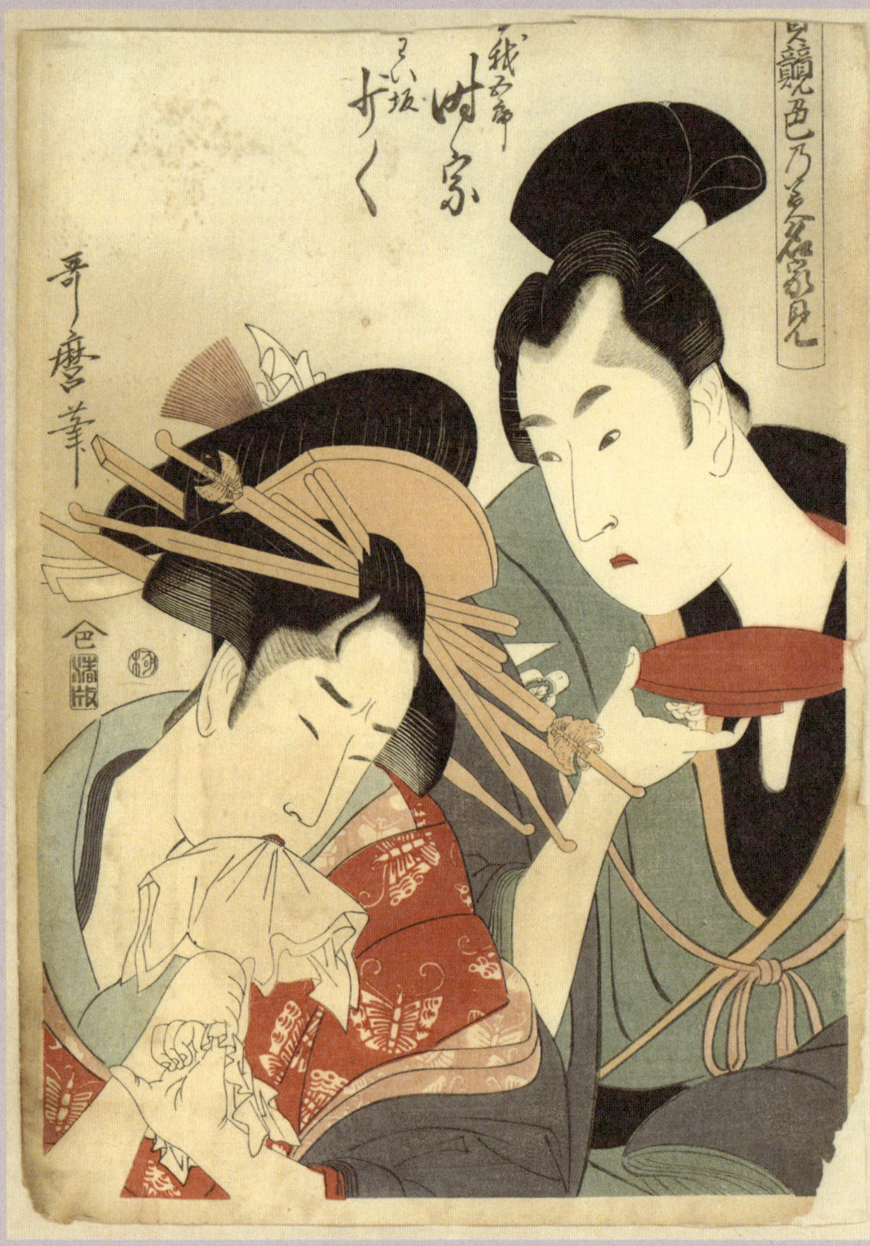

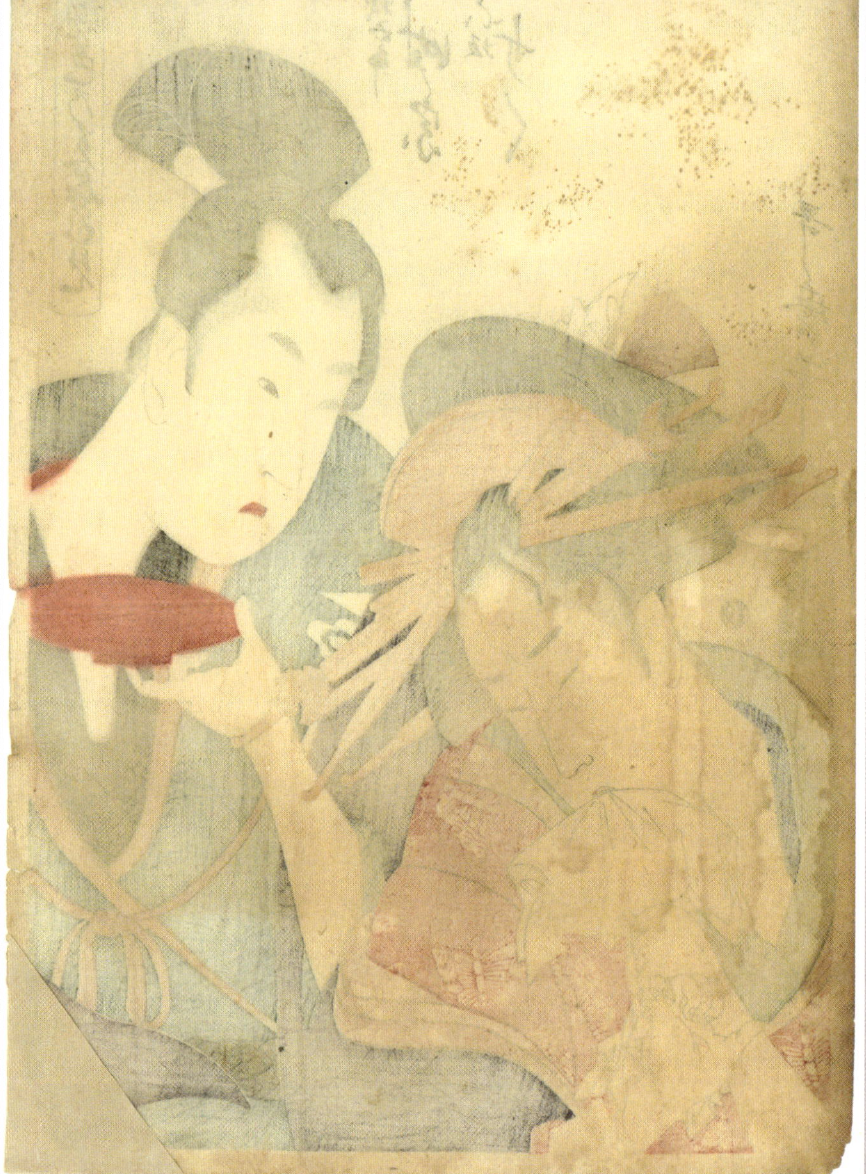

One can also check the seals and signatures. There are websites where you can investigate and so work out the origins of a print - the artist, the period, the publisher, etc.

Also you can check on-line to compare the print you are interested in with others in art shops, auction houses or museums. Some show good quality later editions and occasionally reprints - if they are significant.

Examination can be complicated by some fragile prints being backed by old paper, particularly when there is worm damage - as with this original by **Keisai Eisen** (more of him later).

Worm damage was caused by deathwatch beetle larva in wooden furniture. Sometimes their passage can be tracked as they munch their way through a stack of precious prints.

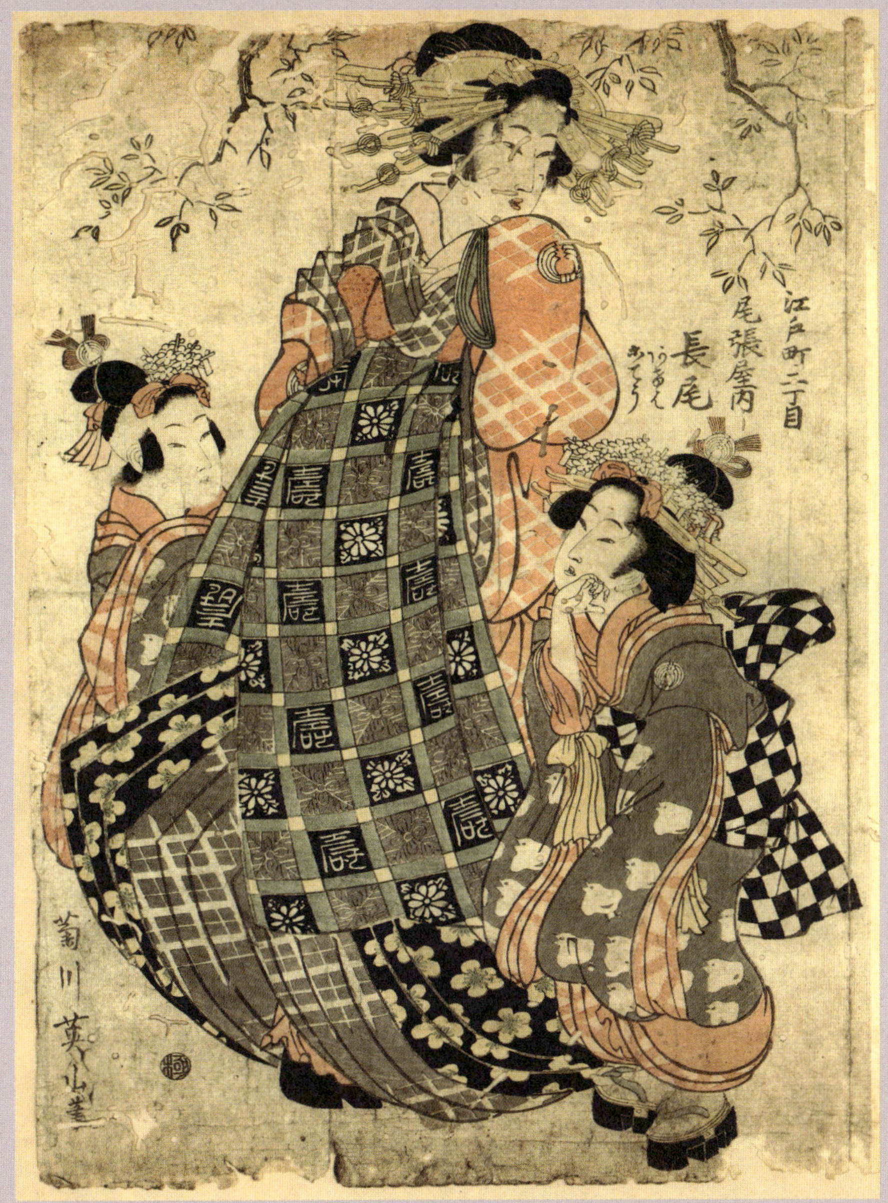

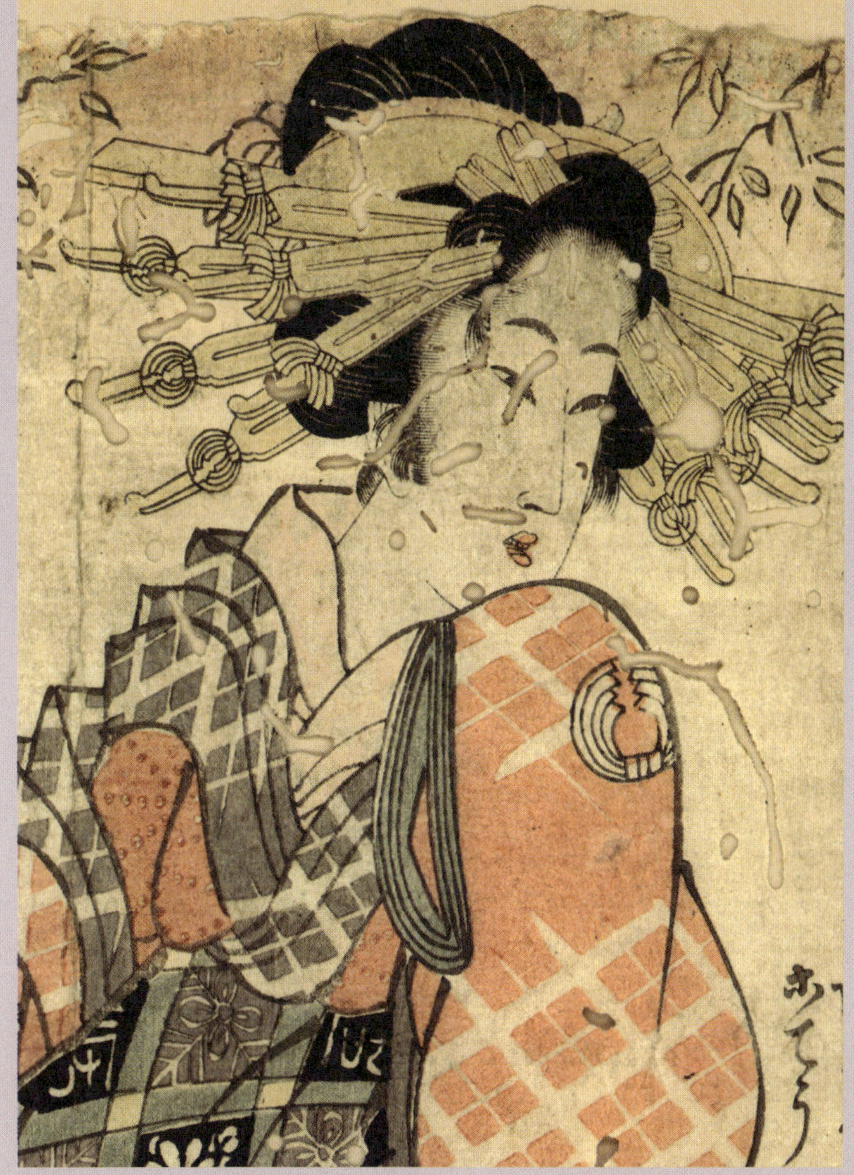

Look at repairs and consider if previous owners would have bothered if the print didn't have some value. The **Utamaro** reprint below has various repairs around the edges with two large patches where it has been considered too fragile - as can be seen on the reverse.

The paper is very brittle and a split has developed top right which needs attention. This is unusual with first strikes as most prints will have softened with age.

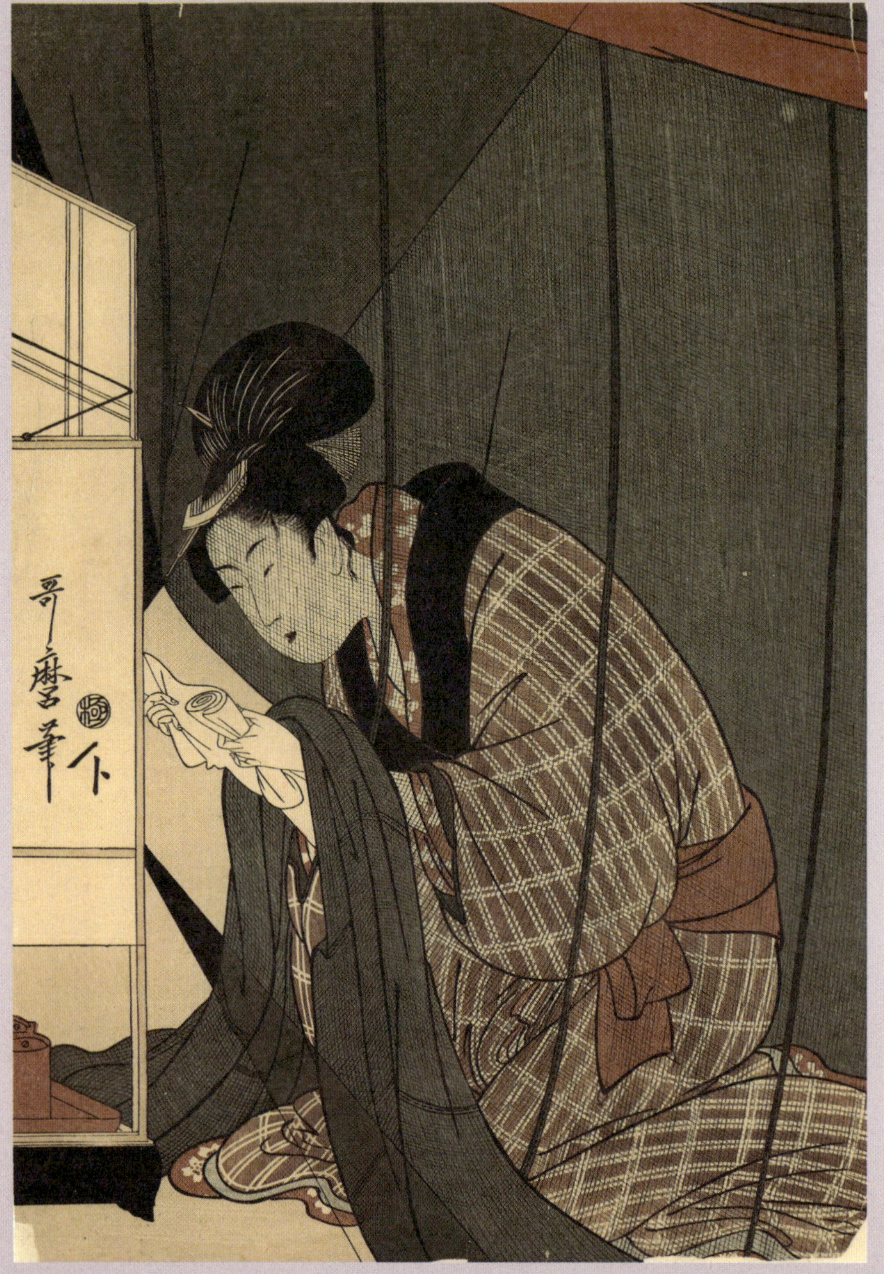

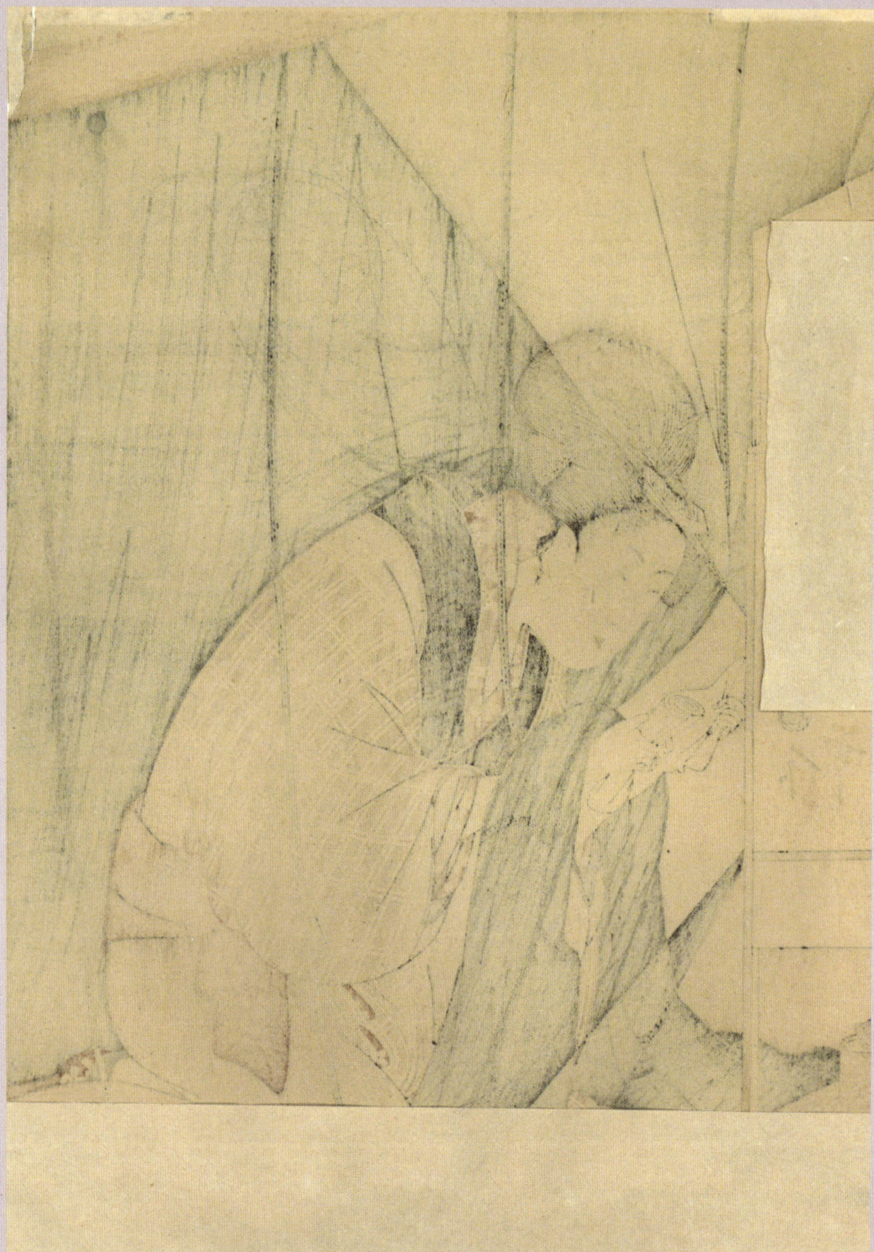

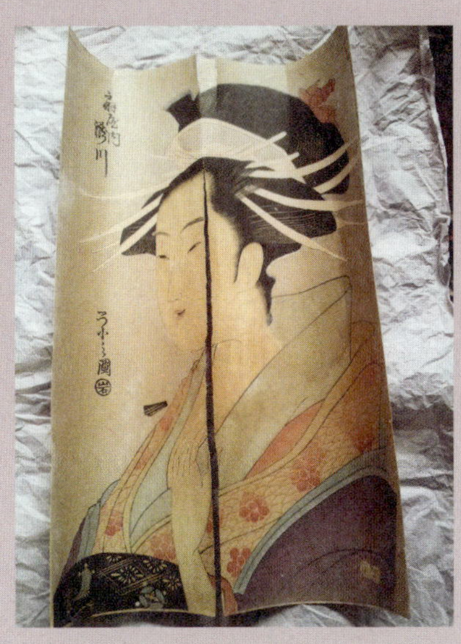

The disaster on this page makes the point most dramatically. I purchased this **Eishi** reprint from an inexperienced seller on Ebay. He sent it rolled up in a tube, apparently safe and sound. But when I came to extract it, the print broke into two halves and bits fell off. I'm pleased to say he was honourable enough to refund, having learnt that it is advisable to package and ship flat.

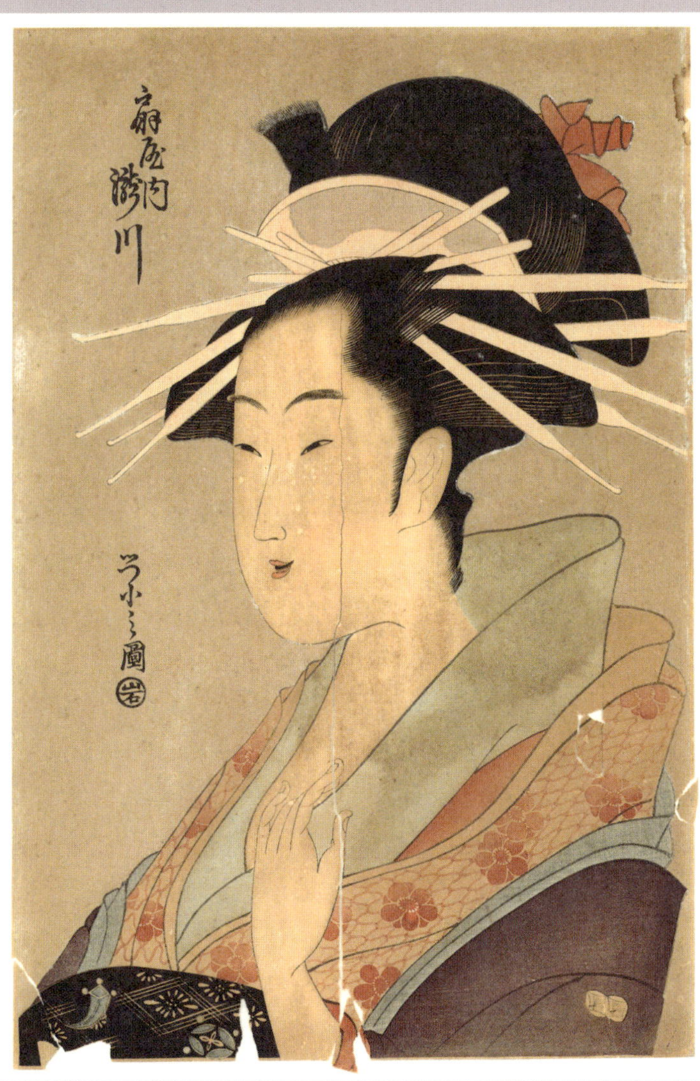

Beautiful original prints are preferred by every collector but I also like to acquire finely crafted reprints, that I can frame and display. Some of these may be quite old and have that special patina of age, demonstrating that many owners have enjoyed the print in the past. There is irony in that the most sought after originals are those that have least evidence of age.

Rare originals should not be displayed for too long, and never in direct sunlight. And the same goes for beautiful old reprints. Many a wonderful treasure has been ruined this way, loosing vibrant colour - and value.

I mix and match, as I like to be surrounded by my collection, rotating them so they are not displayed for too long. However I can understand the purist who will only go for originals with provenance but you do have to have deep pockets - extremely deep if you are going for the very best, rare and valuable. And you can't look at them as often as you might like. I keep my crown jewels locked away for safe keeping!

With the appropriate information, you can decide at what level you want to collect. It is very satisfying to find an affordable original and sometimes it's exciting to find one worthy of a bit more than you'd normally spend.

Chapter 2

THE PEAK

into the 1800's and beyond

WE NOW FEARLESSLY EXPLORE the next century after the experience of Chapter 1. When we pass into the 1800's we enter into the richest period of Japanese woodblock prints - although some detractors see the turn of the century as the beginning of the end - much of the work being 'decadent' and of little value. I do not hold that view.

Utamaro passed his influence on to all the great artists of this time, and they are mostly inter-related in some way, as contemporaries, masters and students, even a father and daughter. It is fascinating to observe the changing culture, styles and fashions.

Katsushika HOKUSAI (1760-1849)

It is difficult not to begin with **Hokusai** so let's plunge into the choppy waters of his most well known image before exploring his shunga & bijin-ga, which come mostly from earlier in his career.

'The Great Wave', created around 1830-32 is a reference point for most collectors and originals never become available these days - so a good reprint is the best one can hope for. This was printed for my television programme and provides the opportunity to show how woodblock prints are made.

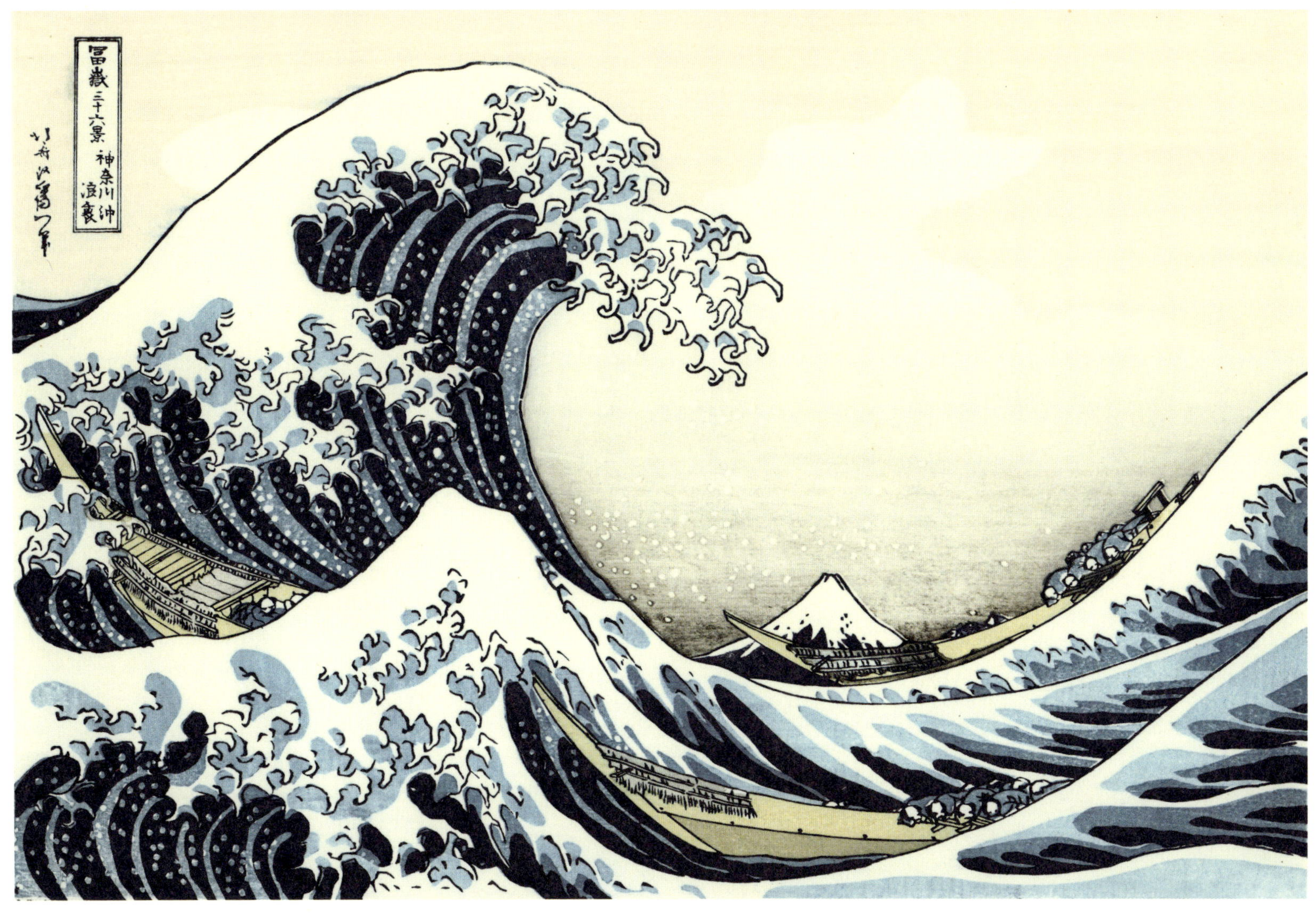

From an original drawing on almost transparent paper the image is transposed on to a block of cherry wood. This key-block line image is supplemented by multiple colour blocks. In this version eight impressions on top of each other make up the eventual finished article, so a mistake at any time can result in a worthless print.

Here we see the progression from the drawing to the finished print - and below a woodblock - showing how the image is reversed.

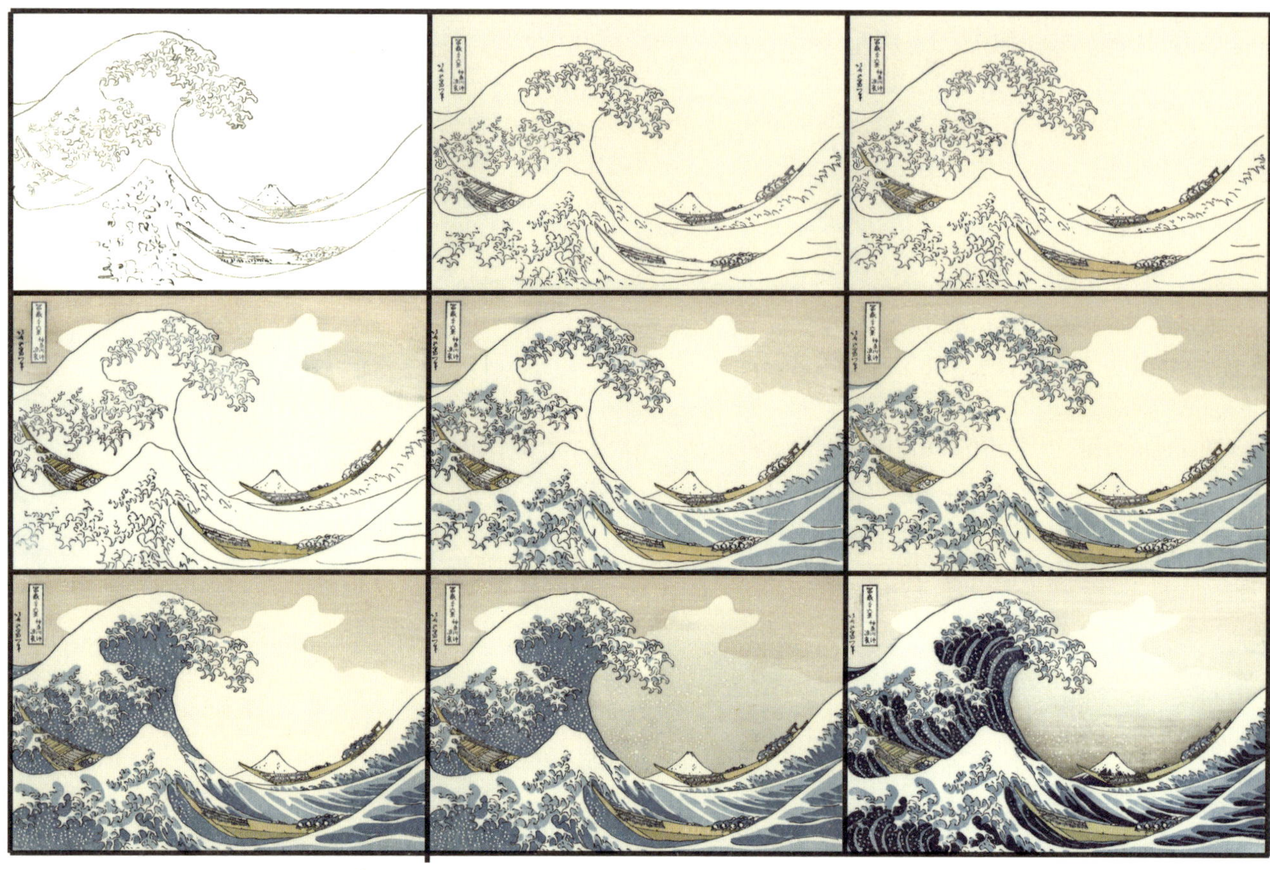

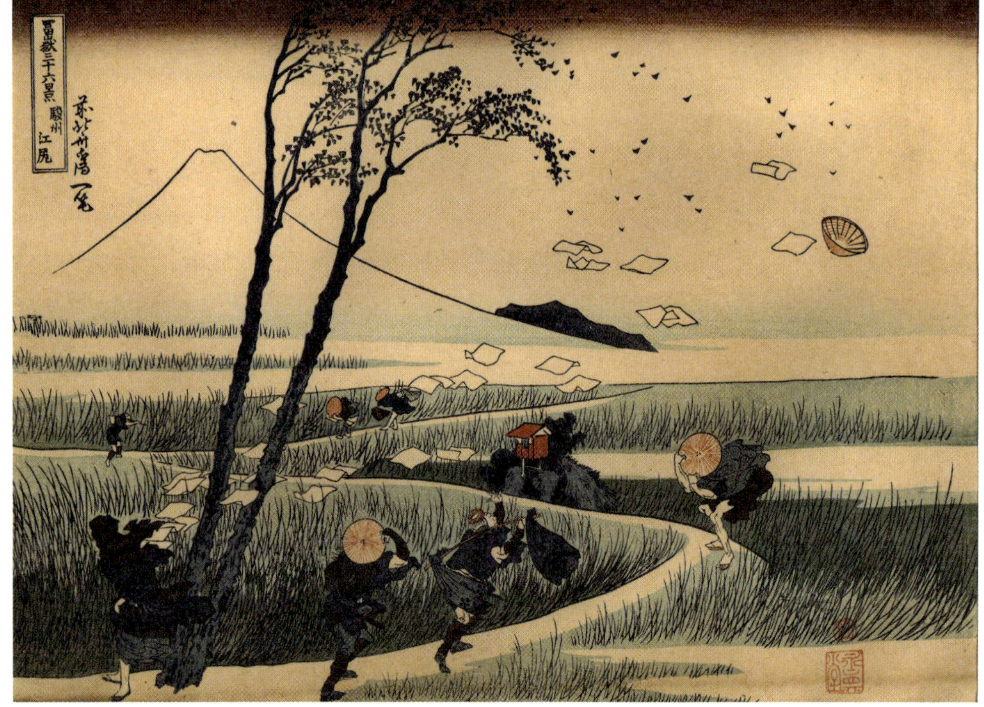

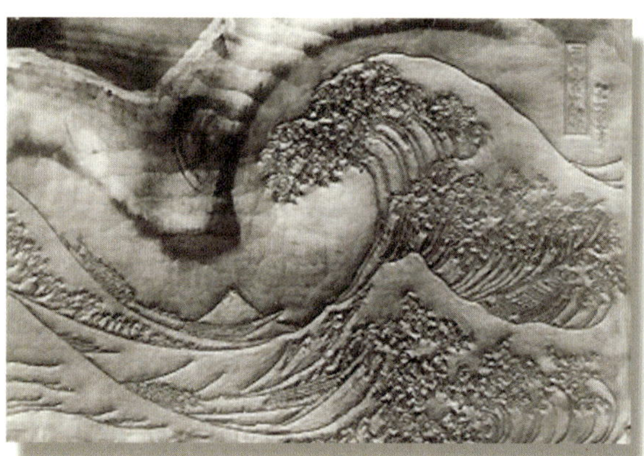

Just about all the prints featured in the book are produced this way, be they original first editions or humble reprints - like this one from the same series *36 Views of Mount Fuji.*

Shunbaisai HOKUEI (active 1827–1836)

At the time of printing, *'The Great Wave'* was just one of many **Hokusai**'s images, but it's success soon resonated among his contemporaries. This original bejin-ga of an actor as a courtesan is by **Hokuei**, a student of **Hokusai** (hence his name).

Within this image **Hokuei** uses the **Hokusai** wave imagery in the design of the kimono. Supernatural night-time forces are also at work, indicted by a floating flame. The print was created in 1836, only a few years after *'The Great Wave'*, so it is possible that **Hokuei** was paying homage or perhaps just reflecting on his mentor's new found popularity.

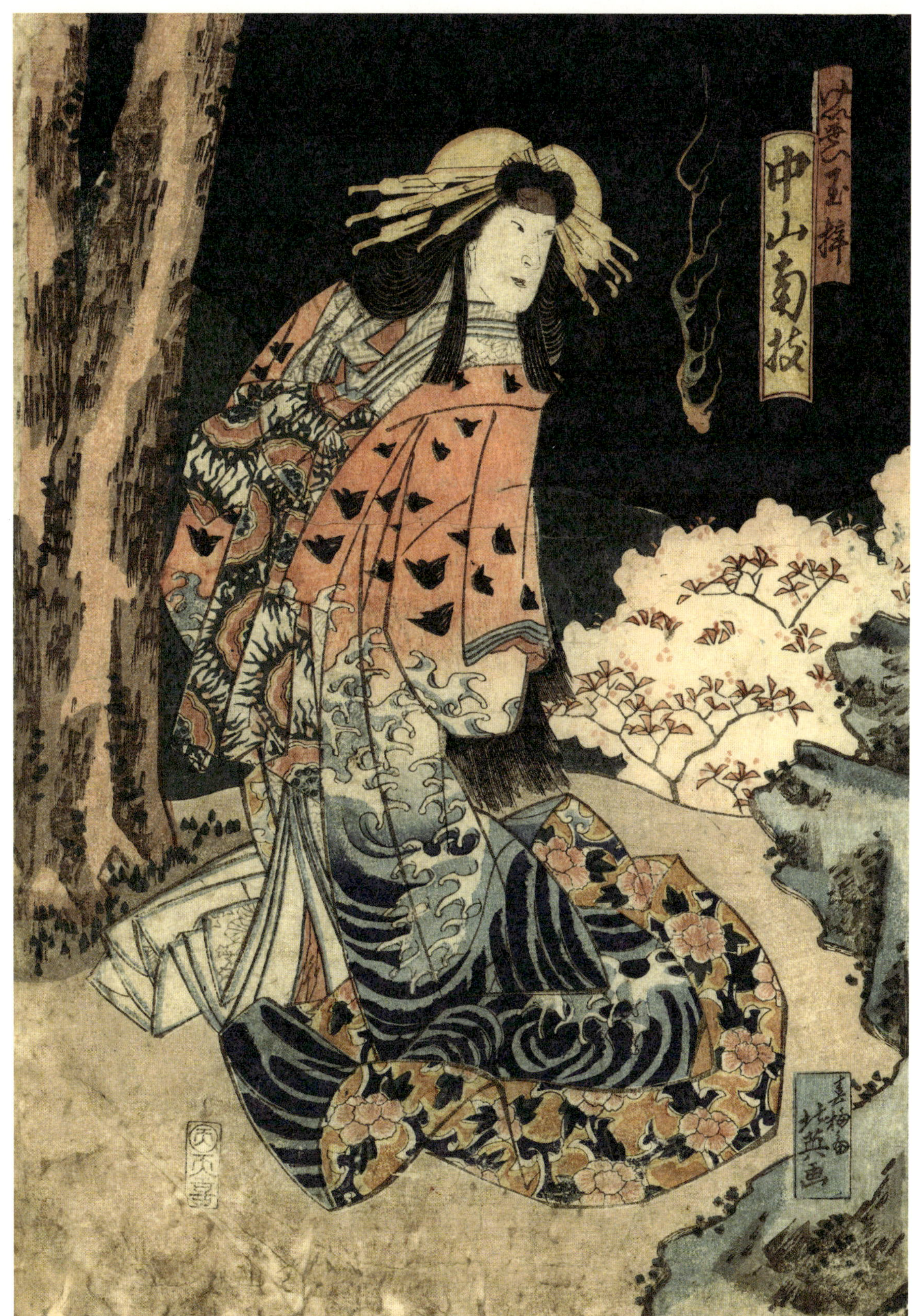

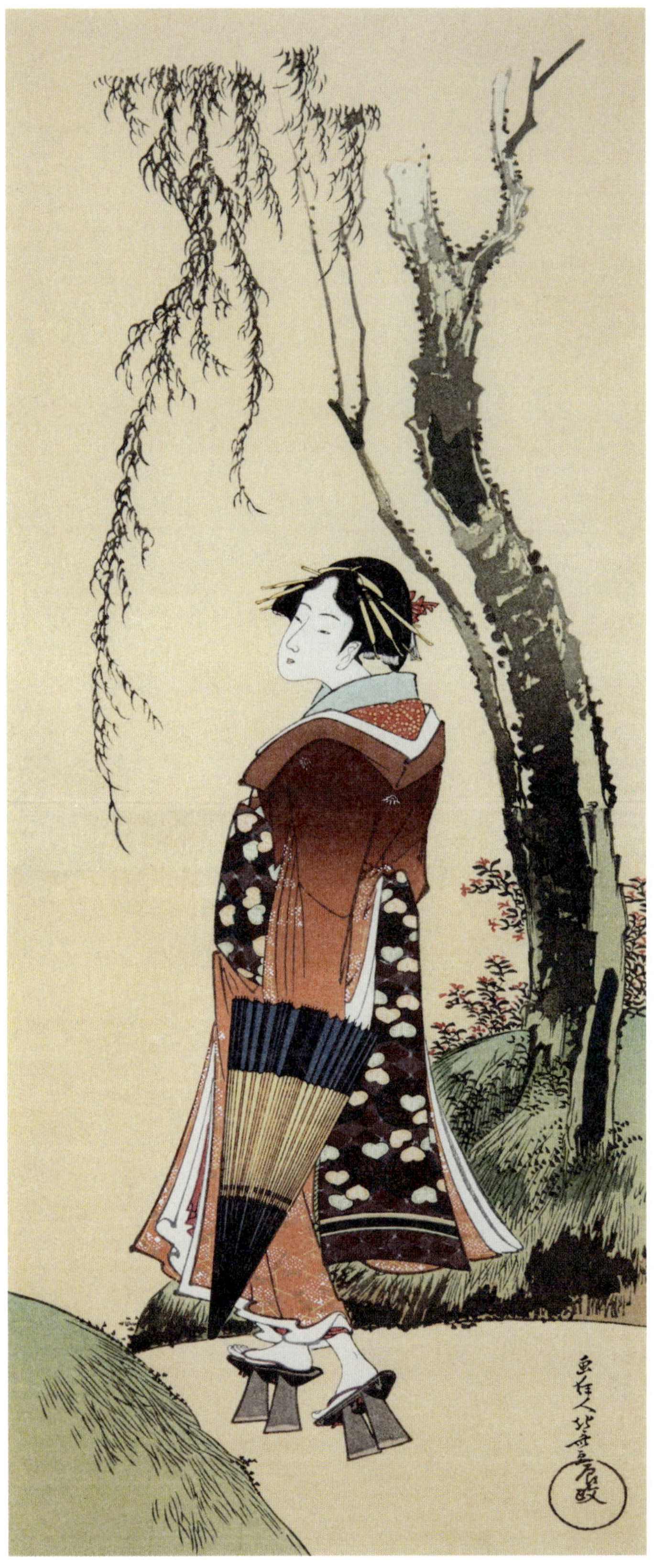

Hokusai produced most of his bijin-ga and shunga a couple of decades before *'The Great Wave'*. At the beginning of the century he created the lovely *'Girl with Umbrella under a Willow'* (c.1801-04). Originally painted on silk it only later became a popular print - and was the first 'beauty' to captivate me.

The facing page shows a couple of **Hokusai** from early on in his career in the series: *Seven Fashionable Bad Habits* (1798). He is doing the **Utamaro** thing of reflecting on the social manners and mores of young women, but in a bolder style, perhaps influenced by his contemporary **Choki** (who we have already met).

The series title may make him seem a little patronising to the modern western sensibility but nonetheless these reprints have real charm. They have intricate compositions and there is a delicacy in the expressions and hairstyles - complimented with metallic mica backgrounds.

The first print is known as *'Girl with a Hozuki in her Mouth'* or alternatively **'***Two Girls'*. It is an image of two young women, possibly teenagers, indulging in activities deemed frivolous - one blowing a hozuki (a ground cherry clacker) in her mouth while the other applies lipstick with the help of a hand mirror.

The second has the title *'Woman and Girl with Telescope'*. It shows two young women fascinated by a Western import that would have been the most desirable of accessories - somewhat like a new mobile phone! The younger girl peers through the eye piece as her companion watches intently.

Original **Hokusai** prints from this early period of his career are very rare - in fact there are only two known first edition examples of this second print in existence.

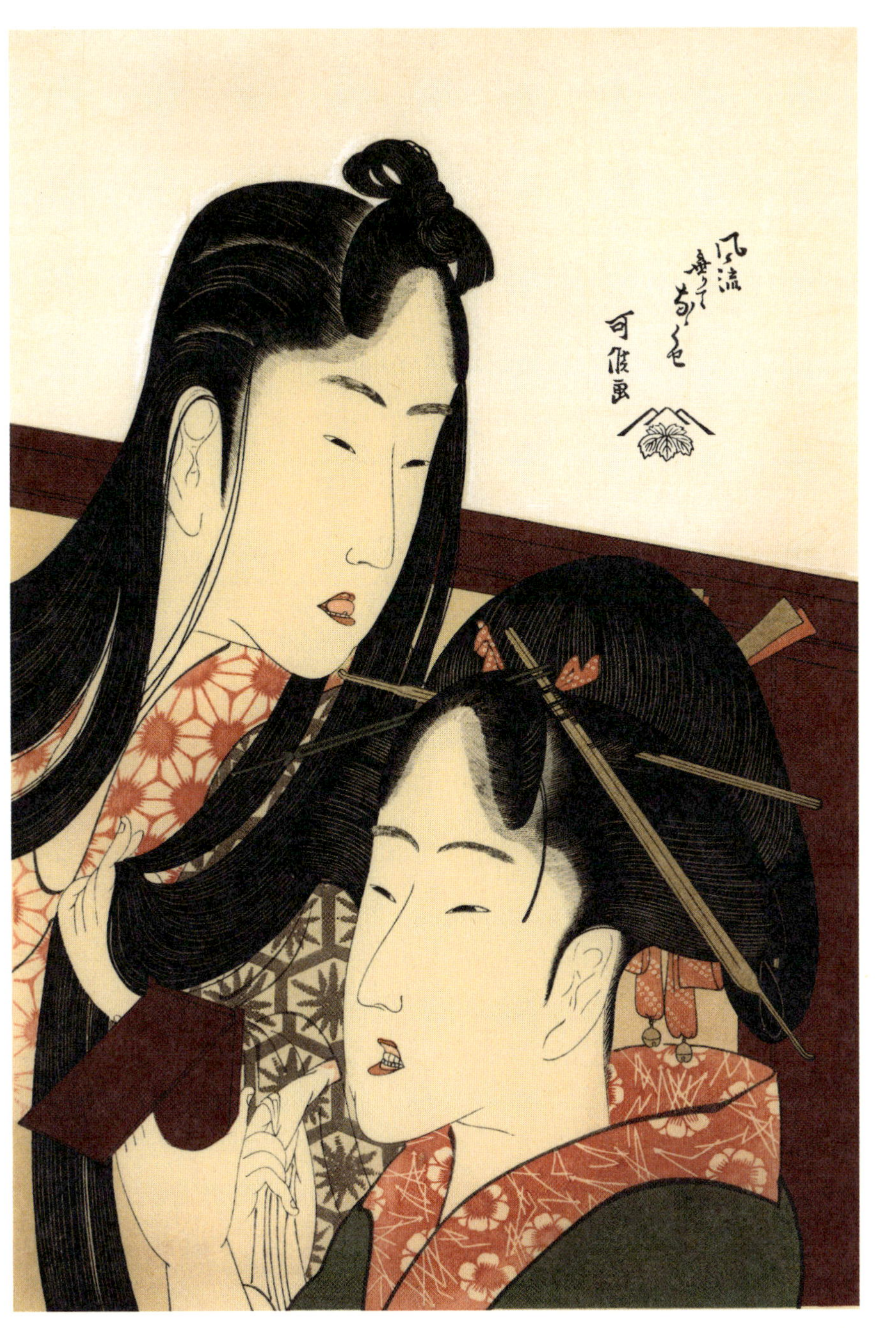
風流
無くてなゝくせ
可候画

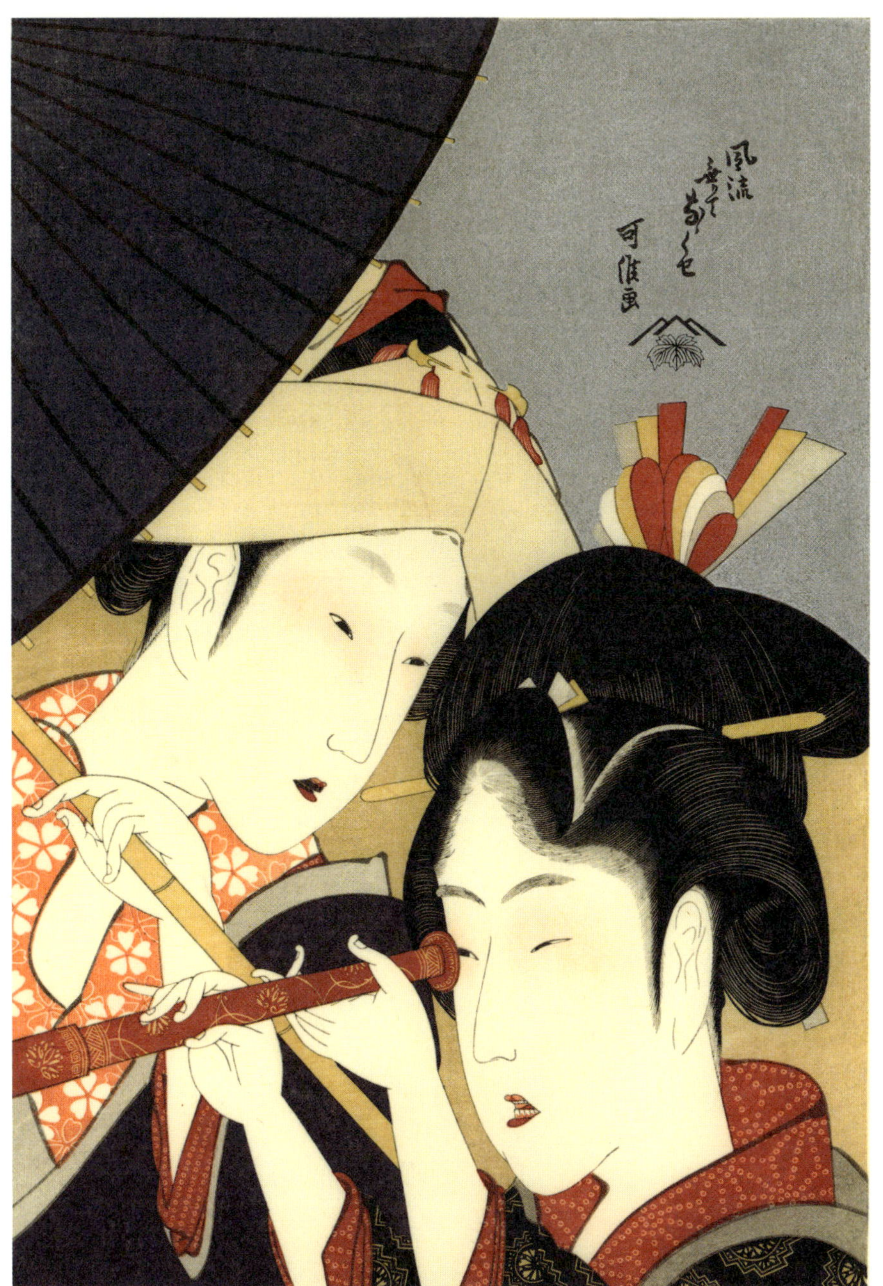
風流
無くてなゝくせ
可候画

With the shunga, his most well known image is *'The Dream of a Fisherman's Wife'* (here to the right), a print so famous that originals never come onto the open market.

I do though have a number of other originals from the same three book series *Young Pine Saplings* published in 1814. *'The Dream'* is in the third book, but these come from the first.

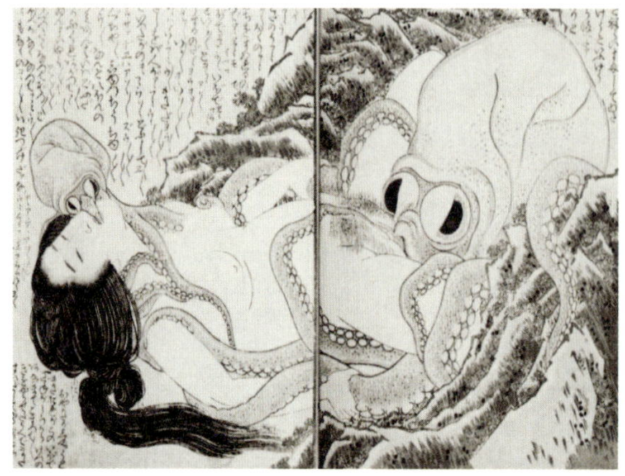

In the print below the woman is writing on the man's member: 'This belongs to ...'.

The idea seems to be that such writing will discourage infidelity. He holds the ink stone for her but doesn't look happy about it.

In the background is a rope commonly used as a sex aid - to keep lovers together during strenuous and active love making.

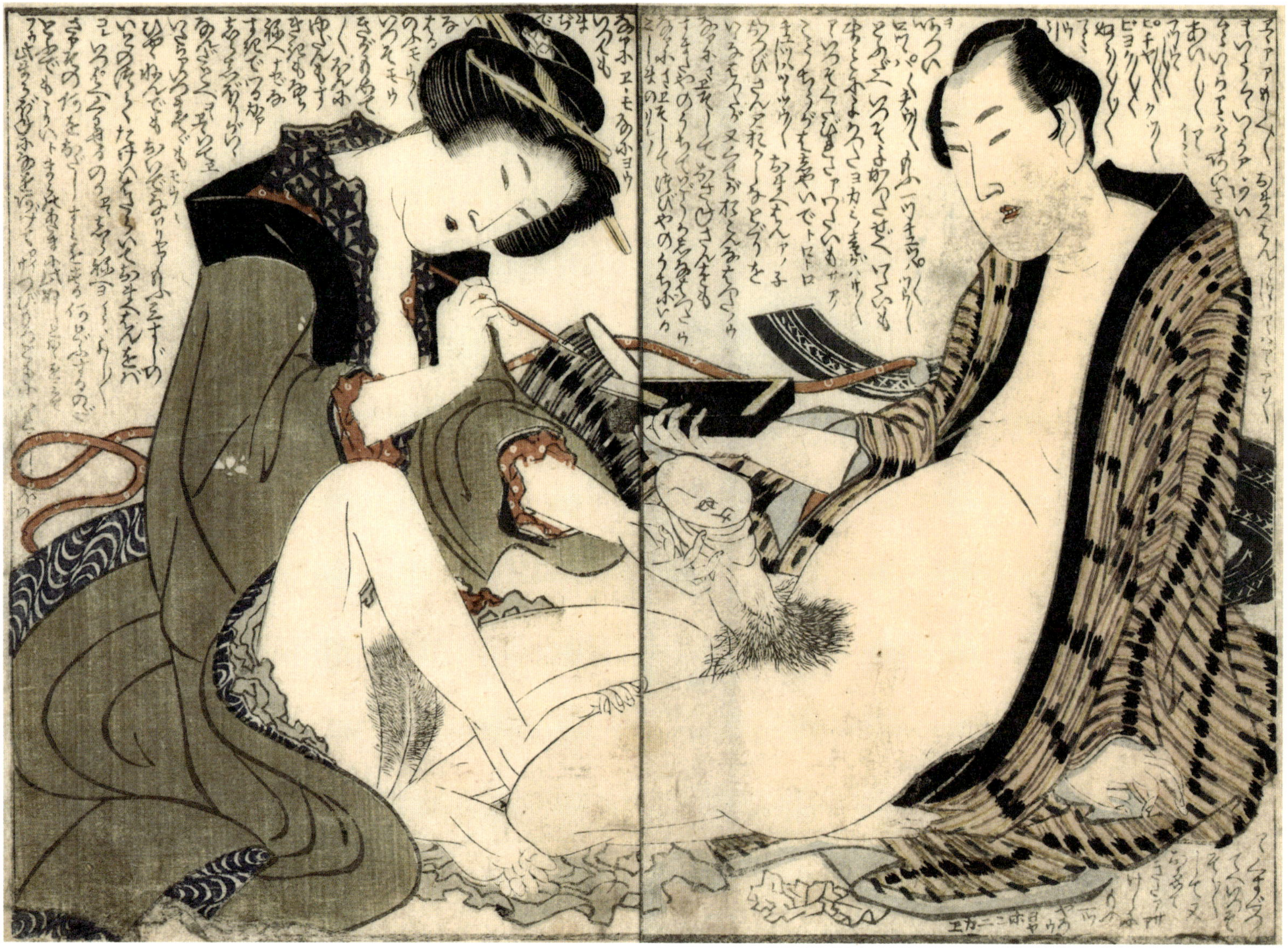

In the main image the man has a thin cord tied round his member. The couple are locked in a high tension position with him providing the action but it is the woman that is in ecstasy.

The clothing reinforces the narrative, with the strong firm lines of the man's garments against the trembling orgasmic depiction of her's.

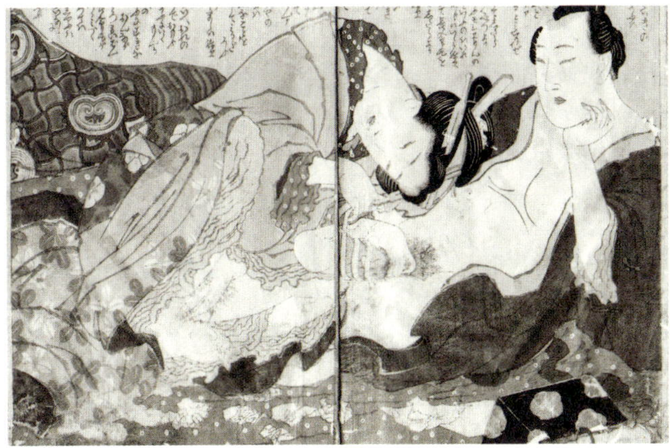

From looking at another **Hokusai** image (shown here on the left), we see the woman doing the tying. It appears the practice was primarily for the gratification of the female partner.

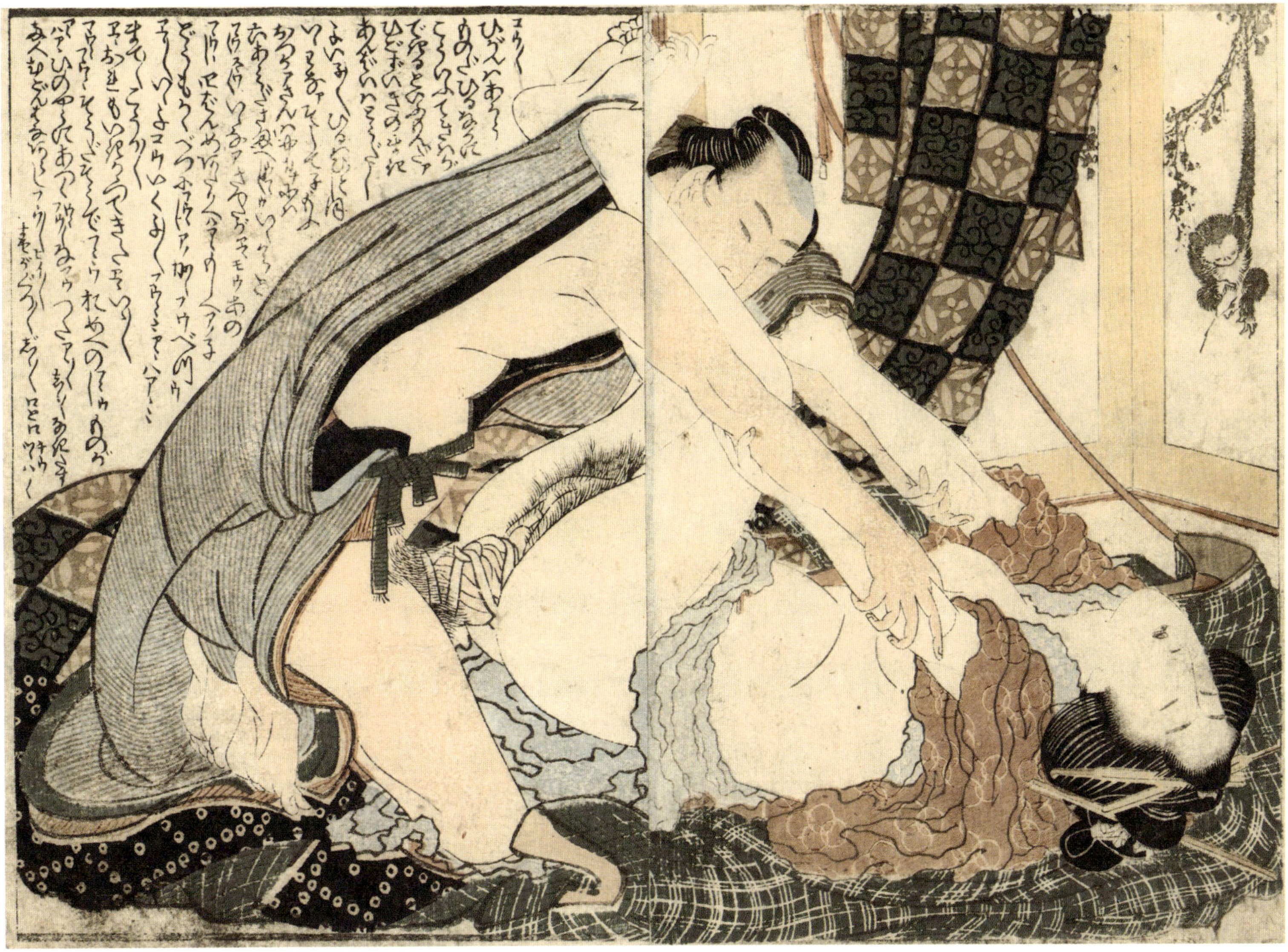

Hokusai didn't work alone - he was a part of a community of artists that was always swapping ideas and keeping up with trends. There is an marked resemblance between a **Hokusai** print from the same series shown below, and our original **Eisen** cover picture shown on the facing page.

Take a look at what the lovers are wearing. The people of Edo were passionate about fashion and style and the prints reflect that, like magazines do now. Everyday designs were important to the townswomen and men, who were not so concerned about the extravagances of courtesan couture.

As the **Hokusai** is dated 1814 perhaps we can date the **Eisen** to that year.

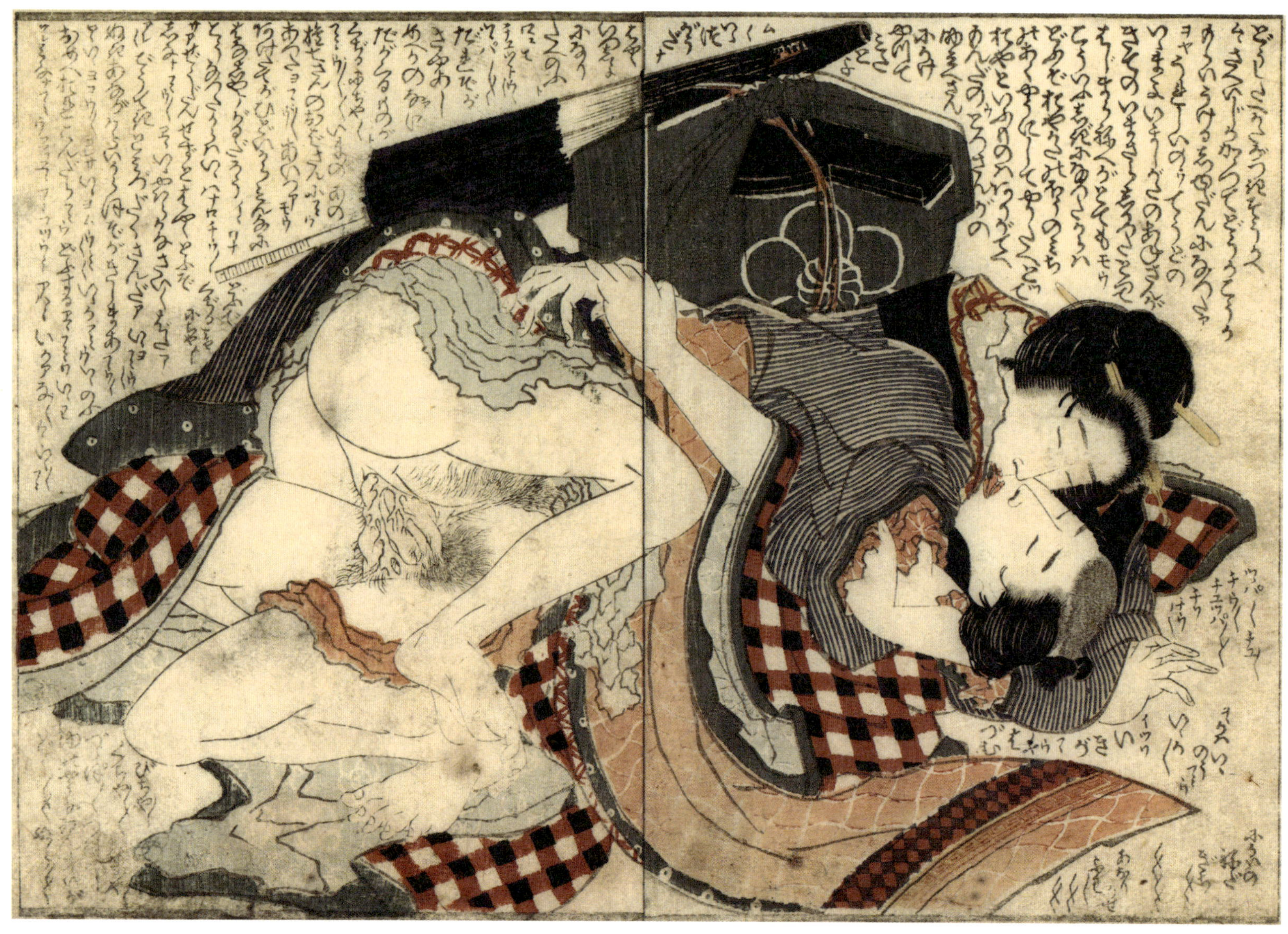

In this **Eisen** titled *'First Love of the New Year'*, the garments dominate the composition with the fabric obscuring the action, to such a degree that the viewer has to seek out the intimacy at the very centre.

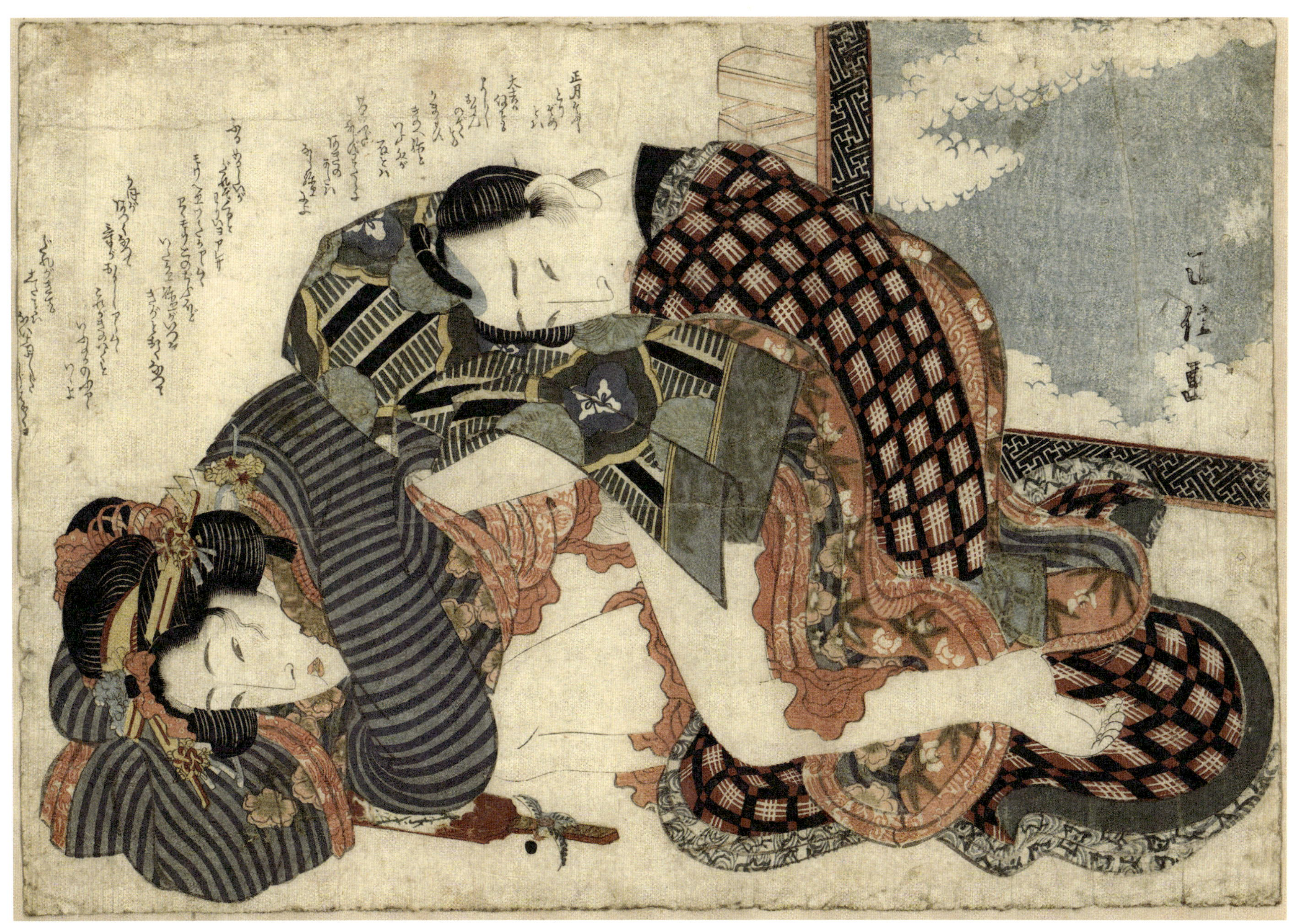

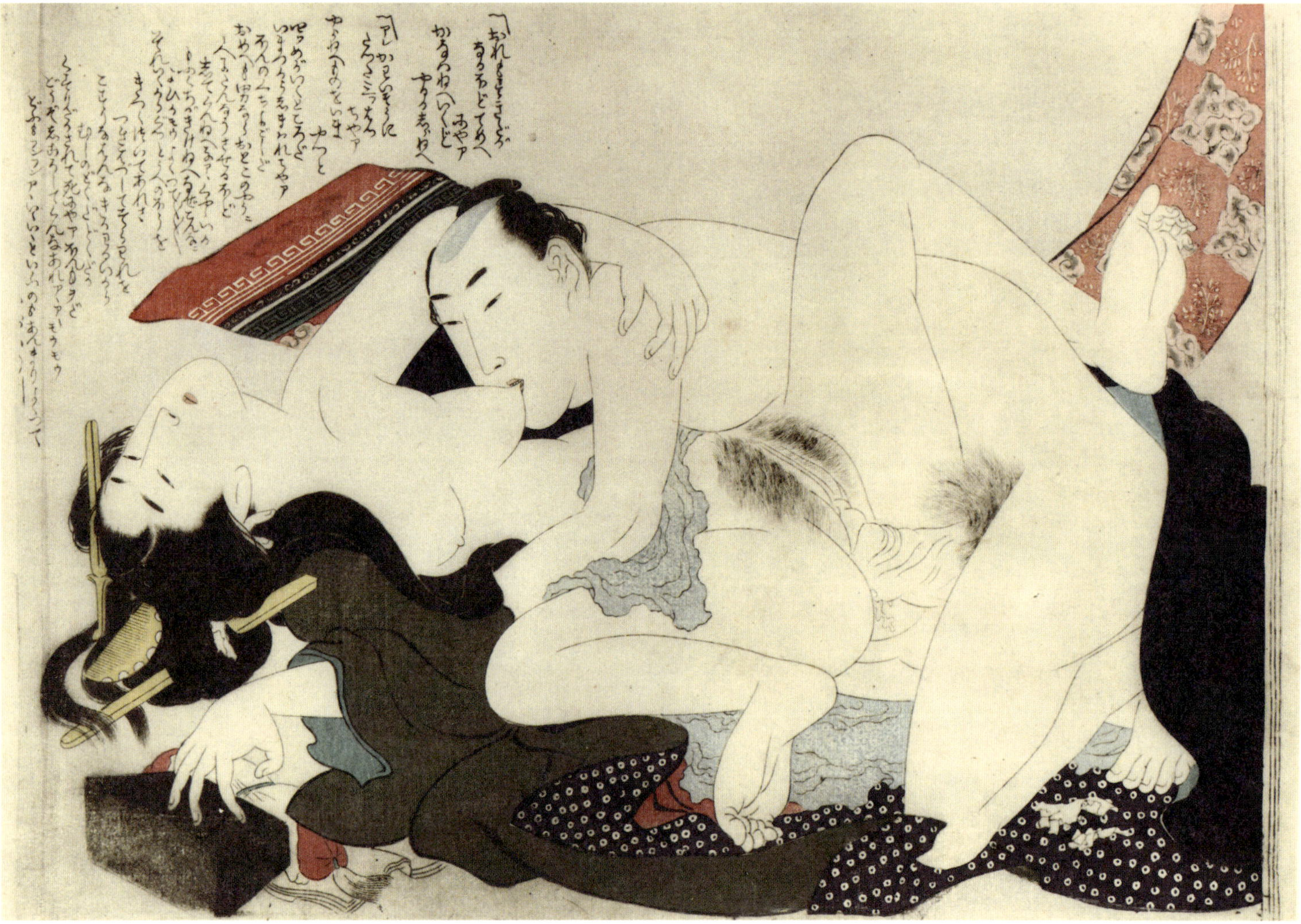

This **Hokusai** reprint comes from the series *Patterns of Couples* (1812-14). It is believed **Eisen**, and perhaps **Hokusai**'s third daughter **Oi**, worked on this picture book - so maybe they contributed on *'The Dream'* books too.

Auguste Rodin had a copy and it is possible to see the influence in much of his sculpture.

There is a lot more to say and show on the work of **Eisen** and we will look at him properly in a moment, but let's digress to discover **Katsushika Oi**.

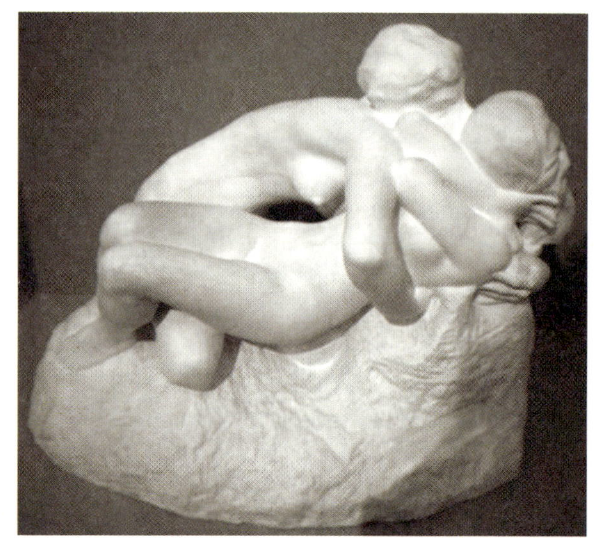

Katsushika Oi (1800-1866 approx)

In this reproduction of an ink drawing created before 1893 by apprentice **Tsuyuki Kosho** we see **Oi** at home with her father **Hokusai,** bundled up against the cold in infested bedding - brush in hand. She looked after him in his later life.

Oi shared her father's artistic talent and also his total disinterest for housekeeping, spending all day drawing with him, never cleaning or cooking. There are reports they ordered food from outside stalls and ate while working. The remains were left on the floor, turning their place into a dump.

No doubt much of **Oi**'s work was passed off as her father's as he had the marketable name (even though he kept changing it). He apparently said 'The bijin-ga I paint myself are no match for **Oi**'s'.

Not much of her known work survives, but what remains is comparable with her father's paintings and prints. She created shunga too and the similarities are noticeable, particularly with the line, some of the fabric details and in the undergarments - see next pages.

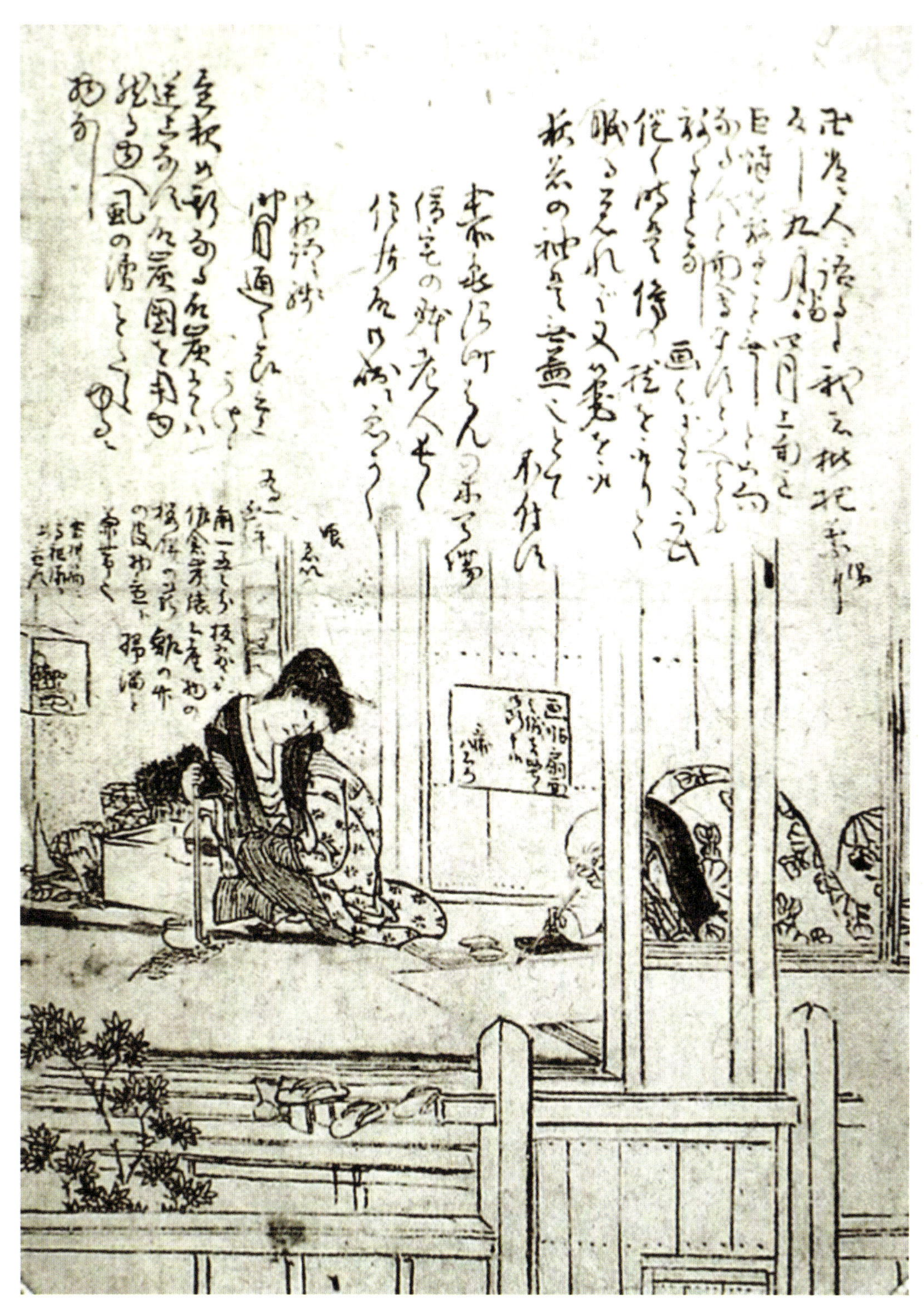

PLEASE NOTE: FROM THIS PAGE ON, WE FEATURE ONLY ORIGINALS - NO MORE REPRINTS UNTIL THE VERY END.

Oi has an individual style and the eroticism in her work has a femininity to it, as in these prints (c.1820). The long slender fingers and curled toes are a special feature.

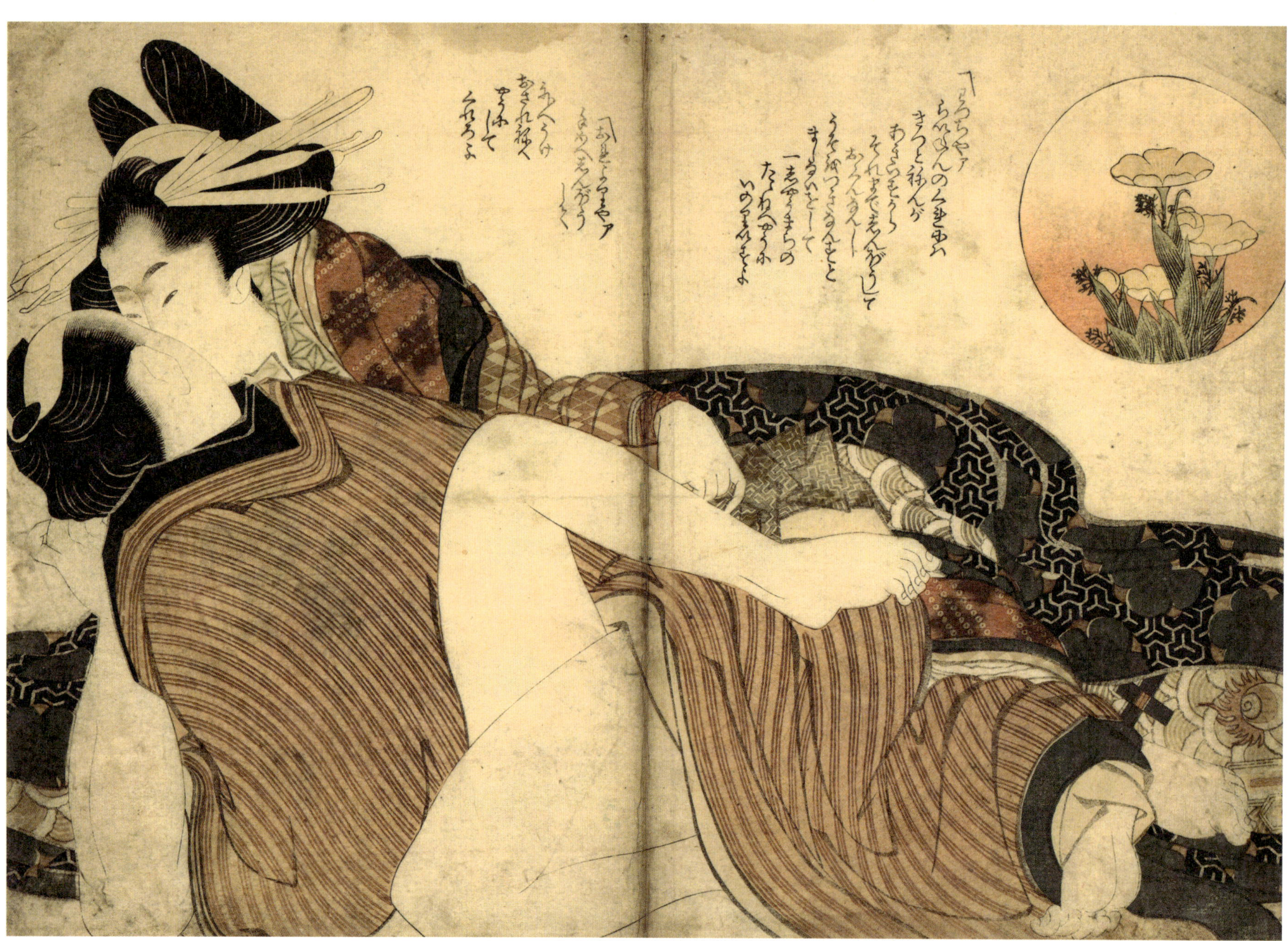

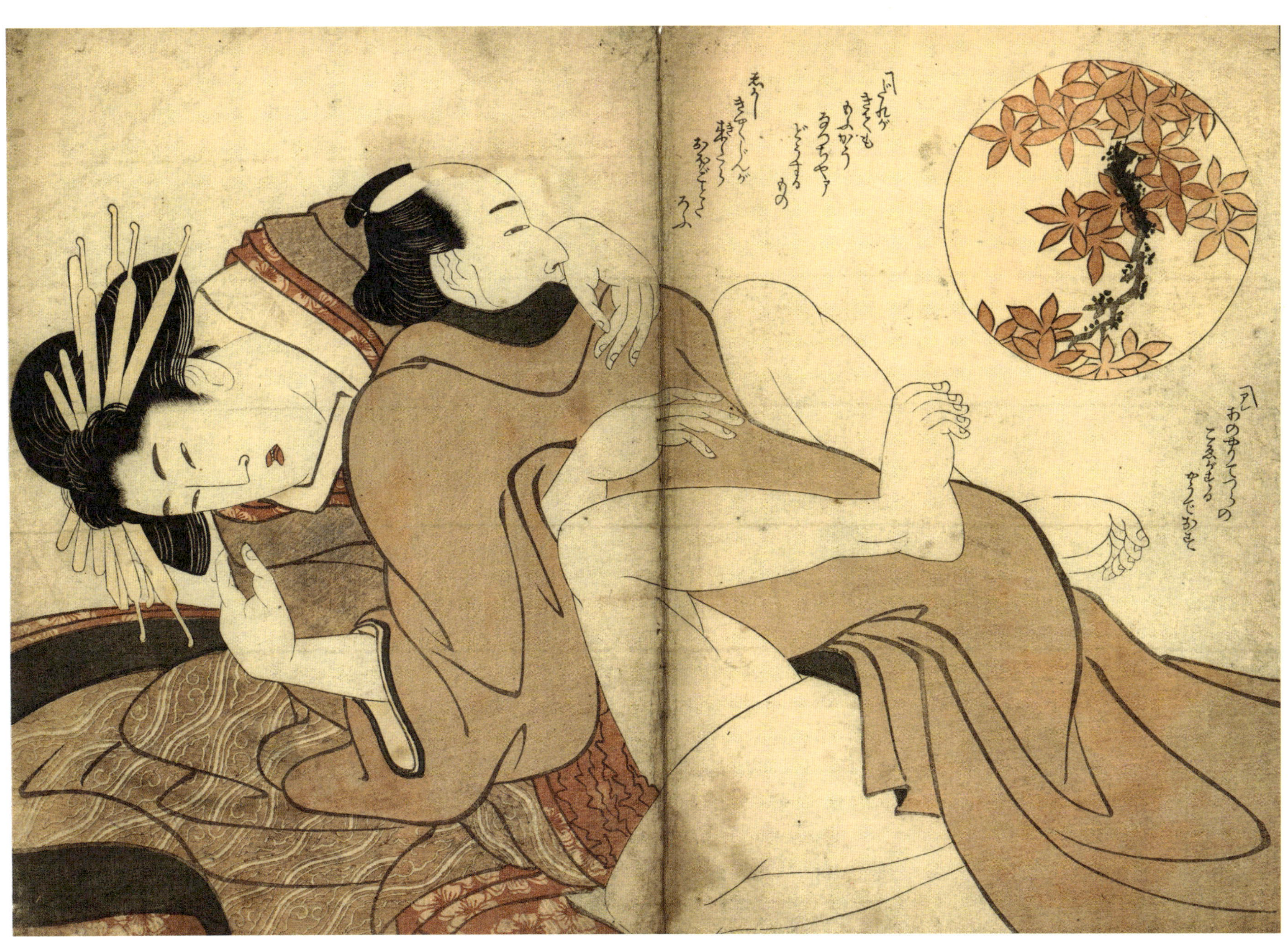

Yanagawa SHIGENOBU (1787-1832)

Another family member was **Shigenobu**,

He was at first the pupil, then son-in-law (not with **Oi**), and finally adopted son of **Hokusai**. He died well before his master. I love his compositional sense and this shunga shows it off so well, particularly when you look at the abstraction in the interior design, fabric, and foot in the top right corner.

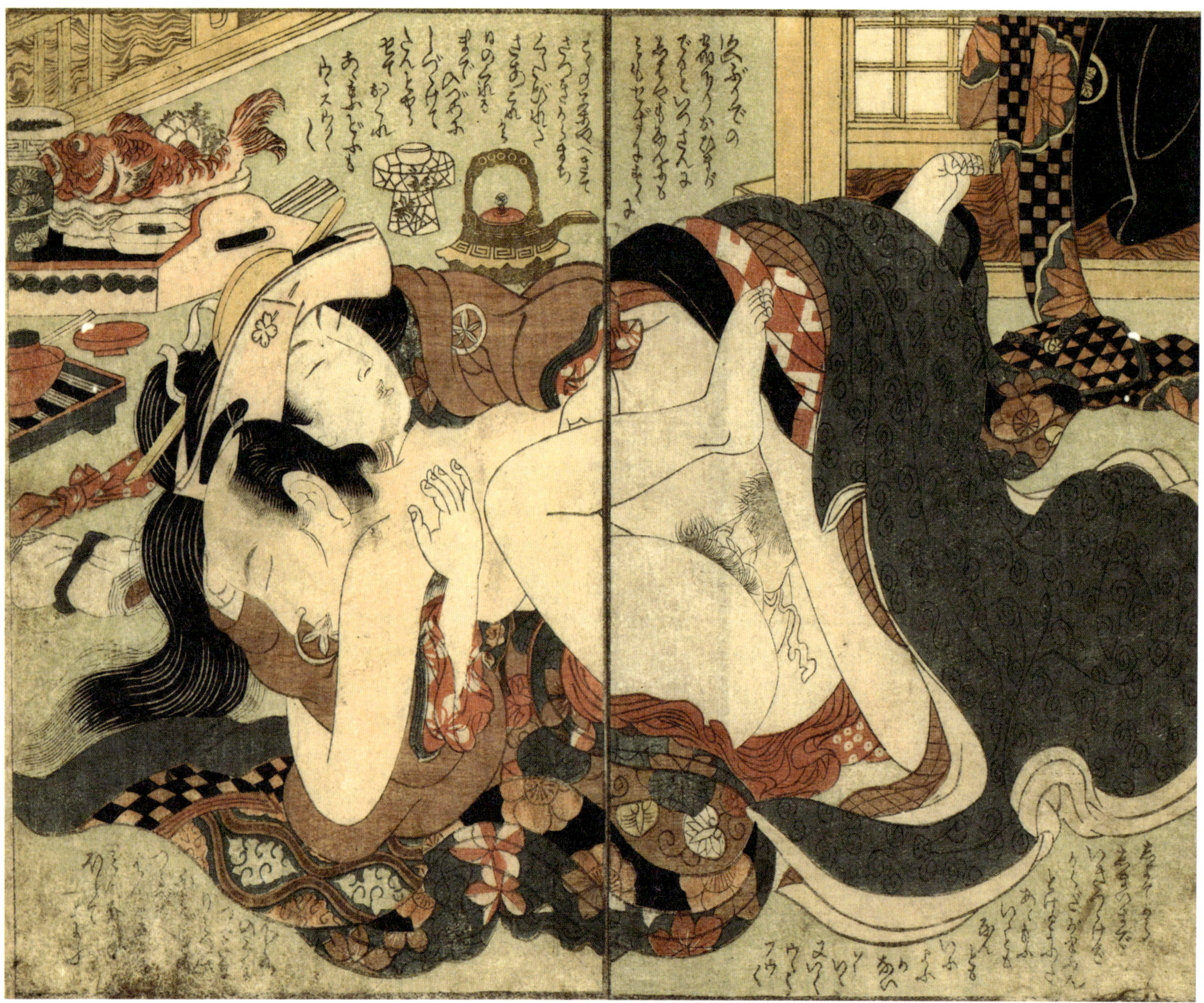

Keisai EISEN (1790-1848)

But back to **Eisen**. He was a friend of **Hokuei** and disciple of **Hokusai,** living and working in Edo.

'*Yaozen Kaiseki Cuisine'* in the series *Famous Products of Today* is my favourite bijin-ga by **Eisen**, It depicts a 'beauty' passing through a doorway, one of his themes. Here she is at the entrance gate to a famous Edo restaurant. The abstract nature of this design really does it for me - a curved striped kimono creating patterns and a sensual face breaking the line of the harsh geometric background. The intricate detail and delicate flesh tones contrast with the brutal black angular shapes.

Eisen was a man of many parts, turning his hand to playwriting, biography and other literary pursuits, mixing with the poets and intellectuals of his day. It is though his depiction of women that he is remembered for.

It is said that **Eisen** devoted his entire life and almost his whole art to women, in particular the 'beauties' of the Edo pleasure quarters. As a young man he was considered disorderly and immoral, maintaining attractive young singers at his house. He justified this by saying, 'What's wrong with spending like water the money I earned myself?' In his autobiography *Notes of a Nameless old Man* he goes on to describe himself as a 'dissolute hard drinker' and claimed to have owned a brothel that burnt down in 1830.

His extraordinary art gives us the opportunity to experience his surroundings and vicariously meet some of the people (usually women) that he got to know.

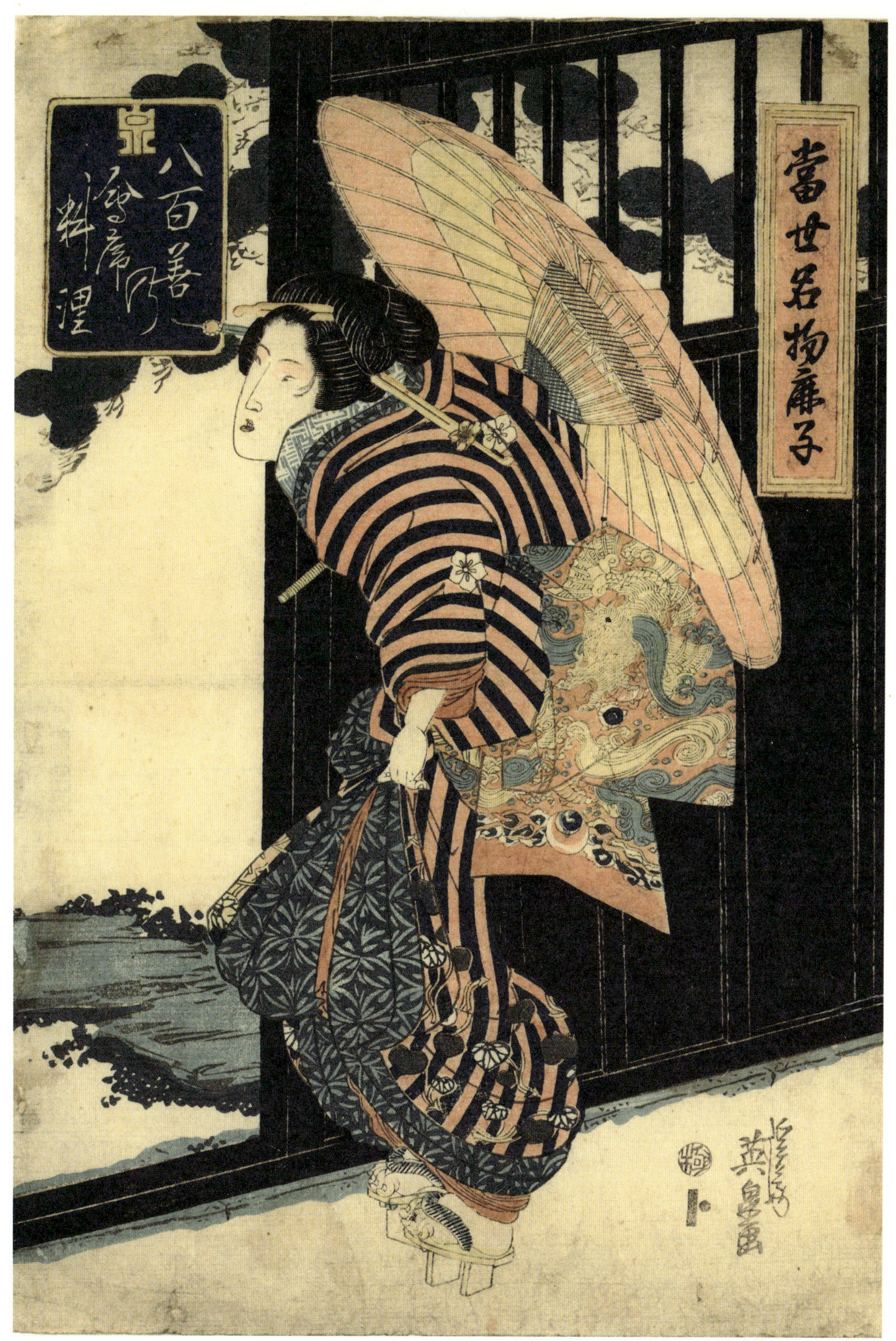

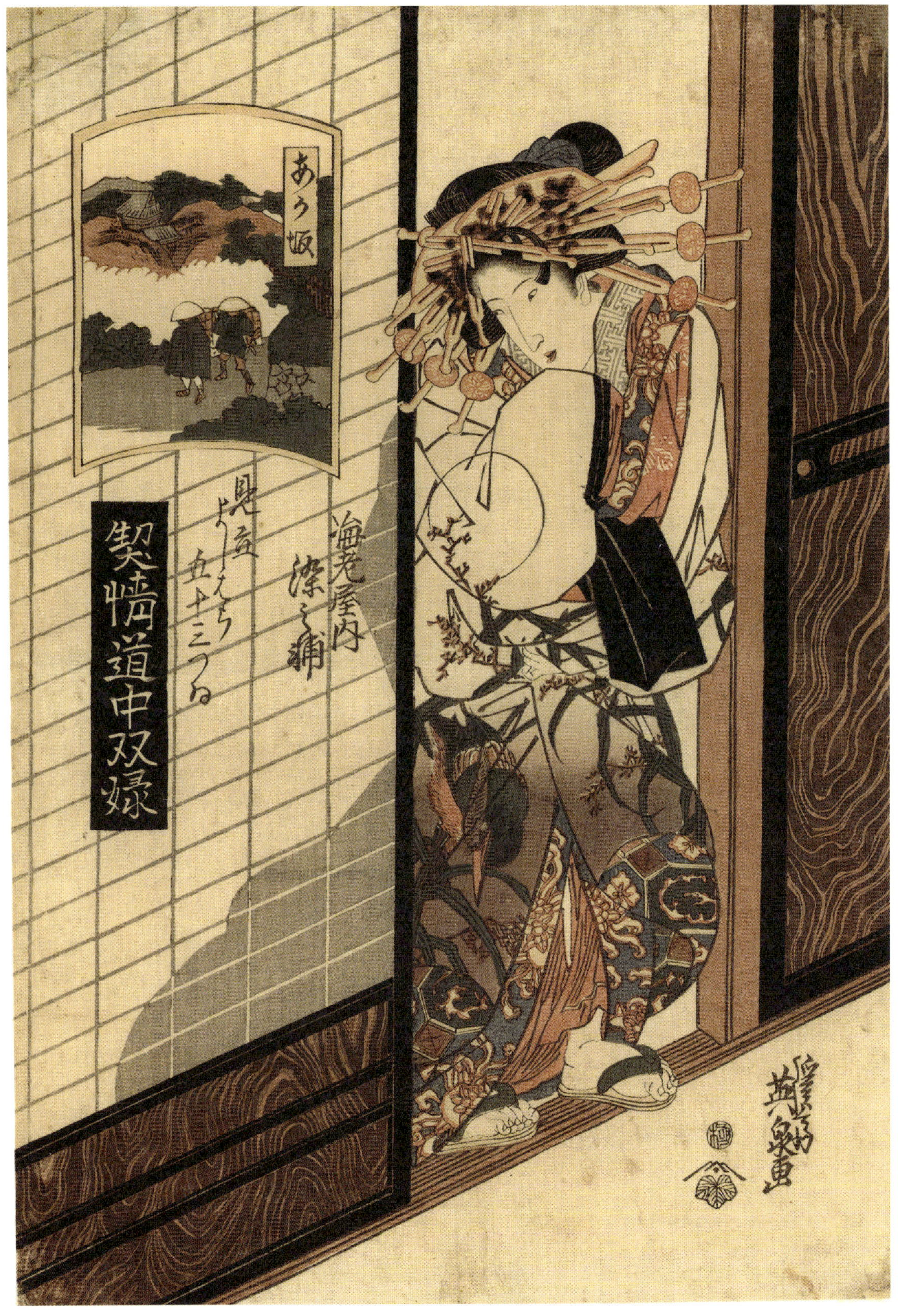

'Wakatake of the Wakanaya,' in the series; *A Tokaido Board Game of Courtesans* (c.1821-23) - is another wonderful threshold image.

Wakatake wears a beautiful kimono with a crested bird and tall grasses. She tilts her head as she looks shyly around the sliding shoji screen, holding a sleeve to her chin. Several tortoiseshell hairpins and combs decorate her hair - and she wears zori sandals - the inspiration for flip-flops! Her robe is silhouetted against the screen, and the inset above shows travellers on the Tokaido Road near Akasaka station.

It is worth making the observation that **Eisen'**s 'beauties' are so different from those shown to us by Utamaro and his contemporaries from only a few decades earlier. Many of them tend to have elongated figures and appear willowy and ethereal. His often have hunched postures and seem much more realistic and down to earth.

This also comes from the series: *A Tokaido Board Game of Courtesans: Fifty-three Pairings in the Yoshiwara* (c1821-23) in which courtesans are matched with stations on the Tokaido Road, which we can see top left.

The courtesan is Sonohama of the Owariya and she appears to have a child on her lap. But I think it is a doll. The rather ghoulish face, the size and stiff pose makes me think it is a mitsuore doll, which were introduced in the late 1700's (the one photographed is from 1840).

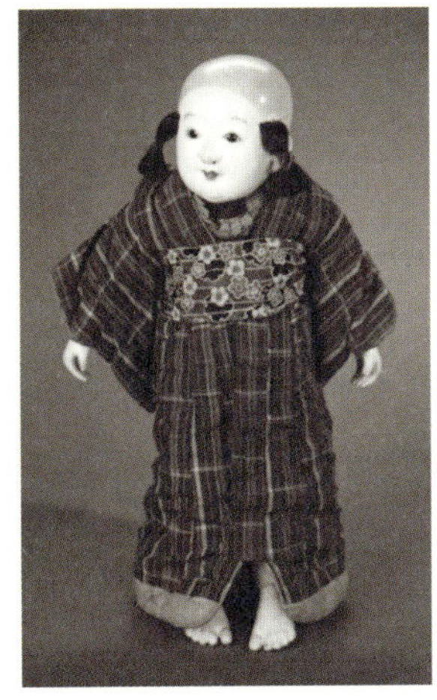

They had intricate articulation, mitsuore meaning triple-jointed, and its construction allowed for dressing and undressing. Although intended for children I've seen other prints in which grown women are playing with them.

It makes me think about the maternal instincts of the courtesans who were living in the pleasure districts. The Yoshiwara was a place where pregnancy was feared and often meant the end of a woman's livelihood and sometime's life. Lovers and offspring were not allowed and suicide was a way out.

Eisen would have been aware of the emotional turmoil that many would have suffered.

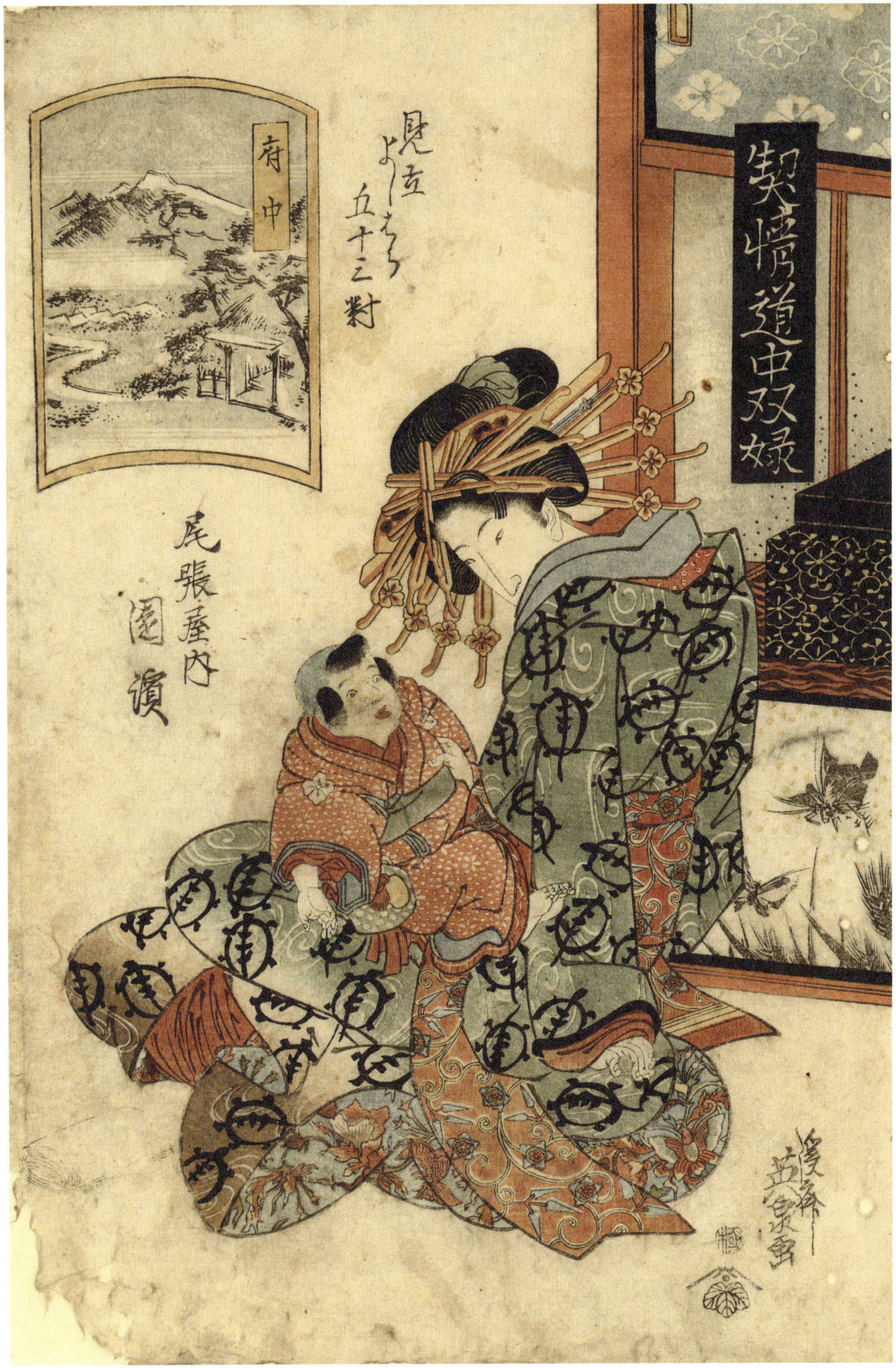

I love this **Eisen** from the series: *Courtesans for Compass Points in Edo.*

The woman is dressed in a red kimono with cherry blossoms with an obi featuring a lion about to spring out - along with peonies and a waterfall. She looks over her shoulder with a concerned expression, the tips of her toes peeking from the hem of her kimono - considered very erotic. A circular cartouche depicts a shrine, so perhaps she is having religious thoughts.

I don't know who this courtesan is, but she looks much older - and very much into co-ordinating her kimono design with the bedding. Standing, as if about to disrobe, she looks a little perturbed, distracted by something we cannot see.

This seems to be a rather affectionate portrait of a somewhat lonely woman who has spent her life pleasing others.

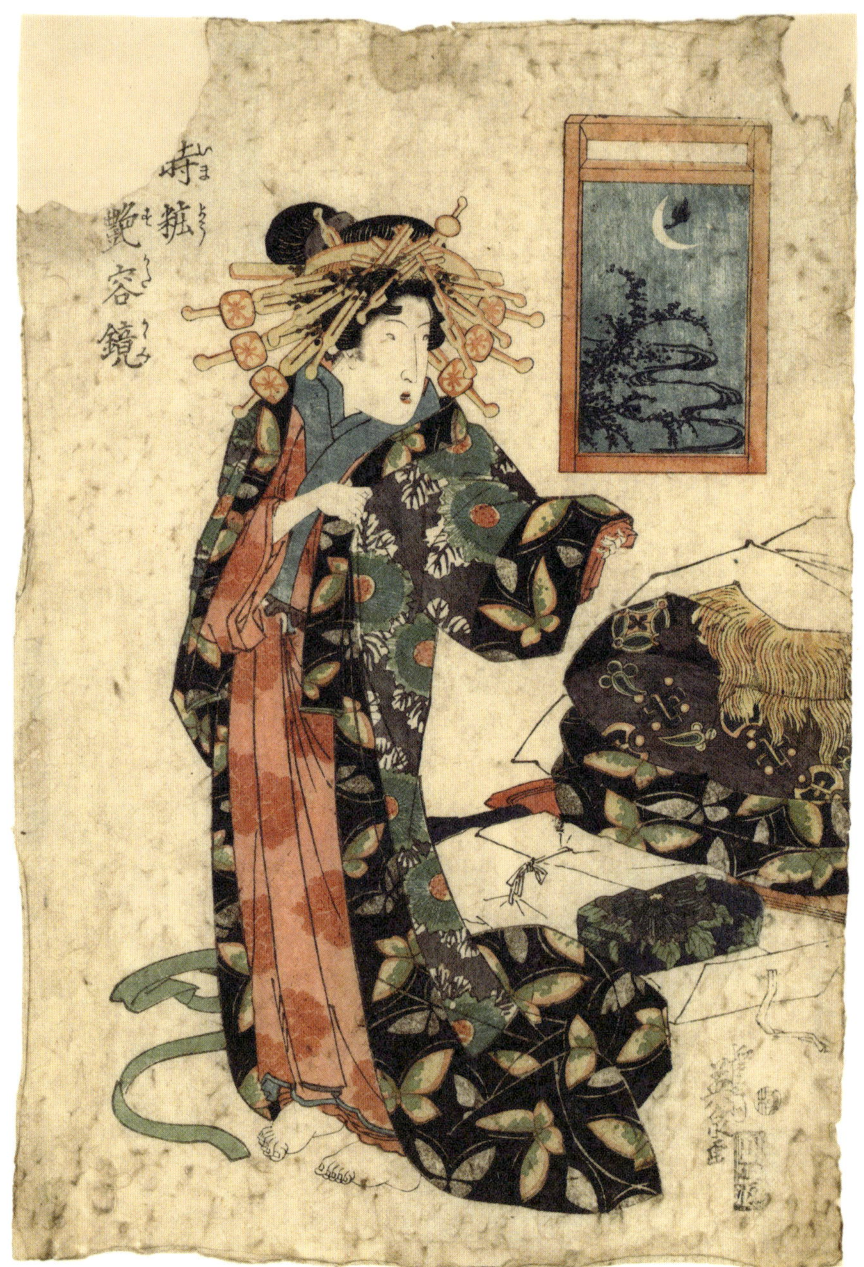

By contrast, this scene shows a first love experience, indicated by plum blossoms on the folding screen. In embarrassment the young woman covers her mouth with the sleeve of her kimono. It is from the series *Grass on the Way of Love* (c.1825).

Another from the series is in Ruminations, after Chapter 3.

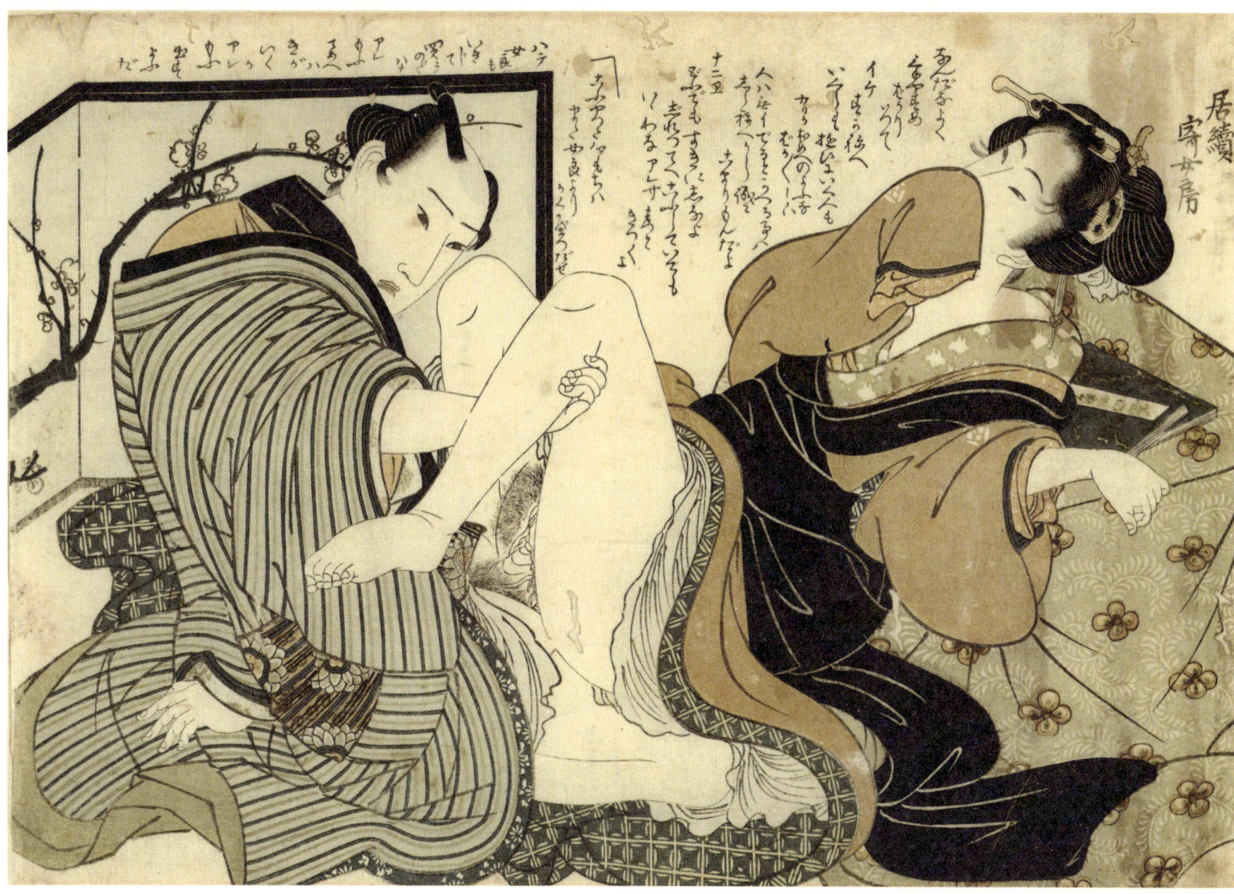

Eisen was fascinated with female attitudes towards the act of love and female sexuality generally. He even created explicit anatomical images - but I don't have any to show you!!

However I do have this much thumbed double page of two women together - lost in the sensual act of joint masturbation. This is not uncommon as a subject in Shunga - perhaps created for the titillation of men.

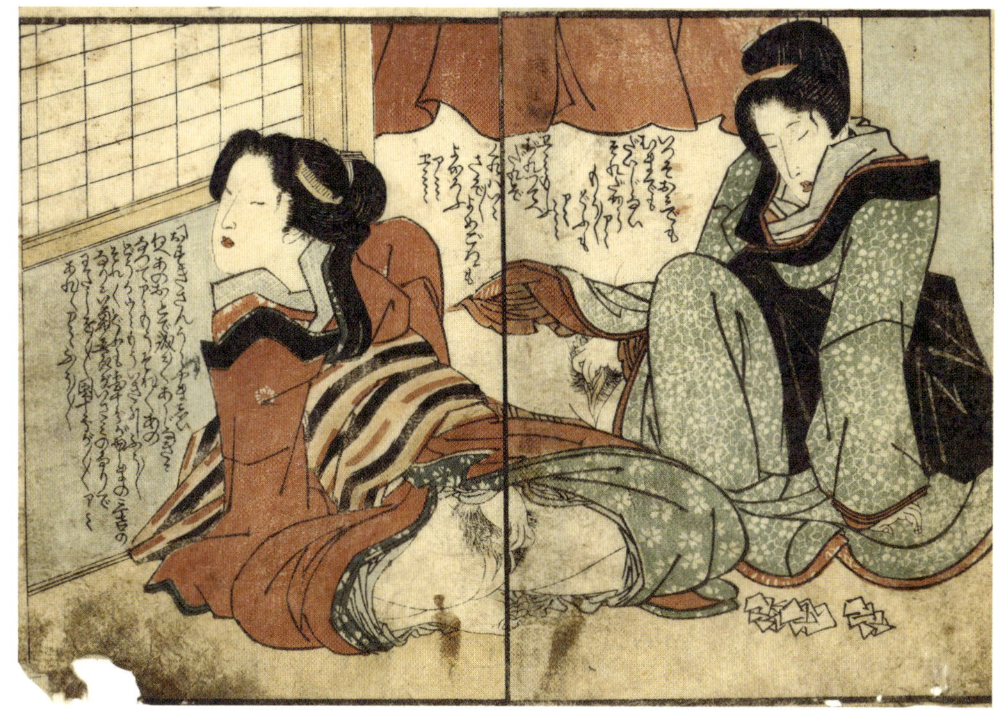

Kikukawa EIZAN (1787-1867)

More complex love scenes were depicted by his colleague and friend **Eizan**. They are inextricably linked and have similar names as they shared the same background, teachers and influences. It is generally believed that **Eizan** was master and **Eisen** his student, although there is some disagreement. Whatever the case they competed for attention as both were supreme artists.

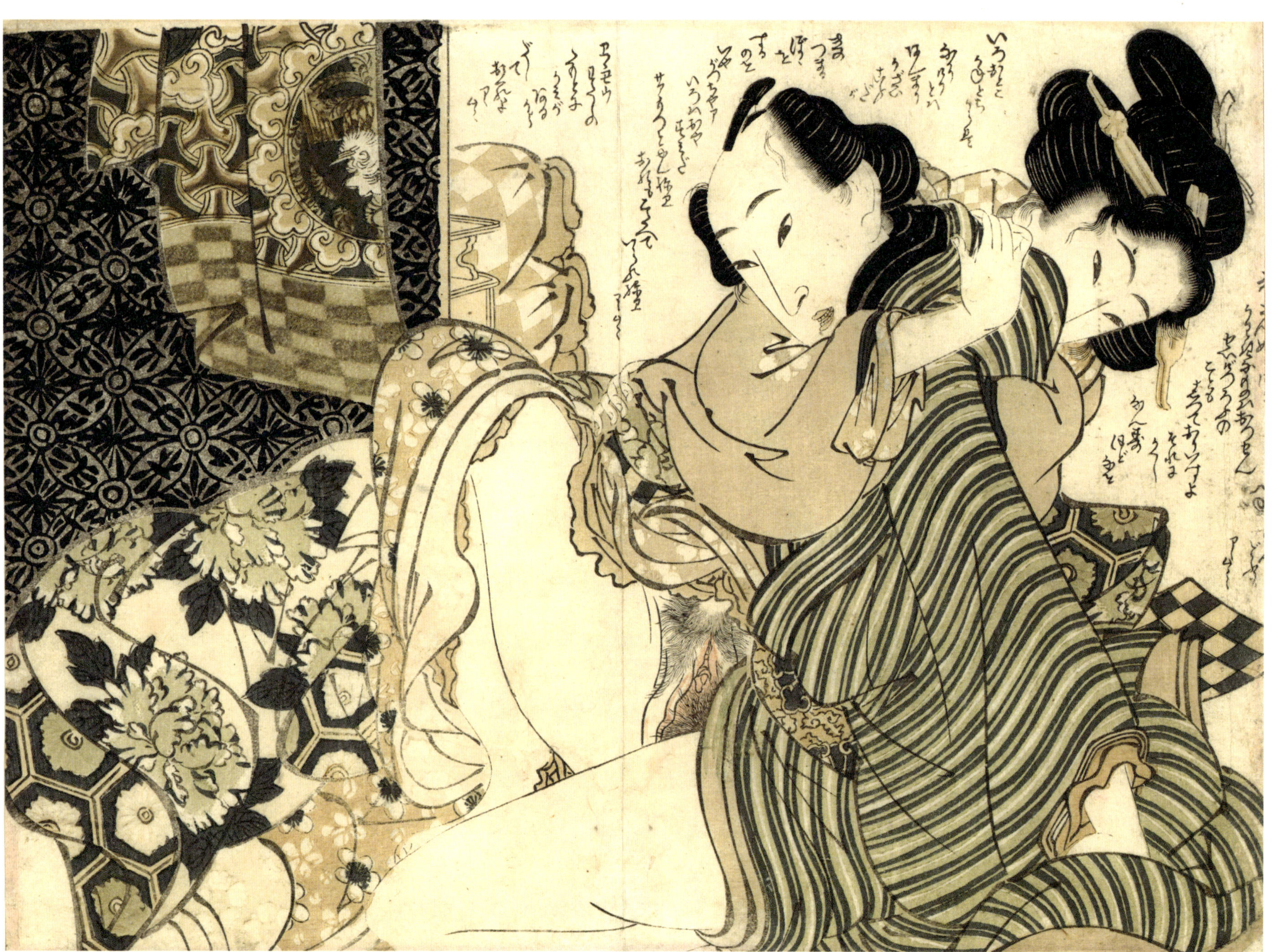

These two come from the same scroll - intended to be carried around in the sleeves of a man's kimono. In the first it is hard to figure out what is going on - such are the contortions. The second is simply about *'Love making after drinking sake'*.

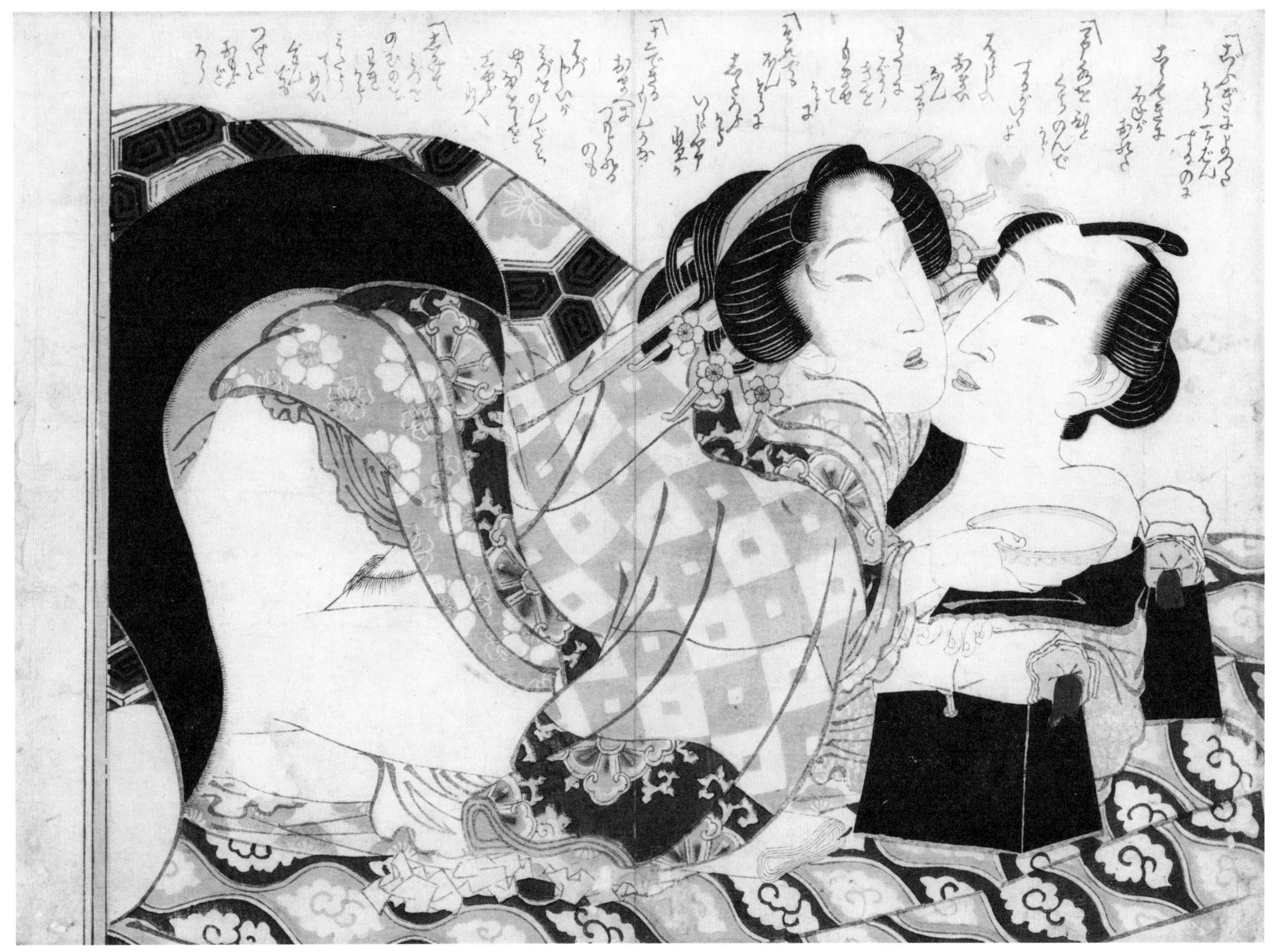

By comparison this could be seen as quite crude - although I find it tender with an overall sense of a couple being consumed in the physicality of love-making - she is cradling his head in a caring post coital moment.

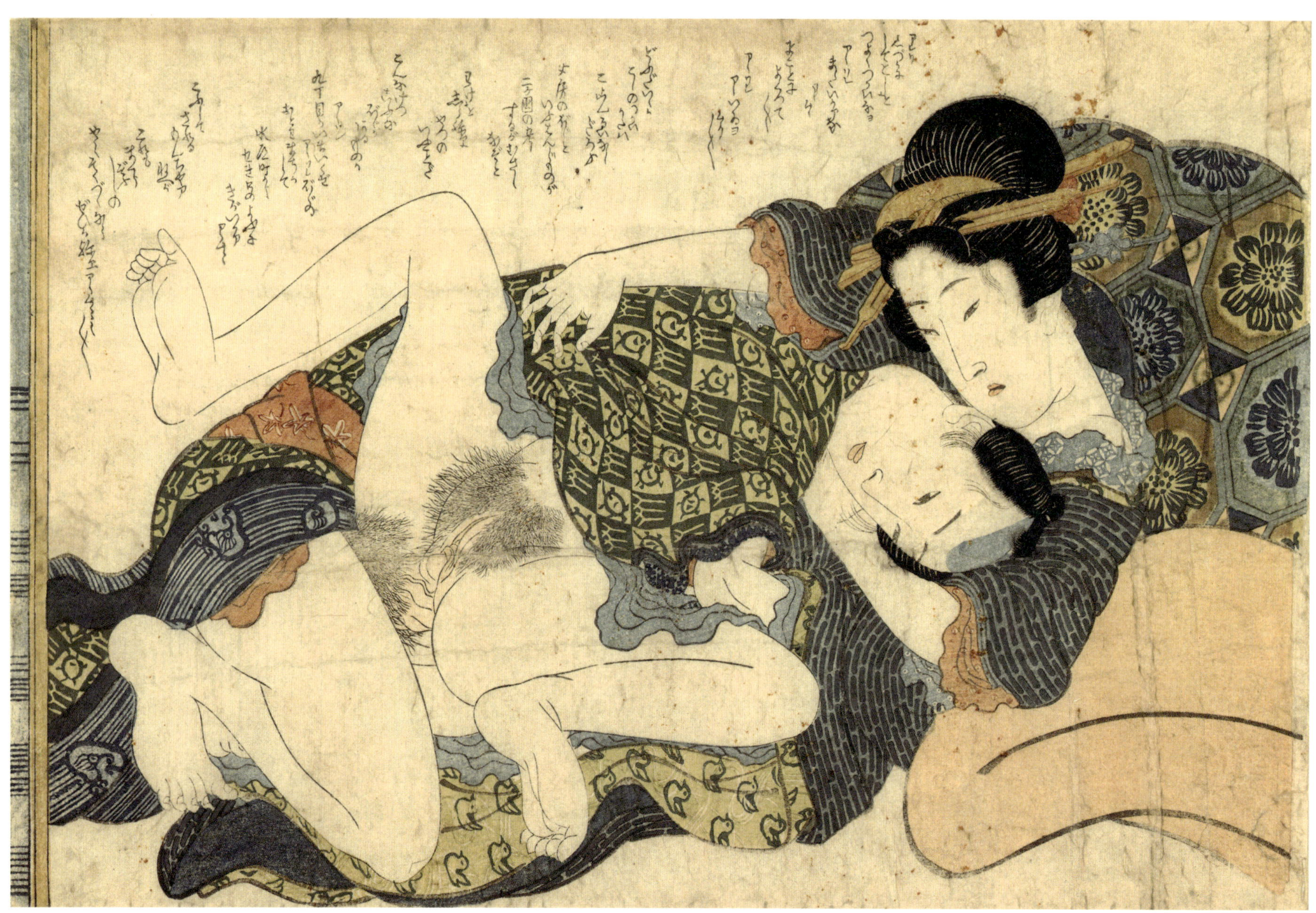

Before we move back into the brothels of Edo, we should take a look at this rather bashed about **Eizan** print from *Spring Pleasures - Scenes from the Pleasure district* (c.1815). In a series of twelve, he romanticised the couplings with fine drapes and costumes - here with a poem on a lantern - In the top left corner.

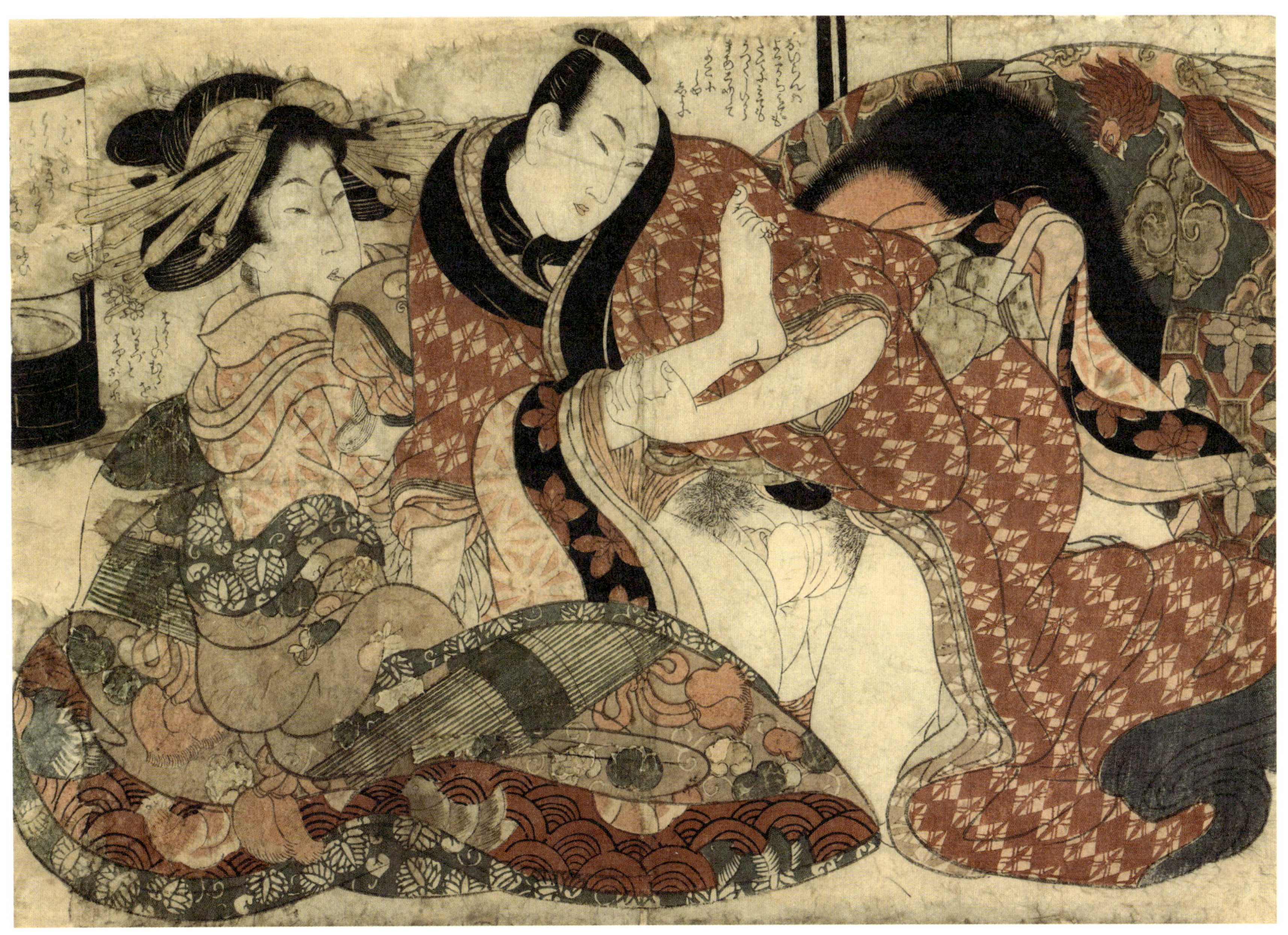

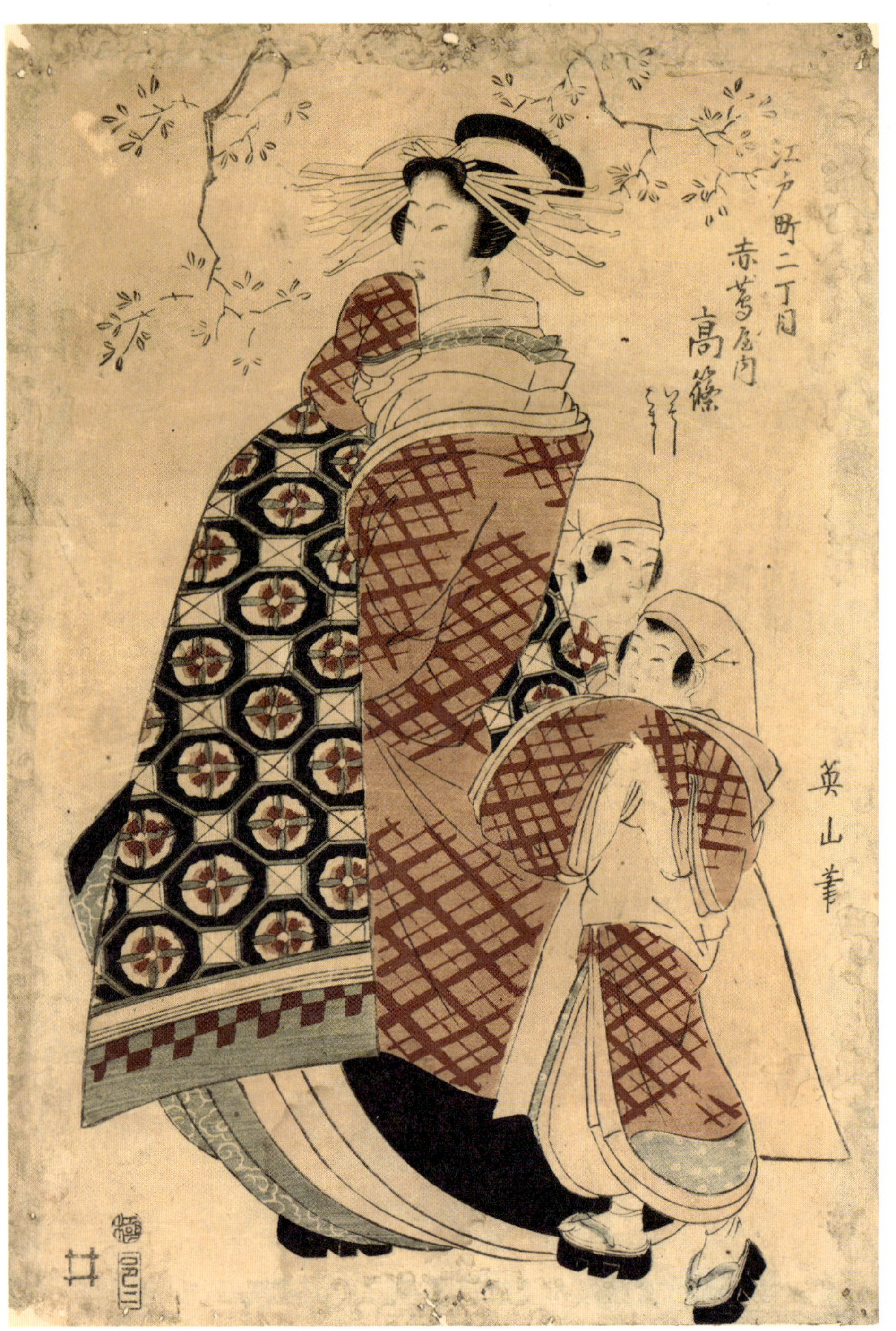

This is the first **Eizan** I acquired in this (almost) sub-genre of celebrated courtesans known as oiran with child assistants, kamuro, dressed in matching outfits. These prints are probably the equivalent of advertising flyers, as with the portraits we saw before.

The two (c.1818-23) shown on the facing page are later **Eizan** acquisitions, equally wonderful. It is sometimes difficult to define where the kimonos and obis of the oiran and the kamuros start and end. It is all one mass of costume design.

It is worth looking into what we are seeing. The women are in effect high class prostitutes, selling themselves on the very lucrative market in sexual pleasure. There was a strict hierarchy with those at the top known as oiran, although until 1761 the highest rank were called tayu. Their child assistants, kamuro, were learning the trade - often sold into servitude by poor farming or fishing families.

The women who worked within the pleasure quarters were rarely allowed out - except for visiting dying relatives. Each major town or city had it's designated area, in Osaka it was Shinmachi, In Kyoto it was Shimabara, and most famously Tokyo had the Yoshiwara, a huge complex just out of town.

The images here represent the glamour of the Yoshiwara, but lurking behind are uncomfortable truths about exploitation, disease and early death.

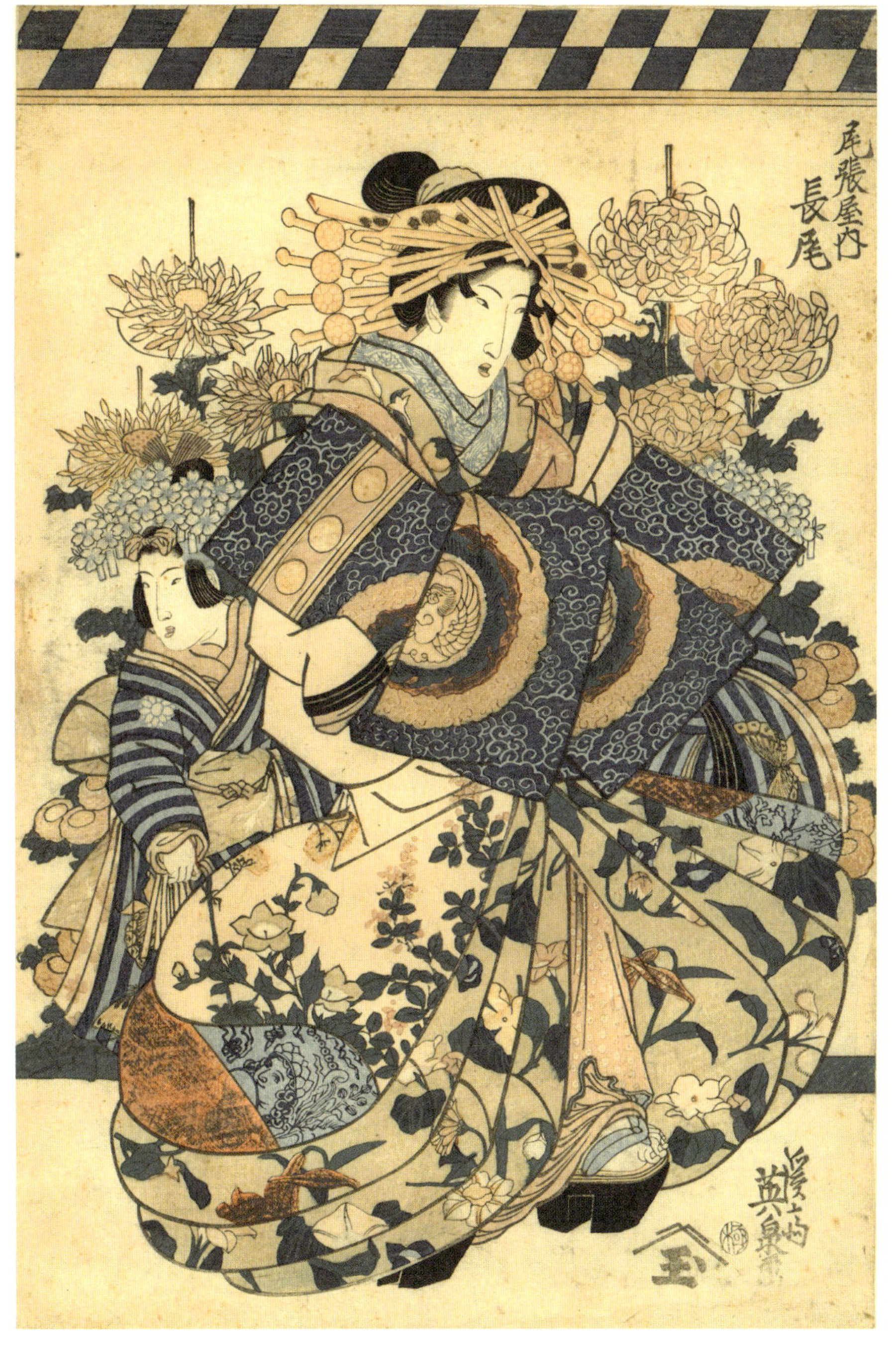
尾張屋内
長尾

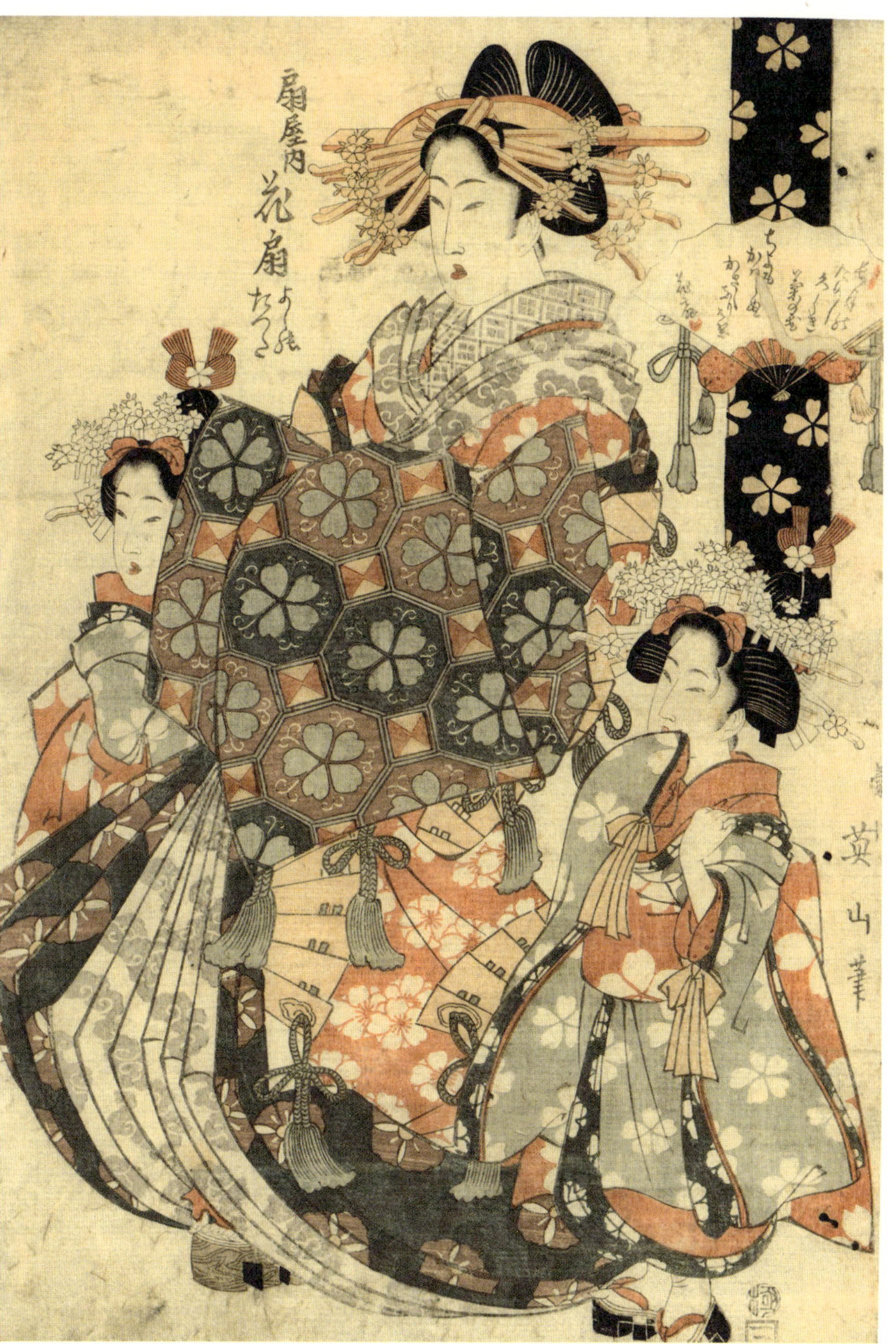
扇屋内
花扇
英山筆

For over three centuries, the Yoshiwara was the centre of a unique sexual culture. It figured prominently in both ukiyo-e in general and shunga in particular. From an early point, brothel owners encouraged publishers, writers and artists to feature their establishments and the women that worked for them, and by the 18th century Yoshiwara courtesans became a primary subject for ukiyo-e. The art was tapping into a huge demand with the number of women in the Yoshiwara swelling to nine thousand in 1893.

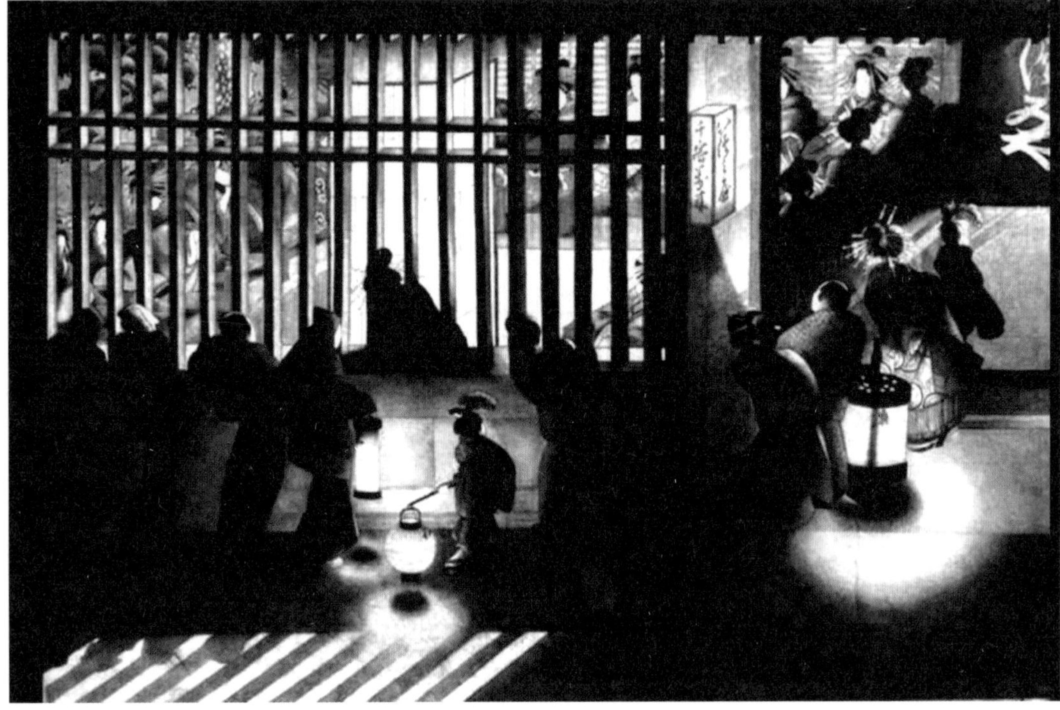

Setting the scene is **Katsushika Oi**, the daughter of the great **Hokusai** who we have already met. In this painting by her we see the women on display inside the brothel, gawped at by men in the street - lanterns lighting the activity.

The goings-on in the 'pleasure quarters' are well illustrated in the small shunga publications which were the porn mags of their day.

On the facing page, first is a cover picture, deliberately innocuous to get past the censors, who supposedly only looked at the opening pages. These two prints (Utagawa School c.1860) are supreme in their detail for such small images.

It is only when you look inside these books (from back to front in the Japanese way) that you get a true picture of the Yoshiwara - although maybe they illustrate pure male fantasy, or perhaps a female nightmare - or both!

You can see where the Austrian artist Gustav Klimt got his ideas.

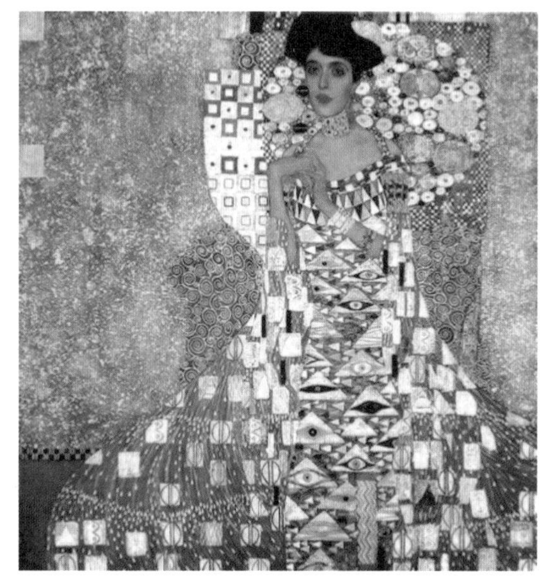

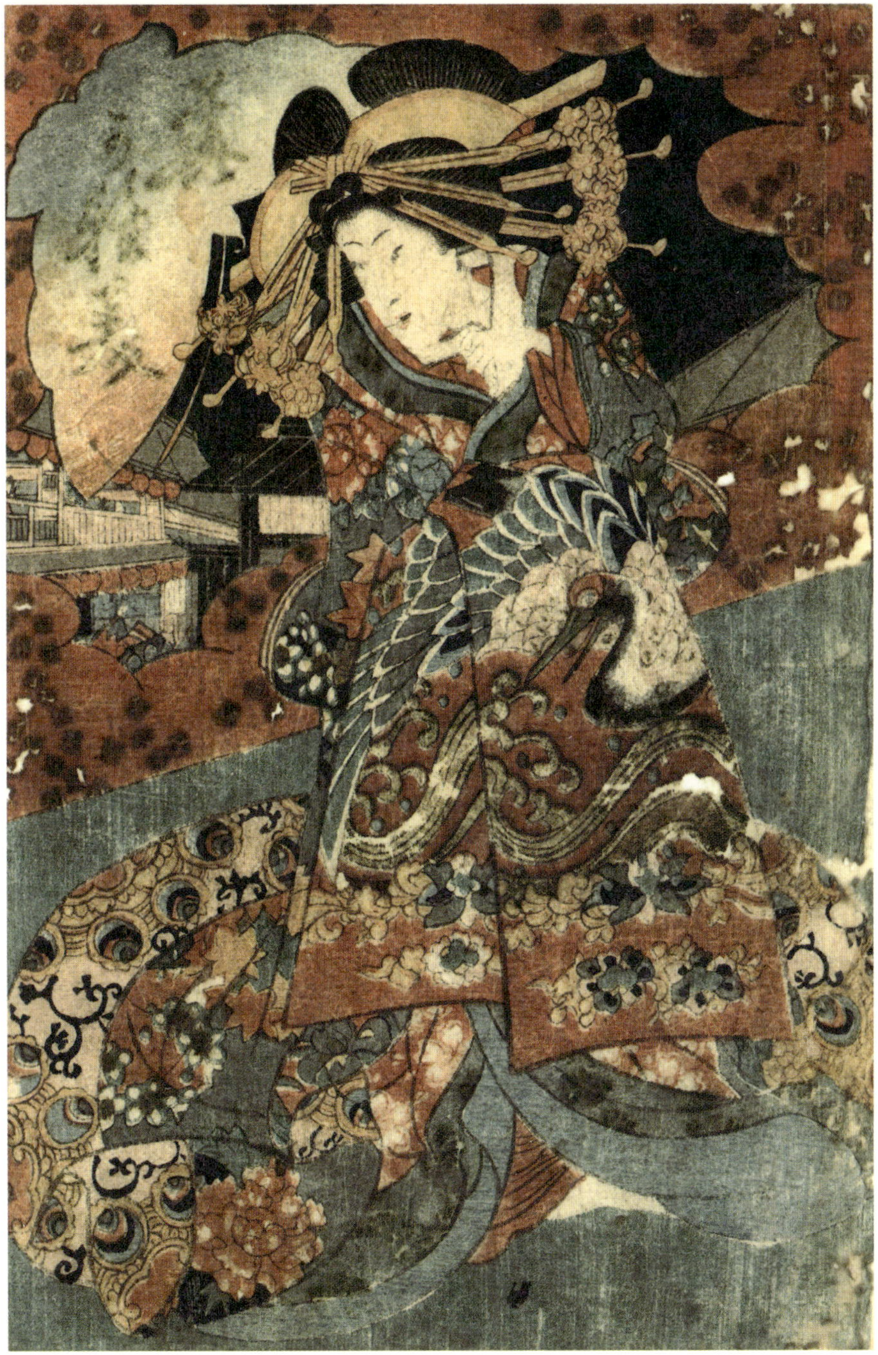

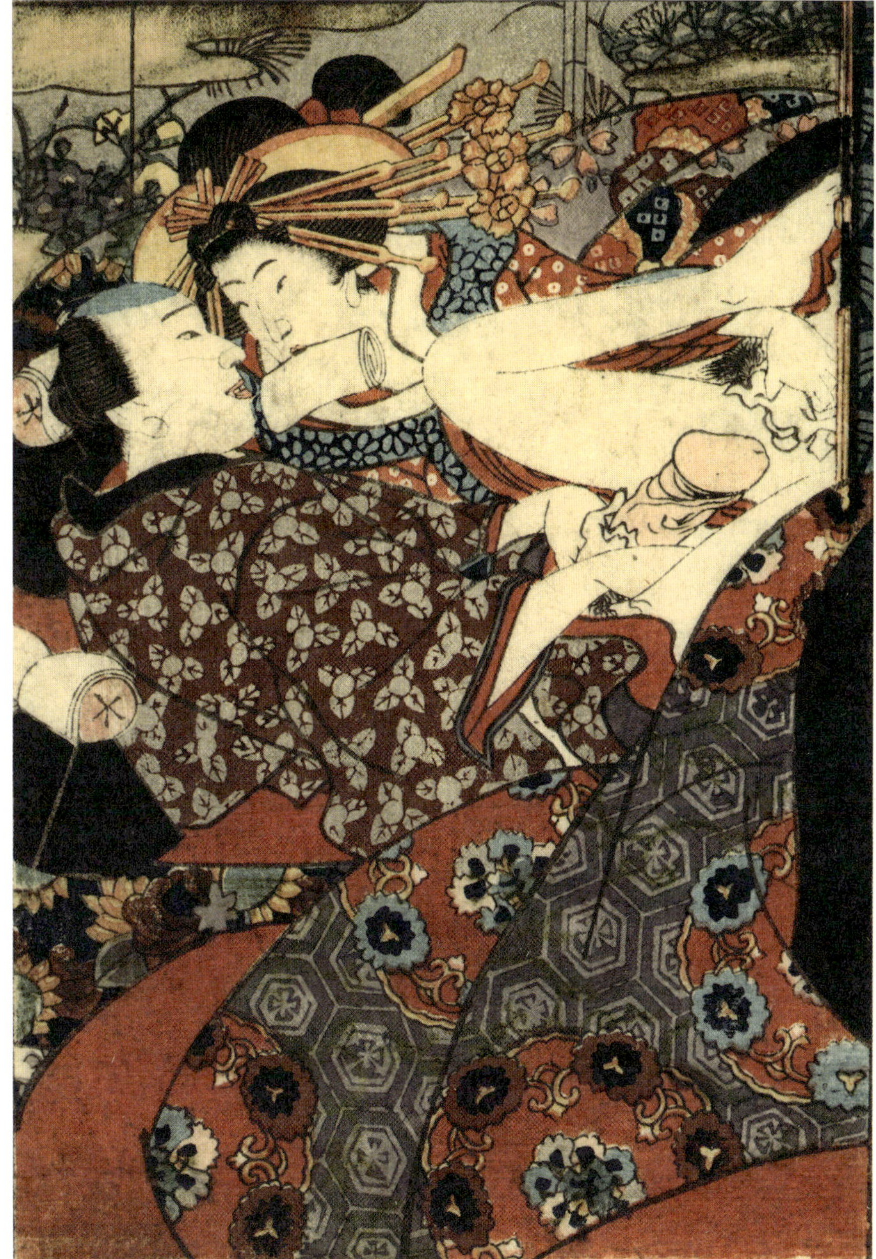

Kiokawa SHOZAN (1821-1907)

This is a book by **Shozan** (c.1850)

The cover is somewhat mutilated by a previous owner who wanted to improve the portrait - which had probably been disfigured by too much touching. It is interesting to see what is displayed behind her.

The narrative appears to be mainly centred on a celebrated courtesan visited in the Yoshiwara by a wealthy daimyo (a high class feudal lord). He arrives with a retinue and then the two are seen indulging in fine food, music and sex.

Inside the book we can follow their progress, interwoven with other participants, in a wonderful array of pages, some fold-outs.

On turning from page to page there are plenty of surprises, including strange hidden thought bubbles - and al fresco shenanigans.

It is an eye opening book, illustrating the many different aspects of the 'pleasure district'.

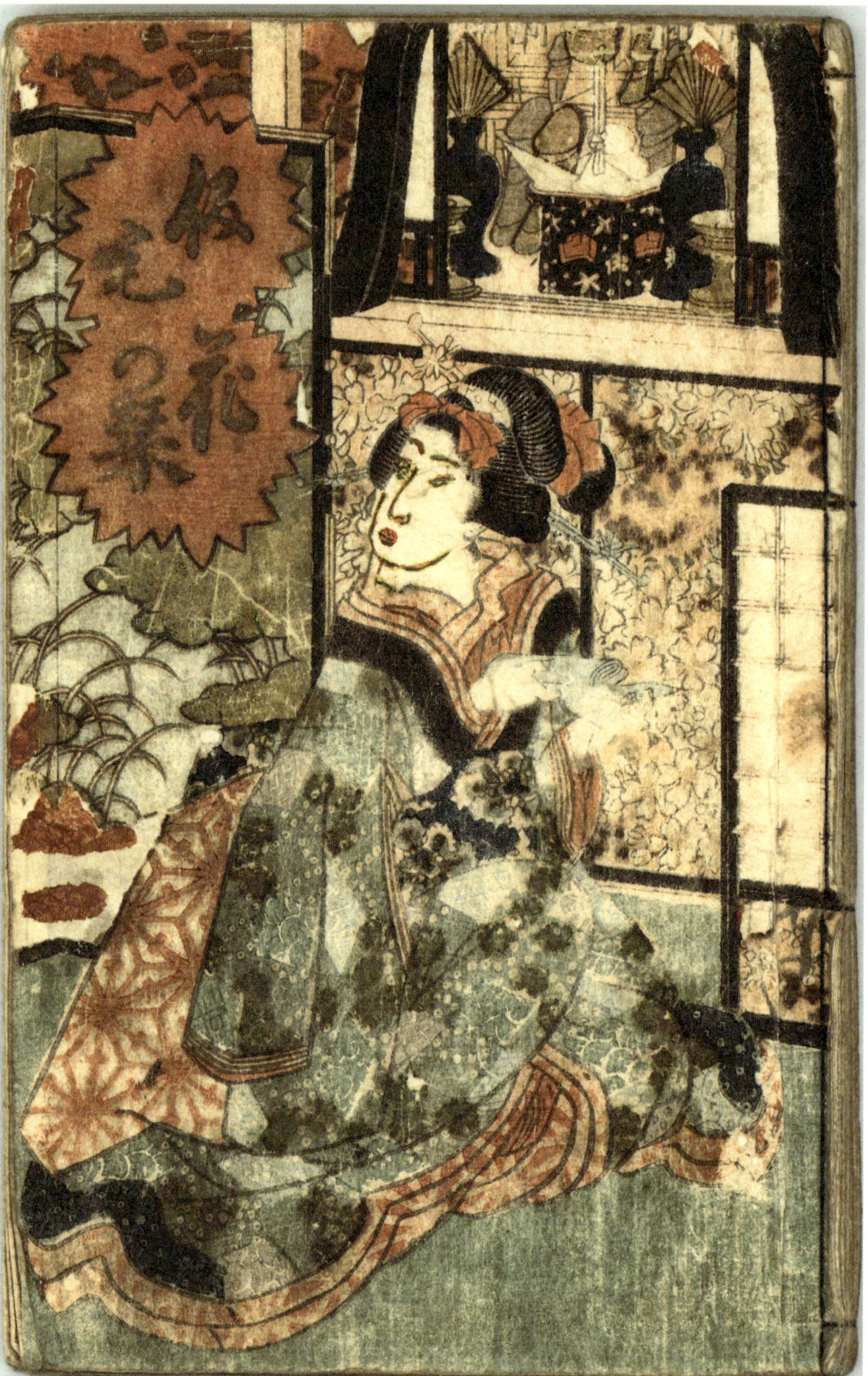

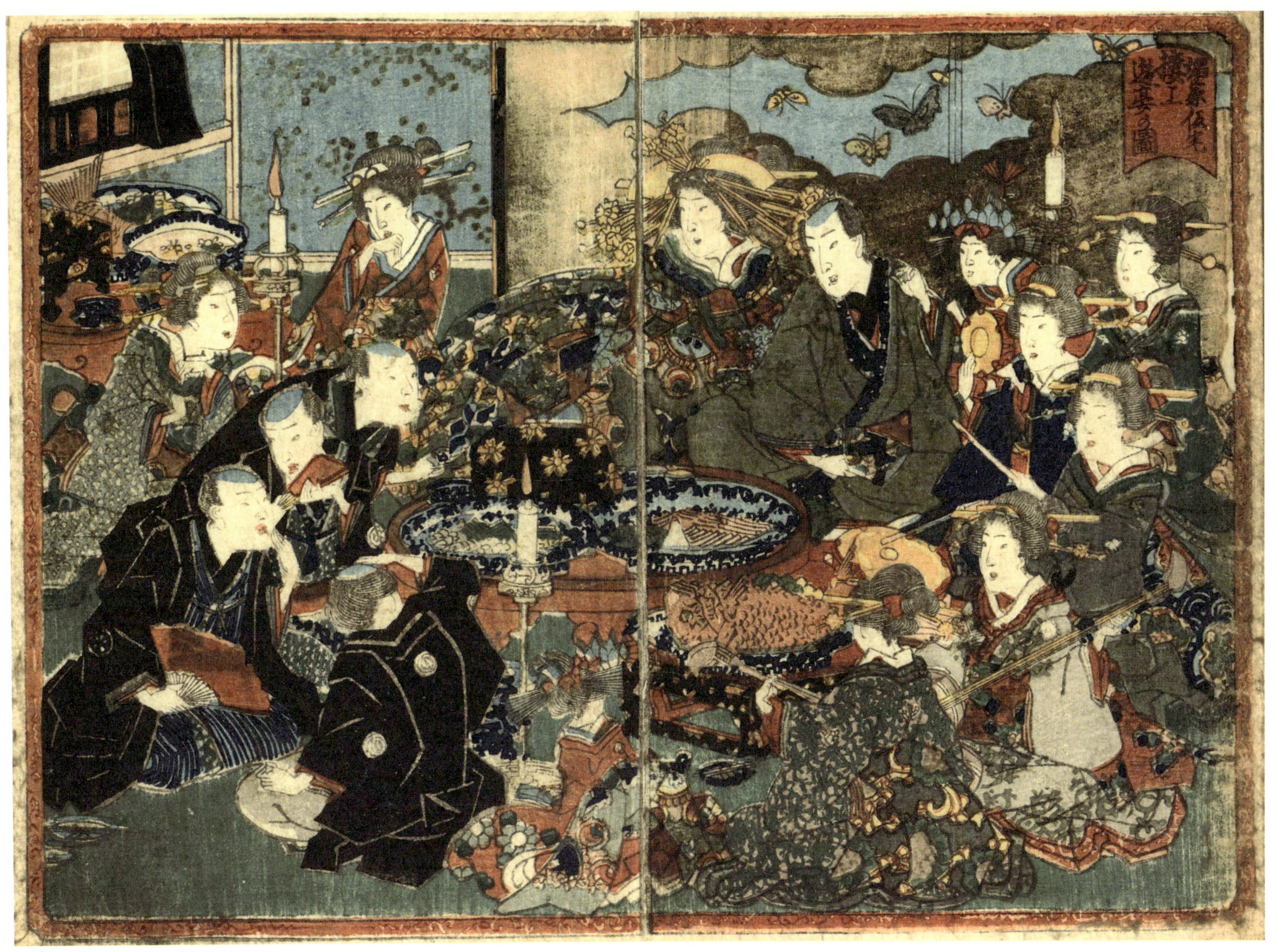

First off, after seeing the daimyo and retinue arrive, we are given the spectacle of a sumptuous banquet, with numerous attendants, musicians - and a huge fish! Turn over the page and we are hit with a panorama on what it is really all about....

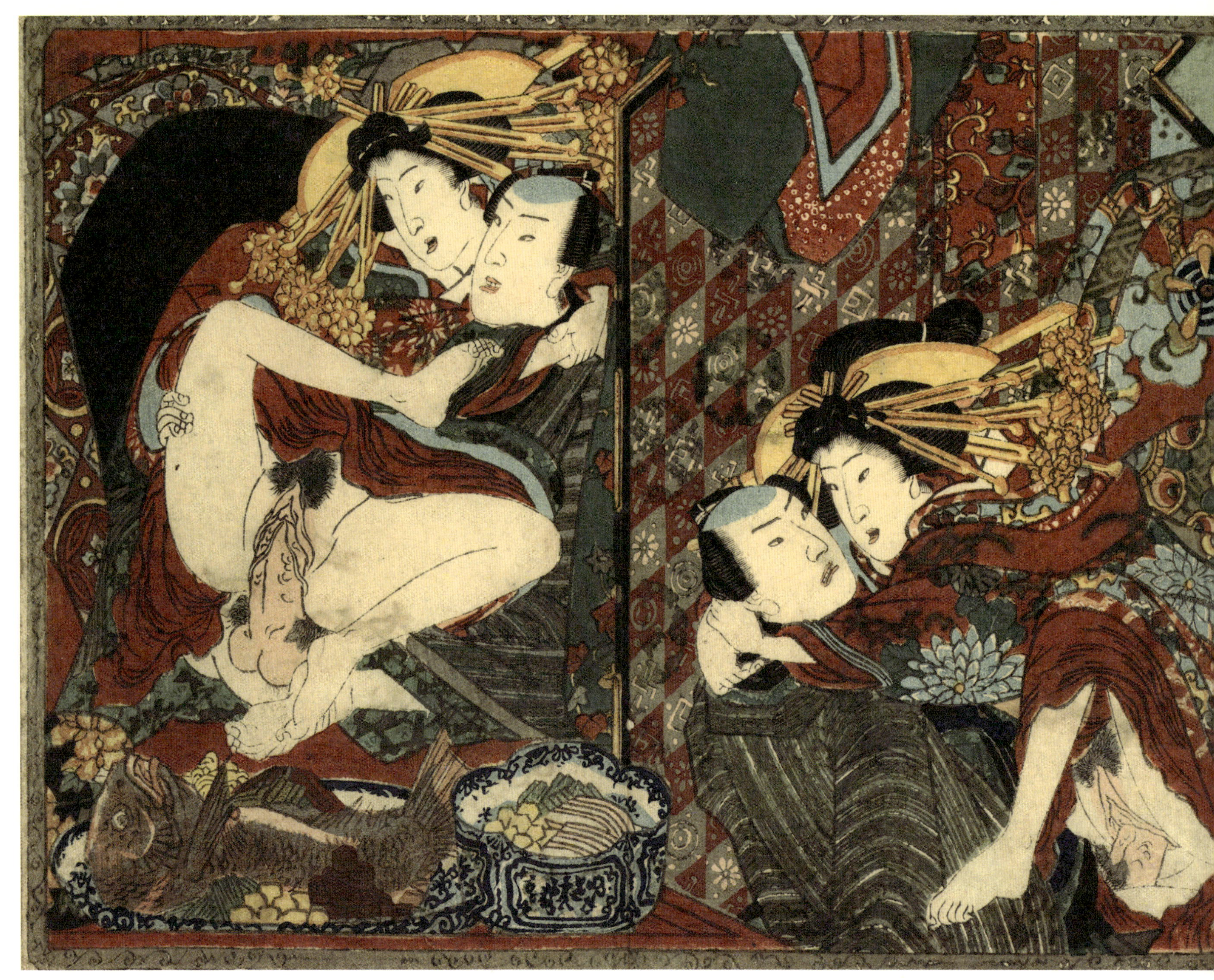

This is revealed by turning over both left and right pages. It seems to depict the same daimyo and courtesan in various contorted love making positions - with her very much in control.

I love the fish, who seems about to comment!

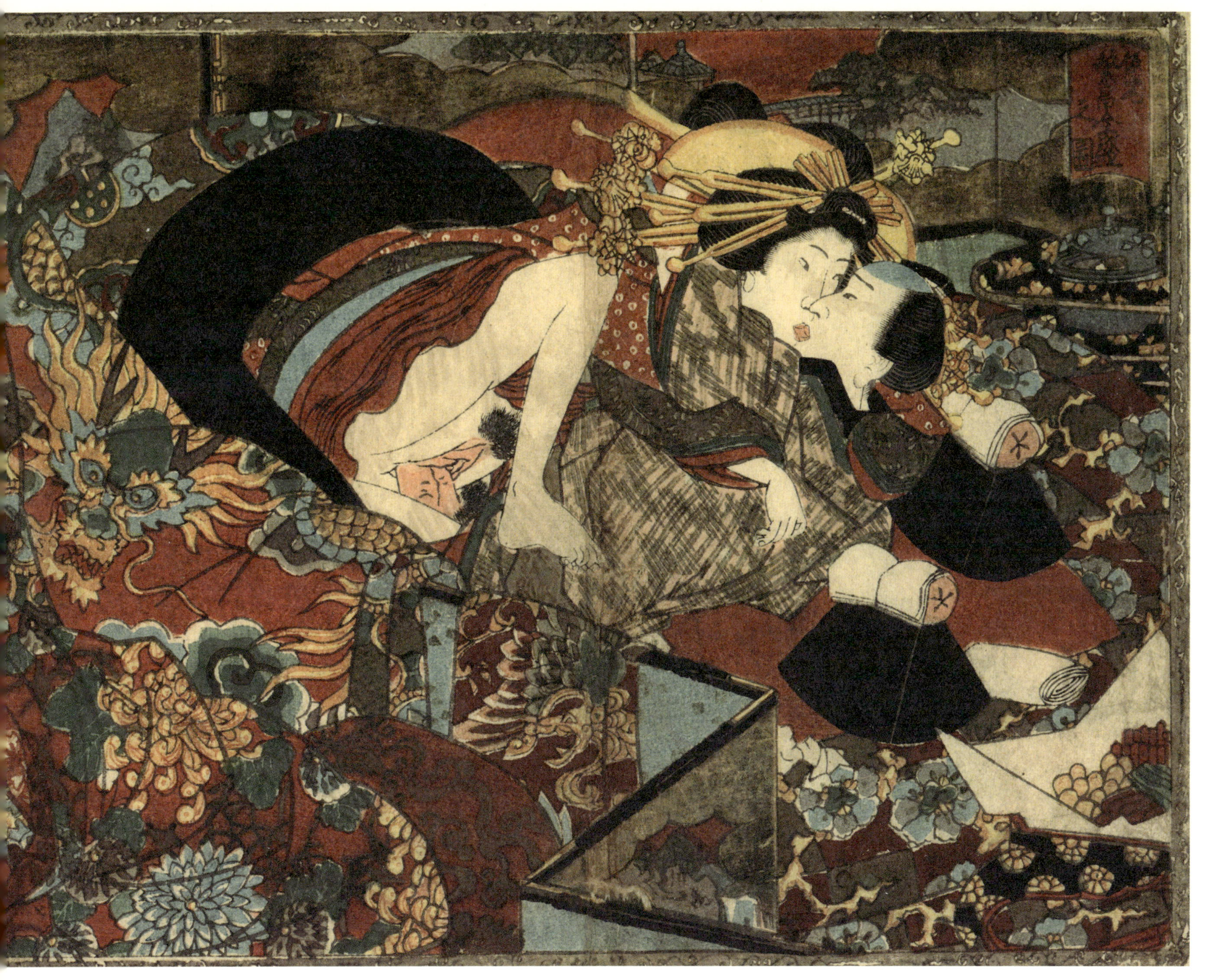

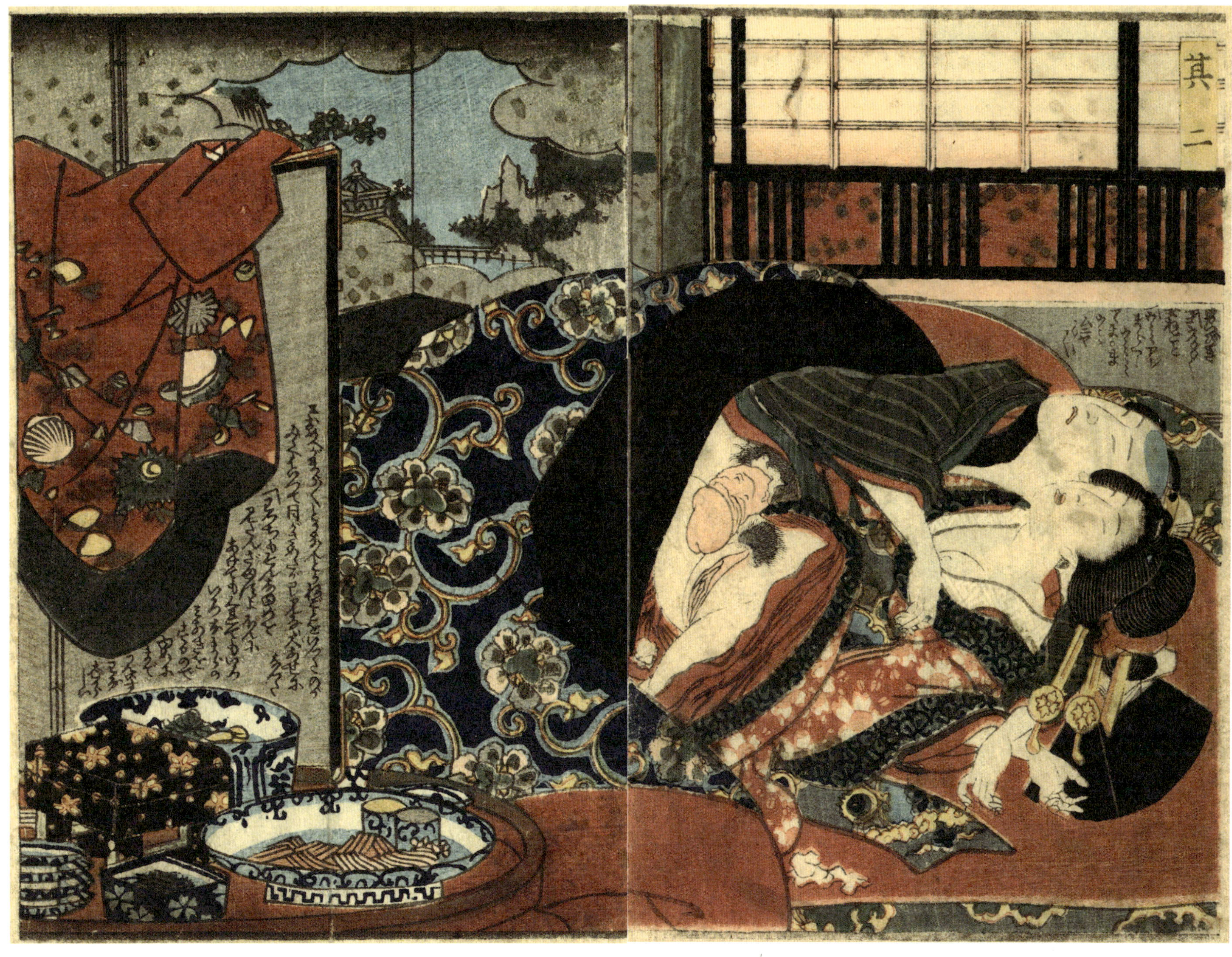

We are then treated to other couples coupling - but here is the most intriguing. On turning to this page the image may be showing an unsatisfactory event, evidence being the flaccid penis. Or it could be a contented scenario, with a couple recovering from a bout of love making.

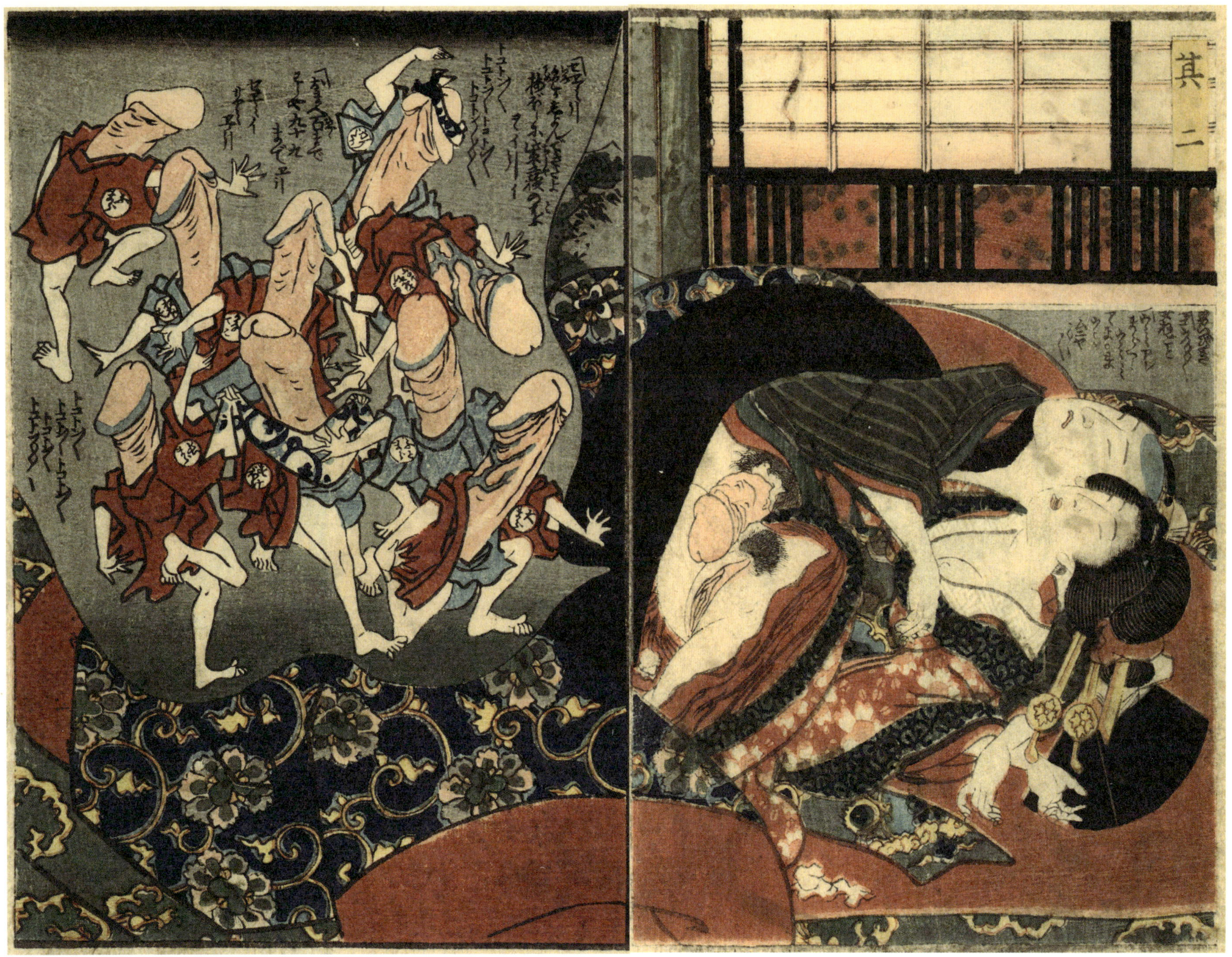

Whatever the case, by turning the folding page on the left an array of stiff members appear, having a riotous time in a thoughts bubble. I leave it to the reader to figure this out further!

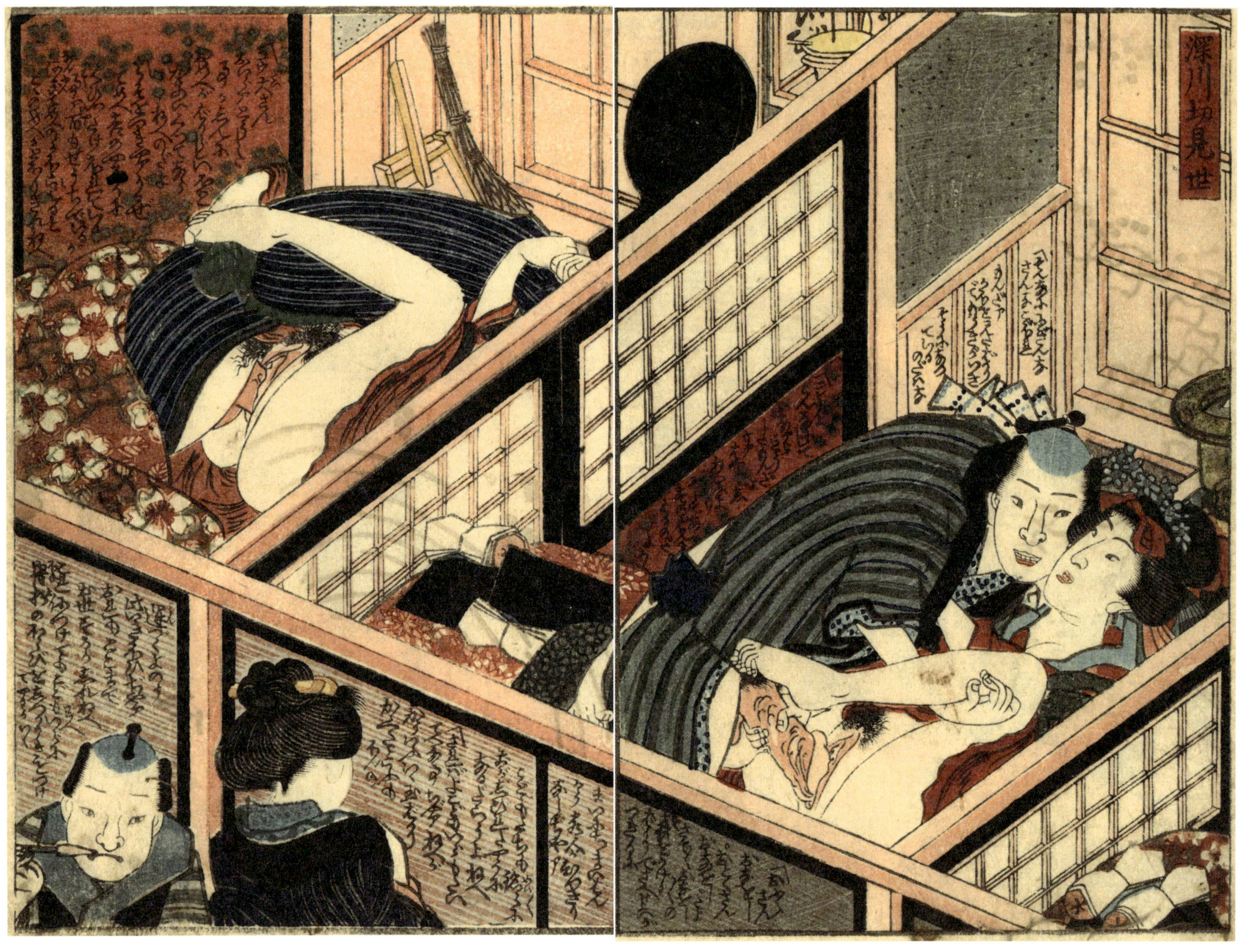

Other images show the less sophisticated side of the Yoshiwara, with clients and prostitutes fornicating in cubicles just out of sight, but presumably in earshot, of men and women in the public areas.

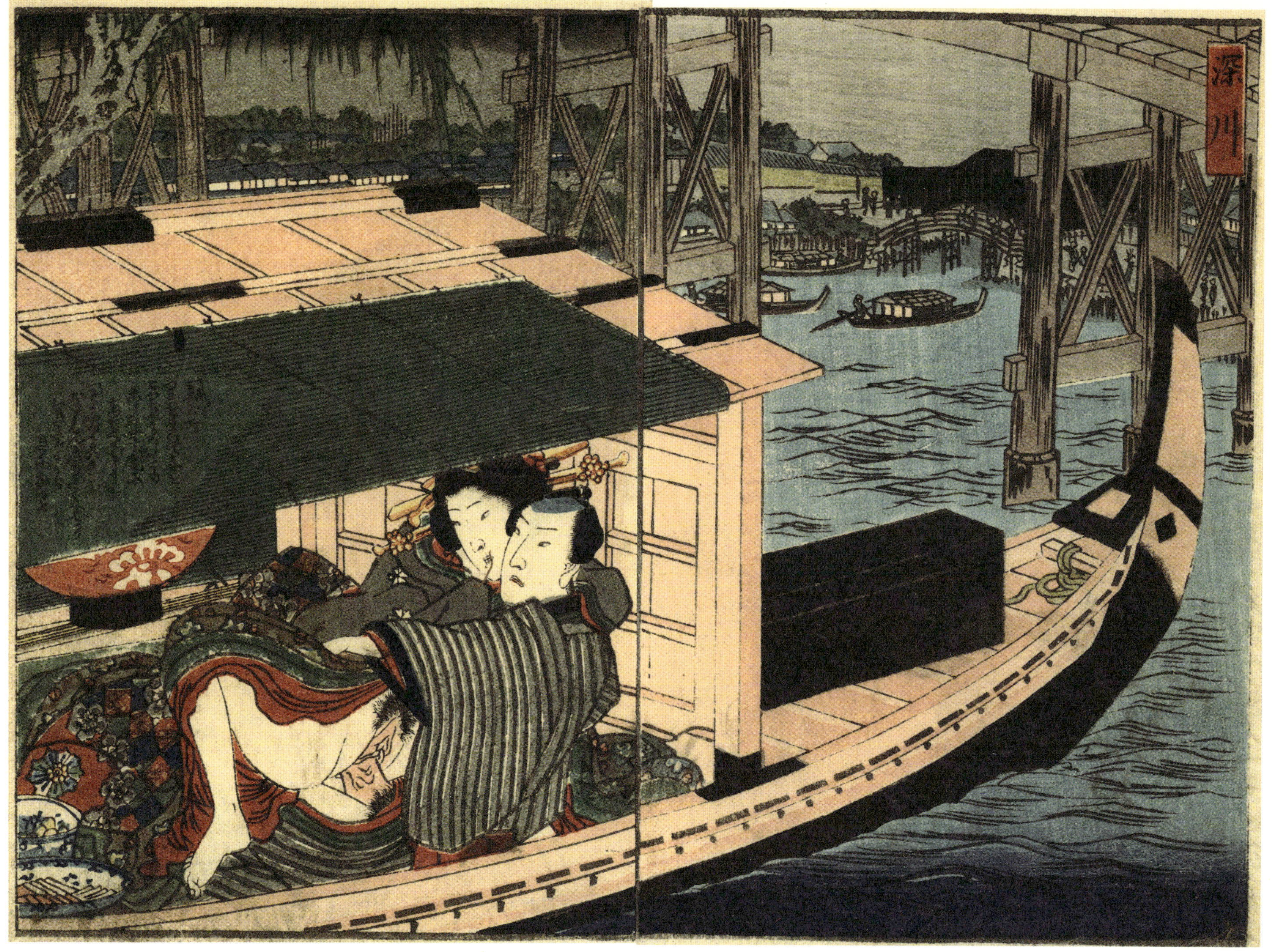

A little more romantic is love making on a boat. Perhaps it is the daimyo and his courtesan lover escaping the frenetic atmosphere of the 'pleasure district' for the purer air on the Sumida River.

EXTRAS & RUMINATIONS AFTER CHAPTER TWO

In this book we have been looking at the erotica of shunga and pictures of beautiful women - bijin-ga. Apart from a few notable exceptions it is mostly male artists and female subjects. In modern western culture this might be seen as the objectification of women in a very misogynist society.

HISTORY

I think it is important to see this art in the context of it's time - and not judge Japanese culture of this period in the same way we might our own. It's worth reflecting on the fact for almost three hundred years the country was cut off from the rest of the world and enjoyed an extended period of peace. This when other countries were embroiled in wars, massacres, rape and pillage.

This extraordinary time started in 1603 when the shogun Tokugawa brought the three hundred warring regional daimyos together in an alliance that managed to defuse their power. Known as the Edo Period, it was characterised by economic growth, strict social order, isolationist foreign policies, a stable population and popular enjoyment of arts and culture - which included free thinking attitudes to sex.

To maintain the peace, feudal lords were required to reside in Edo (Tokyo) every other year, which meant the capital was regularly full of entourages, including samurai. They were eager to be distracted by delights of the big city - where all appetites were catered for.

The southern city of Nagasaki was the only port to the outside world with Dutch traders who had been given exclusive access.

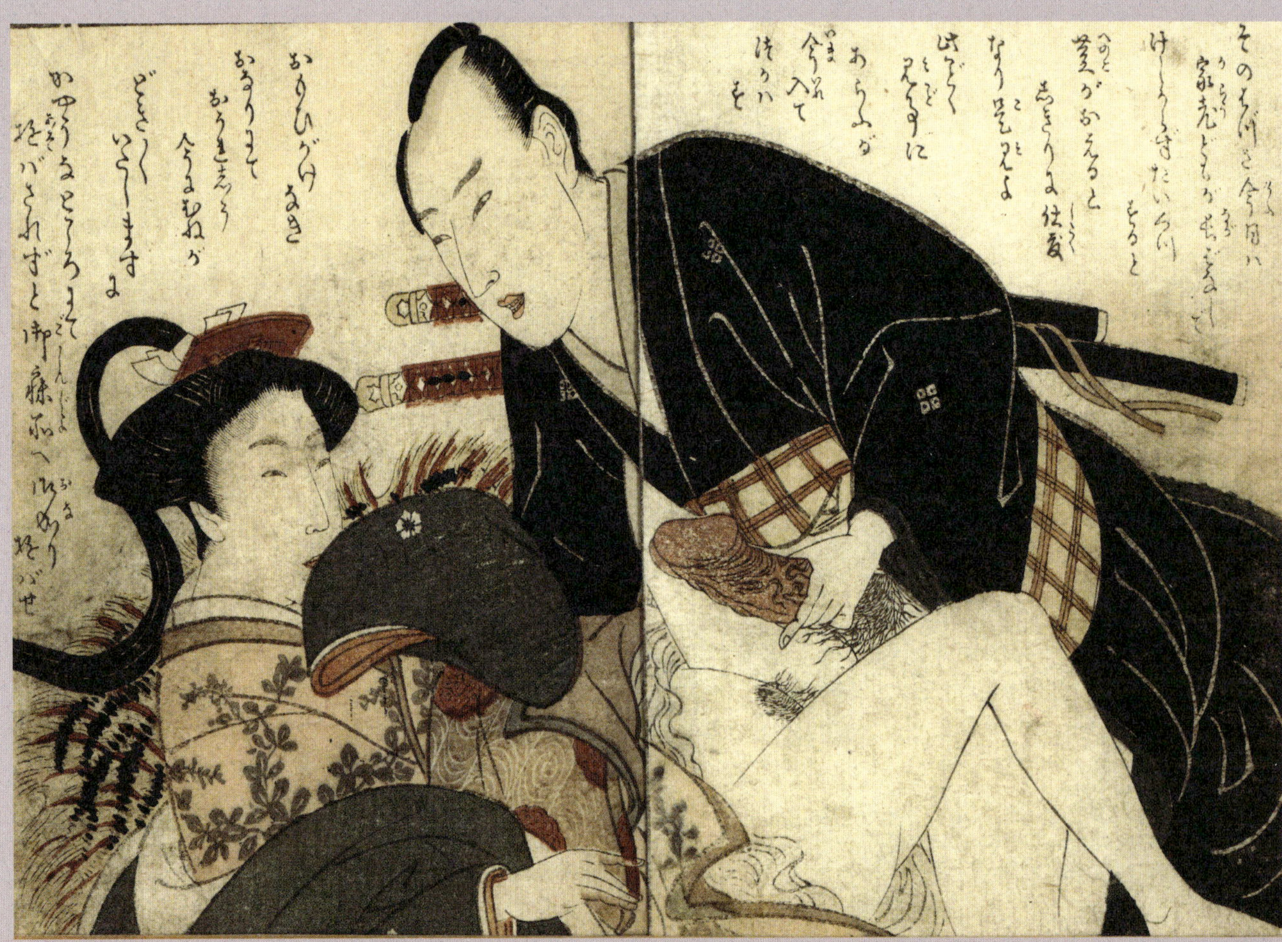

Katsushika HOKUSAI created this print in 1814. It shows a typical samurai indulging in the pleasures of Edo - but it seems not with a courtesan. His swords are neatly placed behind him.

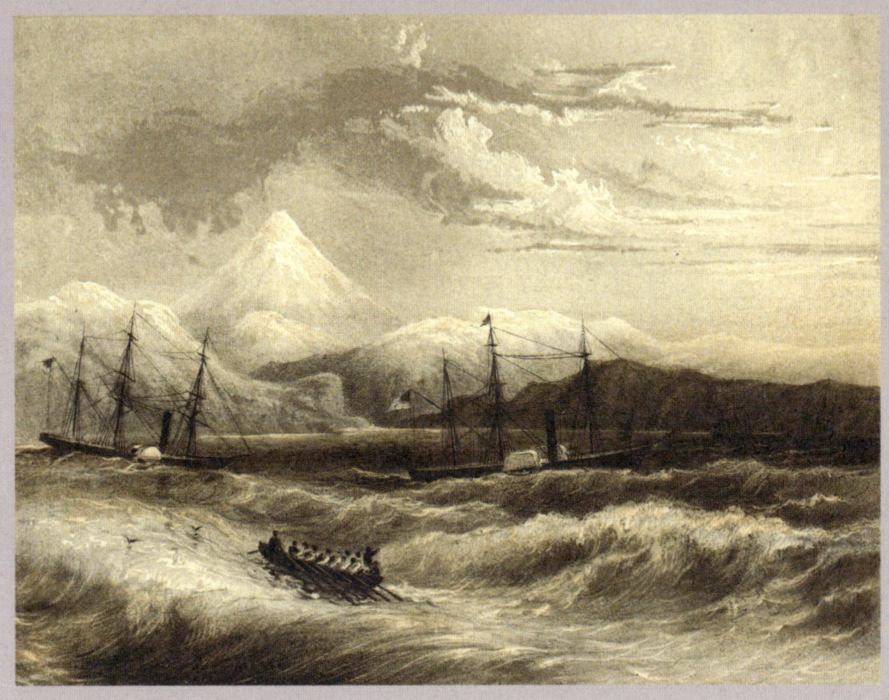

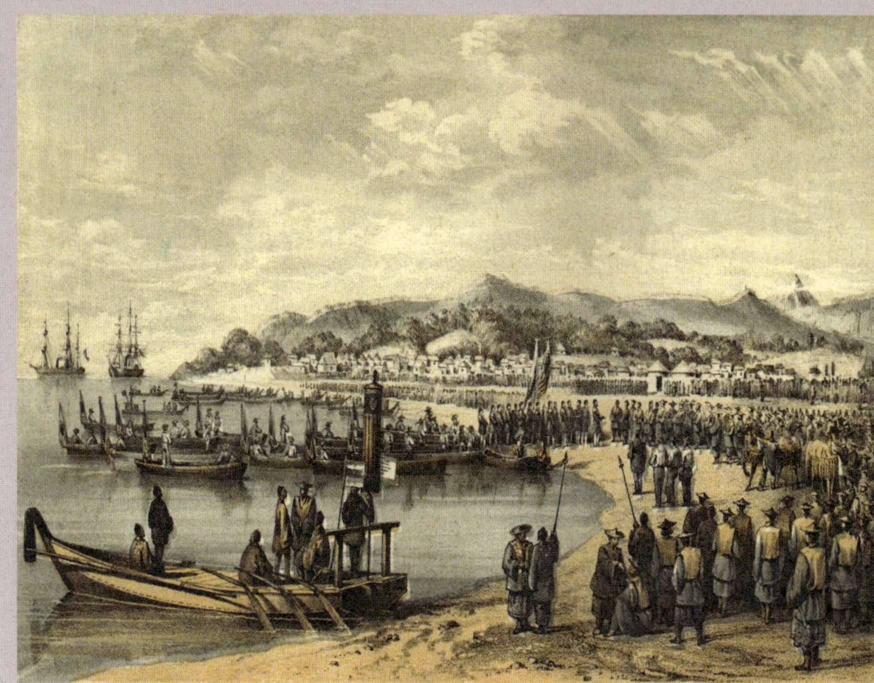

This arrangement managed to continue until the American 'black ships' of Commodore Perry arrived and spoiled the party - in 1854. This was 'shock and awe' and the prize was oil.

The people hadn't seen anything like these ships before, because the shogunate had banned anything but modest one masted sailing ships - for their own internal security. The American warships appeared massive and belched black smoke, something else that impressed, as steamers were unknown to the Japanese.

The defences around Edo were so weak the various leaders felt they had no option but to negotiate deals and open up the country to foreigners. The Americans got what they wanted, which was to establish coaling stations in ports along the coast.

In those days oil meant sperm whales. Good whaling grounds had been discovered in the western Pacific and by the mid 1840's hundreds of whalers were heading there, but without enough coal for their steam engines.

'Regime change' happened in Japan partly because Americans wanted to keep their lamps lit with whale oil! A strong presence in the seas off China was the political reasoning, because the Russians, Dutch and British were already there - gunboat diplomacy!

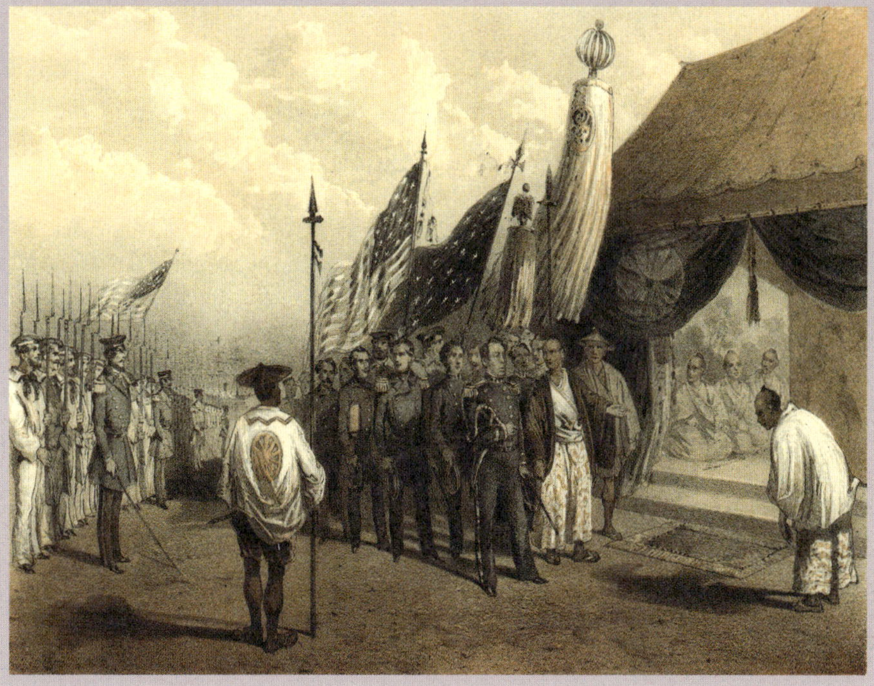

The way of life typified by 'The Floating World' started to fall apart soon after these turn of events.

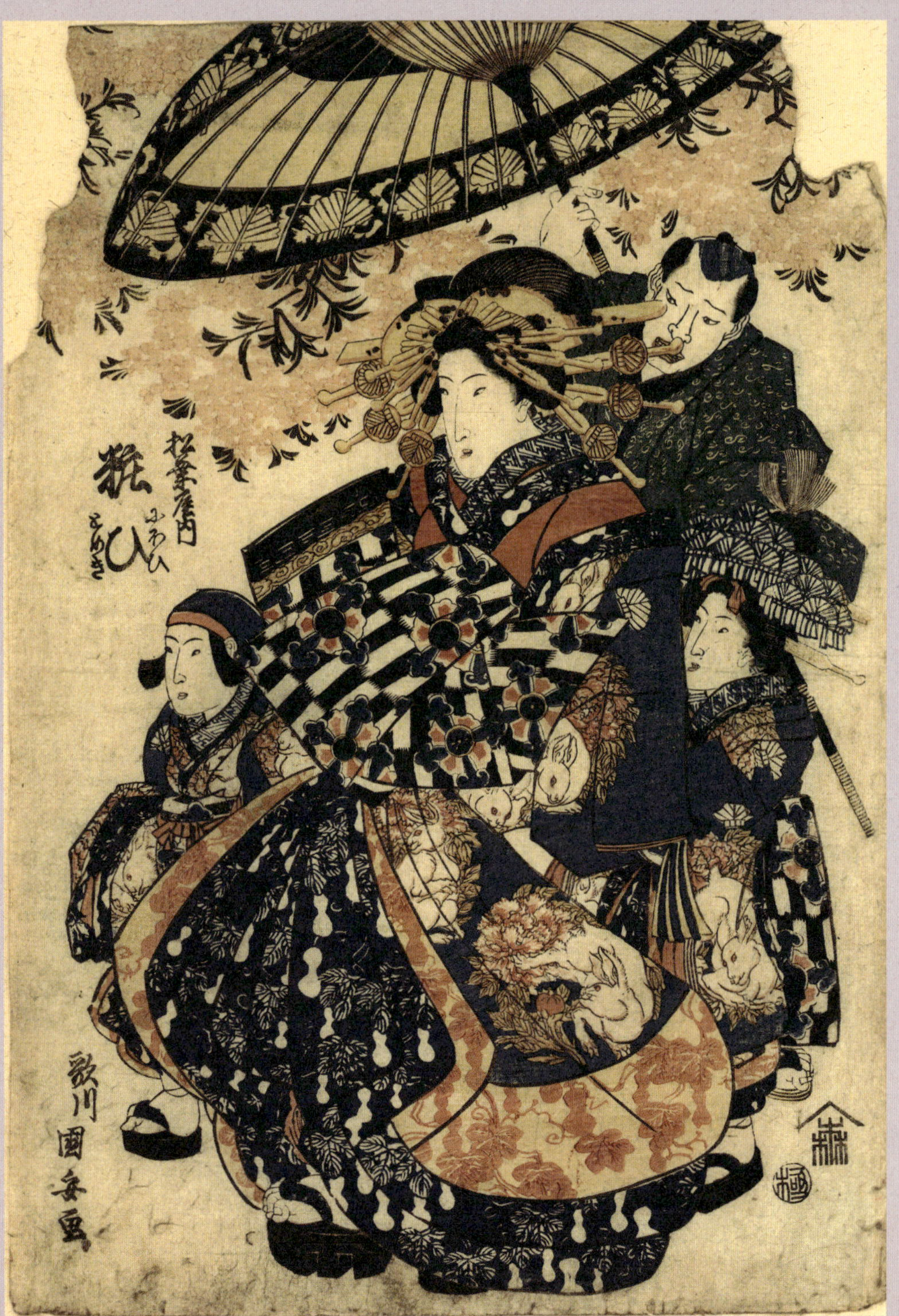

The Yoshiwara just about managed to maintain its exclusive status through the collapse of the Edo period, but shortly after the Meiji emperor came to power in 1868 six other districts, all of which had long been centres of illegal prostitution, were granted licensed status.

Some of the newly arrived western visitors were appalled by these legally approved establishments, seeing a systematic abuse of women. One such observer was Clement Scott who wrote with great passion in support of what he called the 'soiled doves in cages'.

Such criticism from foreigners contributed to the gradual loss of mystique during the late 19th and early 20th centuries, and the Yoshiwara became a ghost of its former self. It was finally closed in 1958.

Utagawa KUNIYASU (1794-1832)

This print shows an oiran on parade wearing heavy platform shoes which made it difficult to walk, so a seductive 'figure of eight' step was devised to help them get around. Dress and elaborate hair combs denote a status that potential clients could decode. As we have seen they were accompanied by child assistants know as kamuro and were often accompanied by attendants with parasols - which drew attention as well as seeing off rain and sun.

The phenomena of parading oiran has been documented in modern times. These photographs date from the early 1900's.

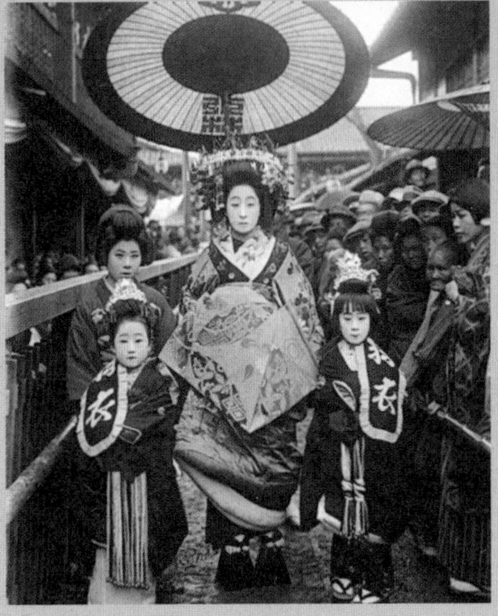

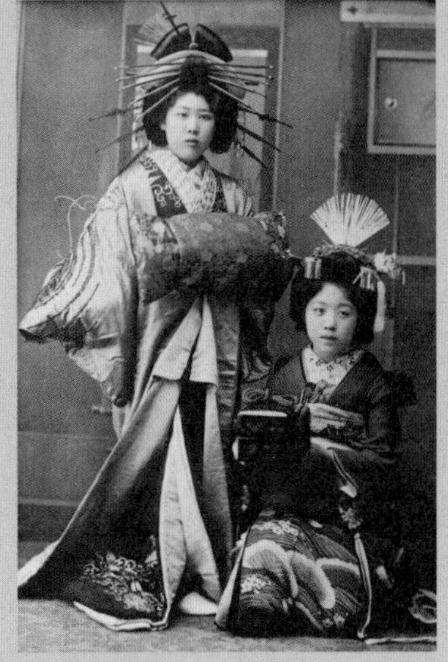

The oiran were historically at the top of a hierarchy in providing sexual pleasure - and that did not include the geisha. But as the allure of the oiran waned, geisha took over as the more fashionable entertainers (below right).

Although originally striving to avoid sexual interaction with clients, the fact that by the 1870's they were required by the shogunate to hold two licenses - one to work as a geisha and another for prostitution - indicates the divisions were somewhat blurred.

It is worth mentioning that in the late 20th century, fictional works loosely based on Japanese history have perpetuated misunderstandings about their duties and practices.

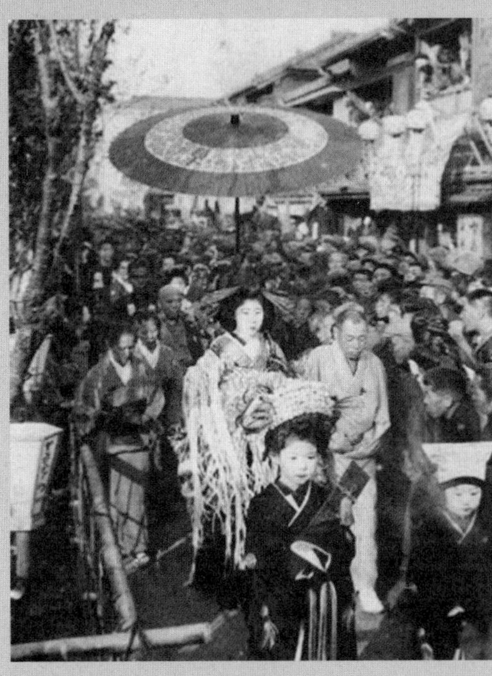

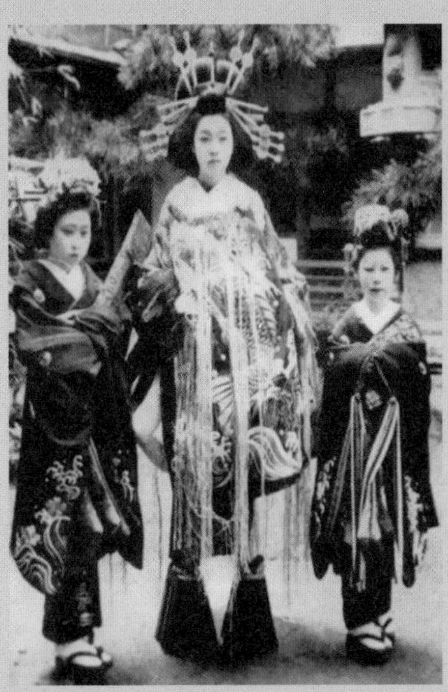

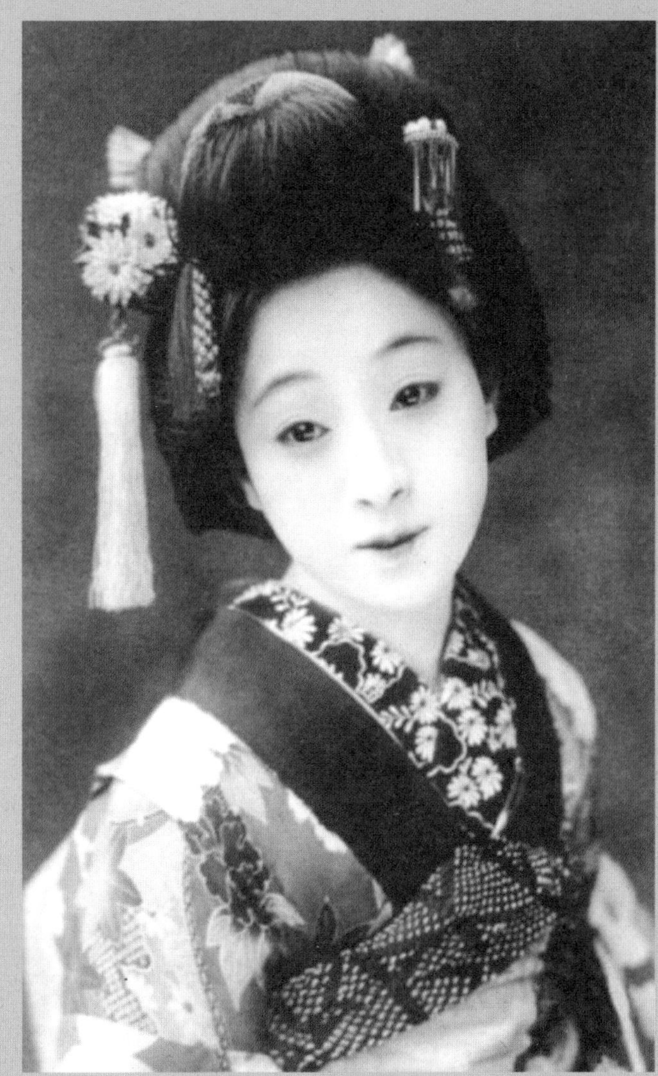

Chapter 3

THE END OF AN ERA

and other mid century masters

THERE WERE MANY OTHER GREAT ARTISTS working during the mid 1800's, right up to the appearance of the American 'black ships', the end of the Edo period and into the Meiji Restoration. They are inextricably linked to the artists we have seen in Chapter 2 and take us through to what many consider to be the end of the greatest period of Japanese art. It is really all one wonderful continuum.

Utagawa (Ando) HIROSHIGE (1797-1858)

One of the most celebrated artists of the period was **Hiroshige**. He was known mostly for landscapes and depictions of forces of nature, like in this iconic image, *'Sudden Rainstorm at Shono'* (1833).

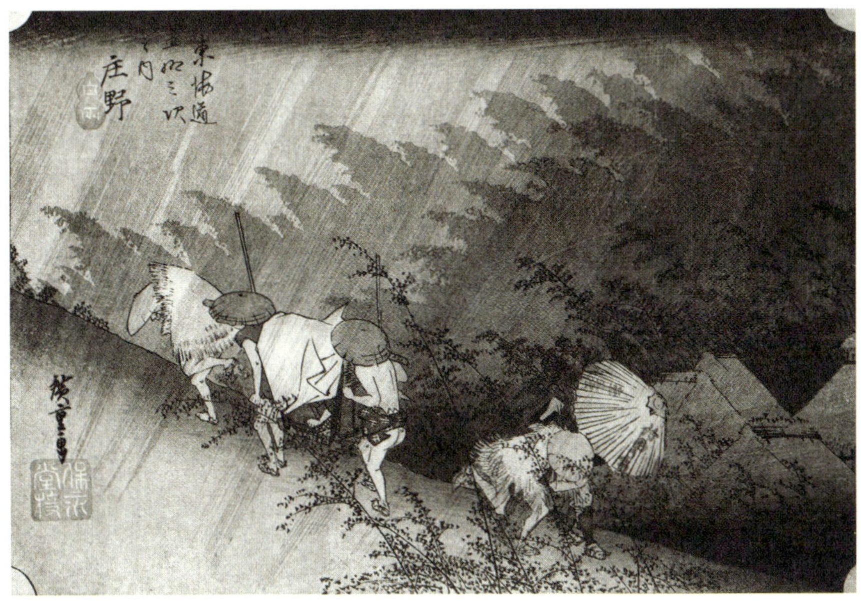

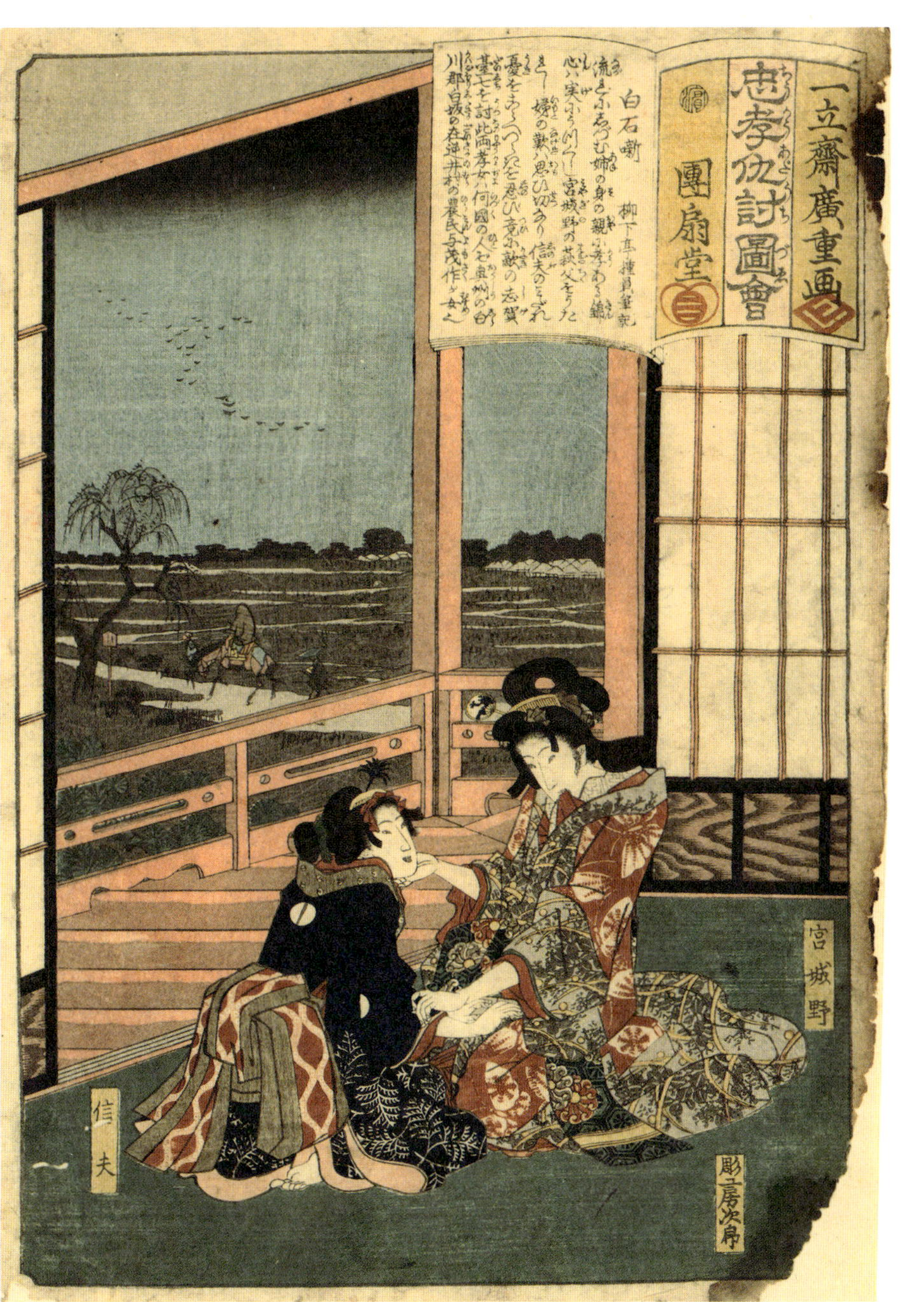

He also did pictures of beautiful women as in this print which shows an intimate moment between female friends. They are nonetheless very much figures in front of a landscape.

It came as a surprise to discover that **Hiroshiga** too did extremely explicit erotica. I discovered individual pages from a book and acquired one of them - on the left.

Several years later the entire publication became available which I was pleased to purchase. So now I have the complete narrative, in a series titled *Genjimon* dated around 1840.

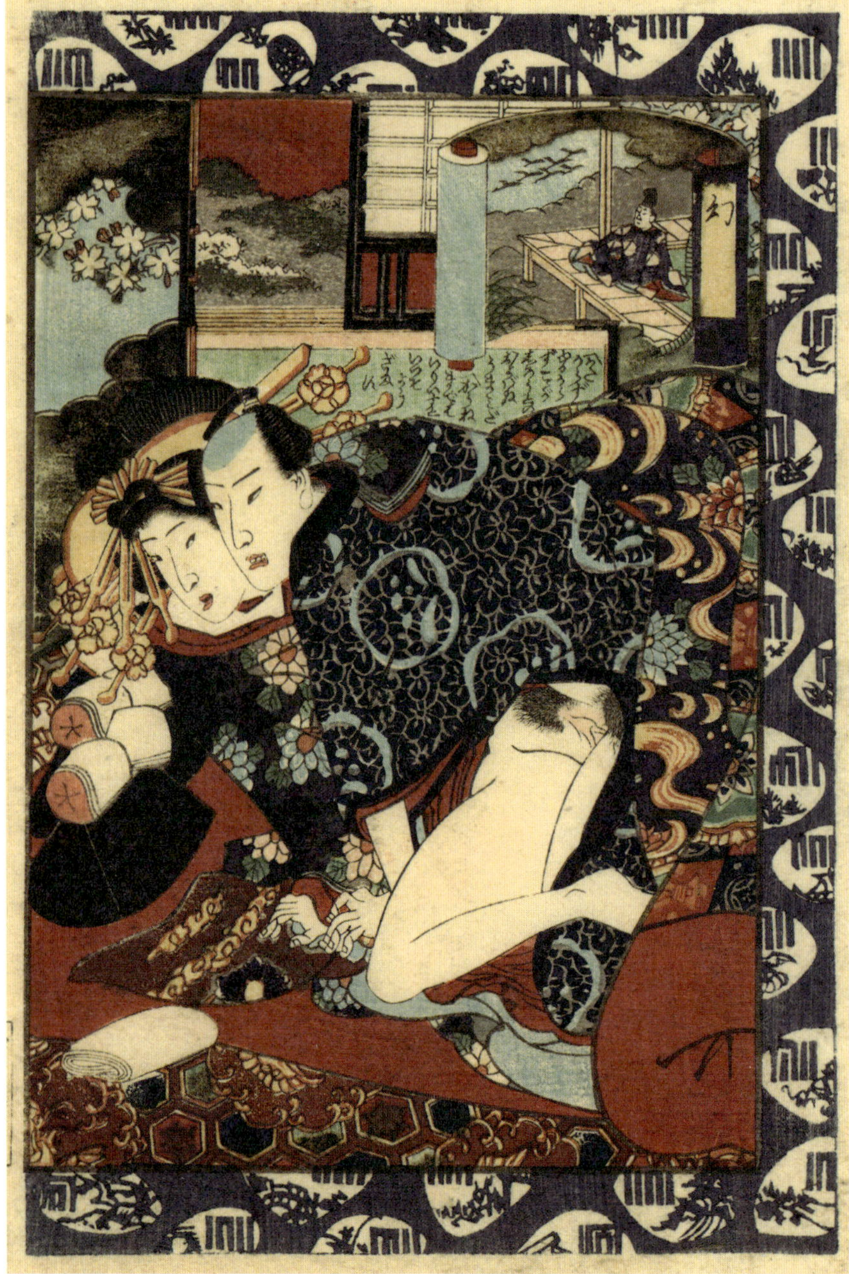

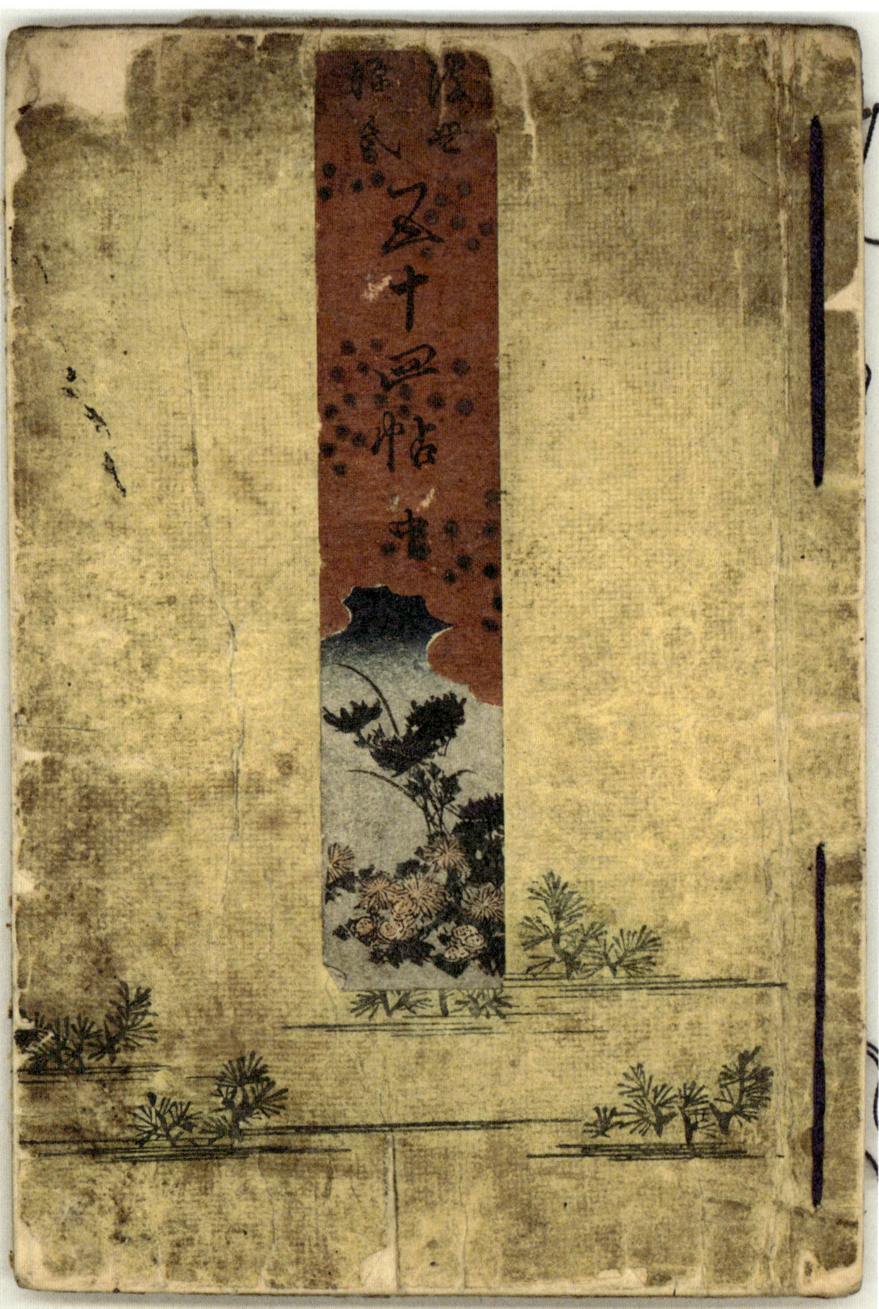

The ornate borders have the motif that indicates that this book is inspired by *The Tale of Genji.* Each picture most likely illustrates a particular chapter, as we will see later with the work of another artist.

This is a selection from the book showing the intricate designs, burnished metallic details - and of course, background landscapes.

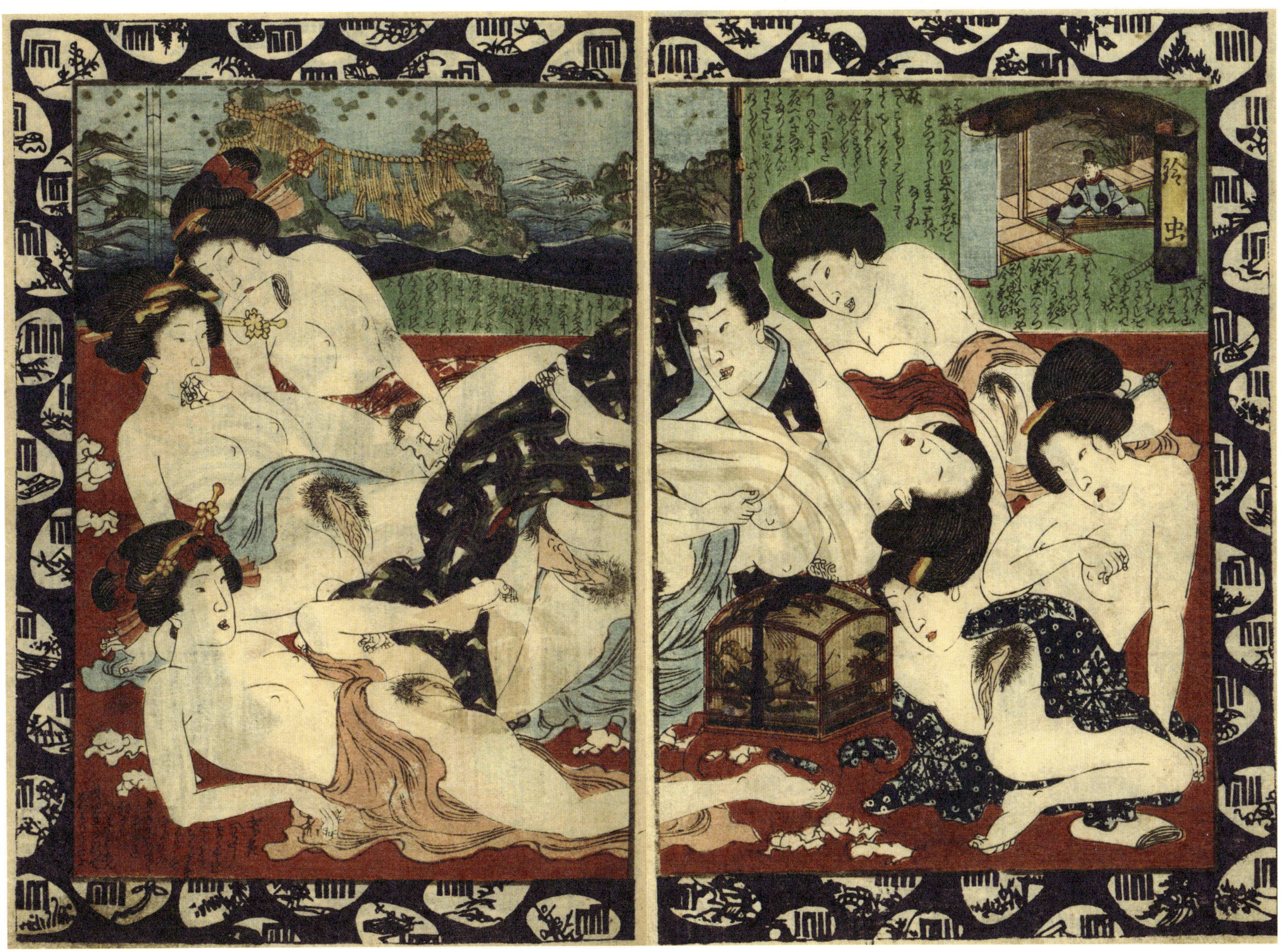

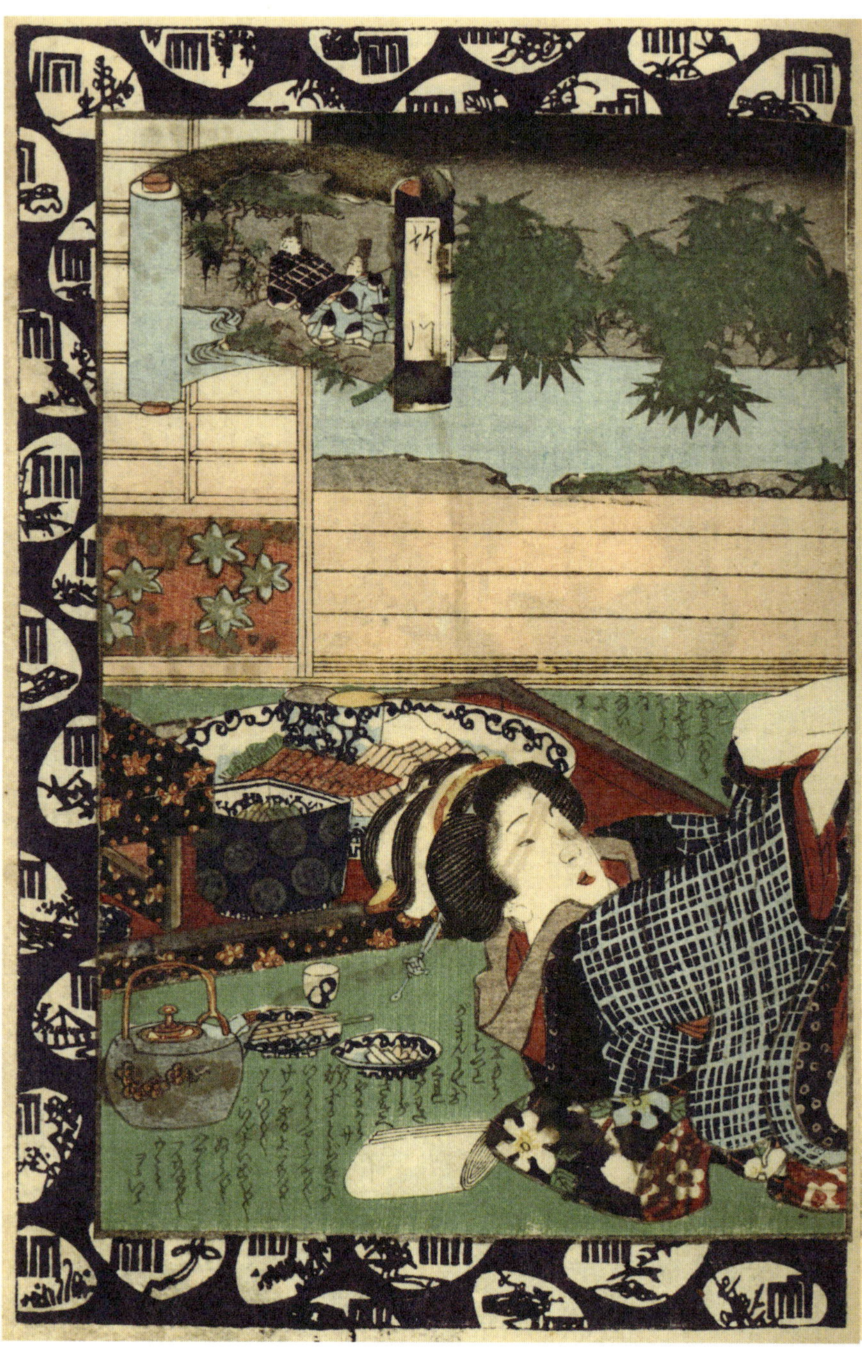

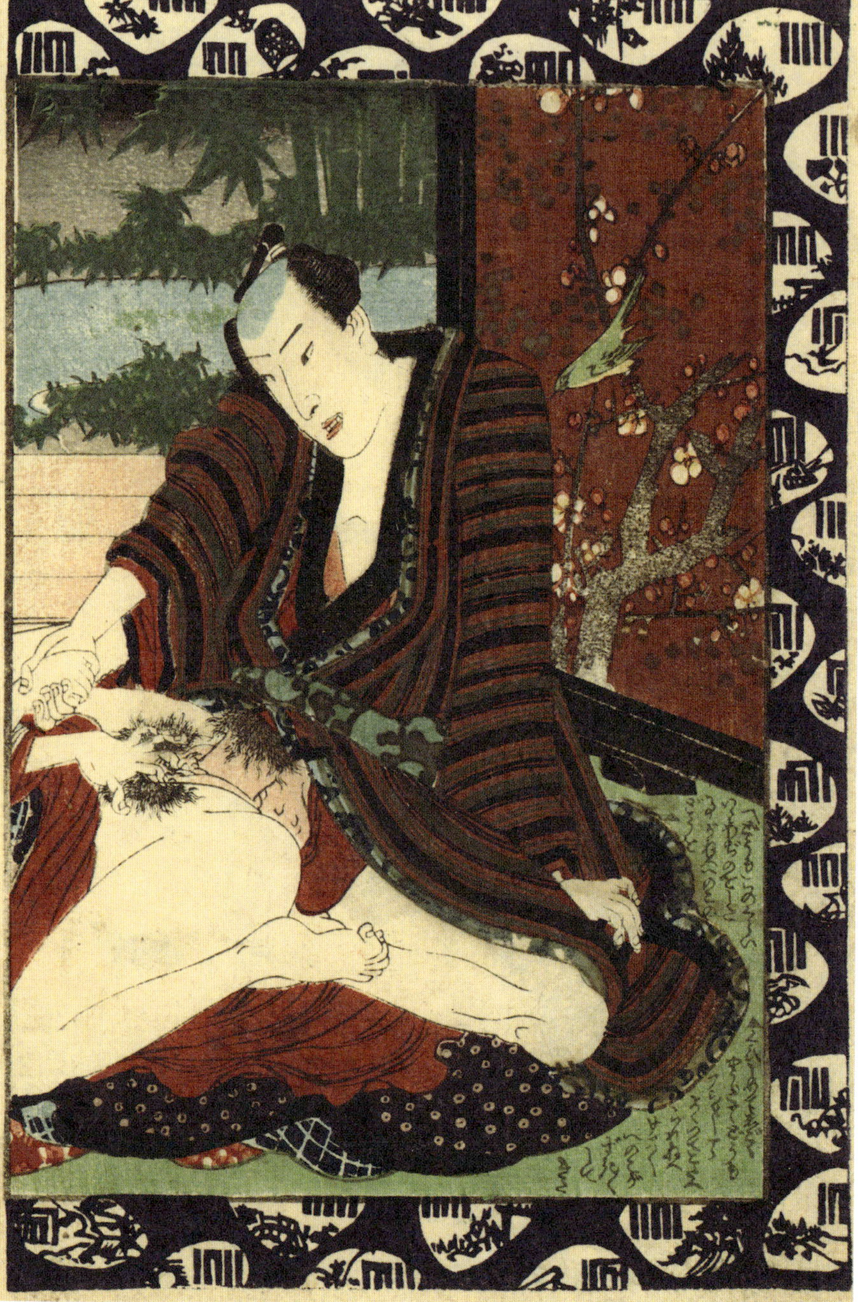

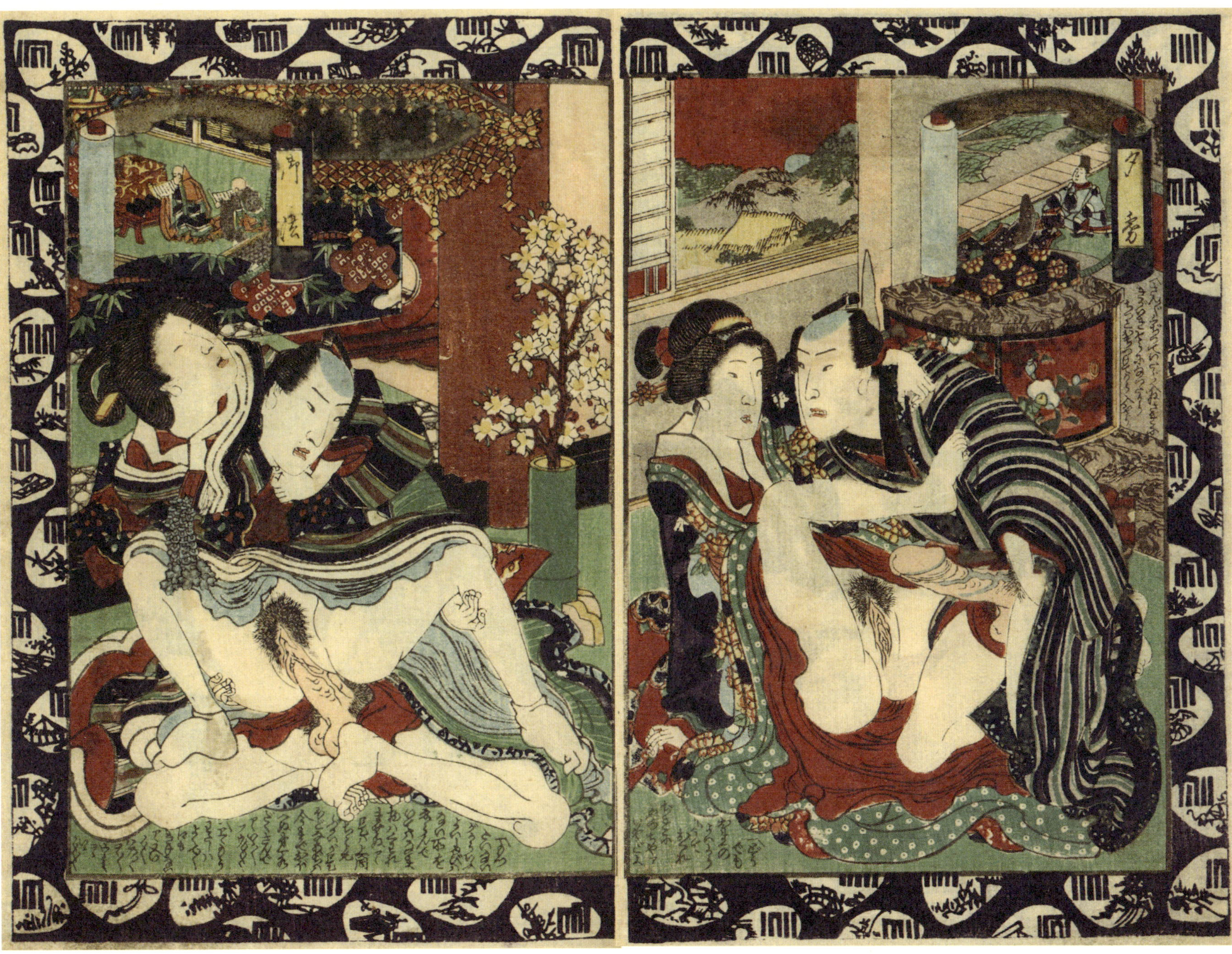

The mid 1800's was a period of great productivity in woodblock printmaking, although a number of specialists in the field are very damning of many of the artists, apart from **Hokusai** and **Hiroshige**.

Much of the work may be lacking the beauty, style and intensity of the early masters but it is fascinating to see how ideas adapted to the times. Much of it is bundled together as Utagawa School but there are other artists that should not be neglected.

Utagawa TOYOKUNI I (1769-1825)

Toyokuni was a student of **Toyoharu** (hence his name) who was the founder of the Utagawa School. They provide the link to the new from the old masters we have been considering.

You can see here that **Toyokuni** has a distinct elegant style with his bijin-ga which was passed on to his popular and most productive student **Utagawa Kunisada** - who took the latter part of his name.

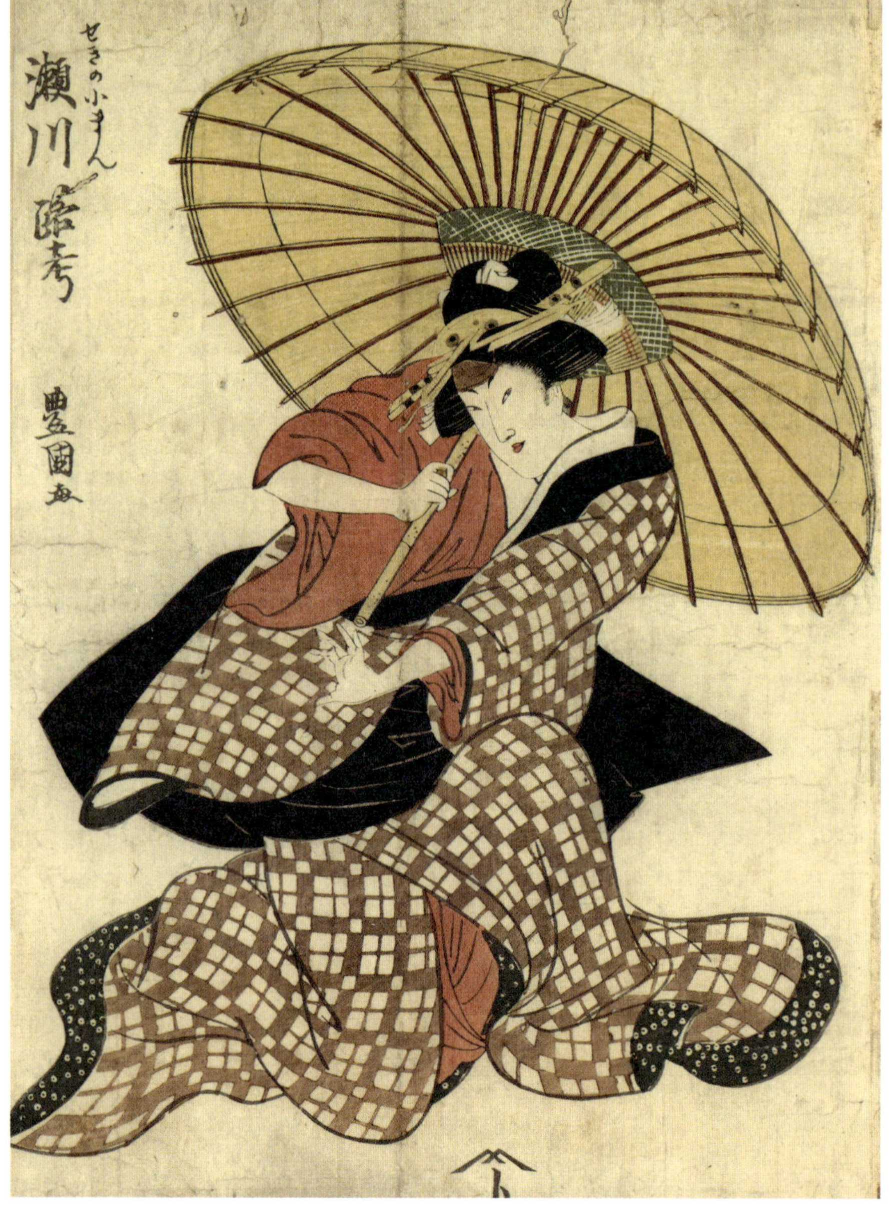

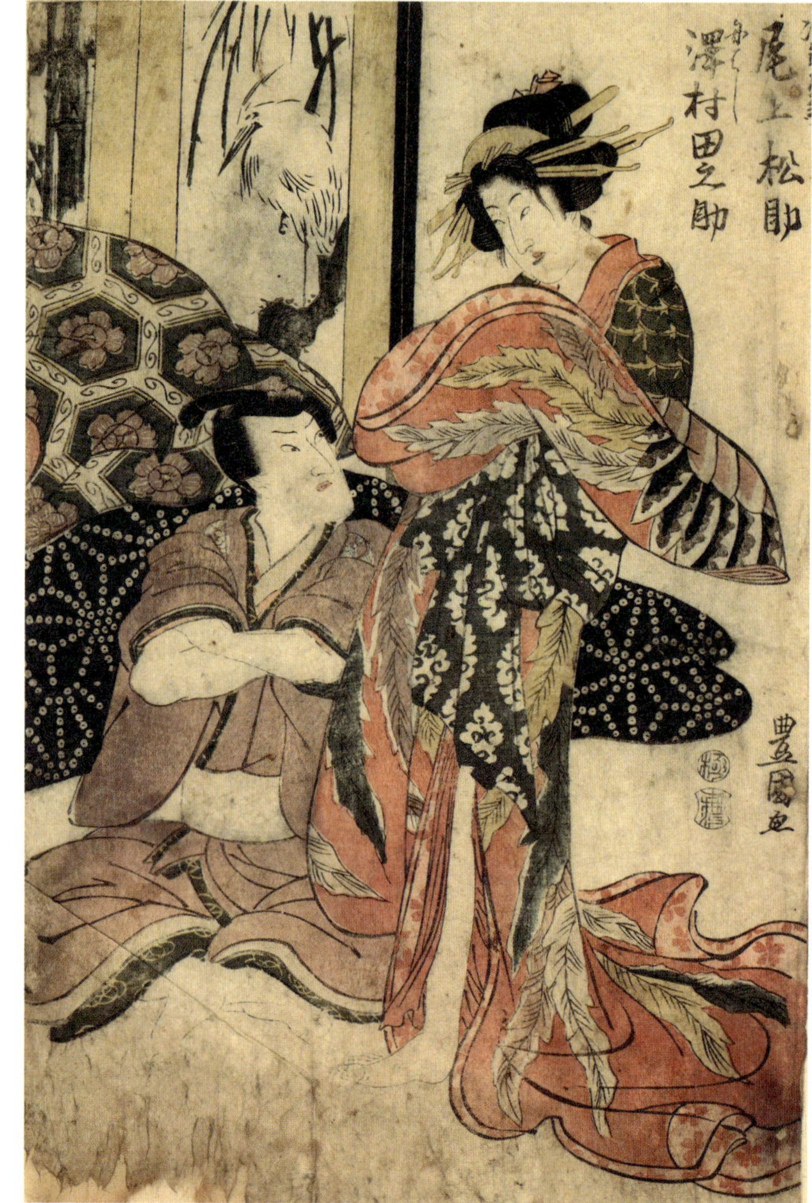

Utagawa KUNISADA (1786-1864)

The transferring of names makes attribution often difficult as like many artists he chopped and changed continually. Some years after **Toyokuni** died, **Kunisada** decided to take the name of his master and also called himself **Toyokuni**. He is now known as **Toyokuni III/Kunisada**.

He did a vast amount of work, some say up to 20,000 images. Once dismissed as being a worthless artist he is now being reassessed.

This is from his series: *One Hundred Poems by One Hundred Poets* (c.1844-45) in which he depicts women in a variety of every day situations. In the print on the left the poem reads:

In a mountain stream
There is a wattled barrier
Built by the busy wind
Yet it's only maple leaves

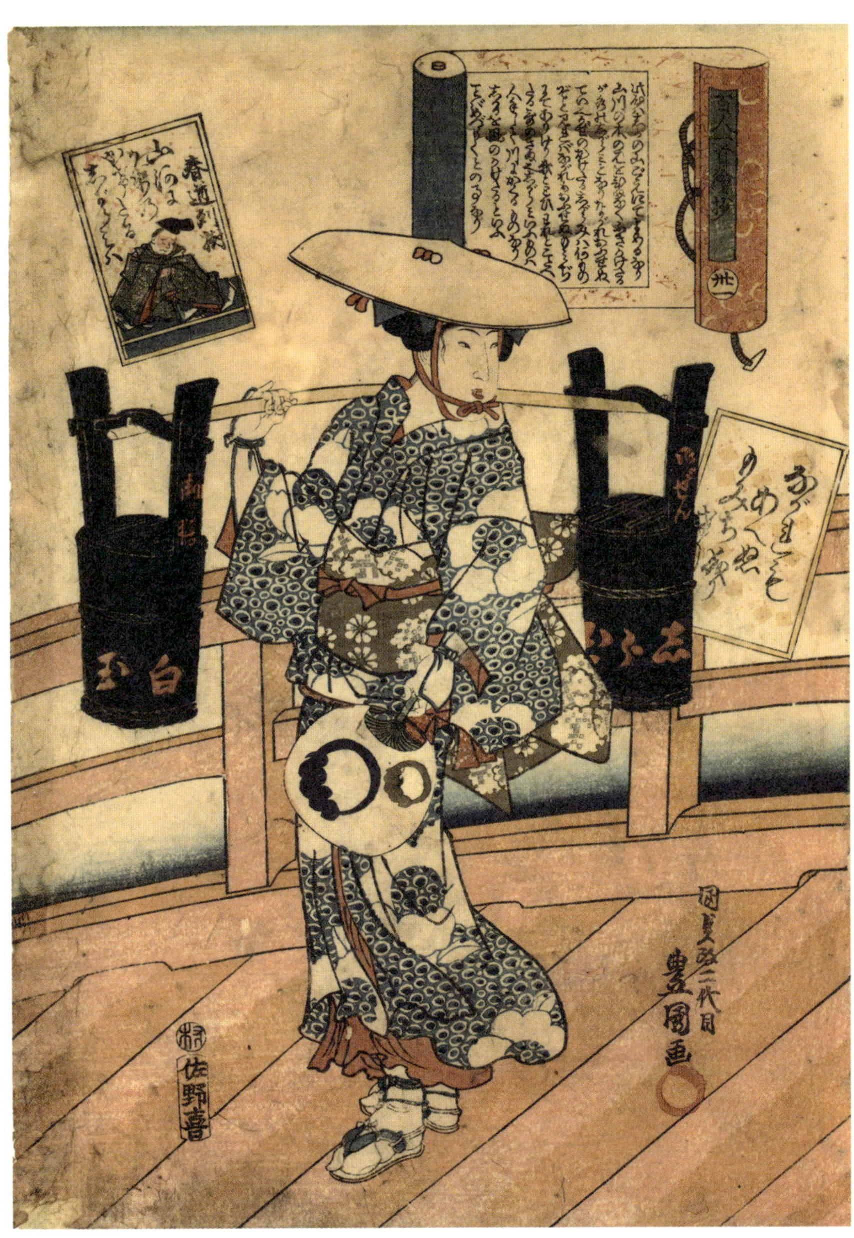

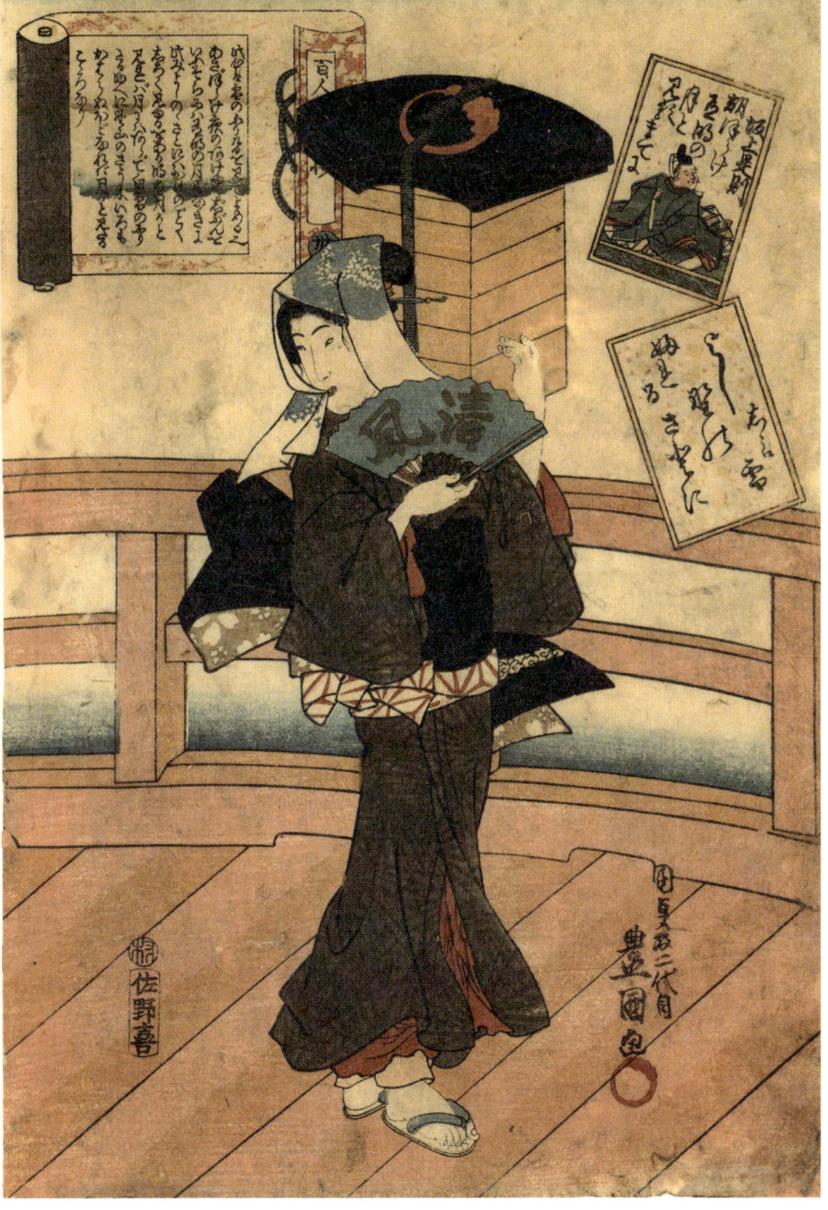

Kunisada liked to explore all manner of people and places, profiling every kind of work.

These bijin-ga are from the series *Meigi sanju rokka-sen* and are called *'Famous Geisha compared to the 36 poets'*(1860-61).

The first is a playful snow scene, but the other on the facing page is one of my favourites - the courtesan Hinazuru and her attendant sheltering from a storm. I love the stylised lightning which is echoed in her kimono - as if the electrical force is being earthed. Also fascinating is the cylindrical toy on the window seat which when turned gives a moving image - very modern.

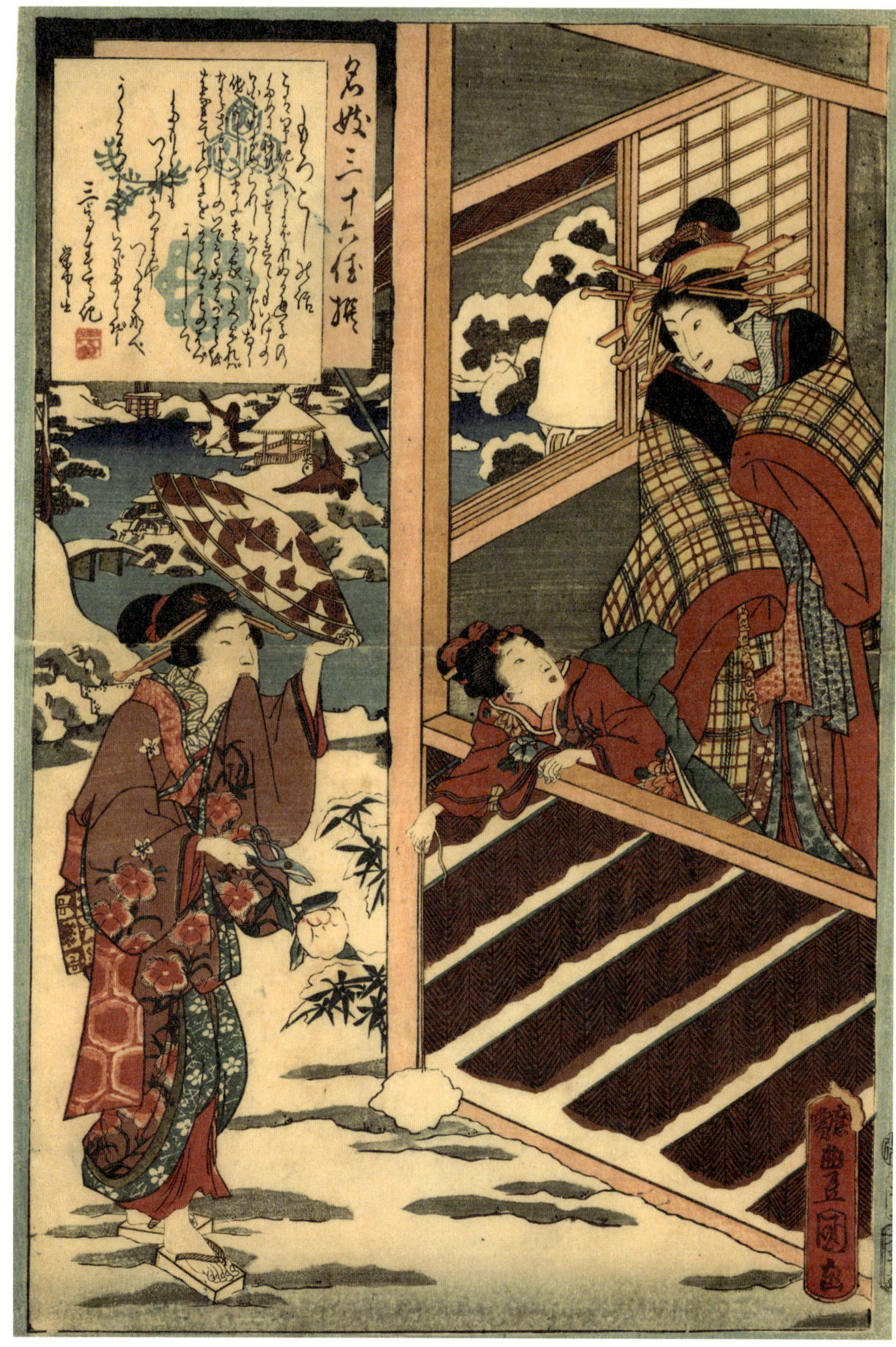

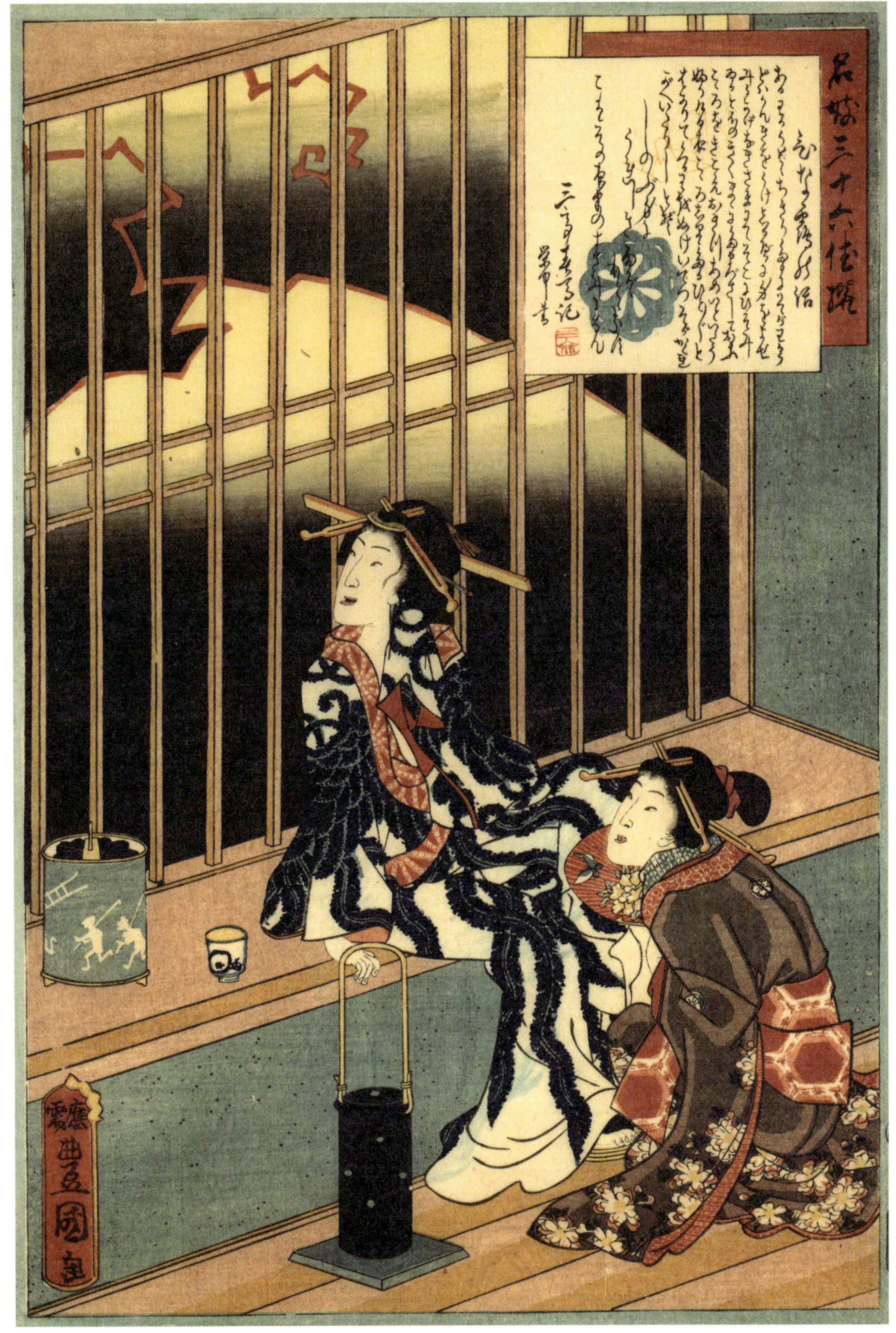

I especially want to include the triptych shown overleaf, which goes under the name *'Eastern Genji: The Wakana Chapter'* (1854). It depicts a moment from the famous book *The Tale of Genji* written in the 11th century by the female author Murasaki Shikibu.

In it we see the wife of Prince Genji in her private quarters with her attendants. Below, three young boys play hand ball in the garden, as the courtier Kashiwagi and his companion watch. The princess is supposed to stay hidden from view behind the reed blinds, but her curious kitten is climbing a wooden pillar in an attempt to catch a firefly and its lead pulls the blinds apart. She becomes briefly visible to Kashiwagi and as their eyes meet they fall madly in love. In the centre, Genji and two companions sit on the verandah, apparently watching the kids playing and enjoying the blossoming cherry trees.

What I love is how the most insignificant and smallest participant - the firefly - is the instigator of this human drama. I didn't notice for ages that Prince Genji's lunch is on its way being delivered by servants who, being in the distance, are the same size as the firefly - the cat's lunch!

The setting has many typical Genji components - including the winding stream and the slightly elevated view point - which we also see in other images.

In the second triptych we see *'Prince Genji attending a Cock Fight'* (1854). He is with numerous 'beauties' some of which are actively involved in the event. You can see two on each side of the fight holding cocks ready for the next conflict - and the next!

I find it a very beautiful image of a brutal 'sport' which is still common in many parts of Asia. I saw one in Bali - and was surprised how quickly it all happened.

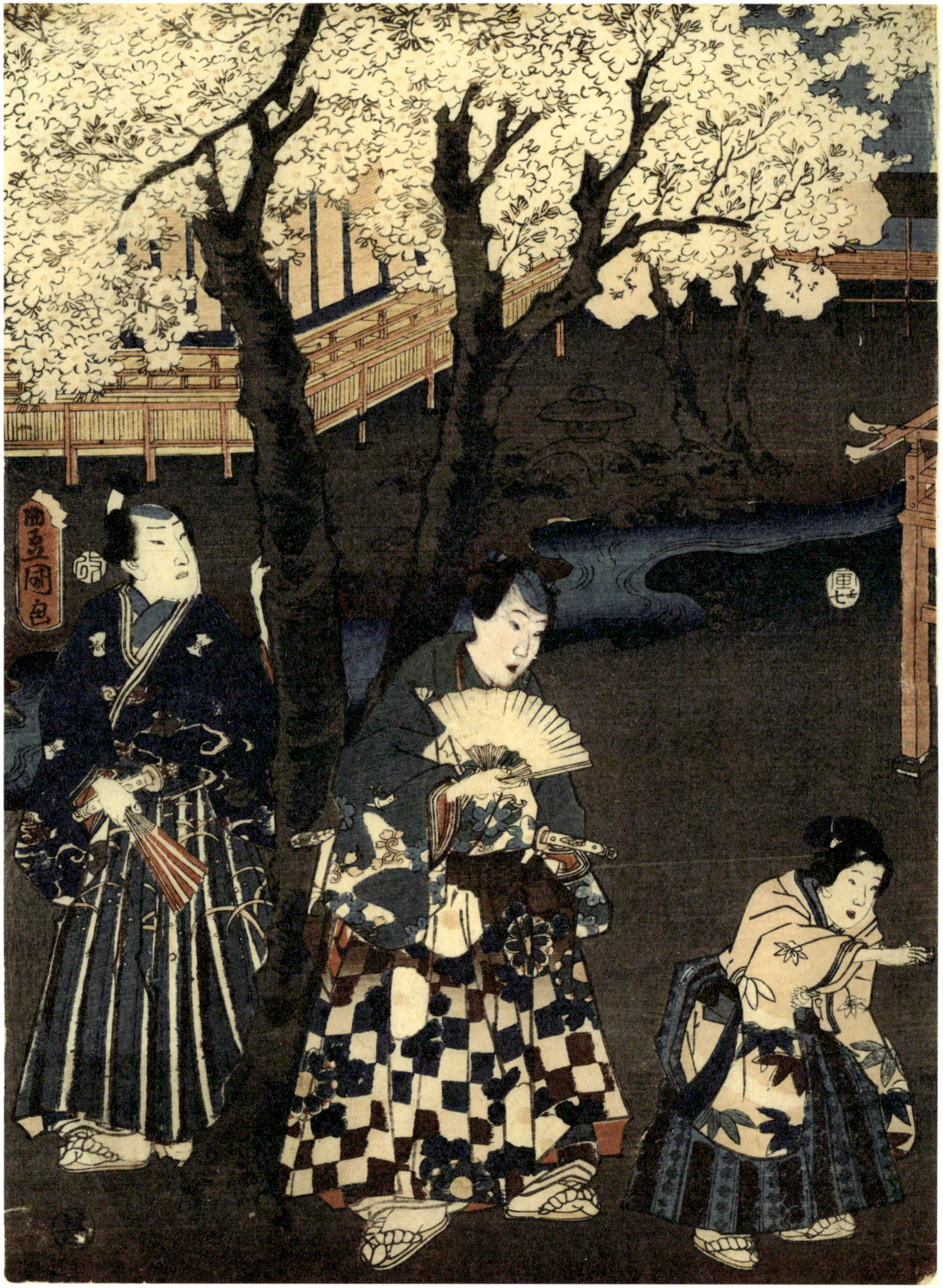

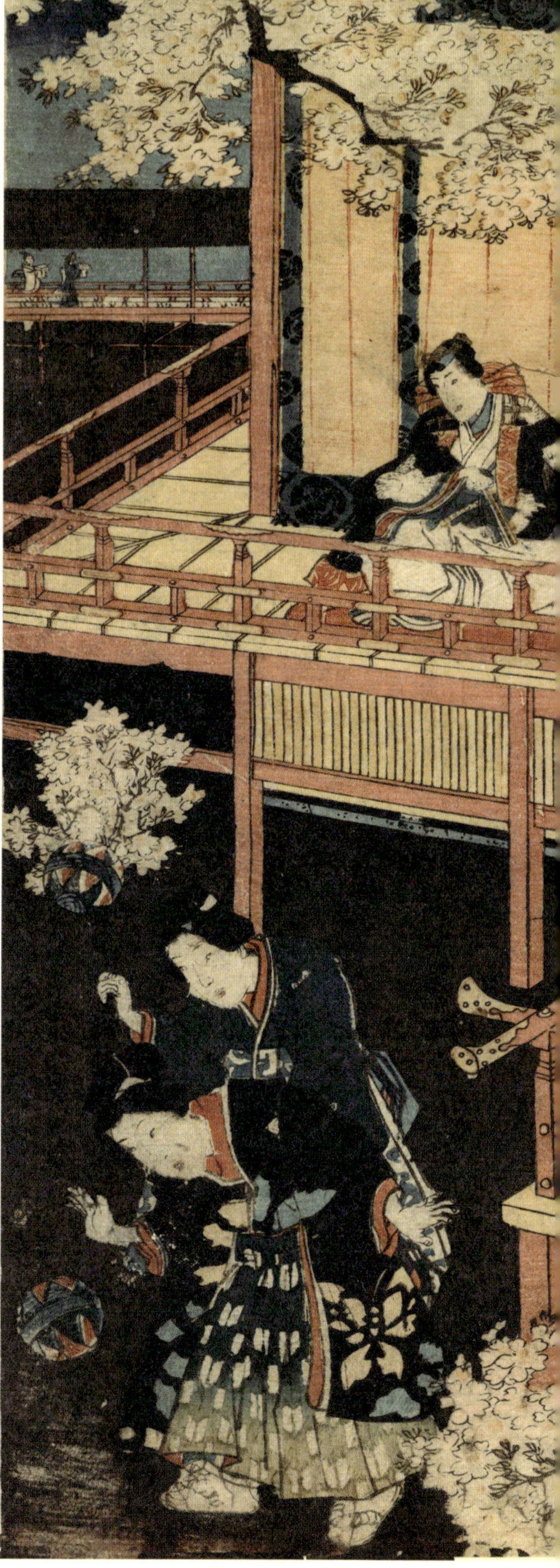

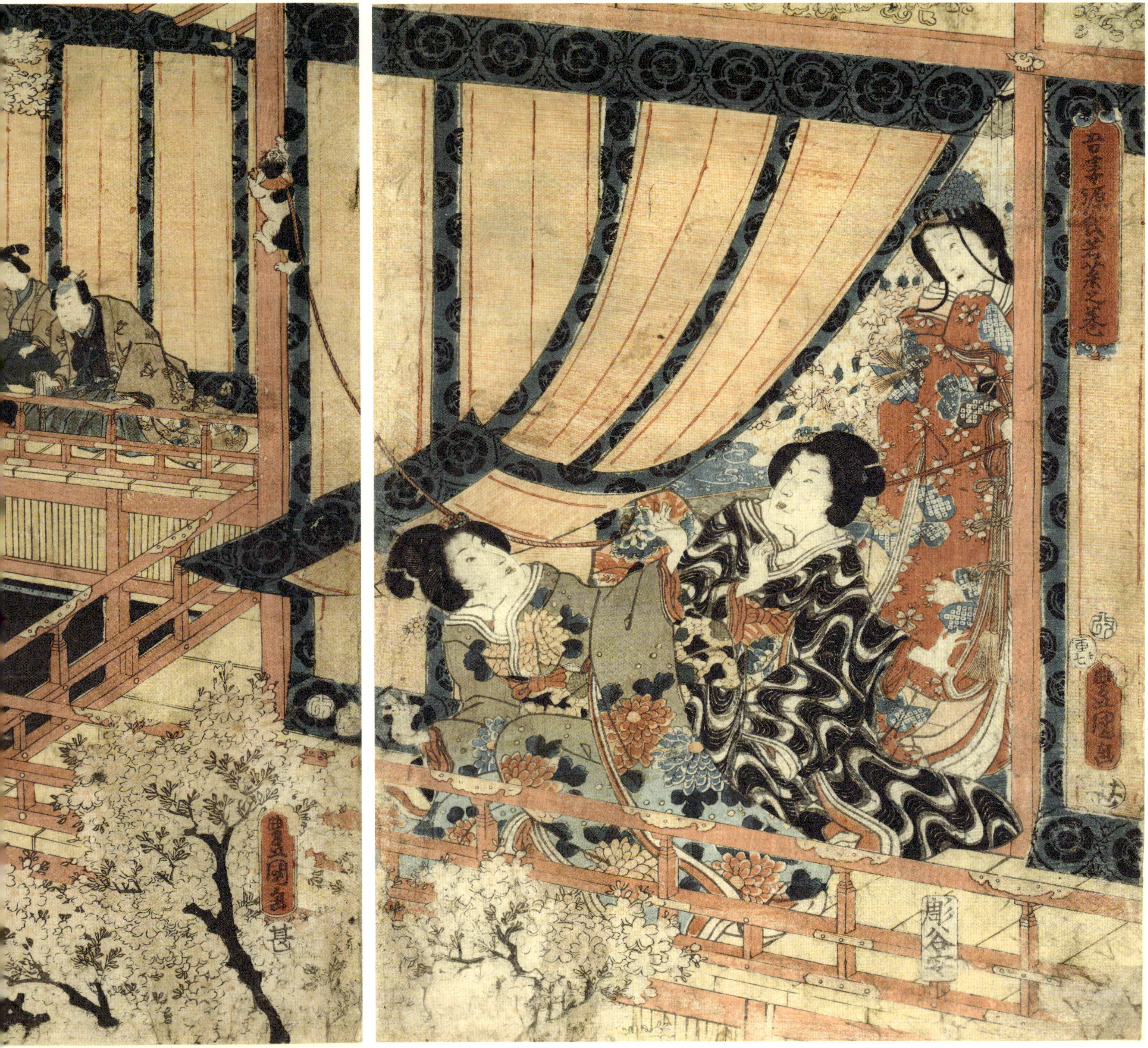

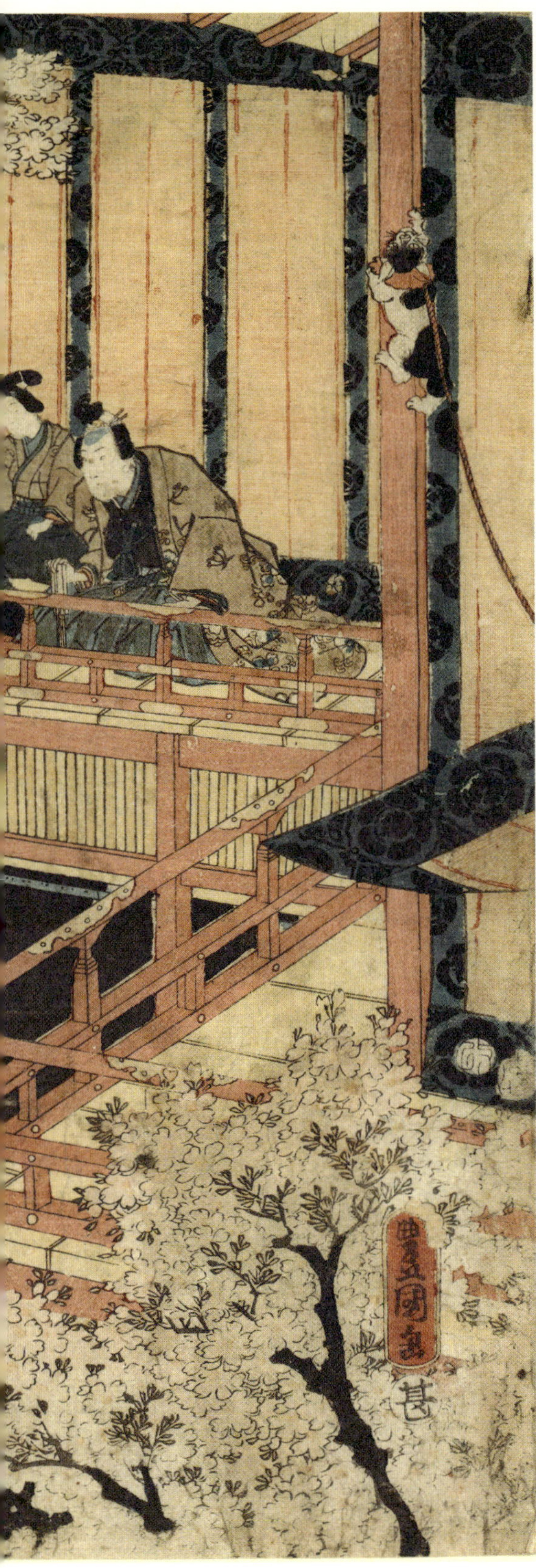
豊国画

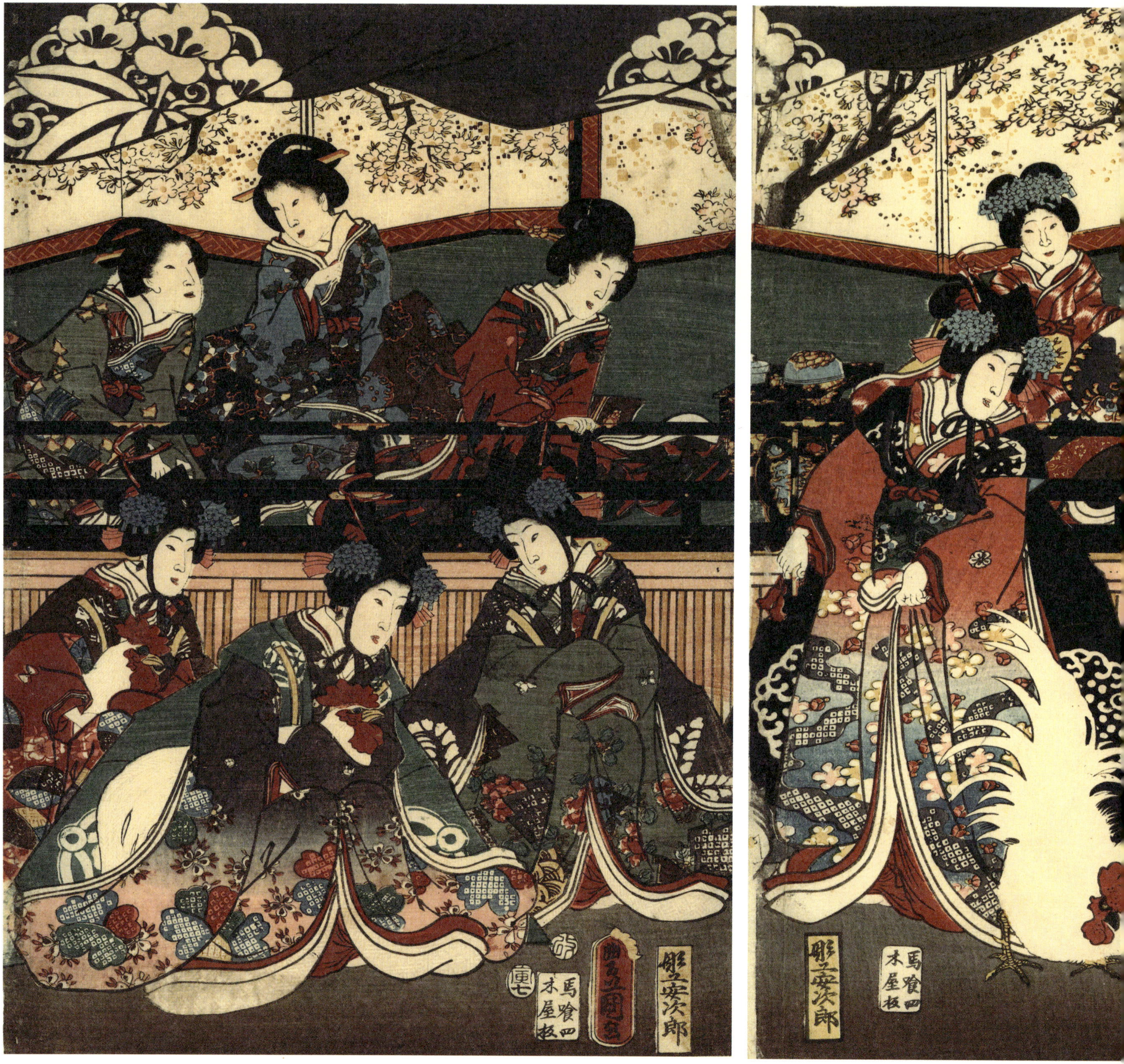

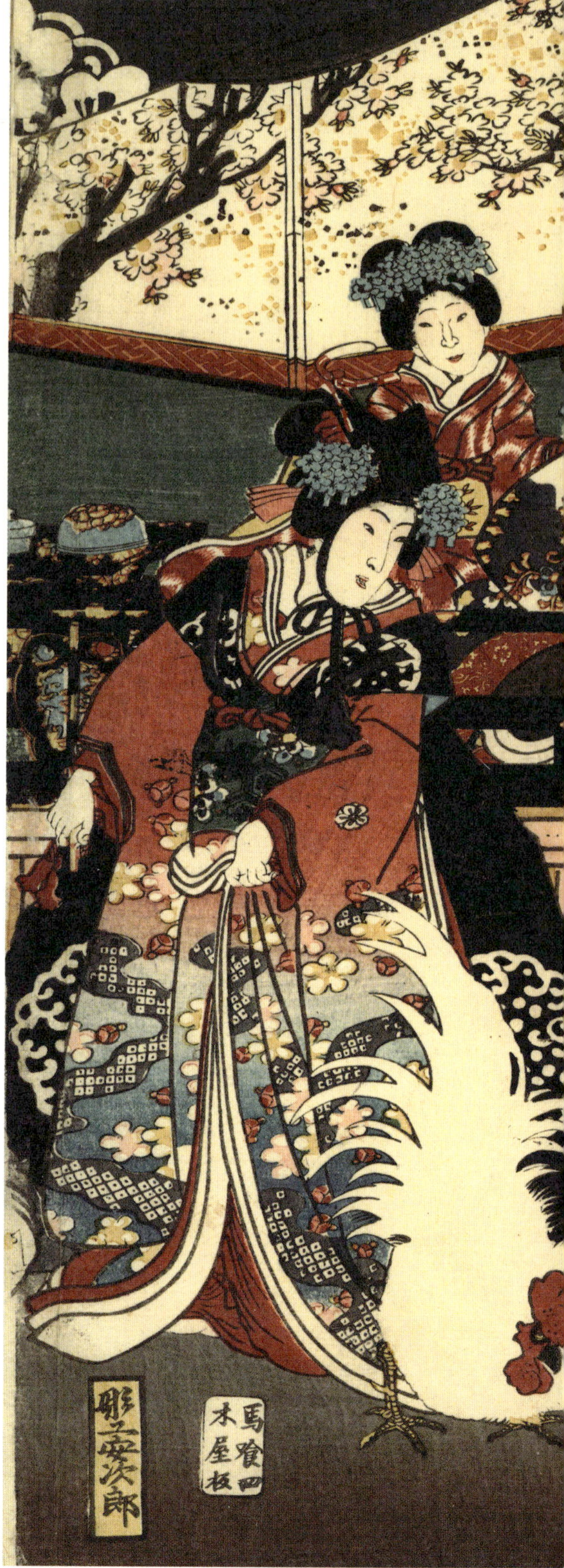
彫工安次郎
馬喰四
木屋板

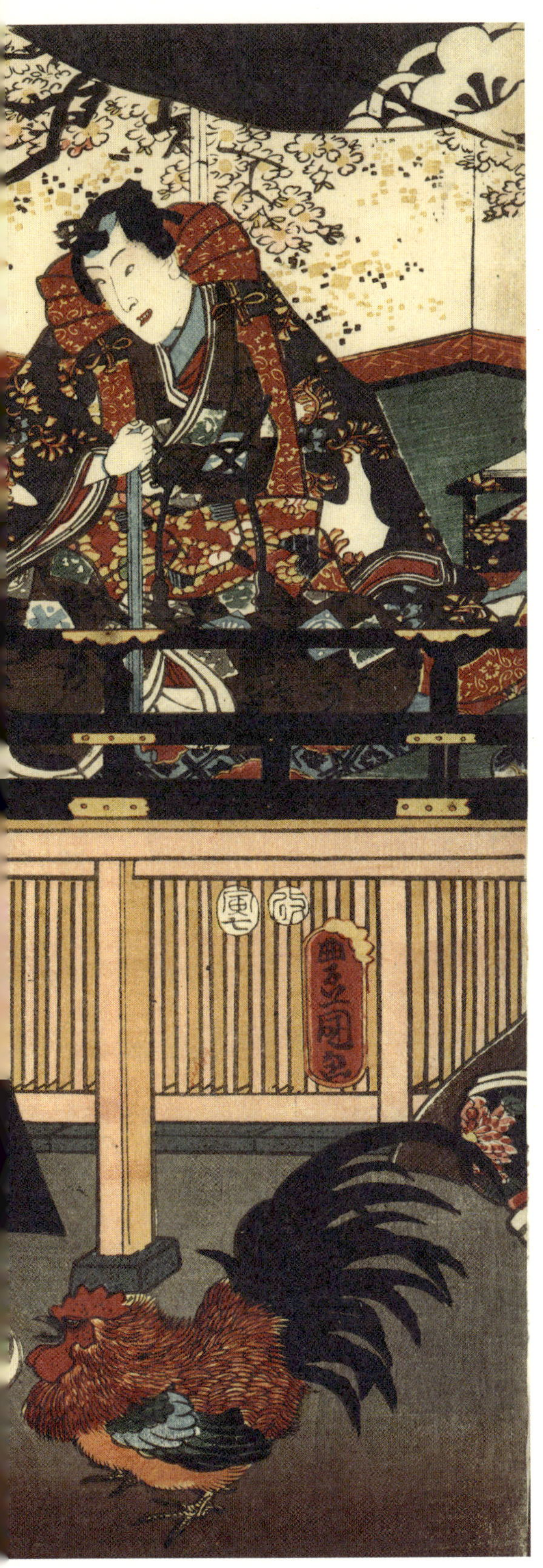
豊国画
鷄合之圖
豊国画
馬喰四
木屋板
彫工安次郎

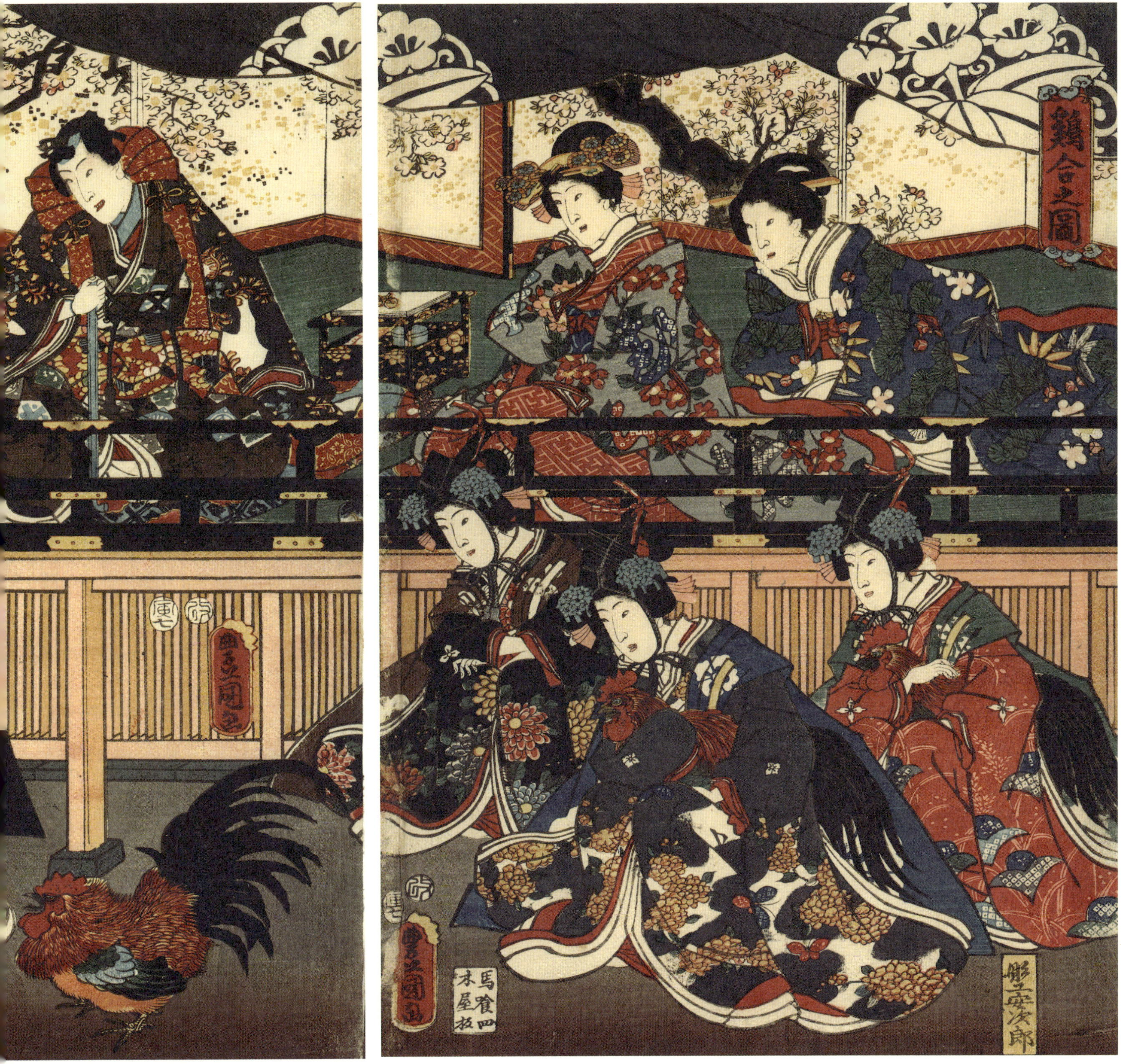

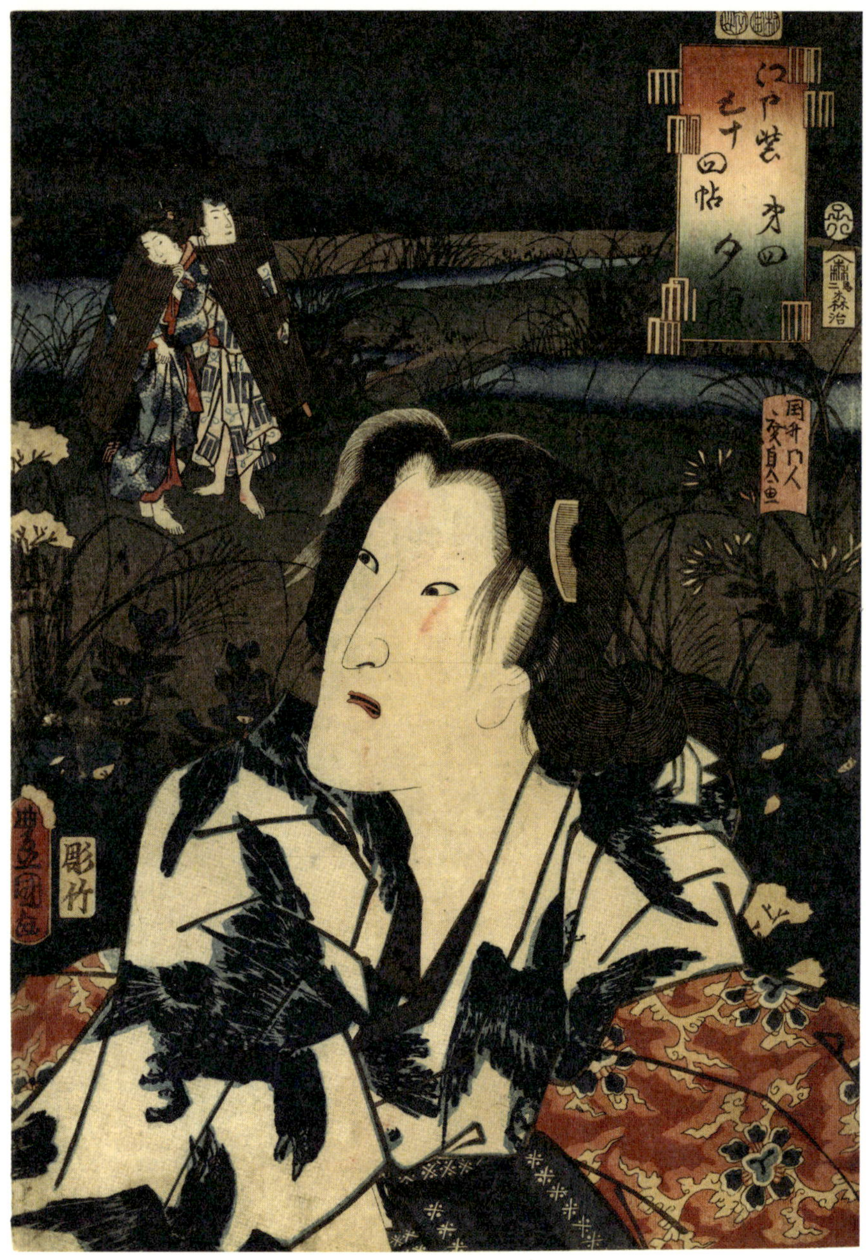

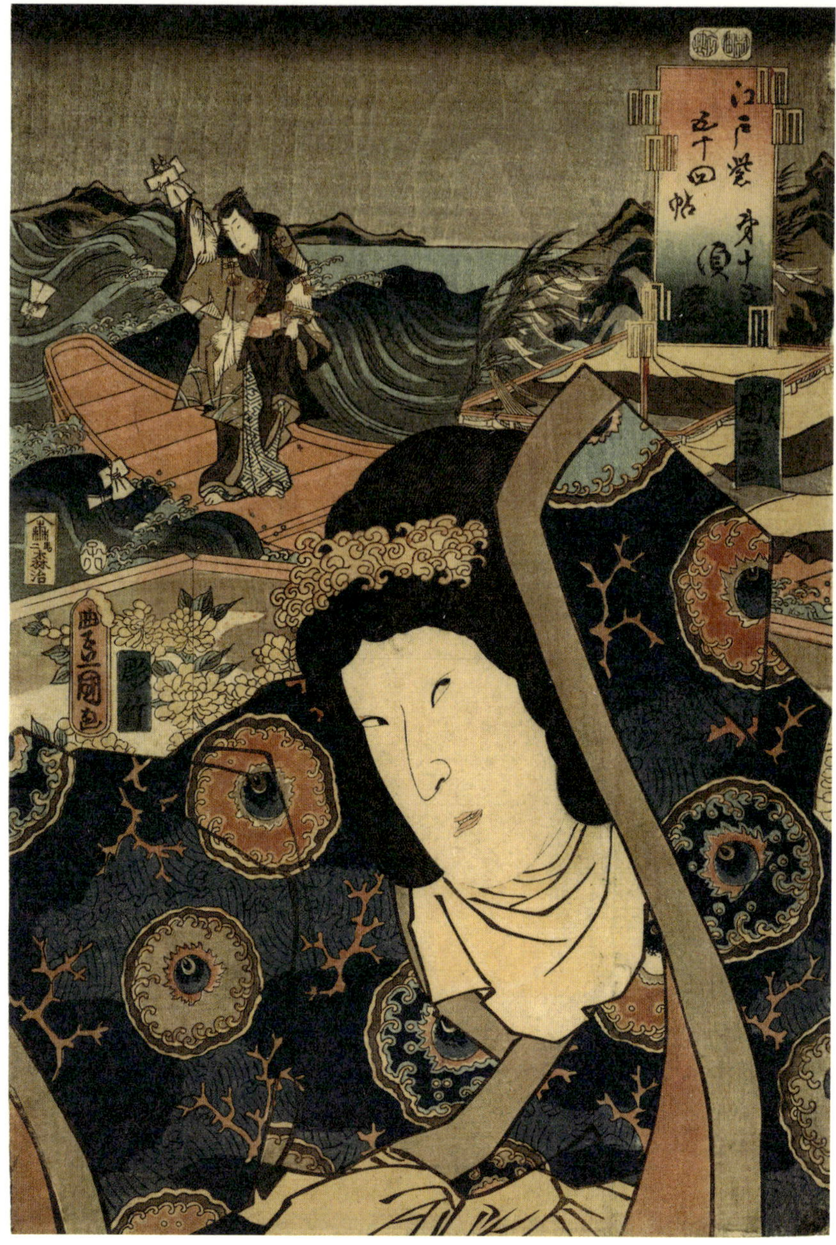

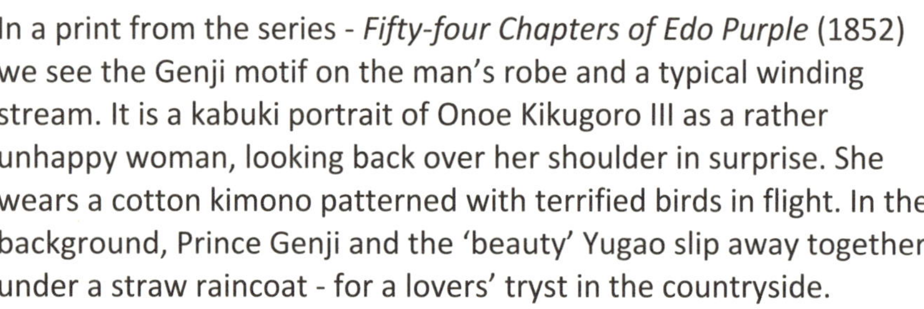

In a print from the series - *Fifty-four Chapters of Edo Purple* (1852) we see the Genji motif on the man's robe and a typical winding stream. It is a kabuki portrait of Onoe Kikugoro III as a rather unhappy woman, looking back over her shoulder in surprise. She wears a cotton kimono patterned with terrified birds in flight. In the background, Prince Genji and the 'beauty' Yugao slip away together under a straw raincoat - for a lovers' tryst in the countryside.

This is from the same series, as indicated by the cartouche. It has a similar composition, with the man placed in the same position - almost in the background. Here the actor Arashi Rikan III is portrayed against a seascape and the aquatic theme is carried through in the depictions of sea life. Anemones and probably scallops are arranged together with fragments of coral on an exquisite kimono.

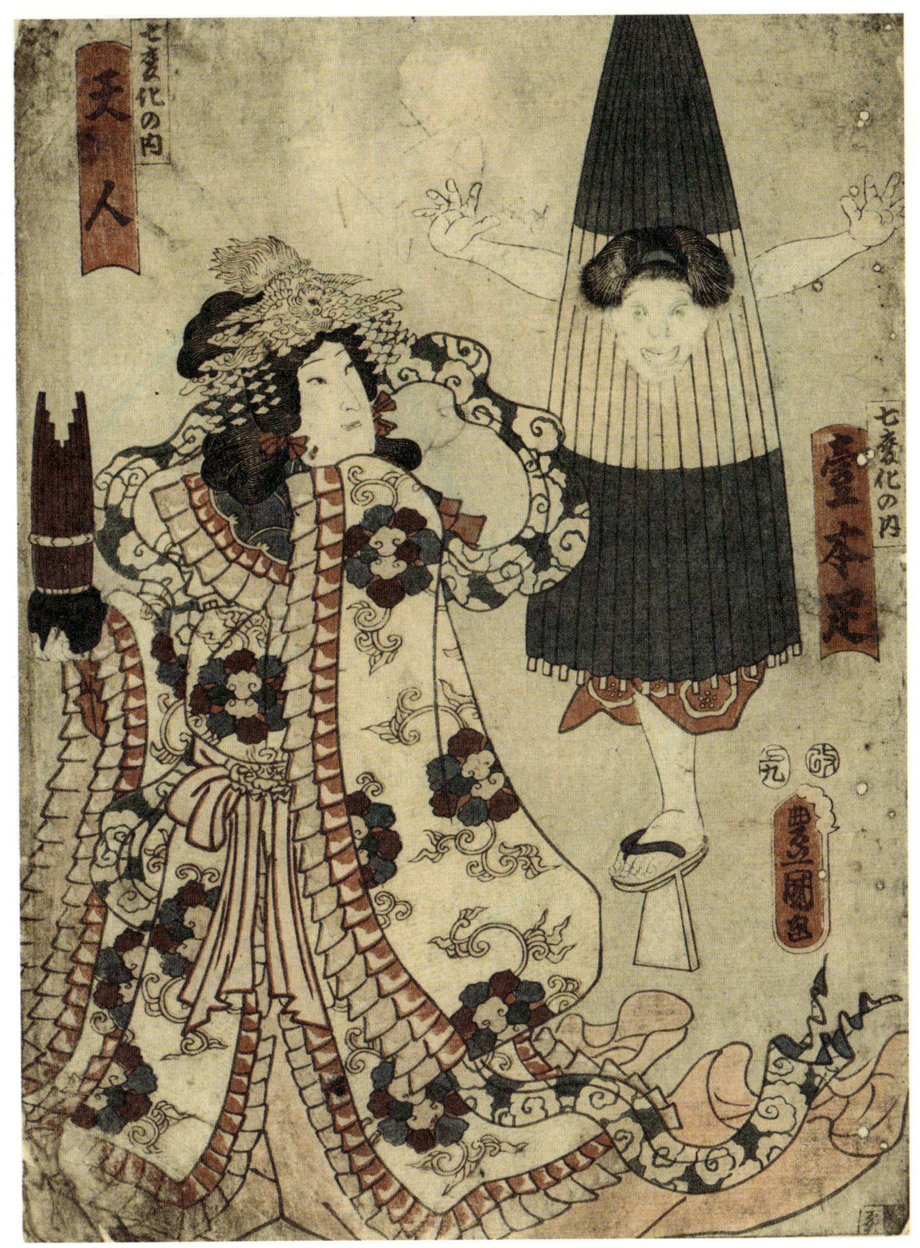

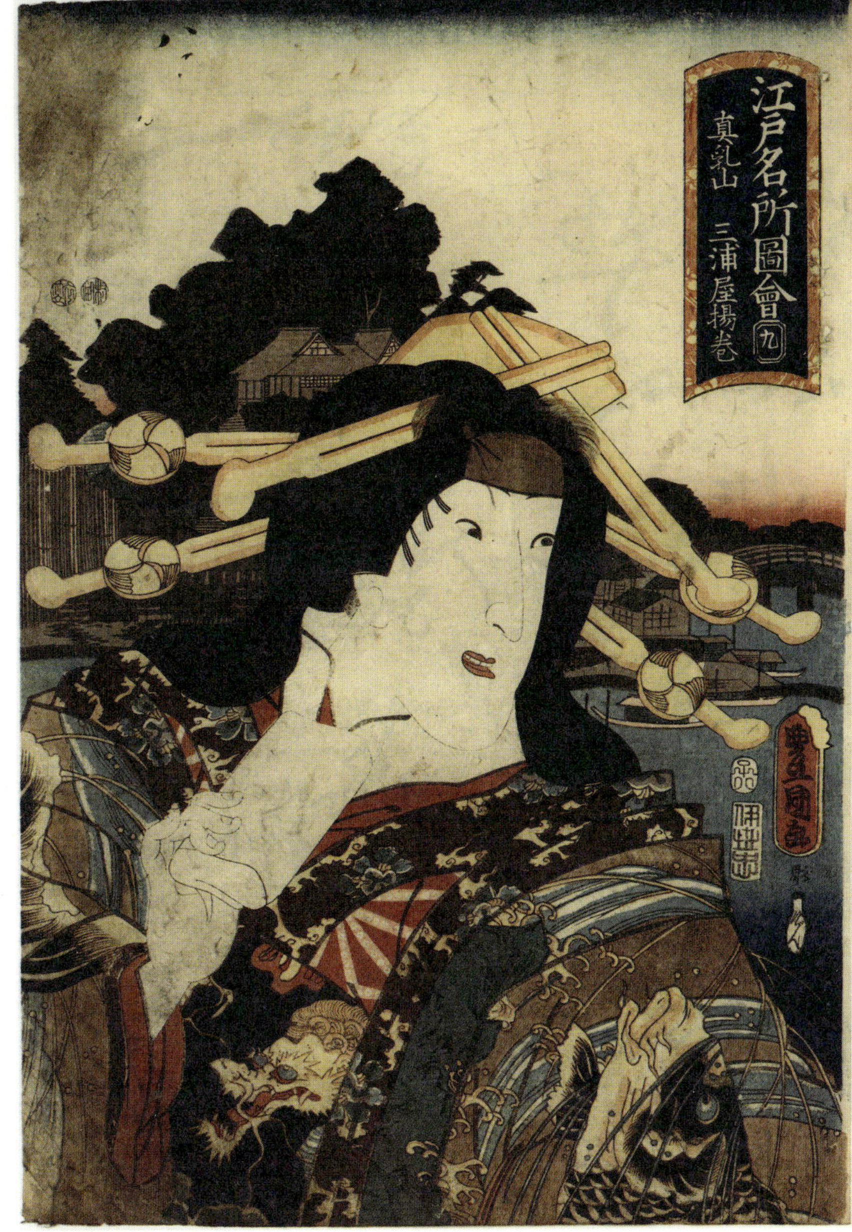

The supernatural looms large in the Japanese imagination, which has offered many extraordinary opportunities to artists. This 'beauty' is surprised by a one legged Umbrella Ghost known as a Tsukumogami (c.1850)

There are wonderful ornate patterns here on the courtesan's kimono - fish, water, dragons - along with huge hair pins and comb. At this time hair ornamentation was the signifier of social status, be it as a courtesan, geisha, a married woman or mother. This is no doubt a courtesan of high status, most likely an oiran.

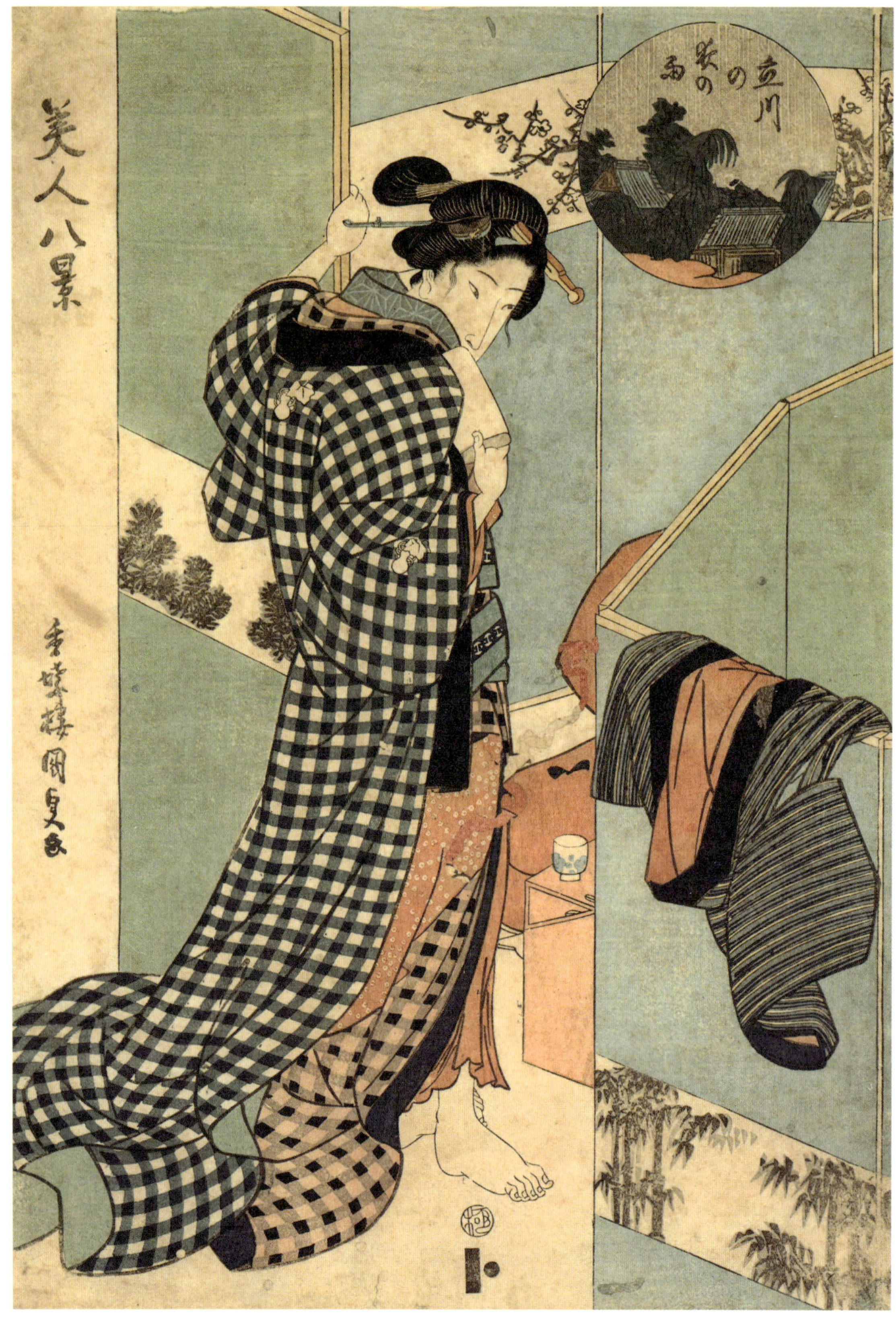

Kunisada didn't only show his lovers in the pleasure districts and the women were not always courtesans.

This lovely bijin-ga is very sensual. With the title *'Night Rain at Tachikawa'* (c.1830s) it is an image of a woman preparing to retire for the evening. Pausing with one hand on the edge of a folding screen she looks down, presumably at a man, a roll of tissues in her other hand. The male kimono draped over the screen suggests that her companion is ready for her.

To add to the eroticism she appears to be about to slip off her blue checked outer robe to reveal a peach and black kimono with red tie-dyed inserts. The green obi loosely wrapped about her waist may not remain in place for long.

To give more atmosphere a circular inset at top right depicts falling rain above tile roof-tops and willow trees of Tachikawa.

Not all the shunga show the most attractive of lovers - or the most erotic of circumstances. This is from the series: *Songs of the Four Seasons: Spring, Summer, Autumn, Winter* (c.1827). Although the series supposedly shows amorous couples throughout the seasons, this print appears to depict a post-coital moment with a woman more concerned with burning the pesky mosquitoes than snuggling up with her lover.

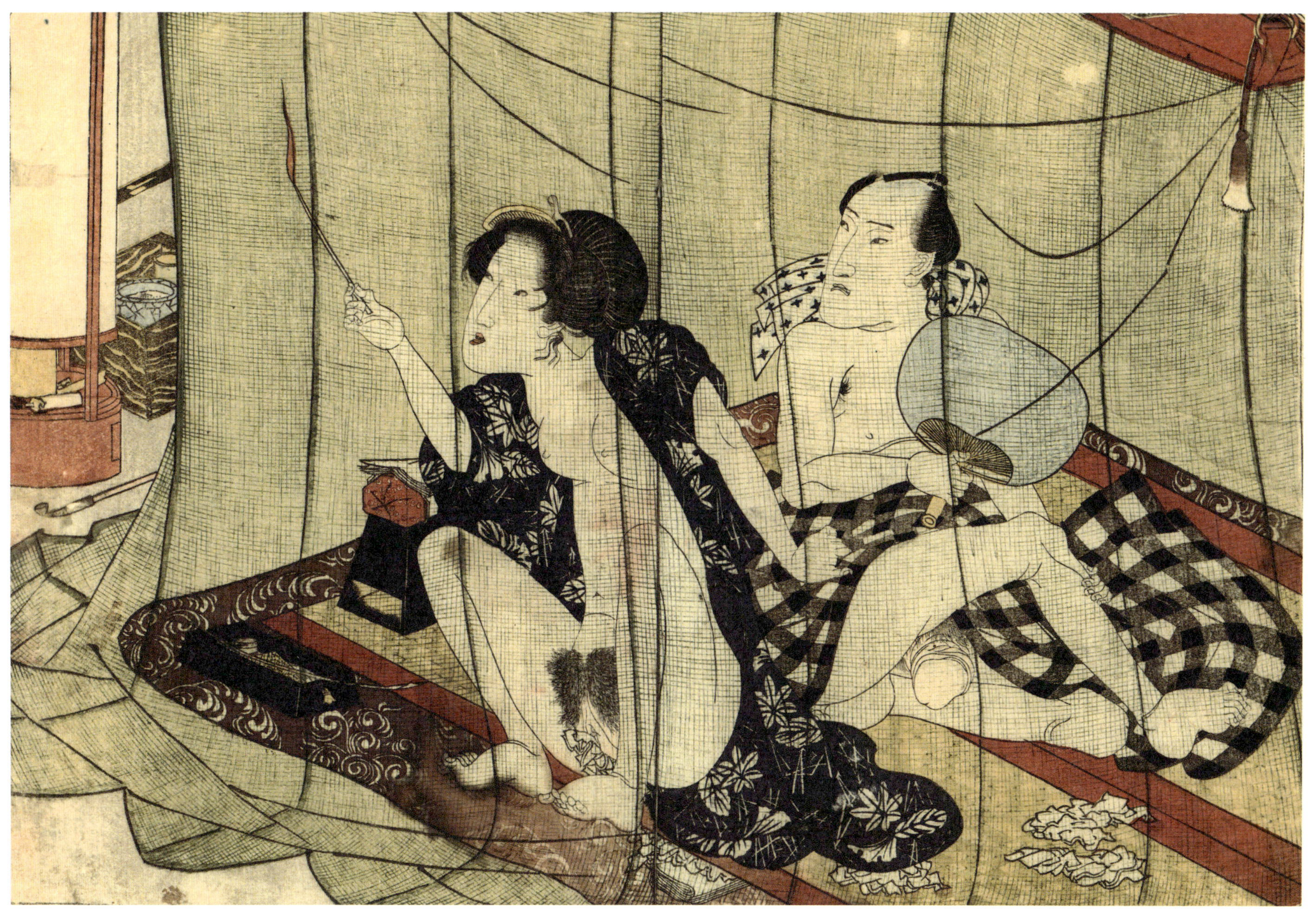

Shunga were often created anonymously so this print is attributed to the Kunisada School (c.1840). It does though have many of the hallmarks of the master - with wonderful textures, abstract shapes and fine detailing.

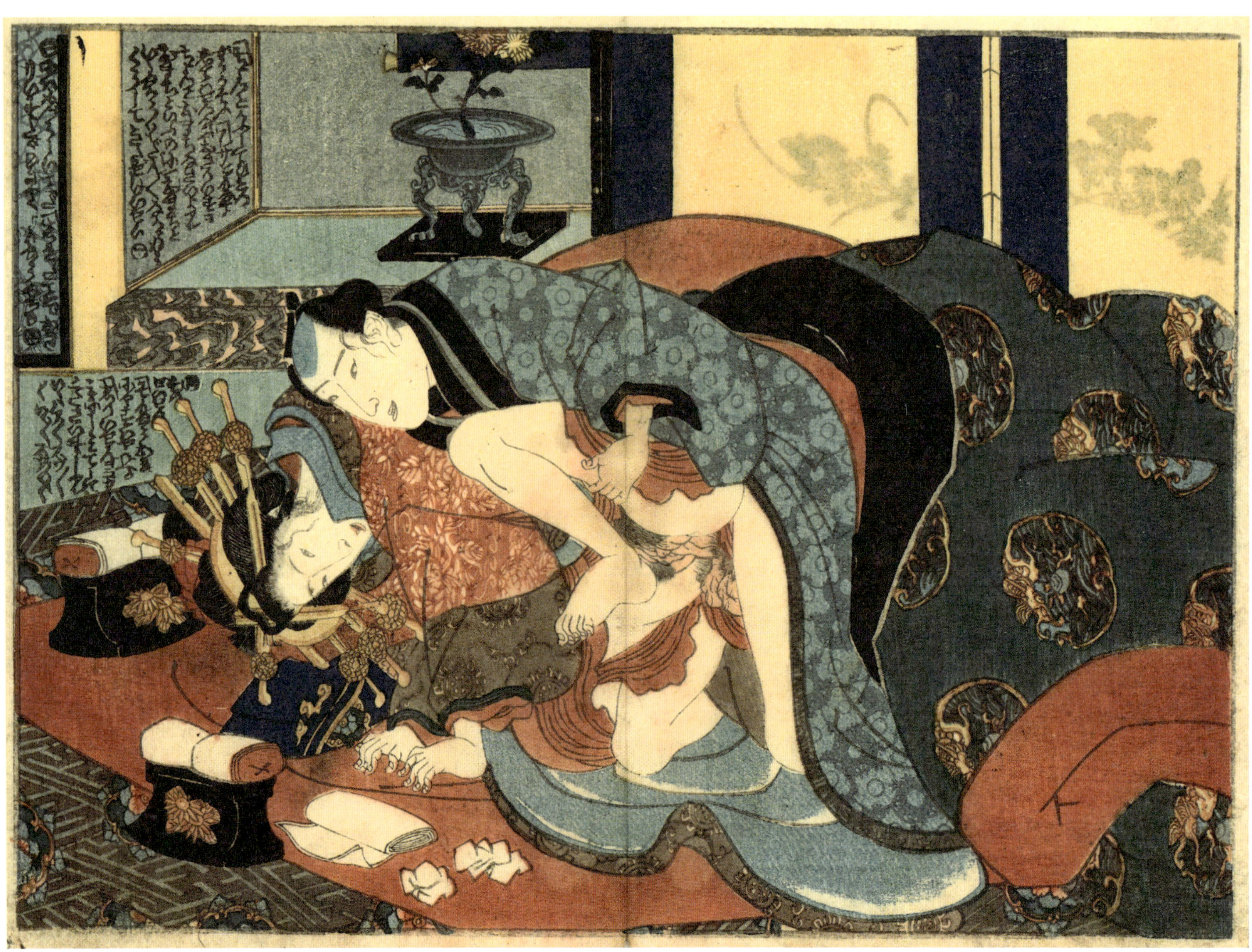

Utagawa KUNISADA II (1823-1880)

Kunisada was so popular he enlisted the services of colleagues, students and employees to satisfy the demand for prints. These portraits are attributed to **Kunisada II** who was a principal student - considered good enough to take his name. He married his master's daughter.

On the left is a courtesan preparing to play the koto, fitting a pick to her finger as her kamuro (child apprentice) offers a small lacquered box. On the right we see a courtesan with a letter, holding a brush in her mouth. She pauses to look over her shoulder as her kamuro gestures up at the cherry blossoms.

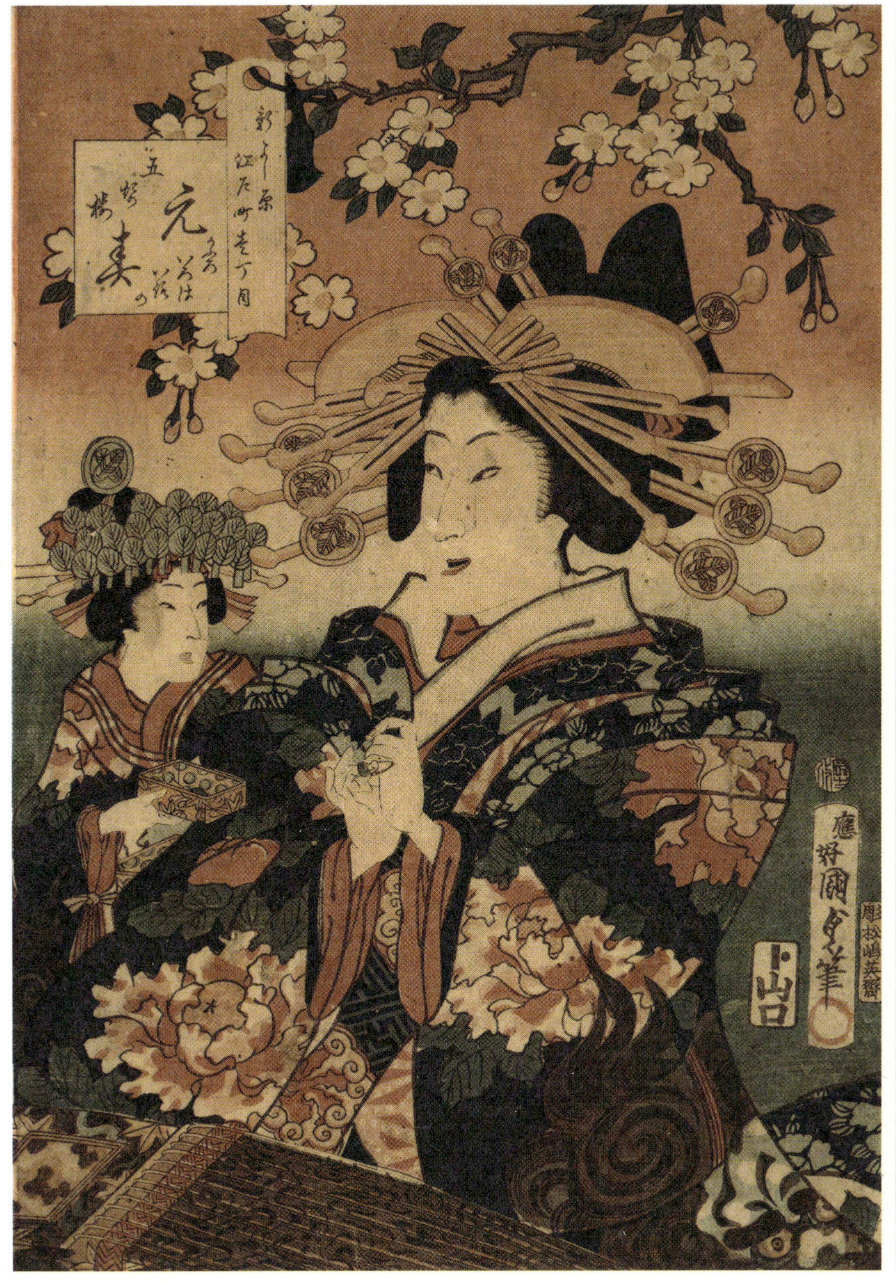

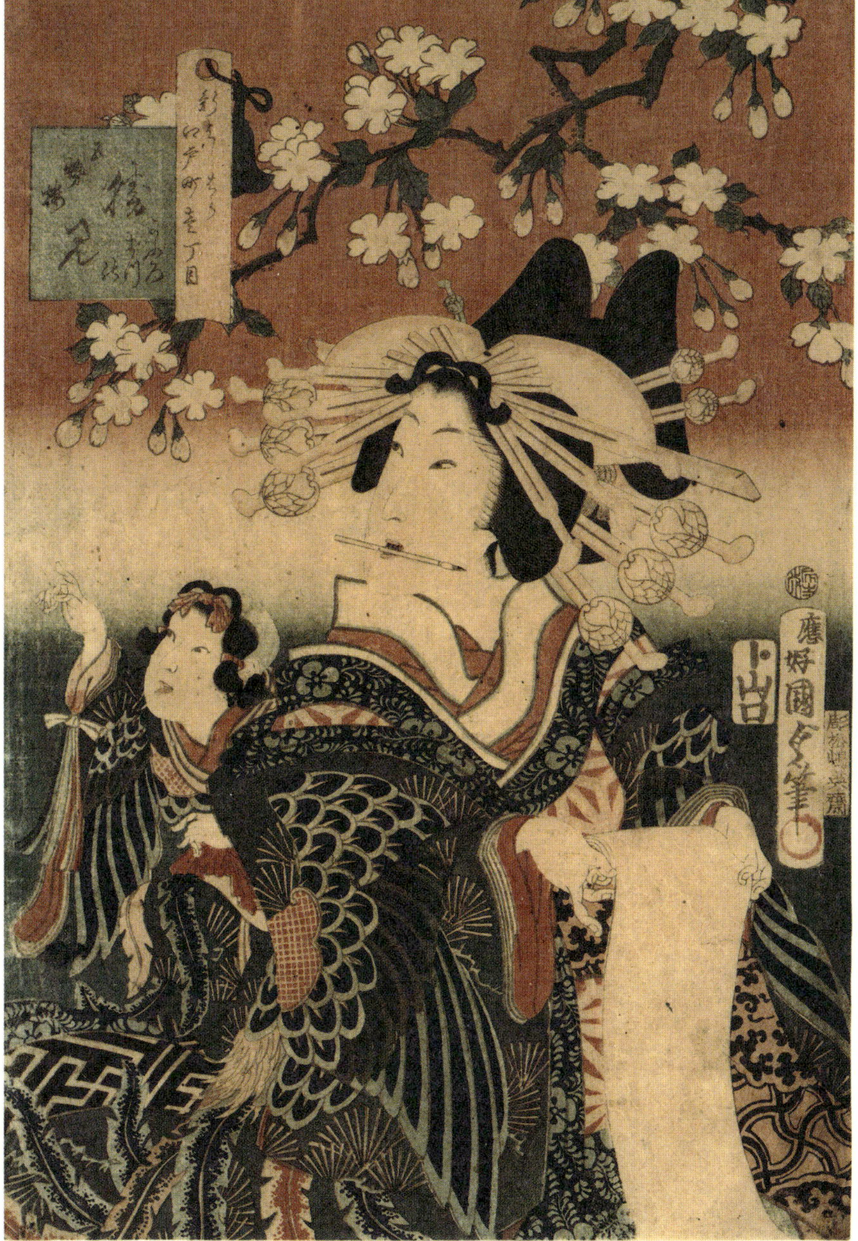

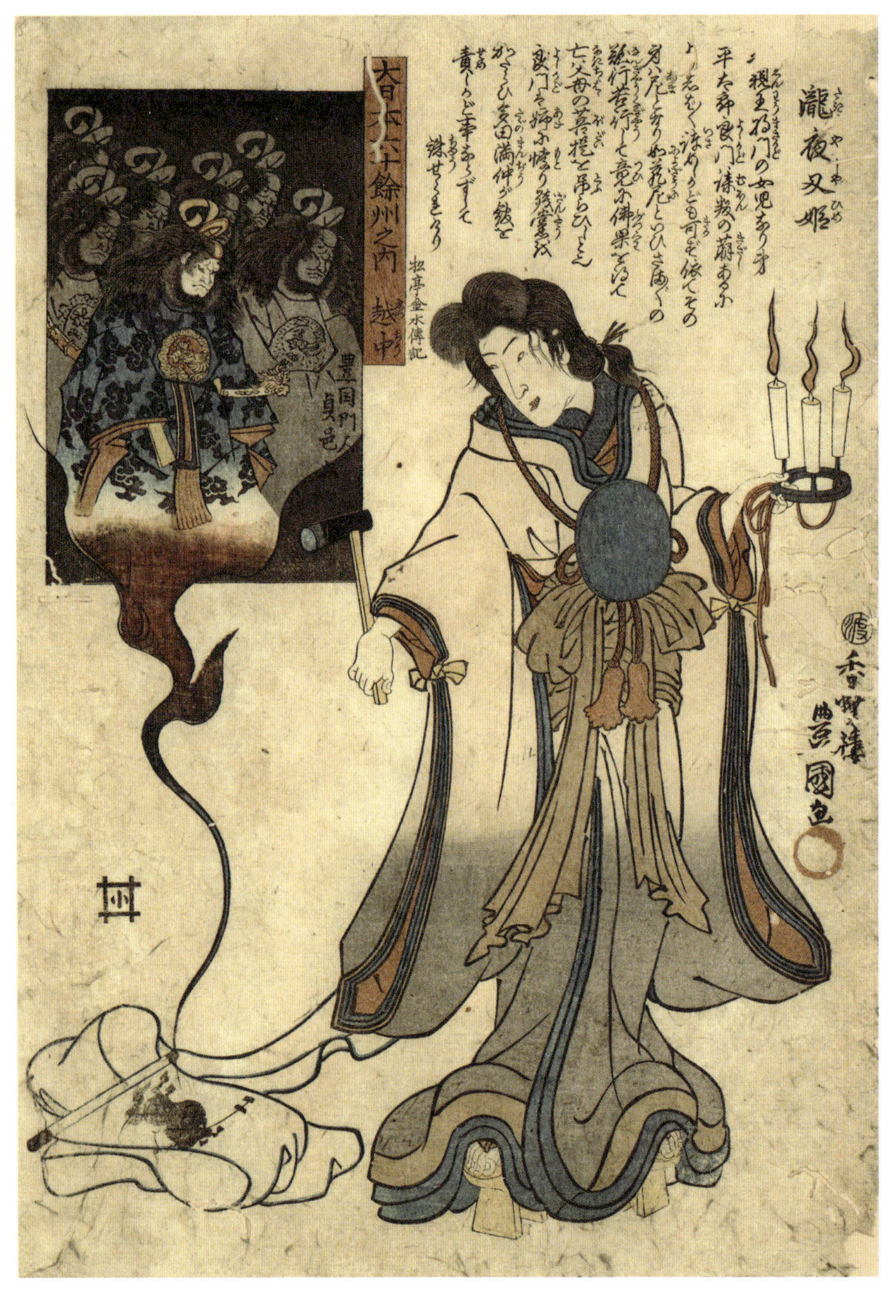
大日本六十餘州之内 越中
瀧夜叉姫
松亭金水傳記
香蝶樓豊國画

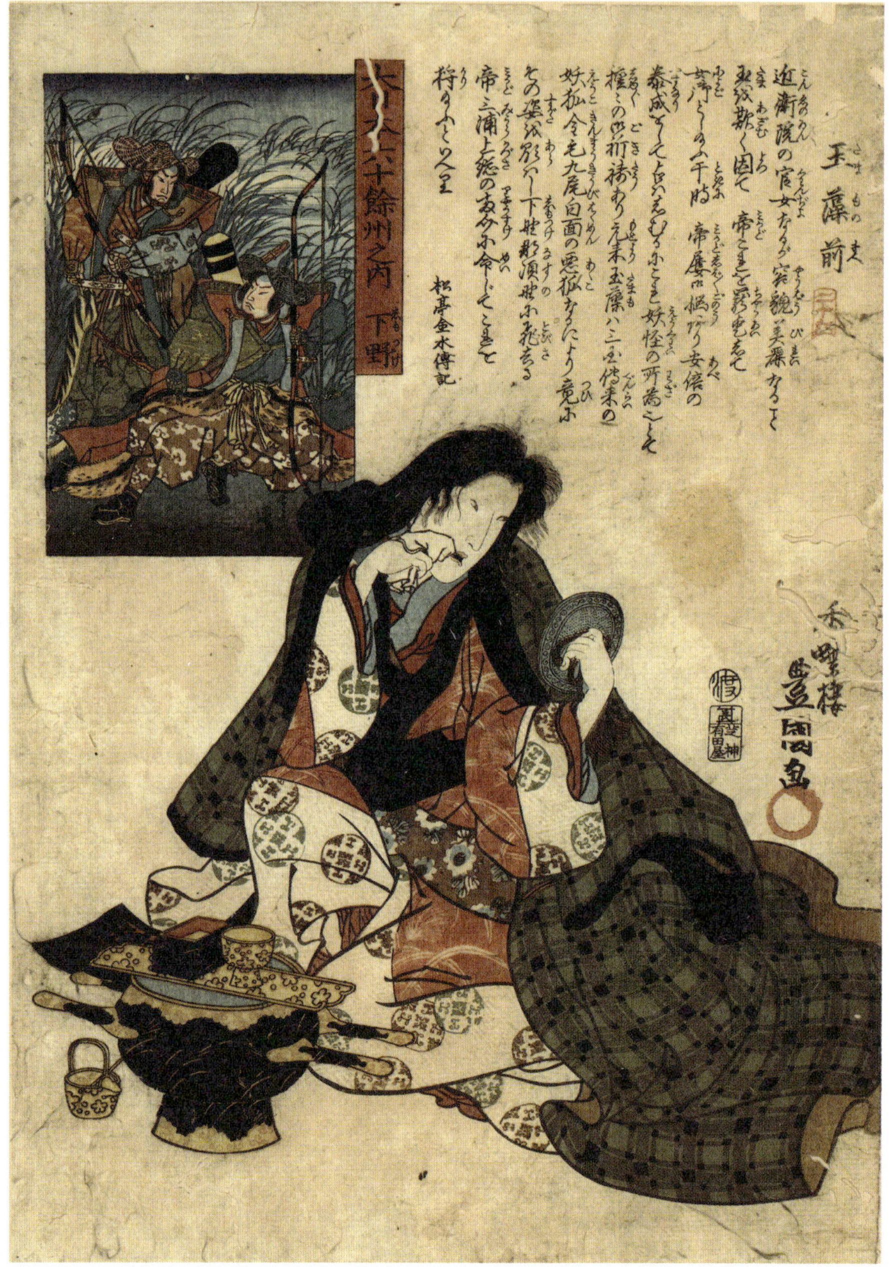
大日本六十餘州之内 下野
玉藻前
松亭金水傳記
香蝶樓豊國画

It is sometimes difficult to work out who did what on any particular series. At the time print artists were not particularly venerated and were considered primarily craftsmen who would not be remembered - hence the name changing. They were always getting in trouble with the censors so joining forces was often a political as well as a practical consideration.

These three images are from *The Sixty-odd Provinces of Great Japan* (c.1845) and are **Kunisada** collaborations with **Kuniyoshi**, one of the greatest artists of the period. They created this series depicting historic men and women, or popular Kabuki characters, one for each of the sixty-odd provinces of Japan. They did the expressive figures with the insets of related scenes done by various students.

From going by the printed signatures the main figures on the left were created by **Kunisada** and the one on the right by **Kuniyoshi**.

He is the next artist I wish to explore.

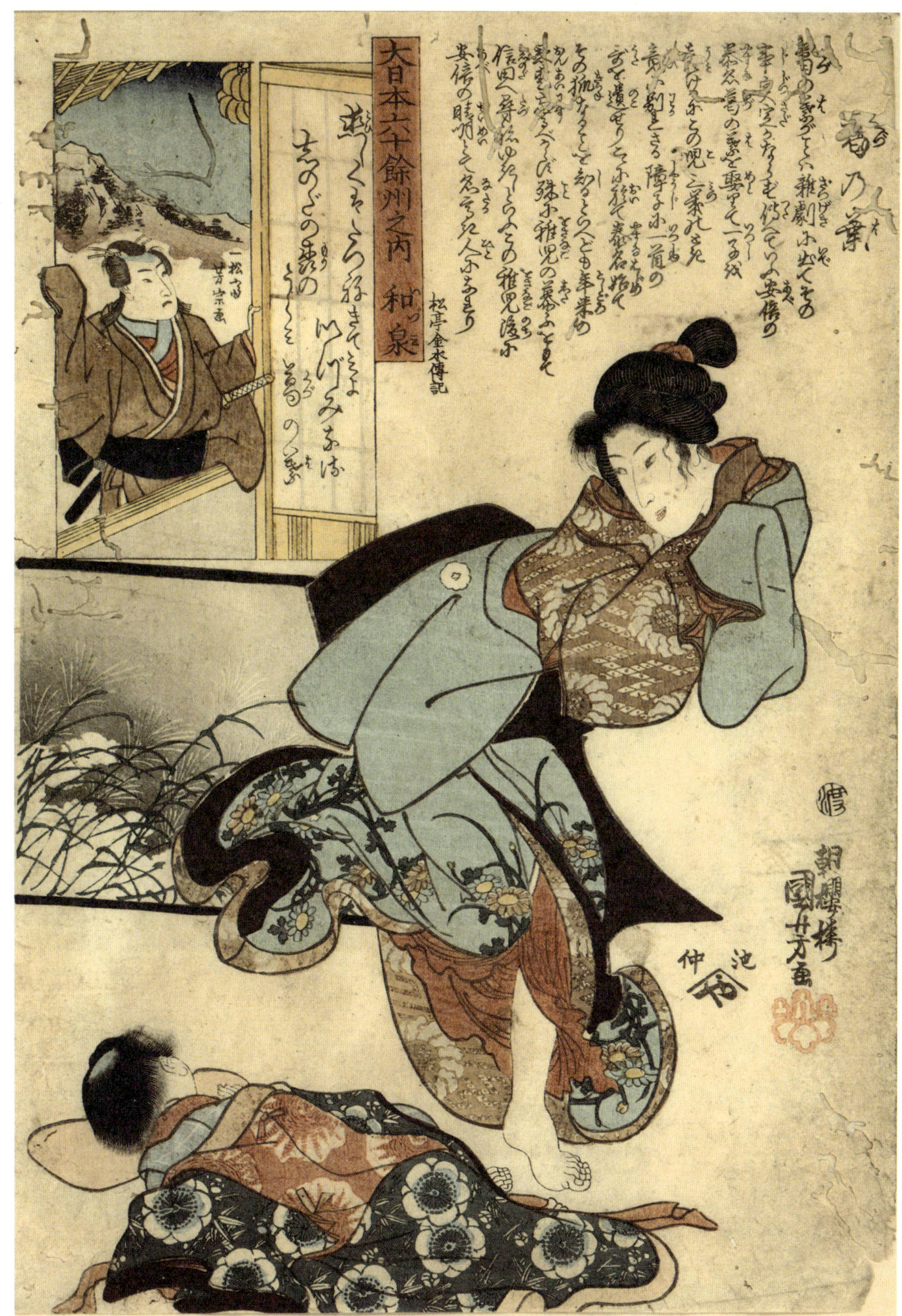

Utagawa KUNIYOSHI (1797-1861)

Like **Kunisada**, the artist **Kuniyoshi** learnt his craft at the studio of **Utagawa Toyokuni** which he attended from the age of thirteen. In 1814 he took on the name of **Kuniyoshi** and became an independent artist. I love his work, particularly the way in which he combines abstraction with naturalism in his bijin-ga.

The dancing geisha (on the previous page) is his - in the collaboration with **Kunisada**. It is interesting to look at the way he depicts the woman's billowing kimono and the angle of her head as she dances - and compare it with the centre sheet of this triptych *'Gathering plants in the Palace Garden'* (1847). It was created only two years later and he appears to be refining an idea, combining two figures.

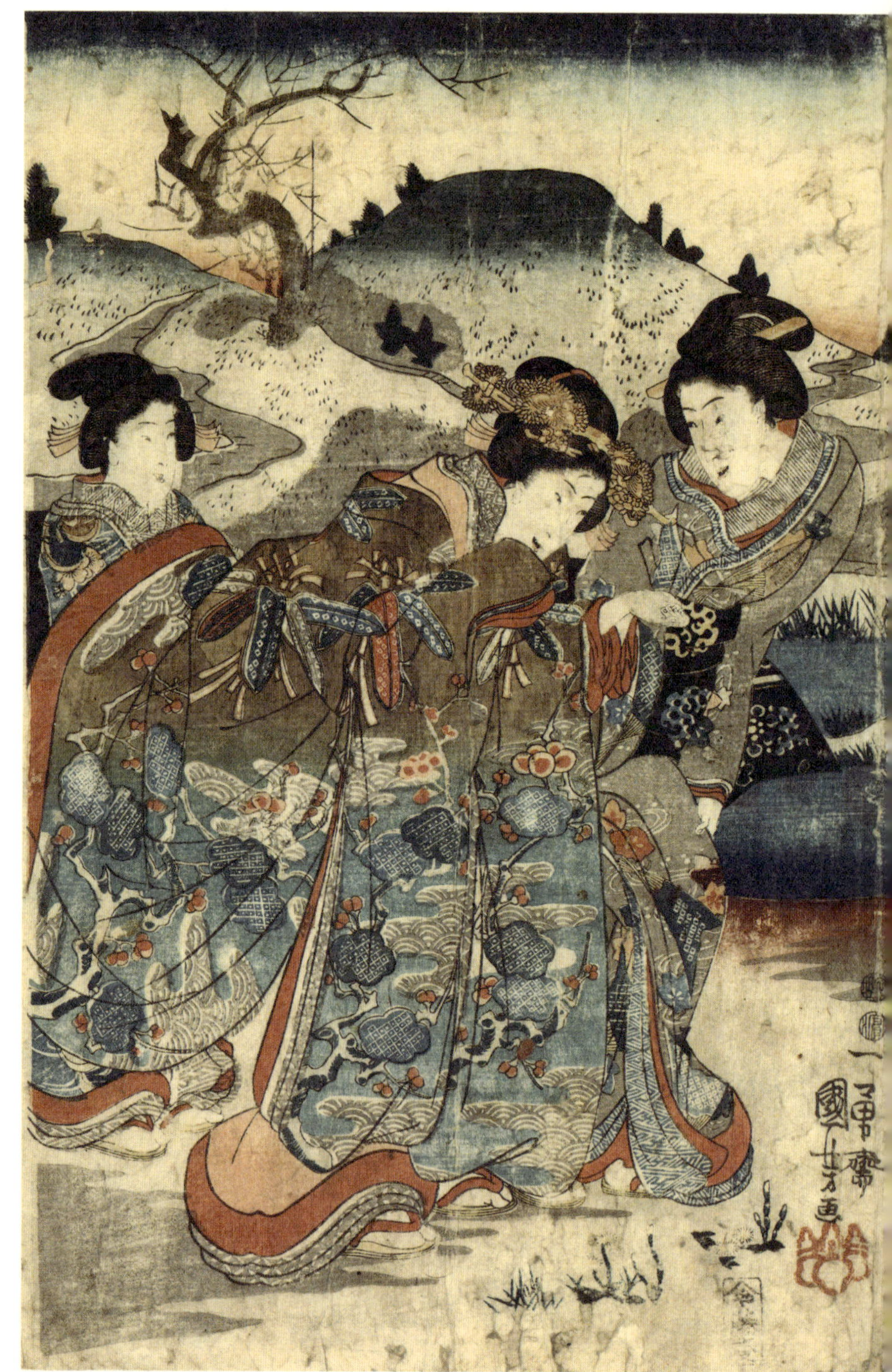

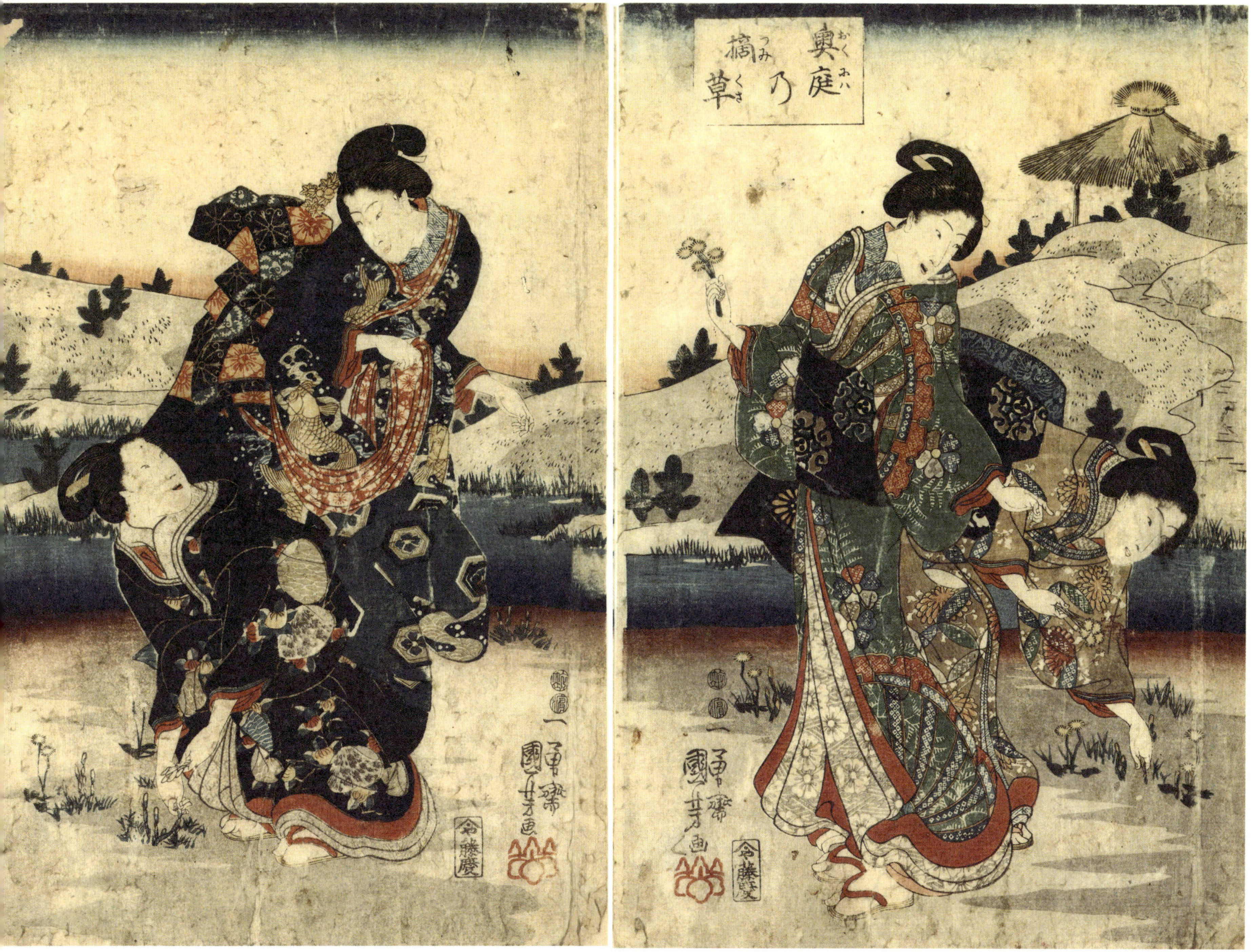

奥庭乃摘草

一勇斎國芳画

藤慶

一勇斎國芳画

藤慶

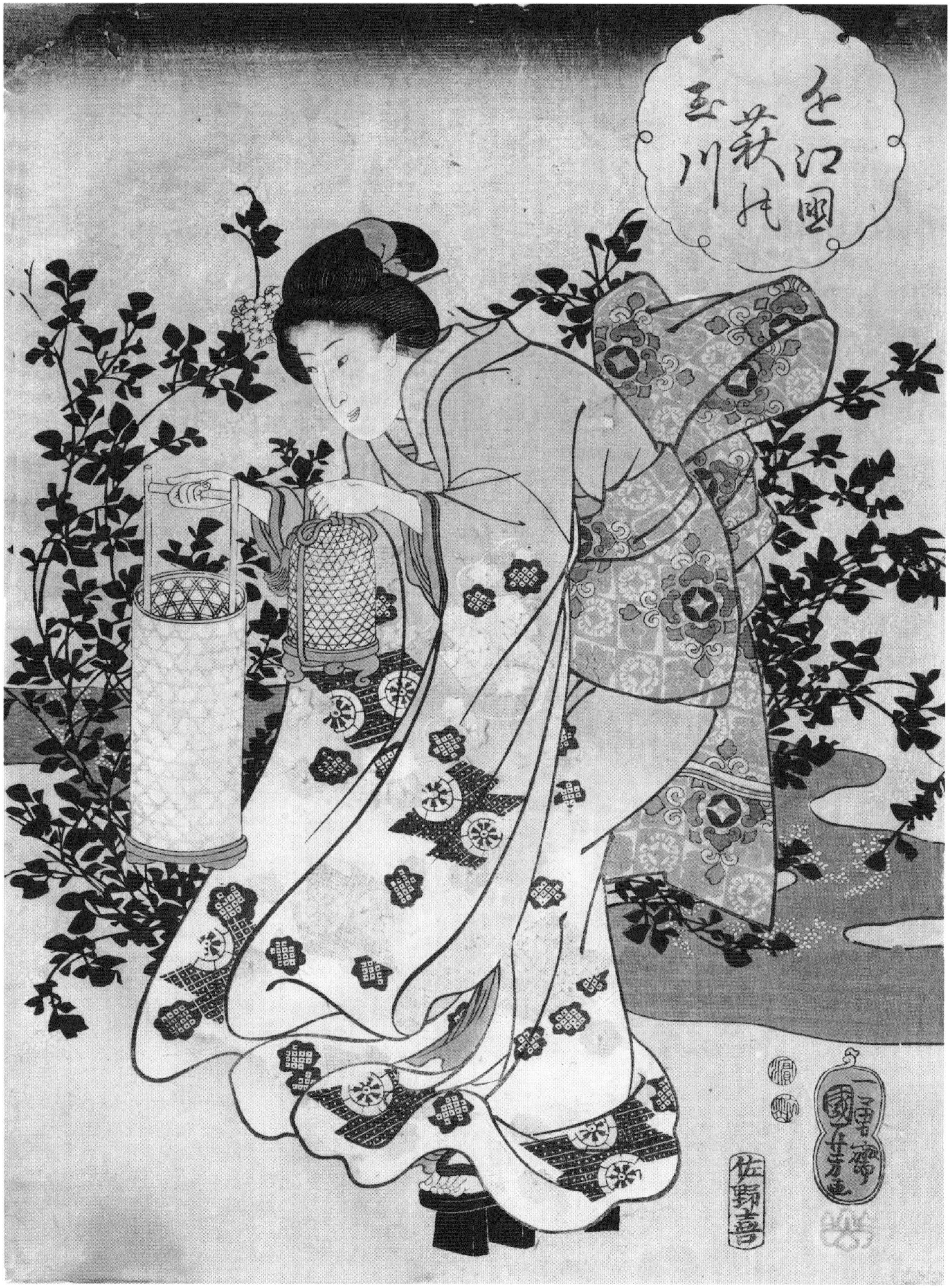

The 'beauty' on the left has a lantern and insect cage, her kimono caught in the evening breeze. It is the right panel of the triptych below *'The Bush Clover Jewel River in Omi Province'* (c.1847-48)

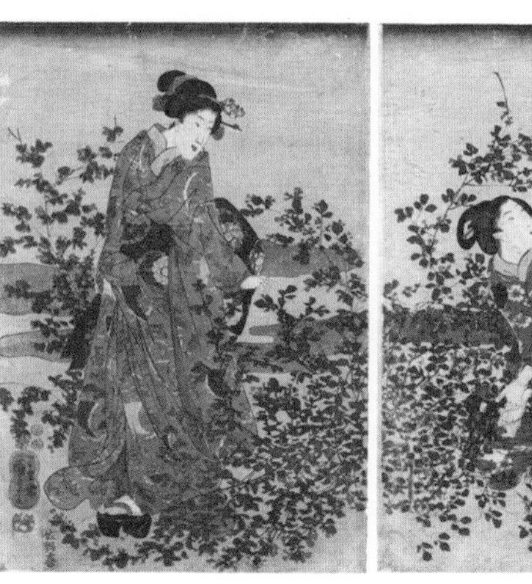

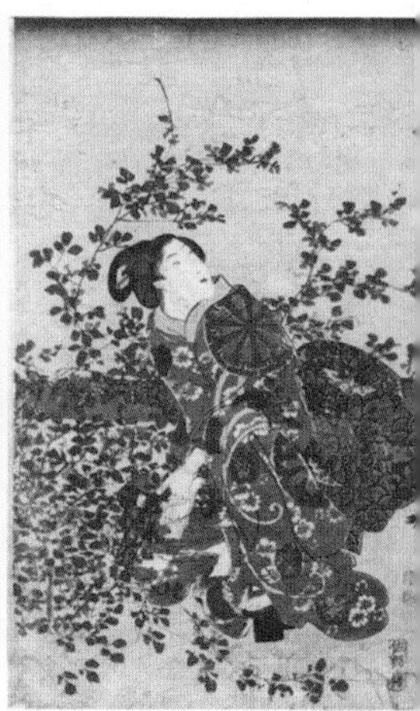

This also demonstrates his obsession with flowing fabric and women in the elements. It shows a ‘beauty’ during Tanabata, the *‘Girls Festival’* (1843) and is in effect a picture of wind. We can tell how strong it is by the way the plants in the background are bending and a cord is flying. The woman is turning away, shielding her face from the stinging blast with a fan.

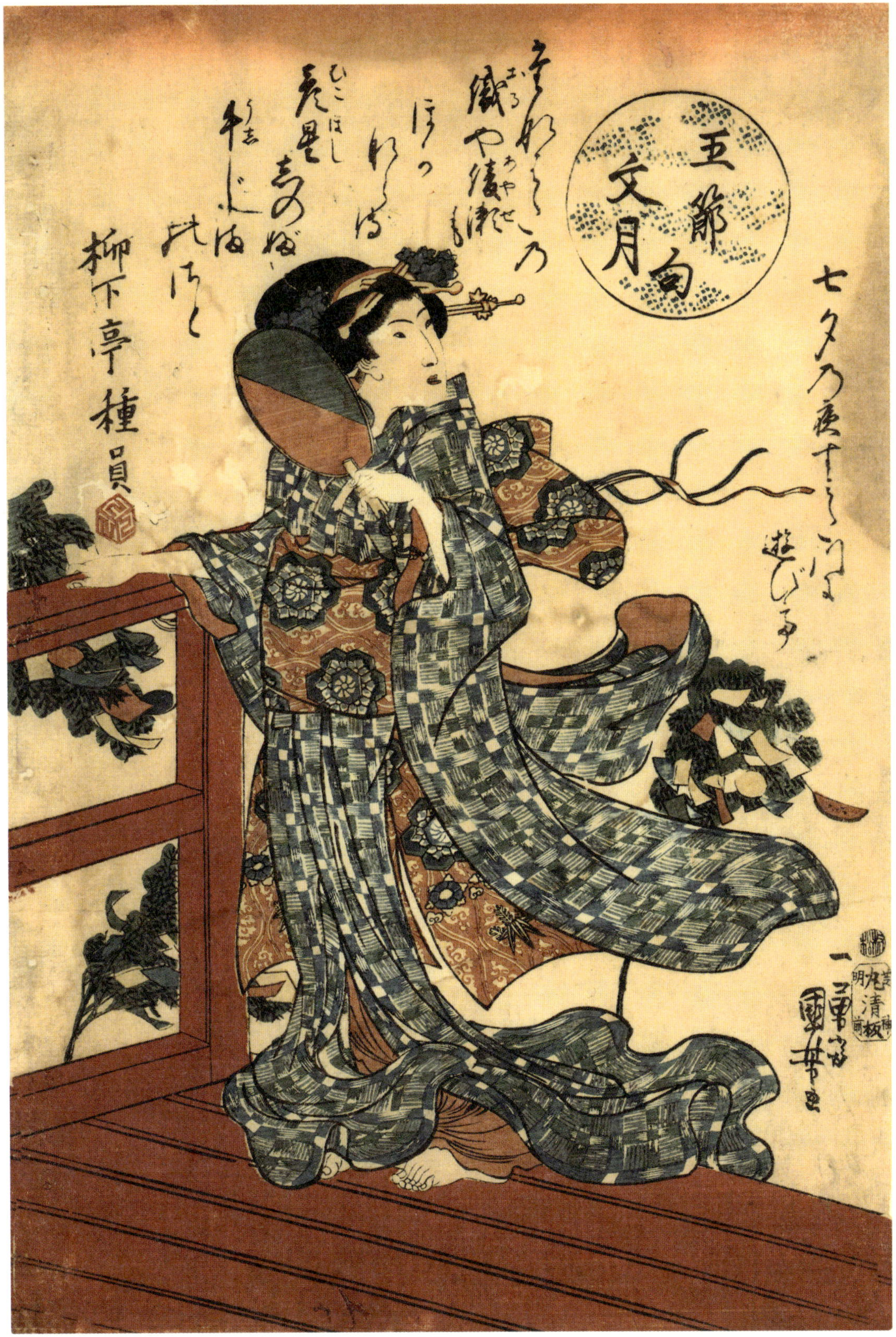

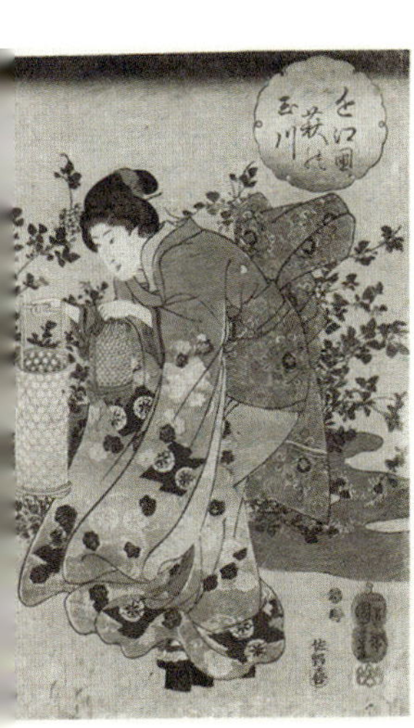

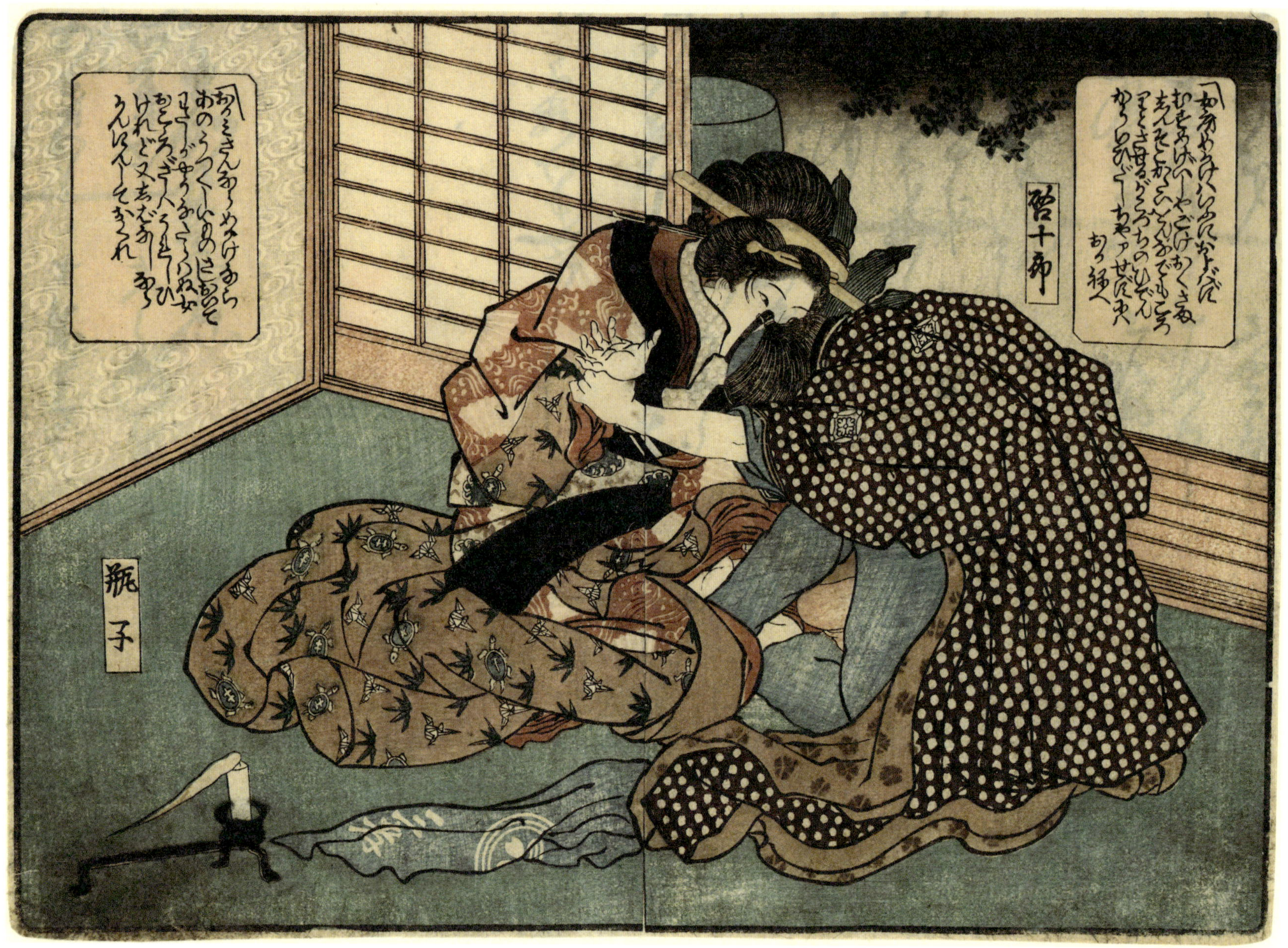

This shunga by **Kuniyoshi** has the breeze at the centre - or rather in the bottom left corner. The candle flame is encouraged by it, but bent so far it must be struggling to stay alight. What it does is set the scene and compliment the other signifiers. The open entrance, the garden outside and the bokashi shading tells us it is probably a warm summer evening - the draught responsible for the displacement of the kimonos as the lovers tussle in a playful way. It is very typical of an erotic scenario some Westerners might think of as being 'inappropriate'. More on the topic to come!

This is from the series: *The Pillowed Boudoir, Chimpen Shinkeibai* (1839).

The story is a parody on the Chinese erotic novel *Jin Ping Mei* which follows the life of a wealthy and lustful merchant Ximen Qing. It was known for both its literary excellence, like *The Tale of Genji* - as well as having a focus on erotic escapades. The series distinguishes itself with his expressive illustration of intertwined figures. This particular image is the least explicit - so probably on page one.

Here we have another bijin-ga that shows his mastery of the genre.

In the series: *Mirror of Eternal Feminine Virtue* (1843) we see full-length portraits of beautiful women likened to Confucius's five cardinal virtues. The characters for them are written in a cartouche above with an accompanying text.

This virtue is *'Good Faith'*. The 'beauty' is probably about to take water from a public basin to wash her hands but is distracted. With a corner of her kimono in her mouth she glances back over her shoulder, partly obscured by a post. Like a snap, the image seems to be tilted as if the photographer didn't have time to level the shot. But this was created in 1853, long before **Kunyoshi** would have seen such things.

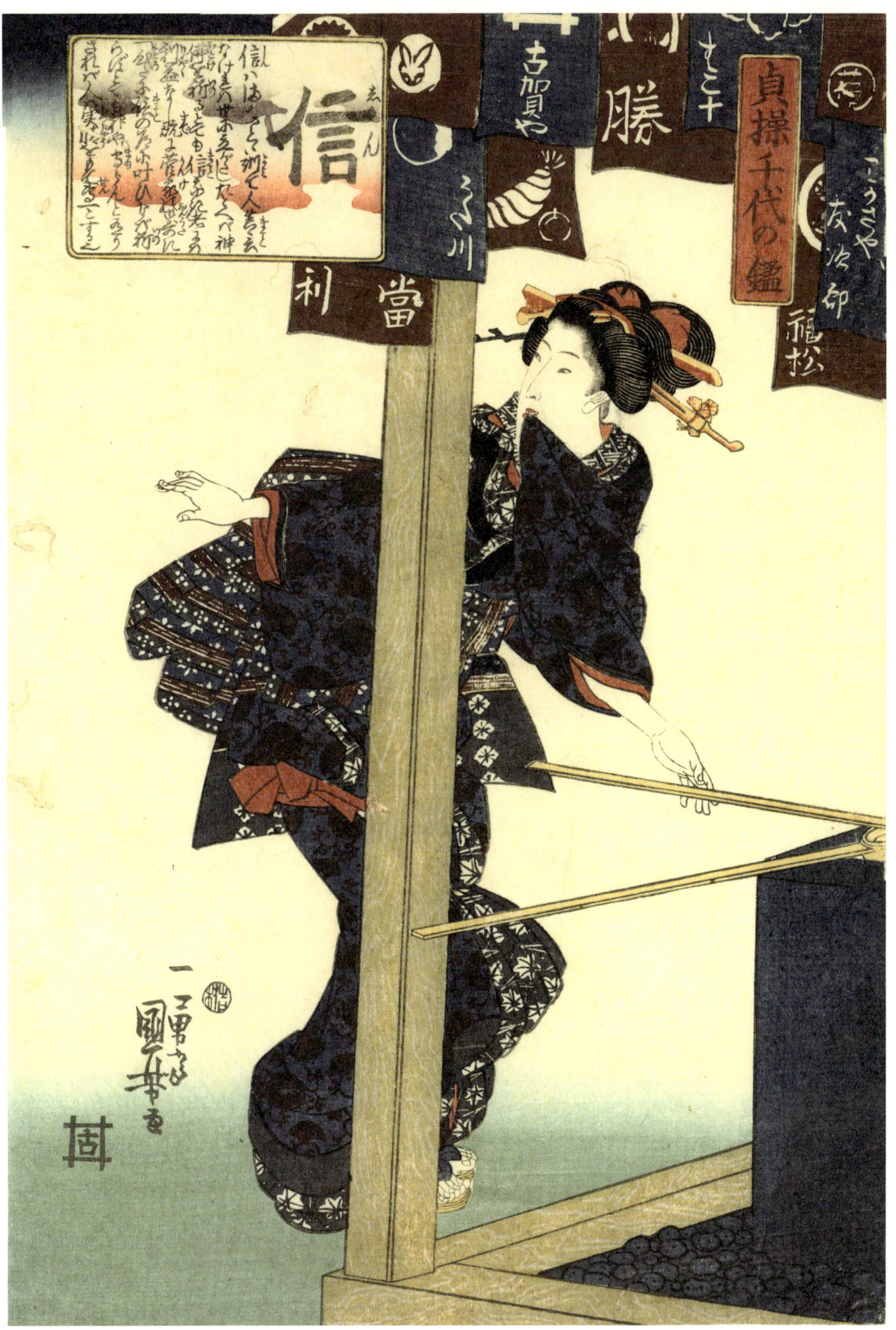

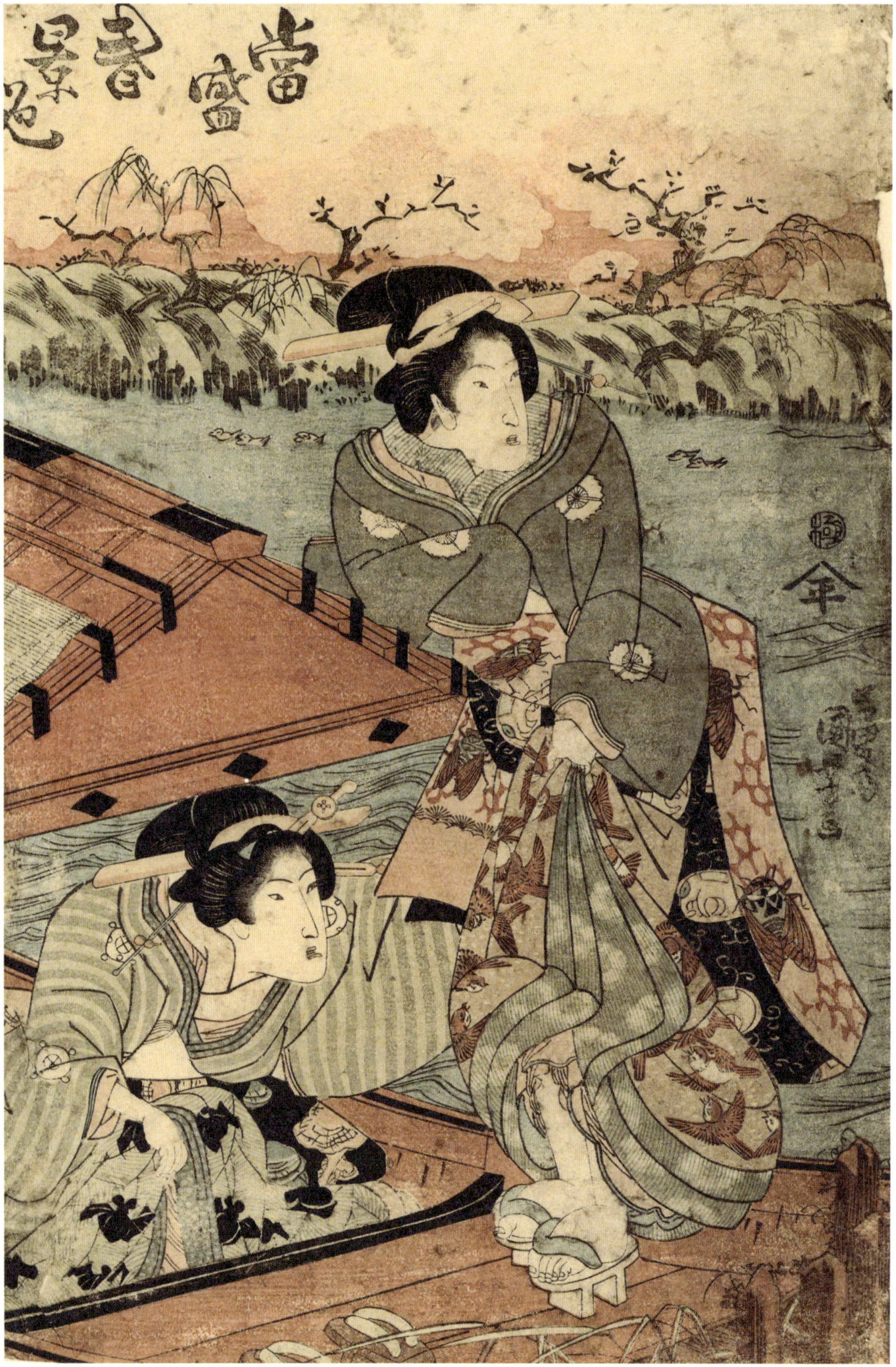

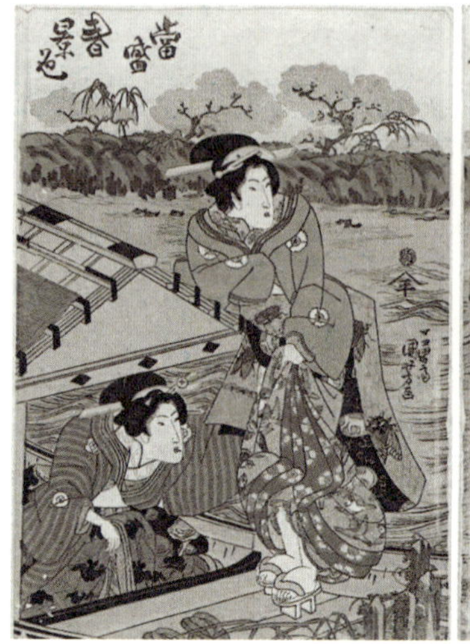

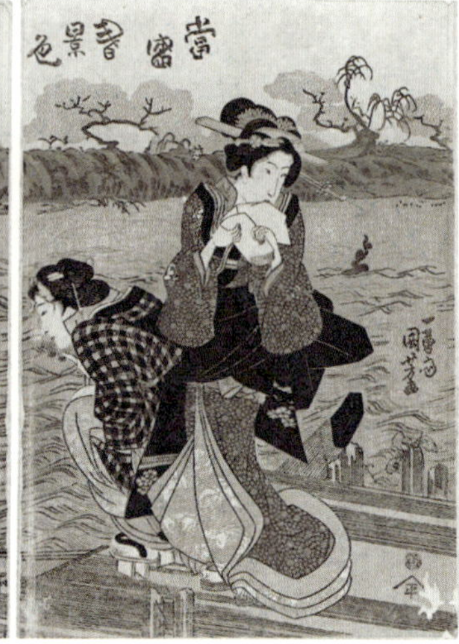

Here we have the left sheet of the triptych *'Up-to-date Spring Scene'* (c.1829). At least we can see how it works with the central image. I have yet to come across the right sheet.

It again shows **Kunyoshi**'s fascination with women in kimonos. There is some fantastic detail - particularly the bats and bees in the fabric. As before, it seems like a moment in time, just captured - similar to a photograph.

This is a fascinating image which emphasises the fabric - but the subject might be somewhat sinister. The woman appears to be secreting samurai swords in her clothing. The advancing figure in the background could be the intended recipient - or perhaps she is fleeing from him! I don’t know the narrative but the motifs in the cartouche indicate that it is from *The Tale of Genji.*

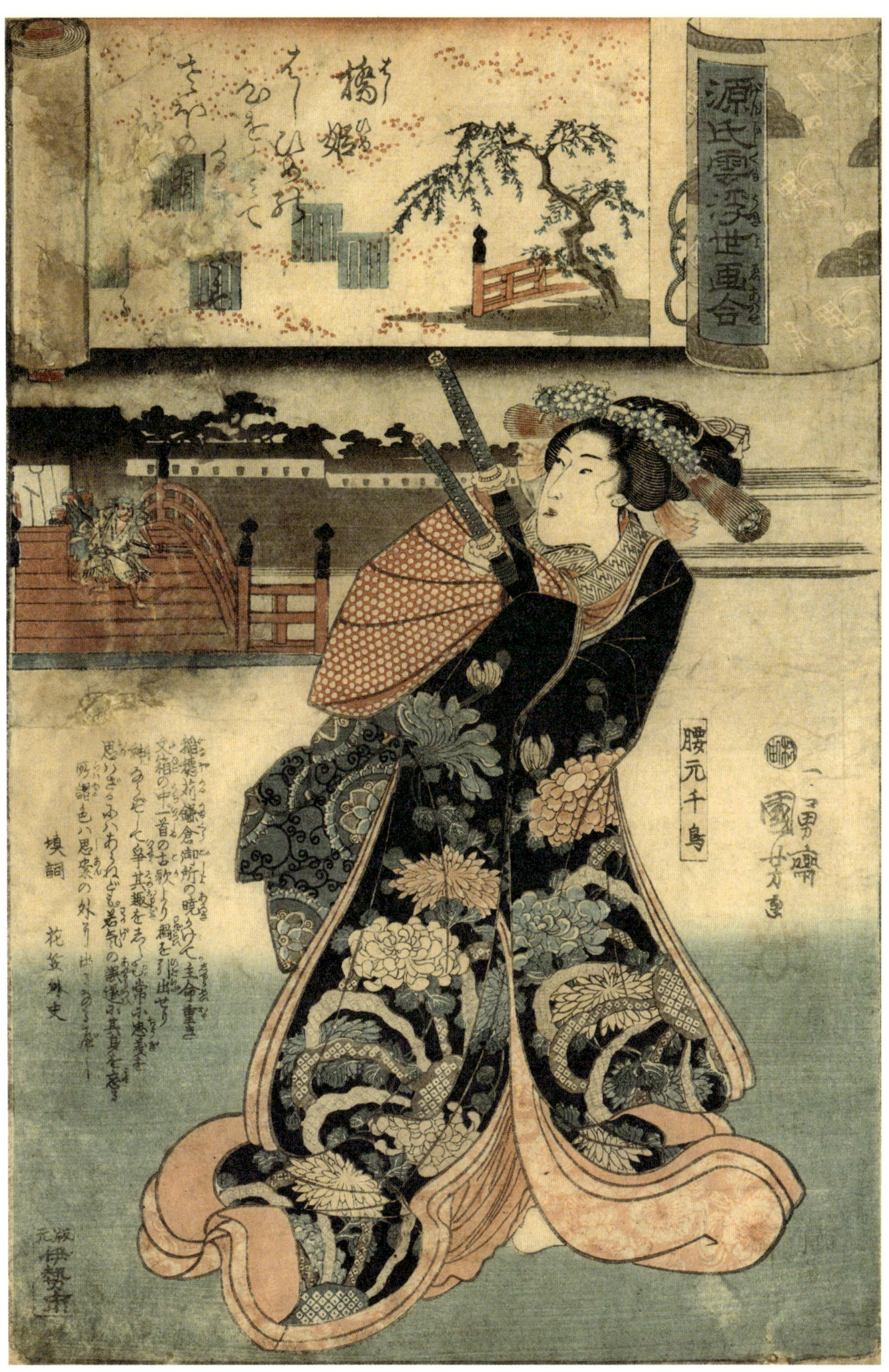

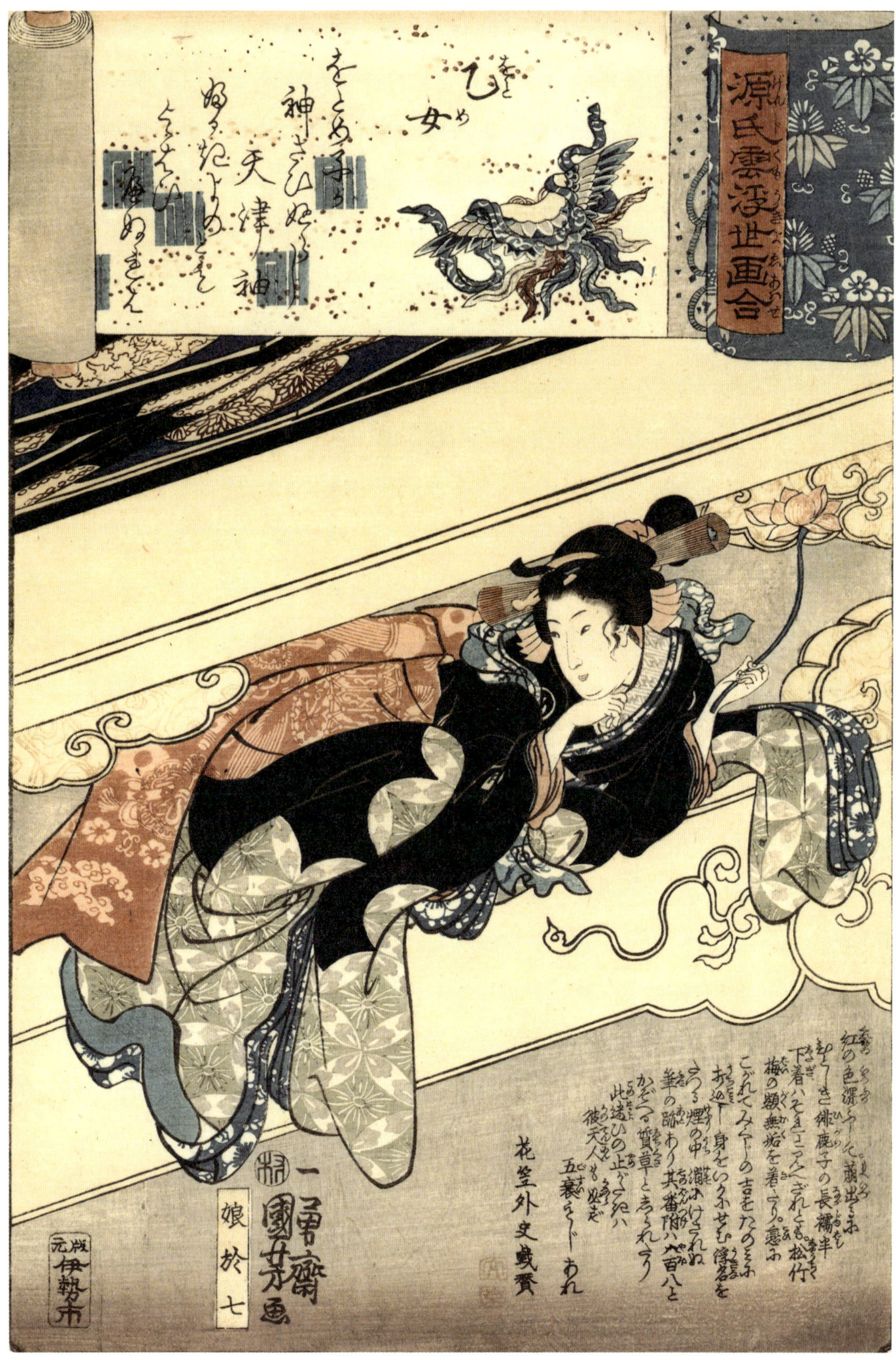

'Otome (The Maiden), Chapter 21' is a depiction of the young 'beauty' Oshichi reclining along the eaves of a Buddhist temple, in the form of a tennin or heavenly Buddhist spirit. The inset above shows a feather robe (hagoromo), worn by tennin, which enables them to fly.

It is from another Genji Series: *Comparisons of the Cloudy Chapters of Genji,* (1845/46). We get a typical **Kuniyoshi** design, with various layers of fabric and contrasting curves set against the geometric structure of the building. She has a lotus blossom in one hand with ribbons and ornaments in her hair.

A lovely print that I was once surprised and delighted to see on display at the Fitzwilliam Museum in Oxford (UK).

Here we see a weird and wonderful print from the series: *Celebrated Products of Mountains and Seas* (1852).

'Edible Seaweed from Shimosa Province' is a fantastic image from this series, which pairs beautiful women with famous products from the various regions.

A 'beauty' is frightened by the enormous mask of a lion dancer looming over her shoulder. She turns away, covering her mouth with the sleeve of her striped kimono. The scene at upper left depicts men harvesting seaweed.

Detailed burnishing in the black areas of the mask and bokashi shading in the background make it particularly special.

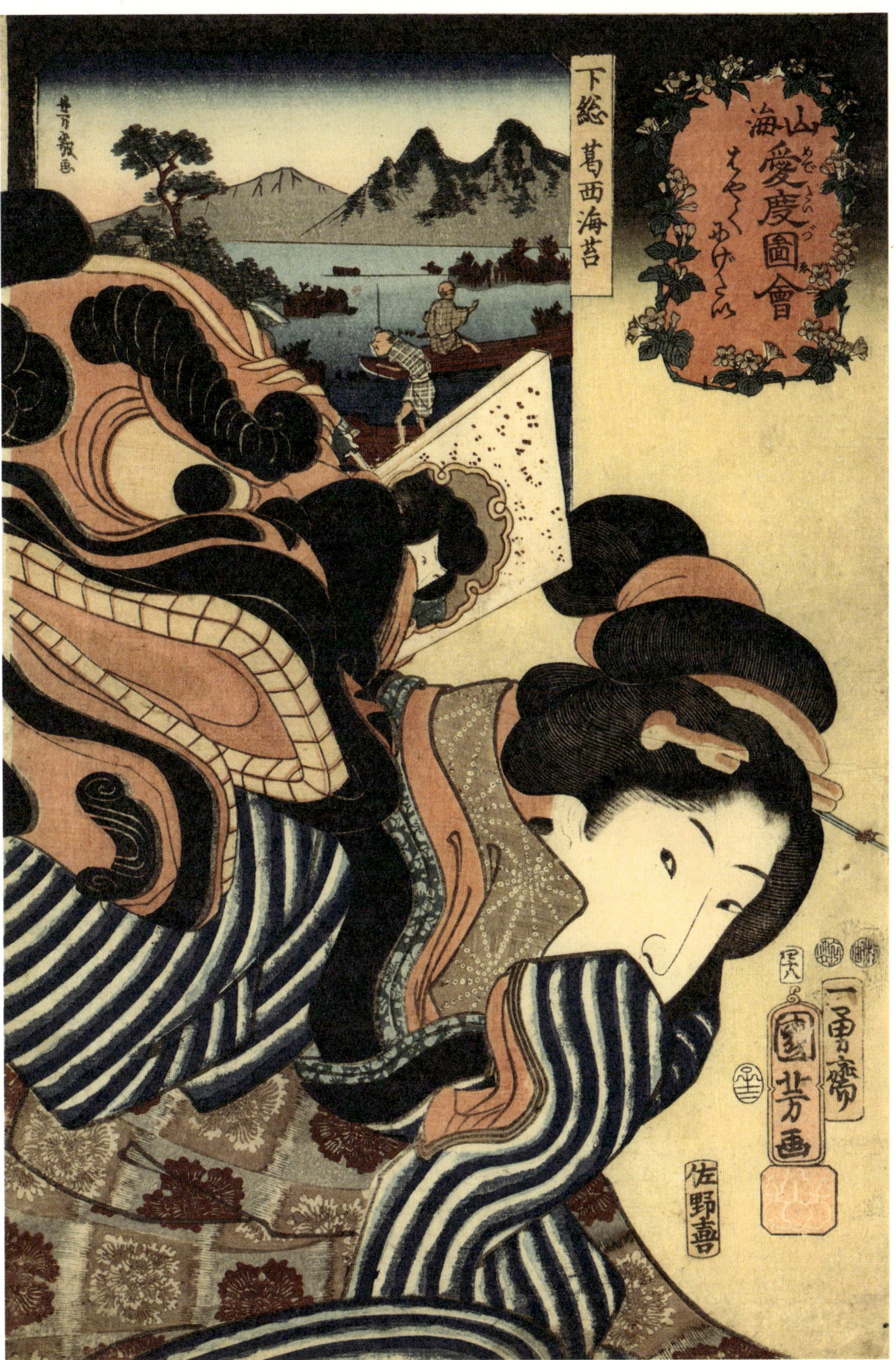

Like all the artists **Kuniyoshi** was compelled to show courtesans, particularly from kabuki performances with famous male actors depicting them.

Bando Shuka is the courtesan Akoya (1849), mistress of the warrior Taira Kagekiyo who escaped following the battle of Dan-no-ura. The Genji commander Shigetada kidnapped Akoya, hoping to force her to reveal Kagekiyo's whereabouts.

Here she sits in front of a koto smiling calmly, dressed in a blue kimono patterned with thistles. The drapery overhead features the butterfly crest of the Taira clan.

Bando Shuka is also found in this second print, but this time as the courtesan Miura no Takao who is being weighed against oval gold coins, some wrapped in paper. It is from the series *Sixty-nine Stations of Kisokaido Road* and titled *'Ageo: Miura no Takao'* (1852-53).

It comes from an extraordinary story. The daimyo Yorikane agreed to purchase the courtesan's contract from the Miura pleasure house for her weight in gold. Giggling into her kimono sleeve she sits on the scale with elegant robes piled up. The proprietor and his wife react with surprise, mouths agape, while more gold pieces are scattered across the floor. The inset shows the village of Ageo with rice fields in the distance.

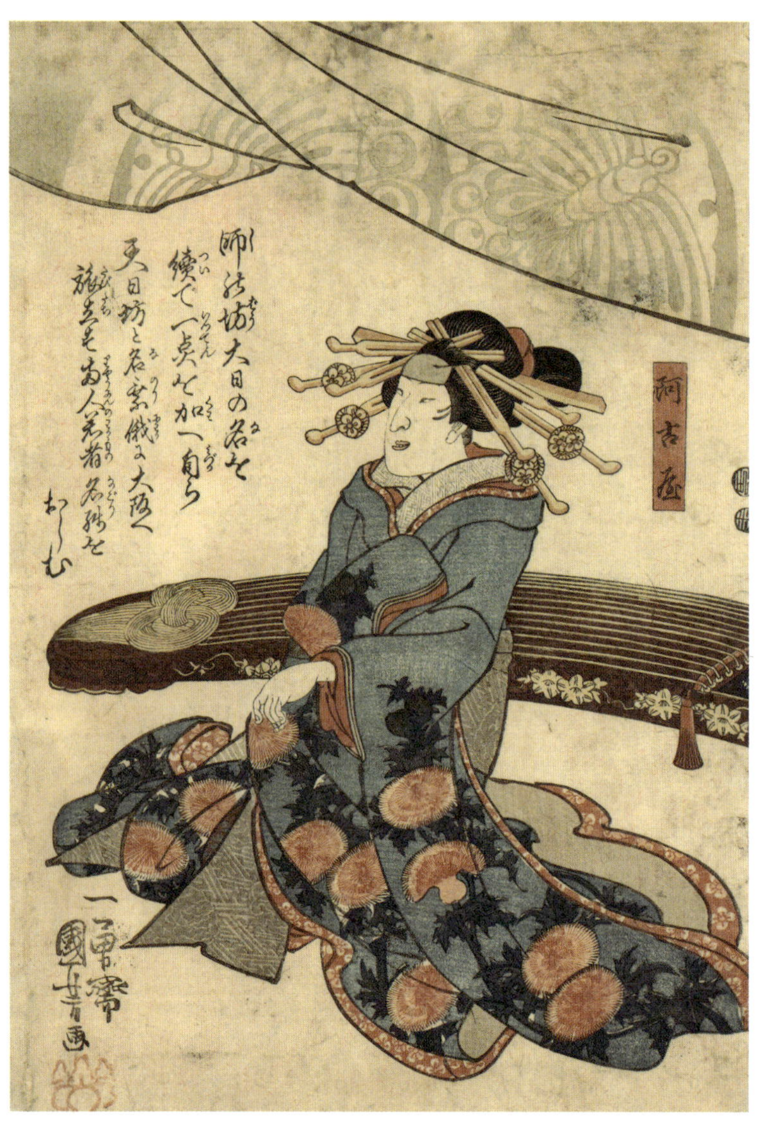

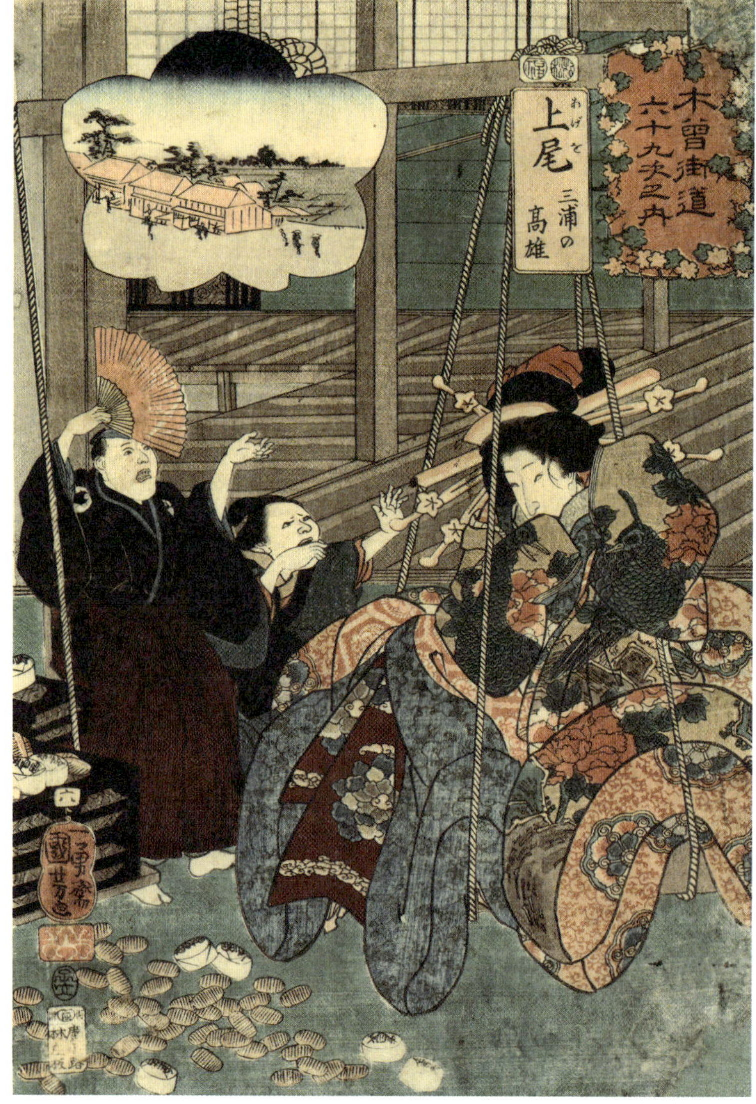

Utagawa YOSHIIKU (1833 - 1904)

Considered very much a minor artist of the Utagawa School, **Yoshiiku** does though provide a link between the two giants of the late 1800's. He was a student of **Kuniyoshi** and then became a fierce rival of **Yoshitoshi** (who we are about to see). I don't know much about these two prints but I like them for different reasons.

On the left a young woman (most likely a man) appears to be dancing - or at least performing in some way. The blue tones together with the red on her kimono are very effective against the background. Also the expressively drawn hands are rather wonderful.

On the right is an intimate study of a courtesan and her attendant as they put up a banner at the entrance of their premises. It matches her kimono.

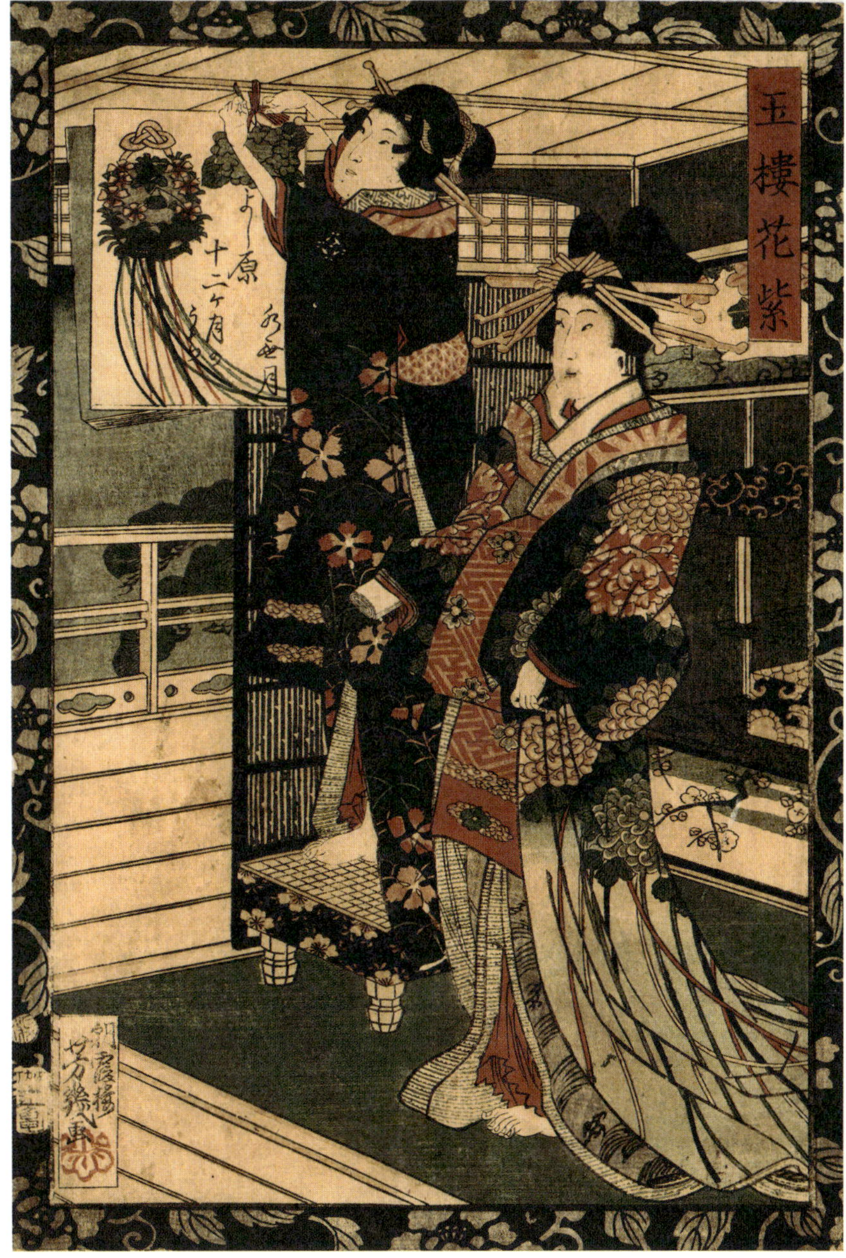

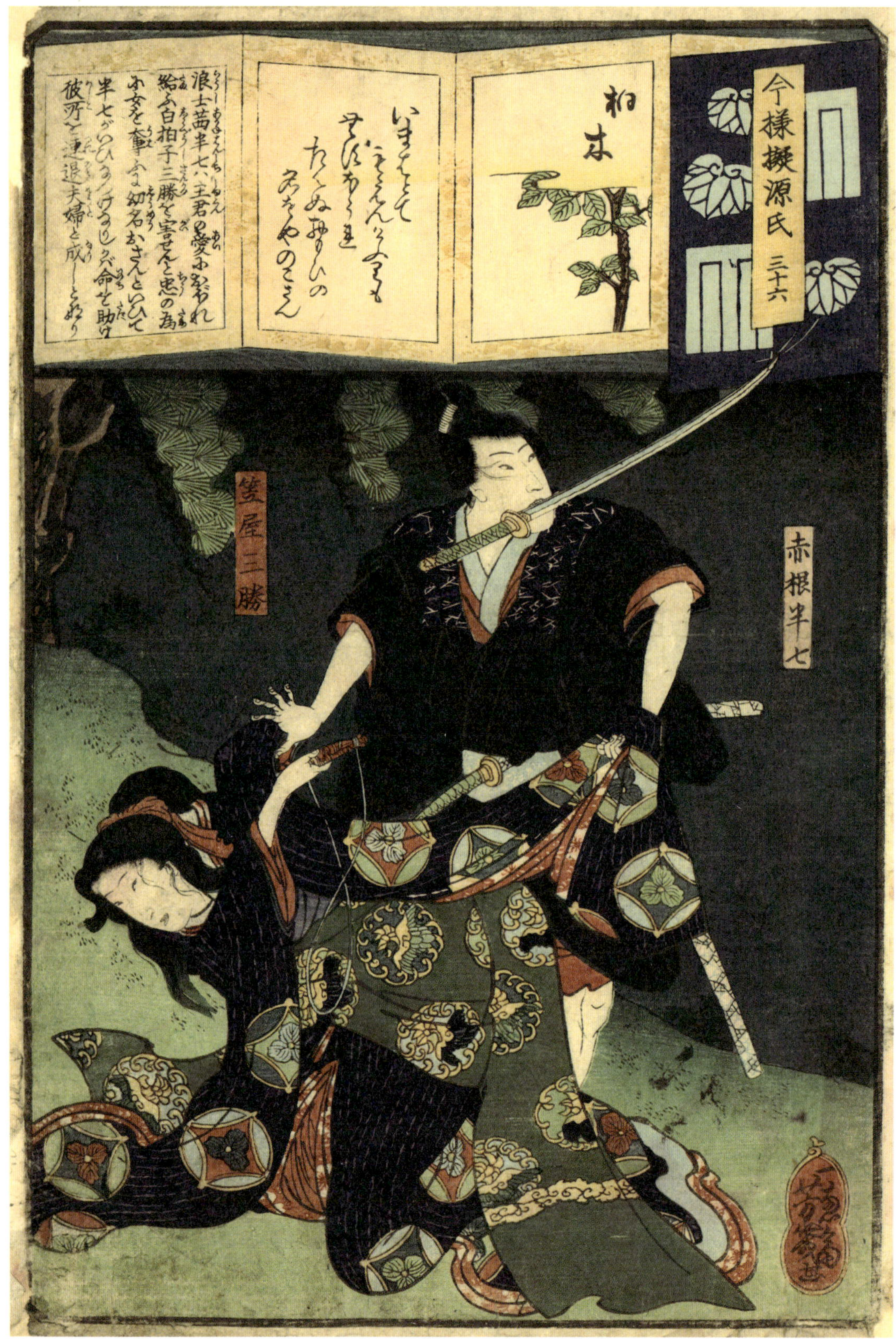

This is from chapter 36 of the series *Modern Parodies of Genji* and is titled *'Kasaya Sankatsu and Akane Hanshichi'* (1864).

It is a dramatic scene from the kabuki play *Akane no Iroba*, based on the true story of lovers' suicide. The young samurai Akane Hanshichi and the 'beauty' Kasaya Sankatsu have decided to commit suicide rather than be parted. Here, he holds one of her kimono sleeves as she hands him a small bag on a cord, a sword clenched between his teeth. The setting is a hillside at night, the dark sky behind a pine tree.

Such suicide pacts were the stuff of theatre - probably because the whole ethos of self sacrifice was ingrained in Japanese culture. We will see another example later.

Yoshiiku fell on hard times with the gradual demise of the woodblock print market and made a living illustrating news sheets - until photography put paid to that.

Utagawa TOMINOBU (1804-44)

This print is attributed to **Tominobu** but very little is known about him, perhaps in part because he is also to be found under the name of **Kunitomi** - and **Kasentai**.

Whatever the name of the artist, I do like this print. It seems to be of a courtesan secretly reading a letter. The shapes and the muted tones are very appealing - and the extra large decorated cartouche behind her is rather wonderful.

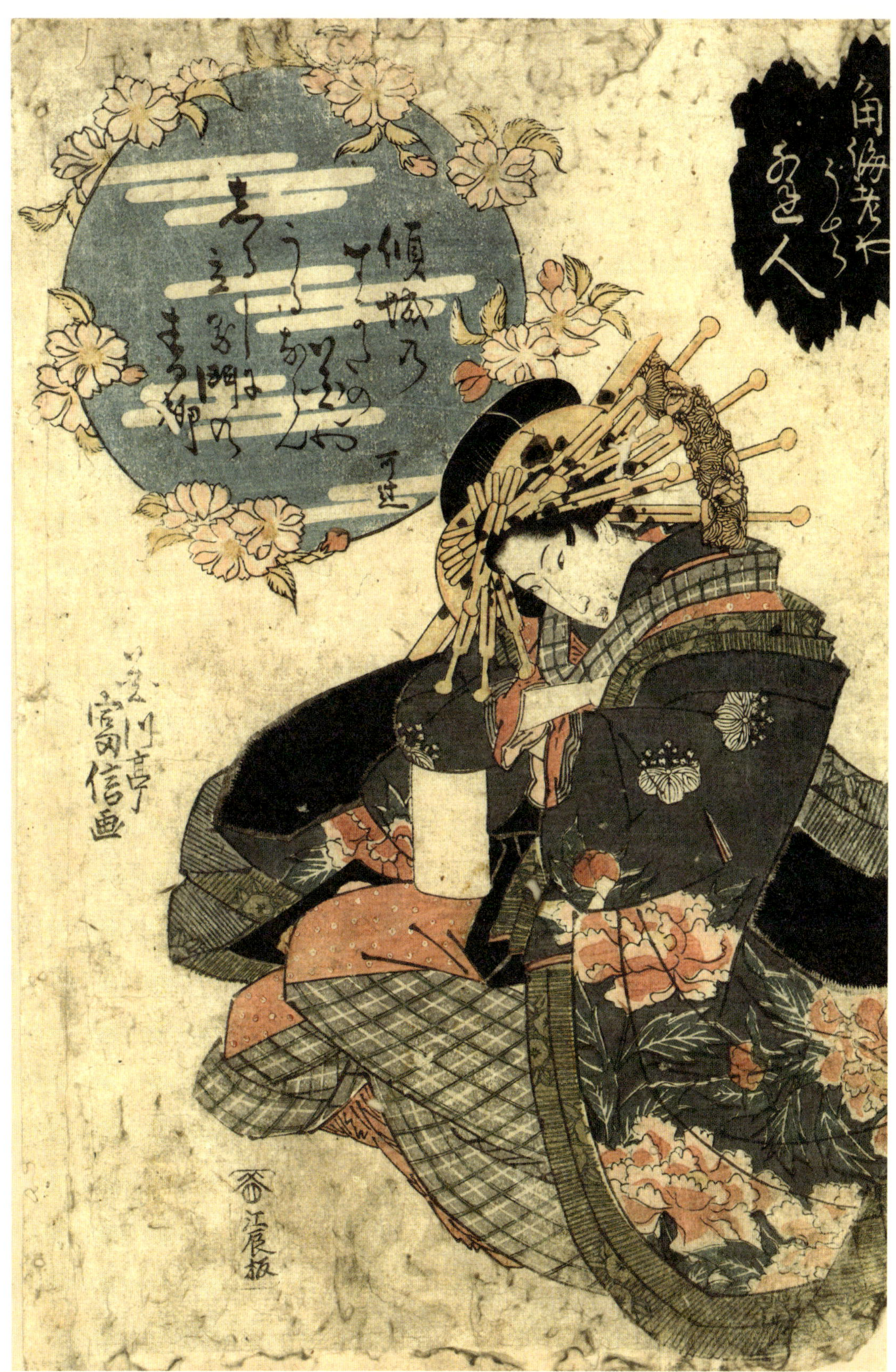

Utagawa School

I'm including a few images by unknown artists as I feel so many are neglected or ignored. There was a wealth of artistic endeavour that generally goes under the heading of Utagawa School, particularly the unattributed erotica.

I like this shunga (c.1840) because it has an element of humour. The couple making love are disturbed by a woman peeking through the damaged paper screen. But look behind her and you will see that she too is being spied on. Despite it being a rather rough and cheap looking print I like the bold sweep of the bed cover design - making a terrific composition.

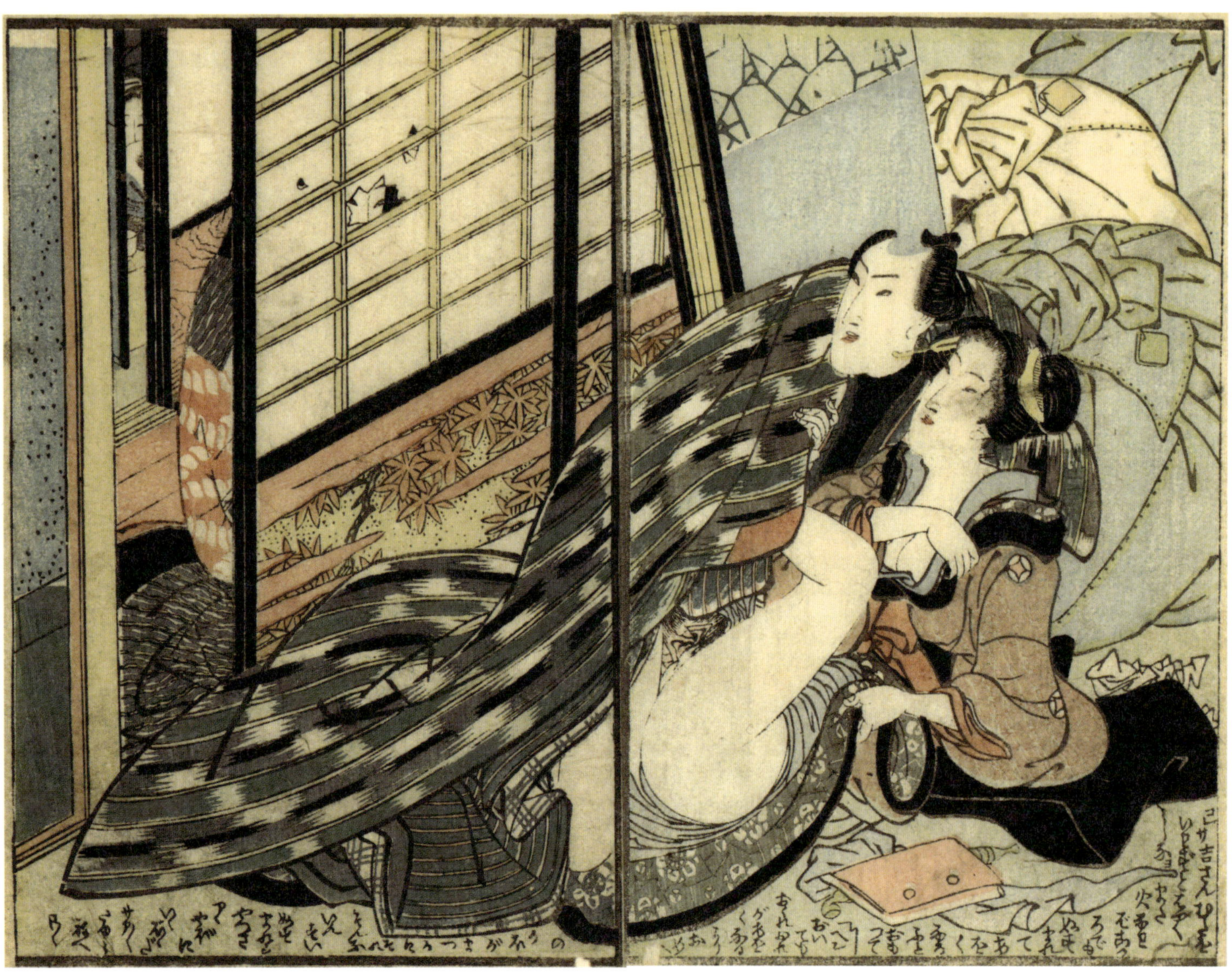

These two are probably Utagawa School sumi drawings - for woodblock designs that may, or may not, have been turned into woodblock prints.

Although done like humorous cartoons, they tap into the fears of many Japanese living in fragile and insecure accommodation - with paper partition walls and entrances. The invasion of a rogue penis while the husband sleeps crops up regularly.

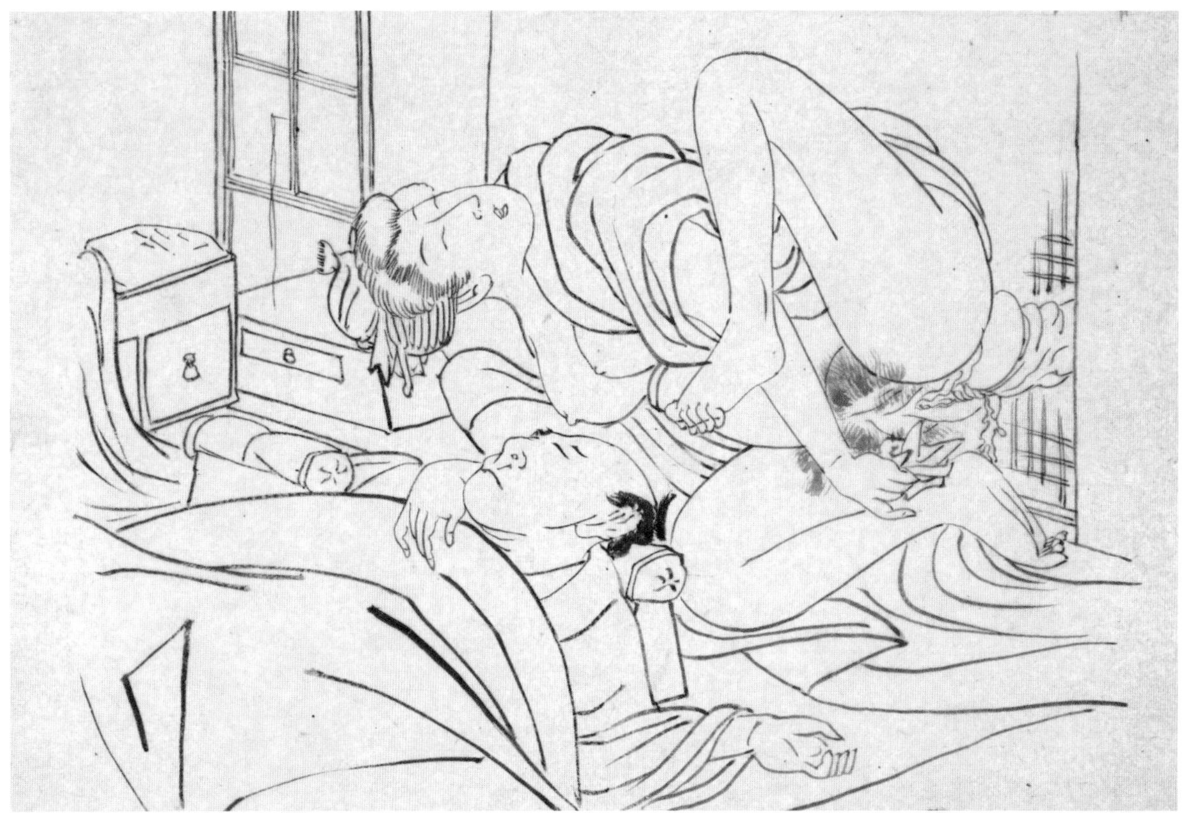

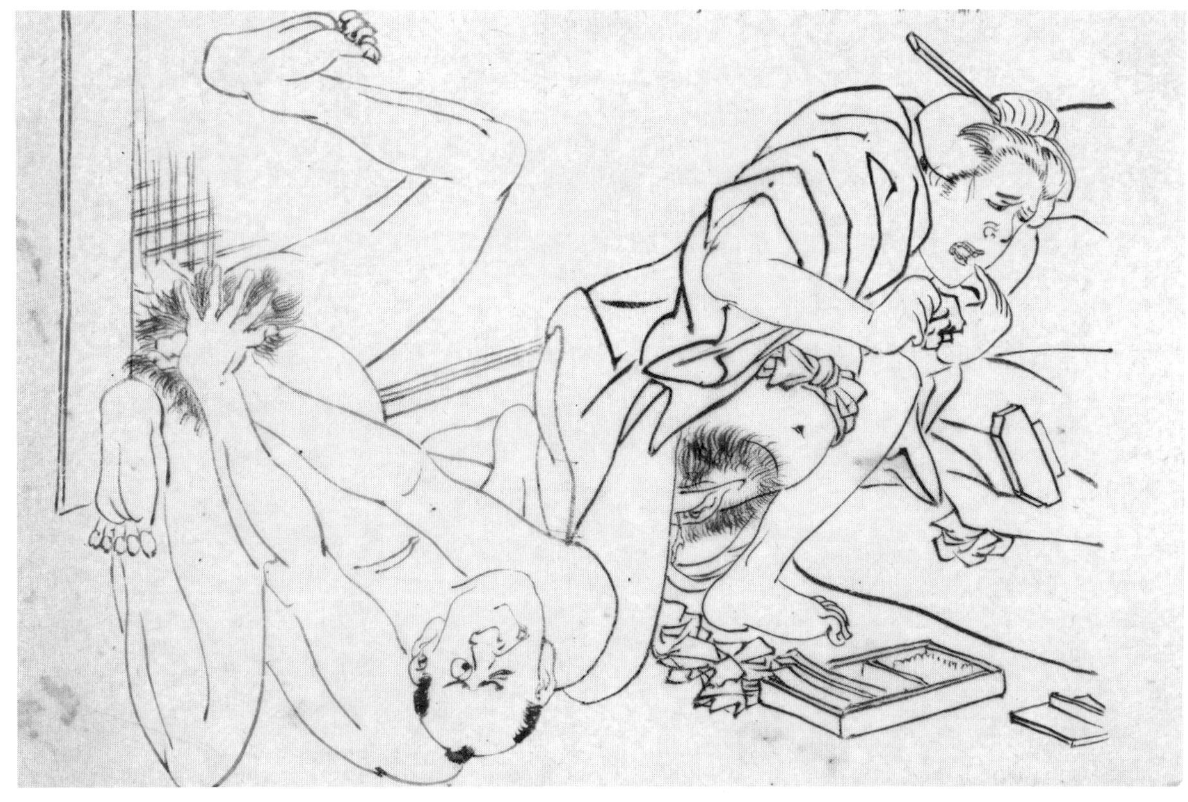

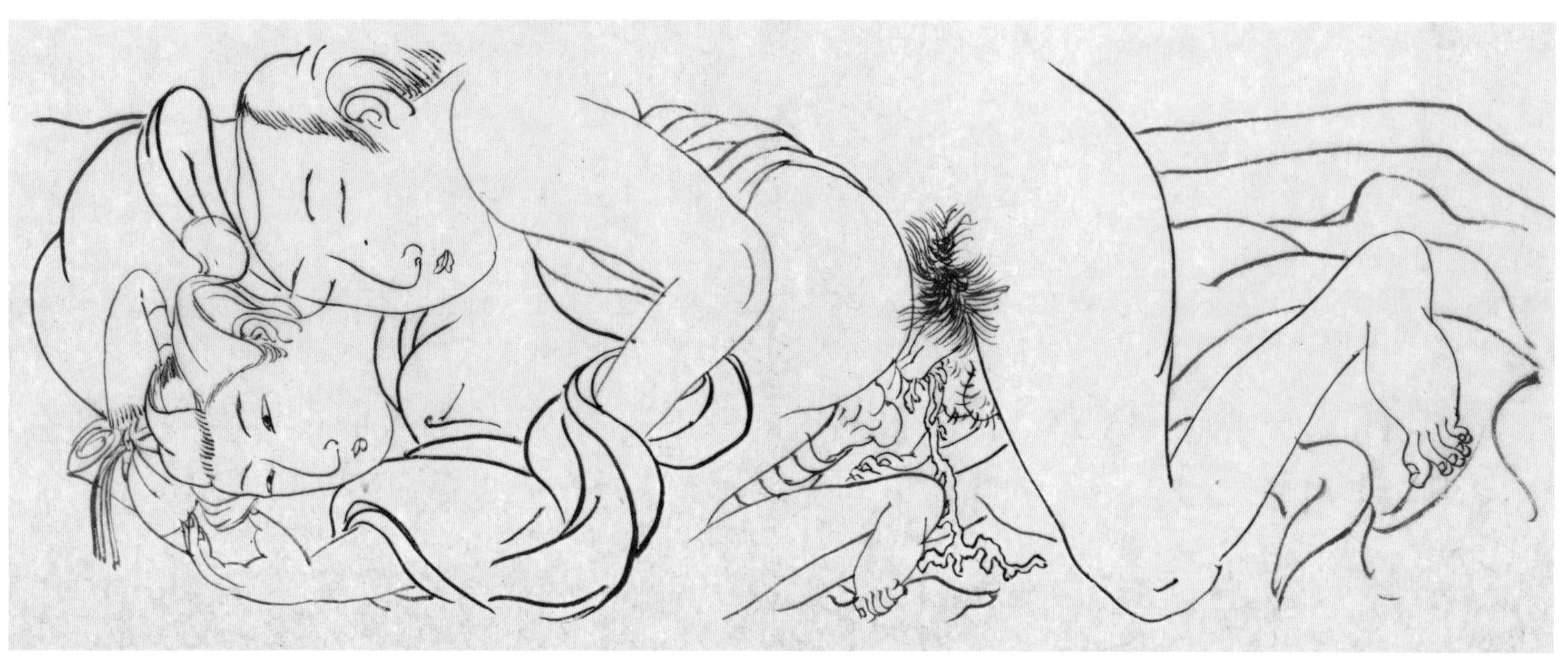

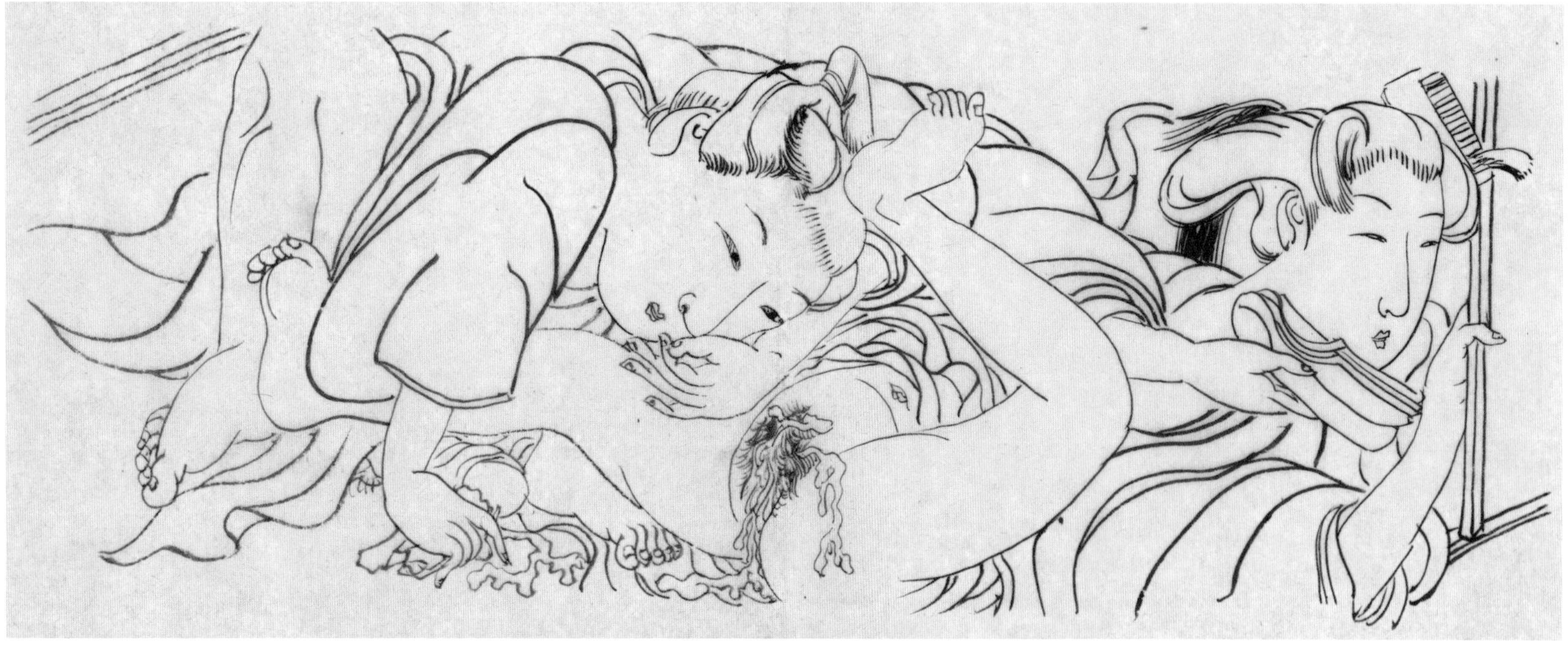

The two shunga drawings on the left are in the style of **Buncho**. The top image appears to be of young male lovers.

The orgy below I have seen briefly on the internet as an unattributed print, so my drawing may be a copy for a reprint.

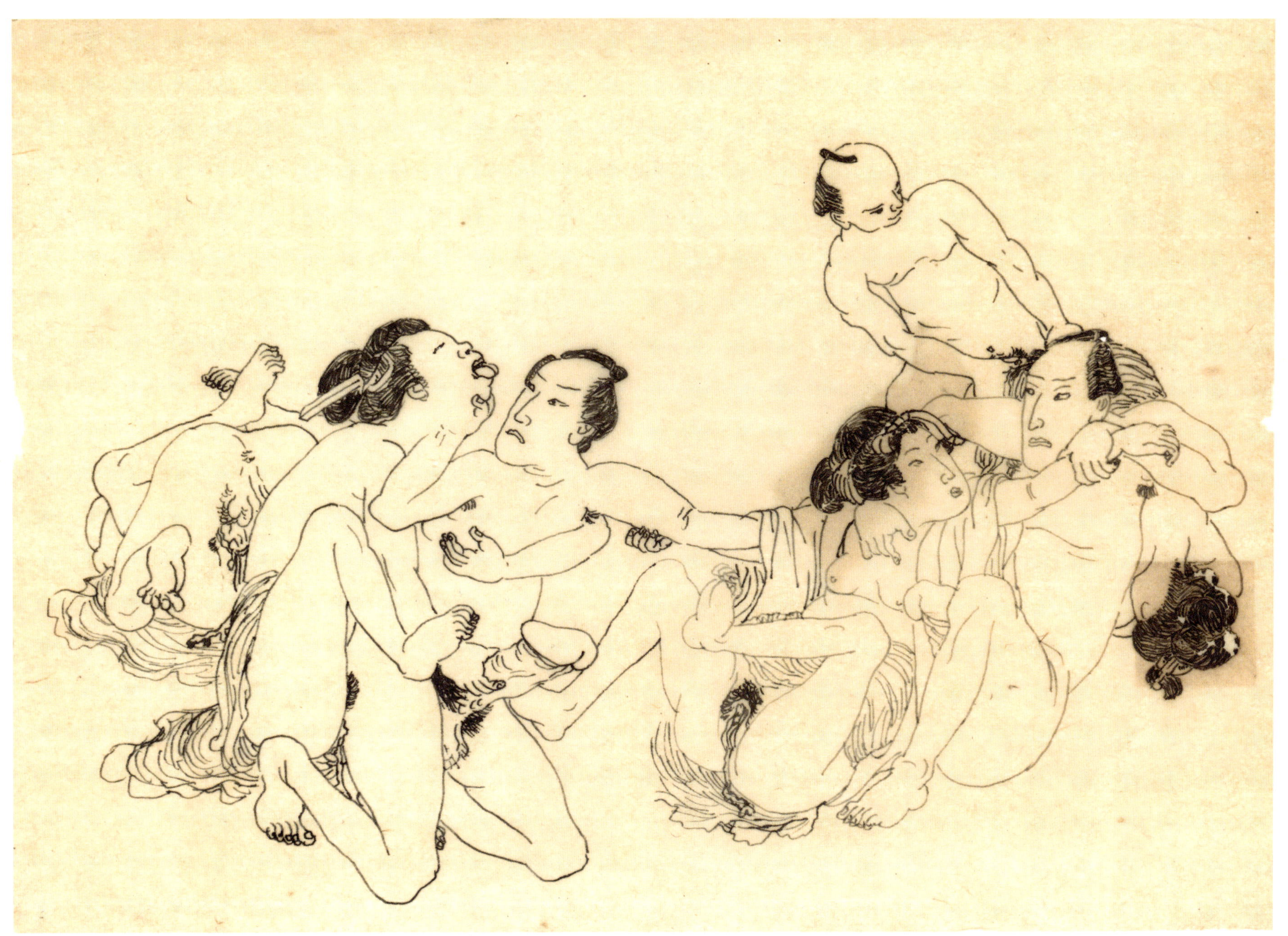

These two are also original ink drawings on thin paper, so they could be preparations for woodblock prints that were never made. The fine line work is extraordinarily deft.

If you look closely at the bottom drawing it perhaps shows that the artist changed his mind - in the depiction of digital pleasure.

I love the rodent action on the side tables - and the smiling long haired cat on a case, watching.

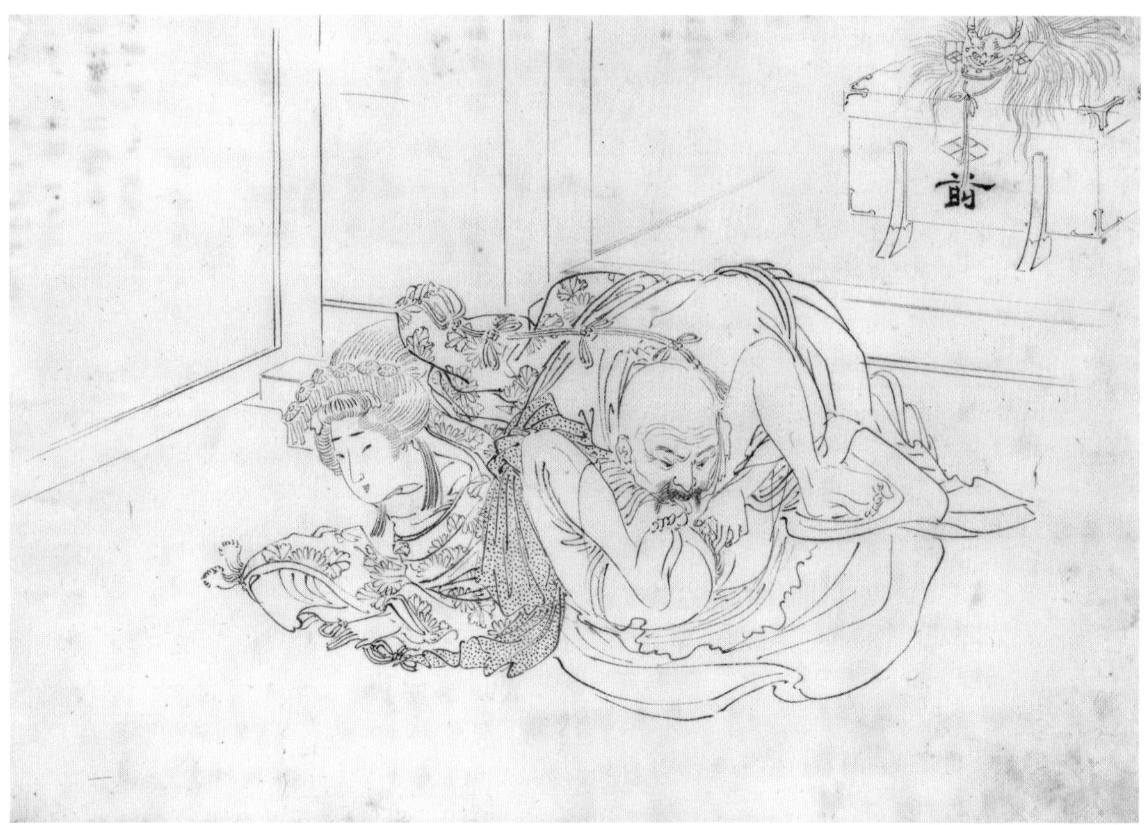

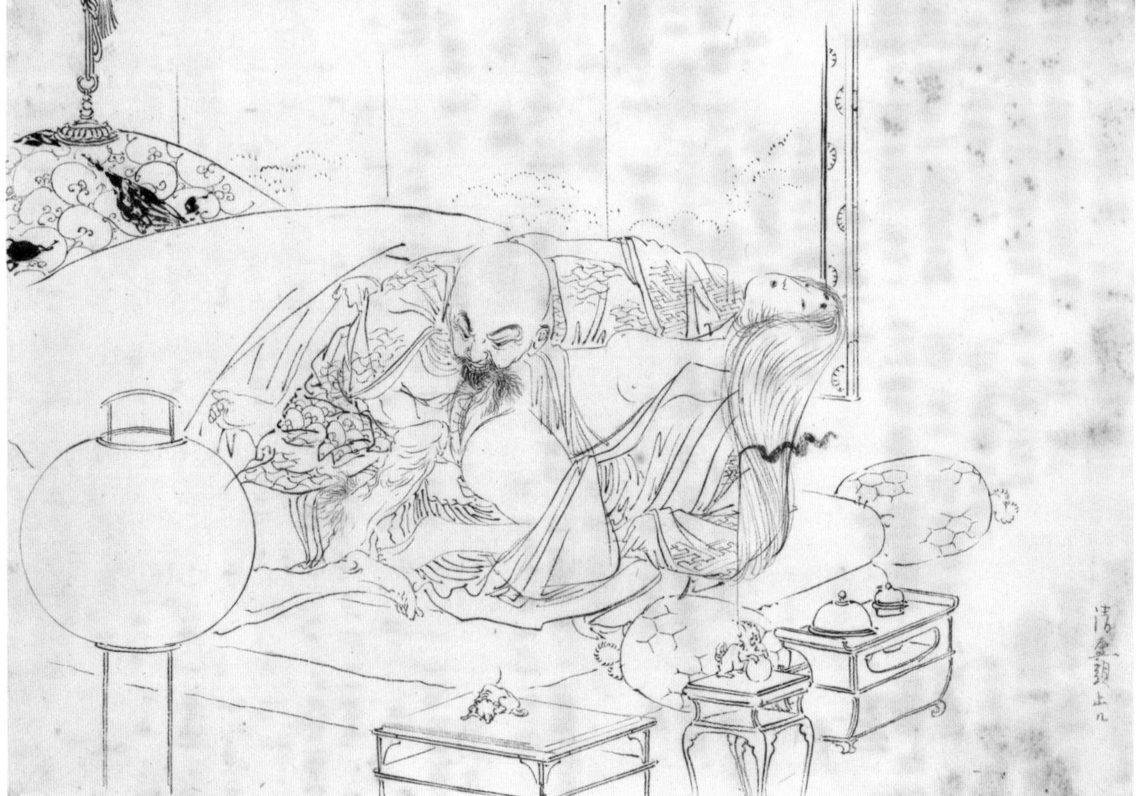

Tsukioka YOSHITOSHI (1839-1892)

Considered the last great master of the ukiyo-e genre of woodblock printing, **Yoshitoshi** is still immensely popular today. It is a constant surprise to me that a print by him can fetch a high price while not being at all rare, while an exquisite rarity by a lesser known artist can get overlooked.

My **Yoshitoshi** 'beauty' is an example, and one of the first bijin-ga I purchased. At the time I really loved this print, although now I find it rather sentimental. Other artists have taken over my affections. It is beautifully printed though.

The print *'Shadows of the Pine Branches'* (1885) is from the series *One Hundred Phases of the Moon* and features a 'beauty' swooning over a shadow. It is an idea that appeals to the sensibilities of the Japanese and we will see another interpretation later.

It was created one year after the 'black ships' arrived, an event that began the process of Japan opening up to the world - thus ending the Edo Period. The Meiji Restoration in 1868 changed the nature of Japanese culture but the arts continued, with the added component of Western influence - which we will see in the next chapter.

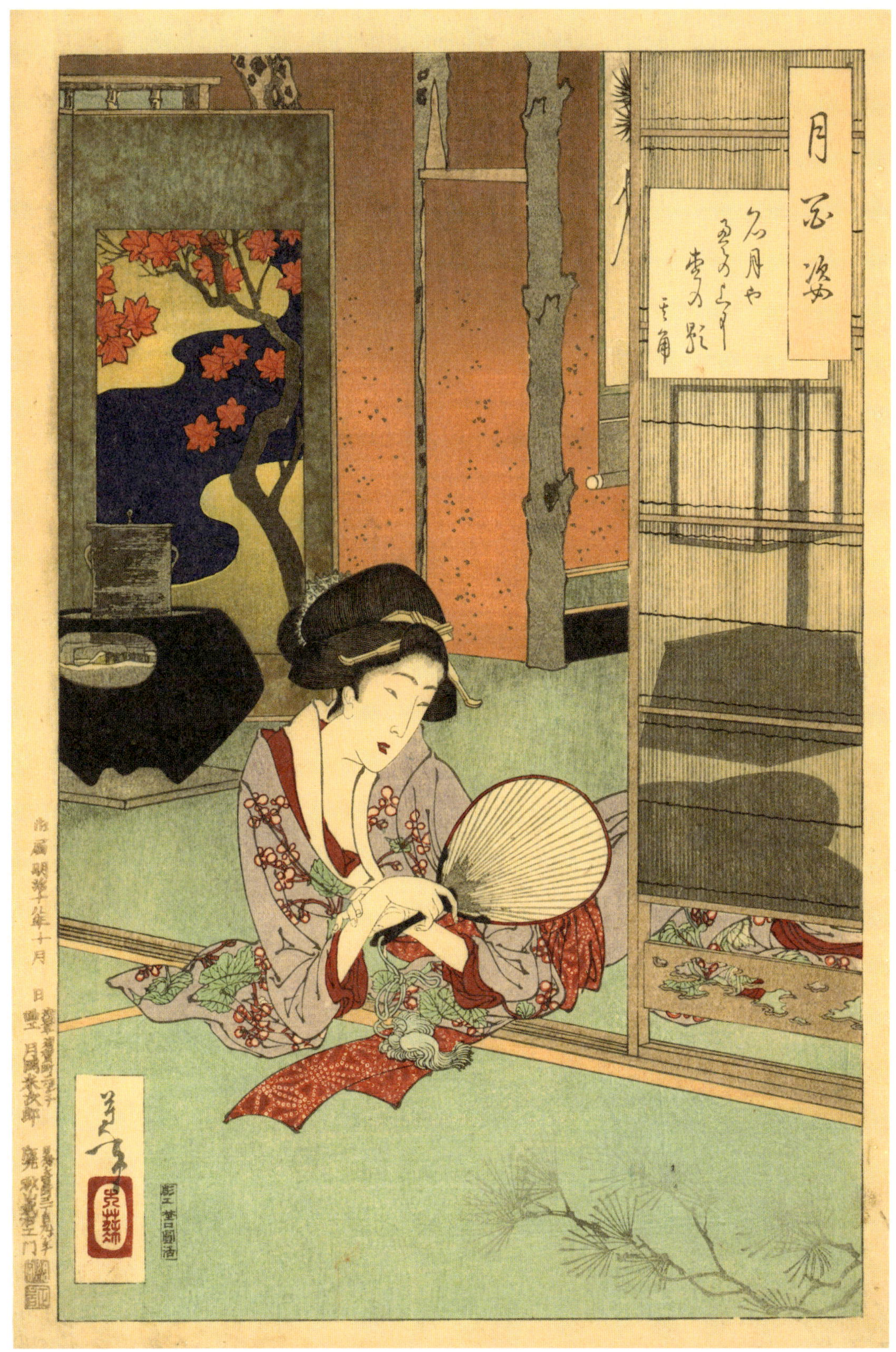

EXTRAS & RUMINATIONS AFTER CHAPTER THREE

Let's review an aspect of the past that we have skirted around. In the Edo Period Japanese society was depicted in ukiyo-e, the pictures of The Floating World. This was a highly eroticised world of art and pleasure, including an indulgence in sex. Mostly this is shown as consensual and for the pleasure of both (or all) participants. We should though look into the darker side too, when this was not the case with many artists we have already met - and a few others. By this I mean from inappropriate behaviour, then grabbing and cajoling, to outright assault and rape.

At the lower end of the scale I'm including this struggle by **Koryusai**, a contemporary of **Harunobu** in the late 1700's. It could just be play fighting - certainly the other woman in the picture doesn't seem too bothered.

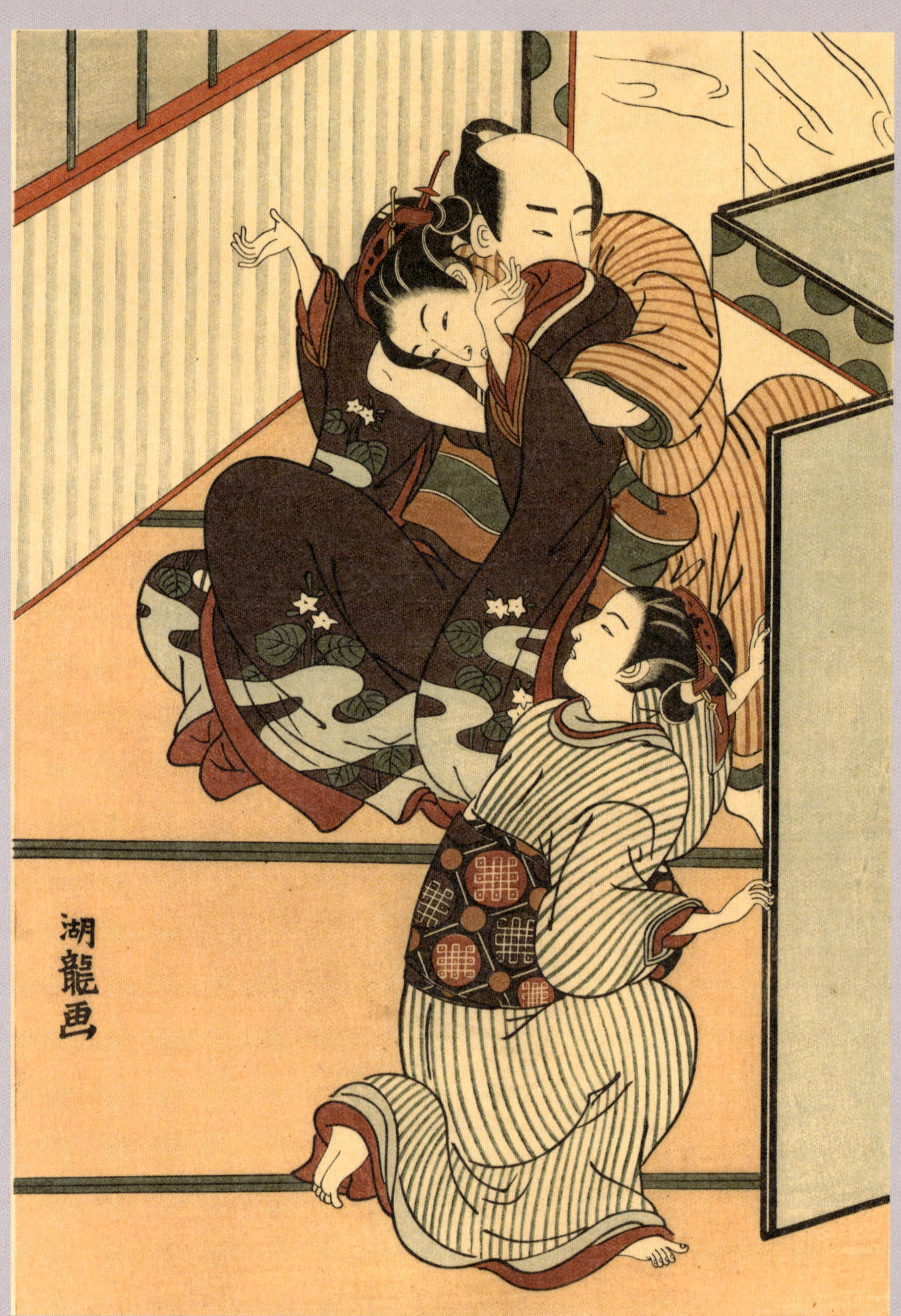

For the next stage we would no doubt see this print by **Eisen** to be depicting a greater degree of unwanted attention. From the series *Grass on the Way of Love* (1825) we see a teahouse waitress as she tries to resist the advances of an amorous customer - with a porcelain cup knocked over in the struggle. The text tells us she is not compliant, protesting 'Somebody might be coming' but he insists 'Take the bottom off' and manages to lift her kimono hem.

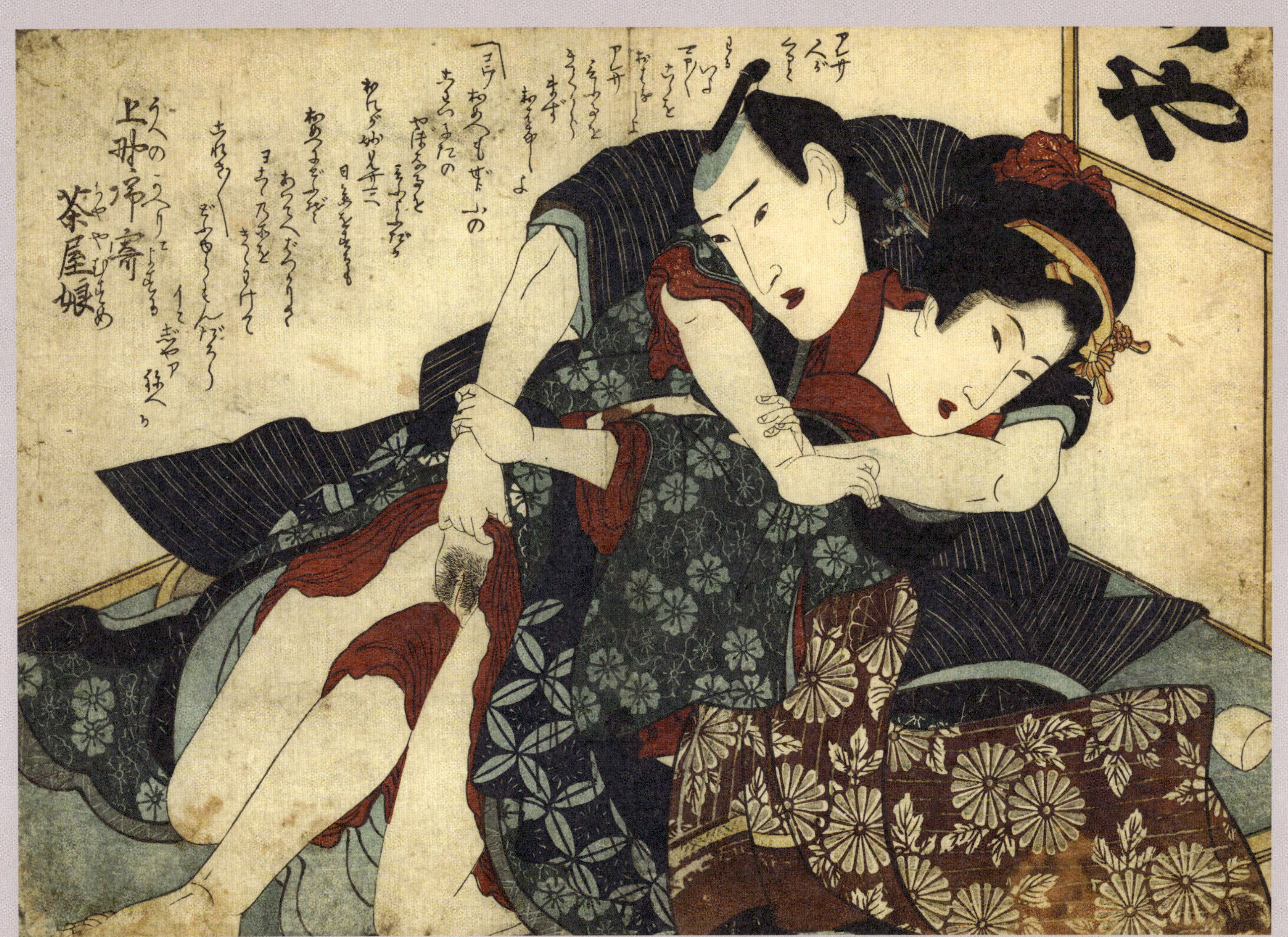

Now we are visiting one of **Hokusai'**s most powerful images - from the series *Young Pine Saplings* which we have already seen (Re: *'The Dream of the Fisherman's Wife'*).

There is no doubt what is happening here - a labourer forcing himself on a young woman. She resists, jabbing her fingers into his face. In the text she cries out 'Don't, don't' and we are told neighbours hear her screams and rescue her.

Hokusai takes care to depict the scene in all it's horror. The man's grotesque face is accompanied by graphically drawn cracked heels and a misshapen member. It has none of the sensuality and harmony of his other shunga - no doubt to make a comment about human nature and the darkness beneath the surface of the male psyche.

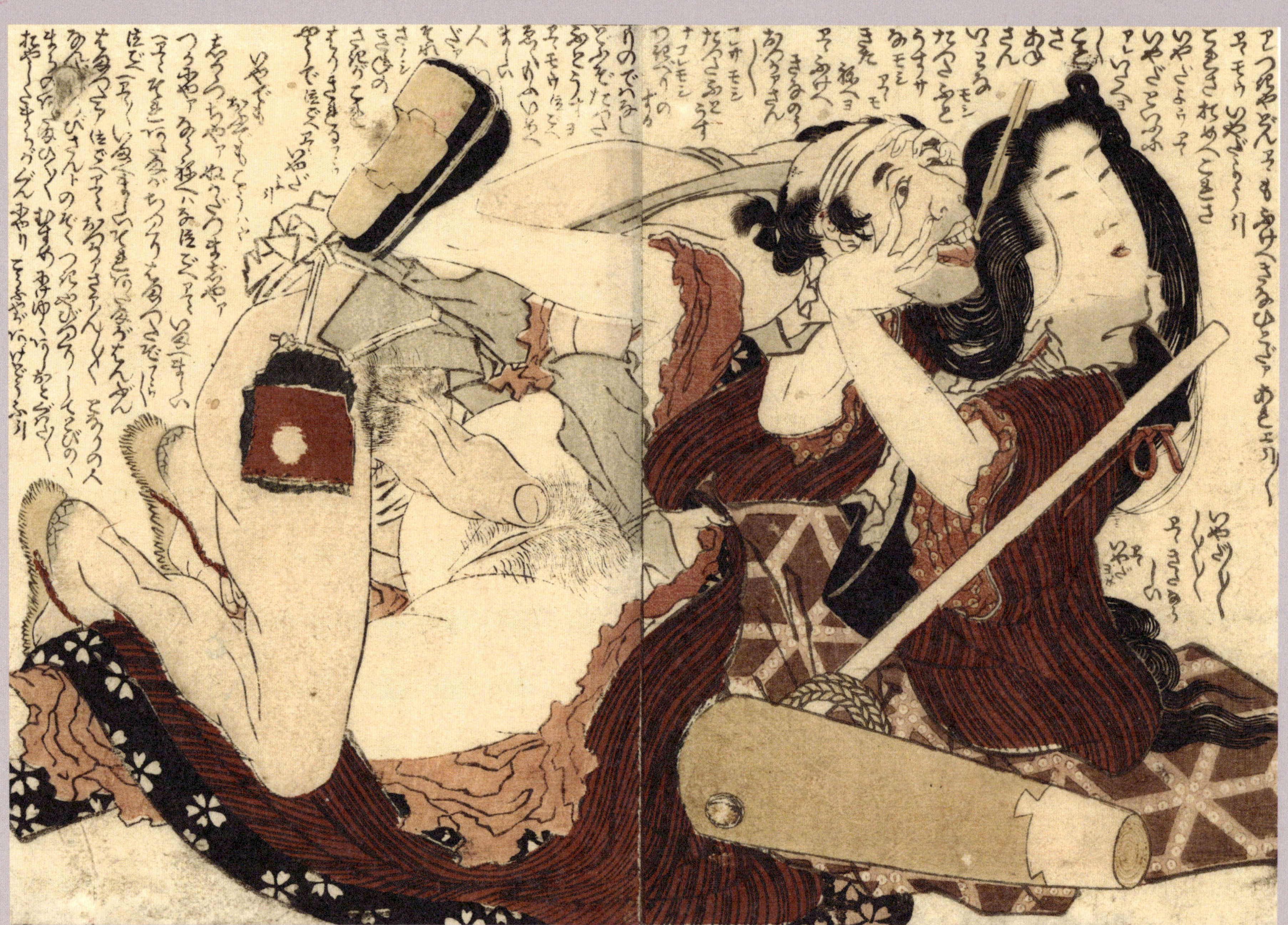

This is another extreme scene, but I don't know who it is by or what the text is telling us. It certainly seems to be a rape - with two ruffians assaulting a woman on a waterfront.

How do we psychologically process such imagery? Can we separate our aesthetic reaction to an artwork from our emotional reaction to the act depicted? Perhaps the artist should be criticised for depicting the topic of sexual violence, or maybe commended for addressing the subject and the ethical issues that on occasions lurk in the subject matter of shunga. And what about the viewer or collector of such images?

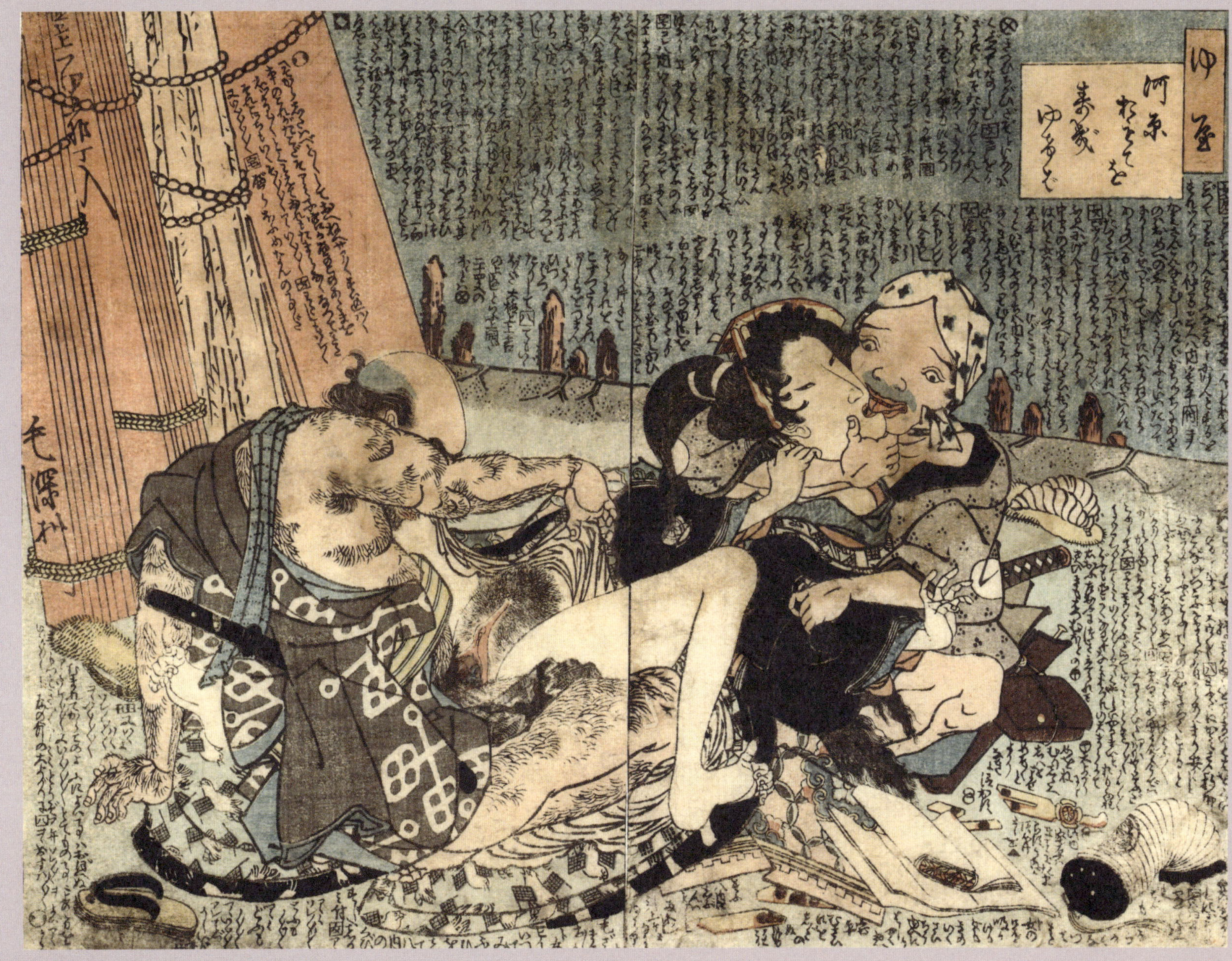

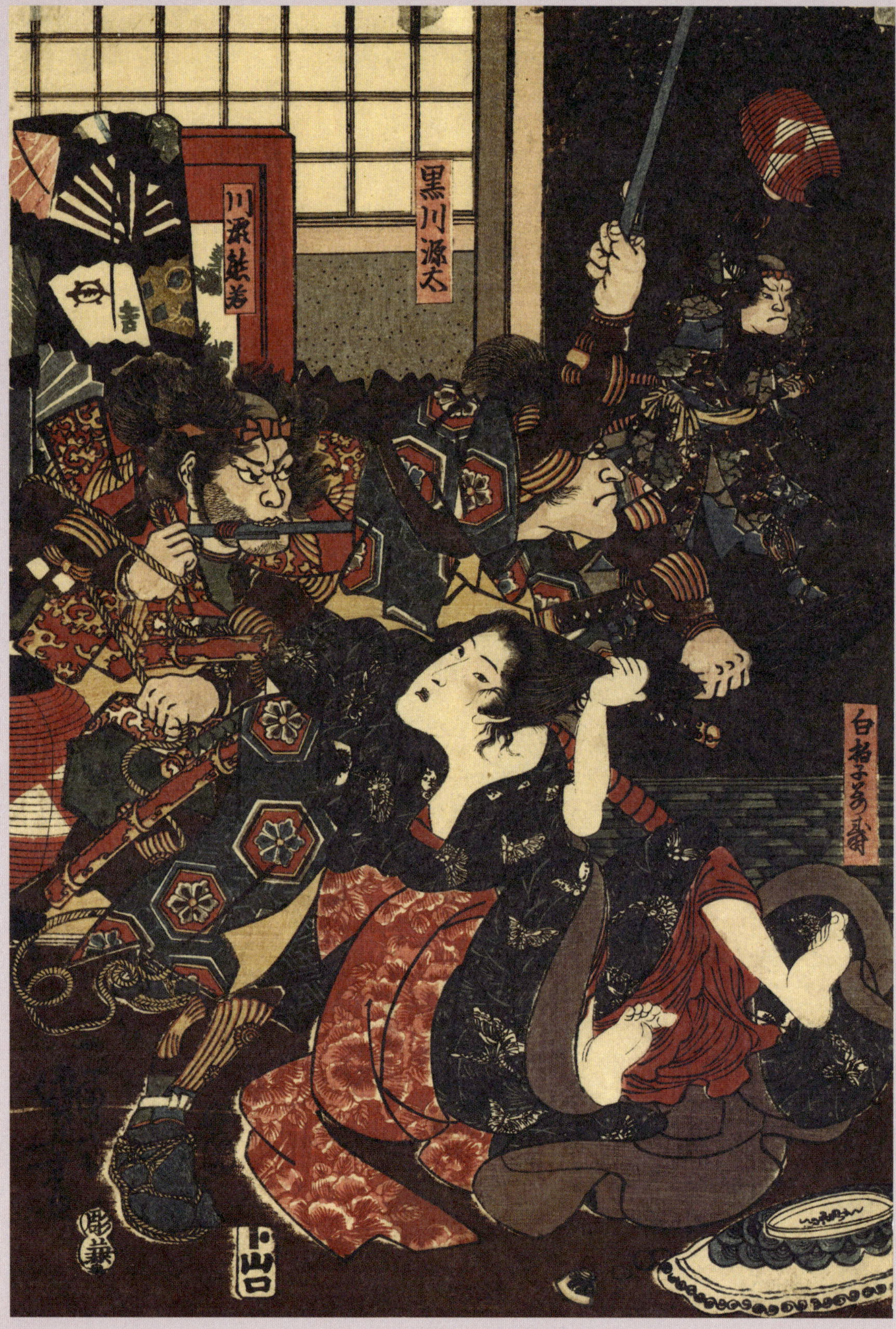

In some works the violence is in the context of other narratives. This would be one sheet of a larger image by **Kuniyoshi**, depicting some battle or other, as he was won't to do. The woman seems to be a spoil of war.

Despite Japan being at peace for so long, there was nonetheless an appetite for dramatising campaigns and battles that took place when the daimyos and samurai terrified the populace - women often being the victims.

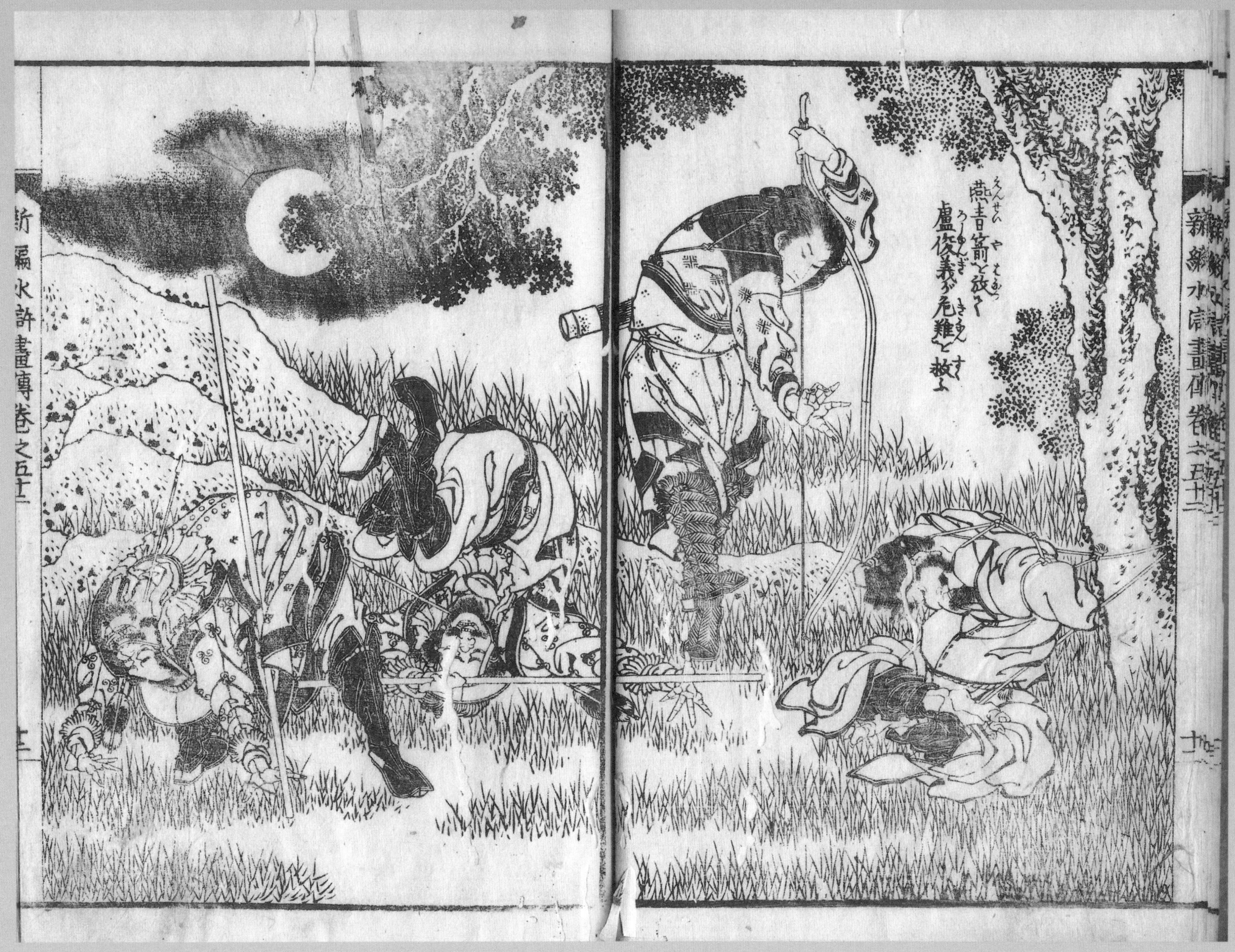

Other influences from the pre-Edo period are noticable in scenes with bondage. Hojojutsu originated with the military and is used here for restraining a prisoner.

The illustration by **Hokusai** is for *The Water Margin*, a classic Chinese story that was also popular in Japan.

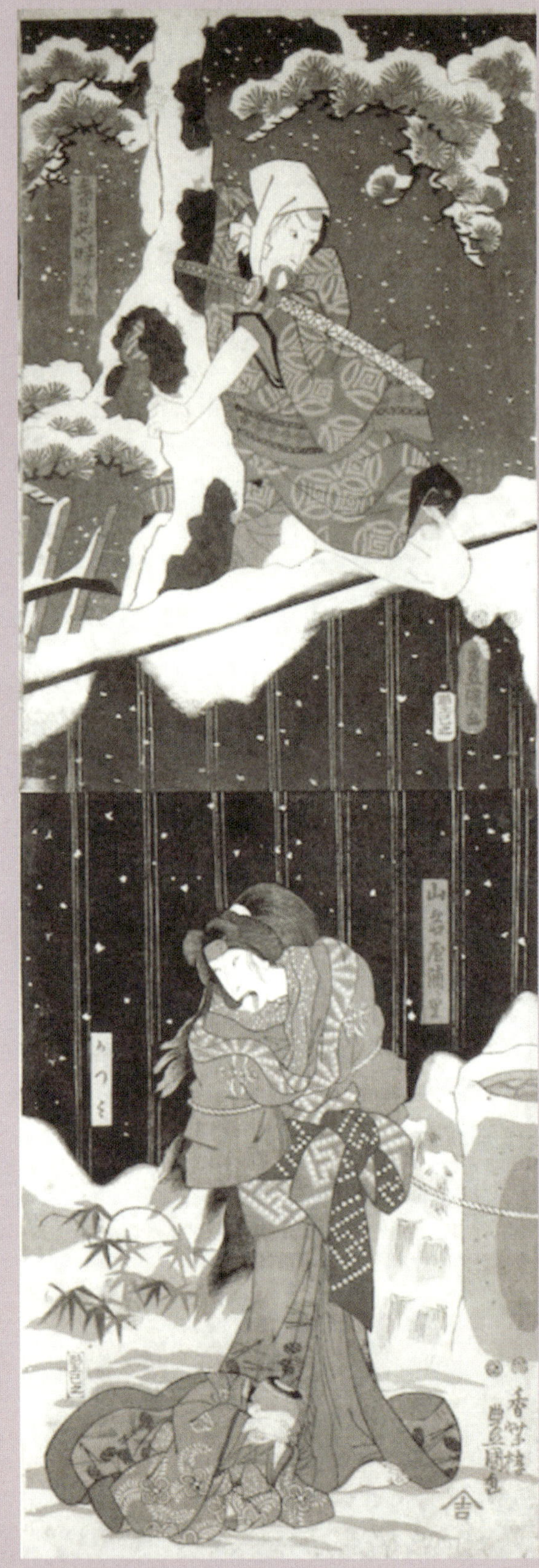
山名屋浦里

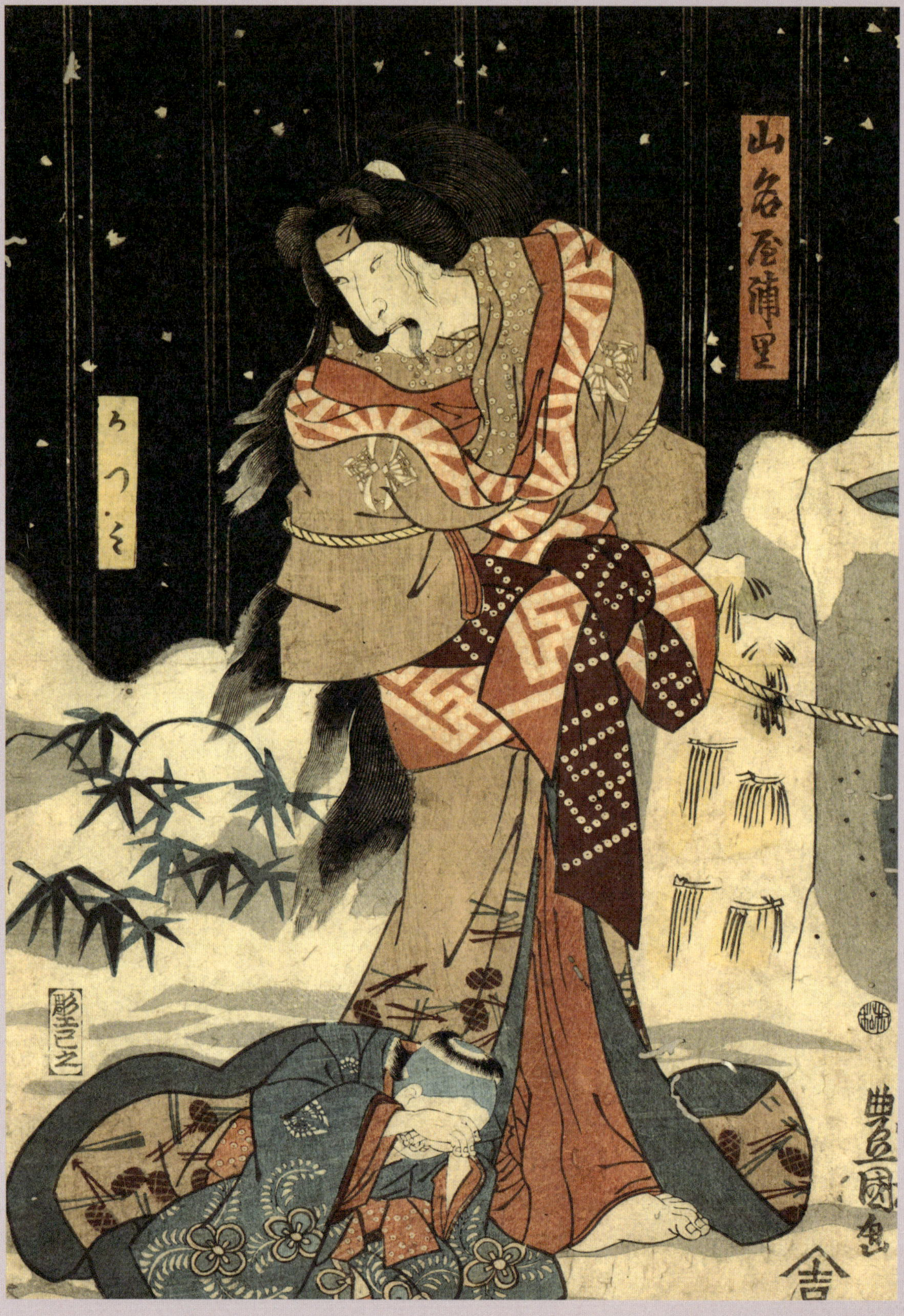

Bondage pops up from time to time and here we can see it in prints by **Kunisada**. *'Snow at Yoshiwara: Urazato'* (c.1857) is a vertical diptych. The two halves tell the narrative but I only have the lower sheet. Ialso have another version, again by **Kunisada**.

The story of Urazato was popular with Kabuki audiences. The plot tells of the doomed love affair between the prostitute Urazato and her samurai lover who cannot afford to buy her out of service. They have a child together and plan to escape. As punishment Urazato is bound with rope and put out in the snow. She is given water by her young daughter (from the butt on the right in both images) whilst her lover waits in a pine tree above. He rescues her but they have nowhere to go and they jointly commit suicide that same night.

Whenever this story is told Urazato always has a strand of hair in her mouth.

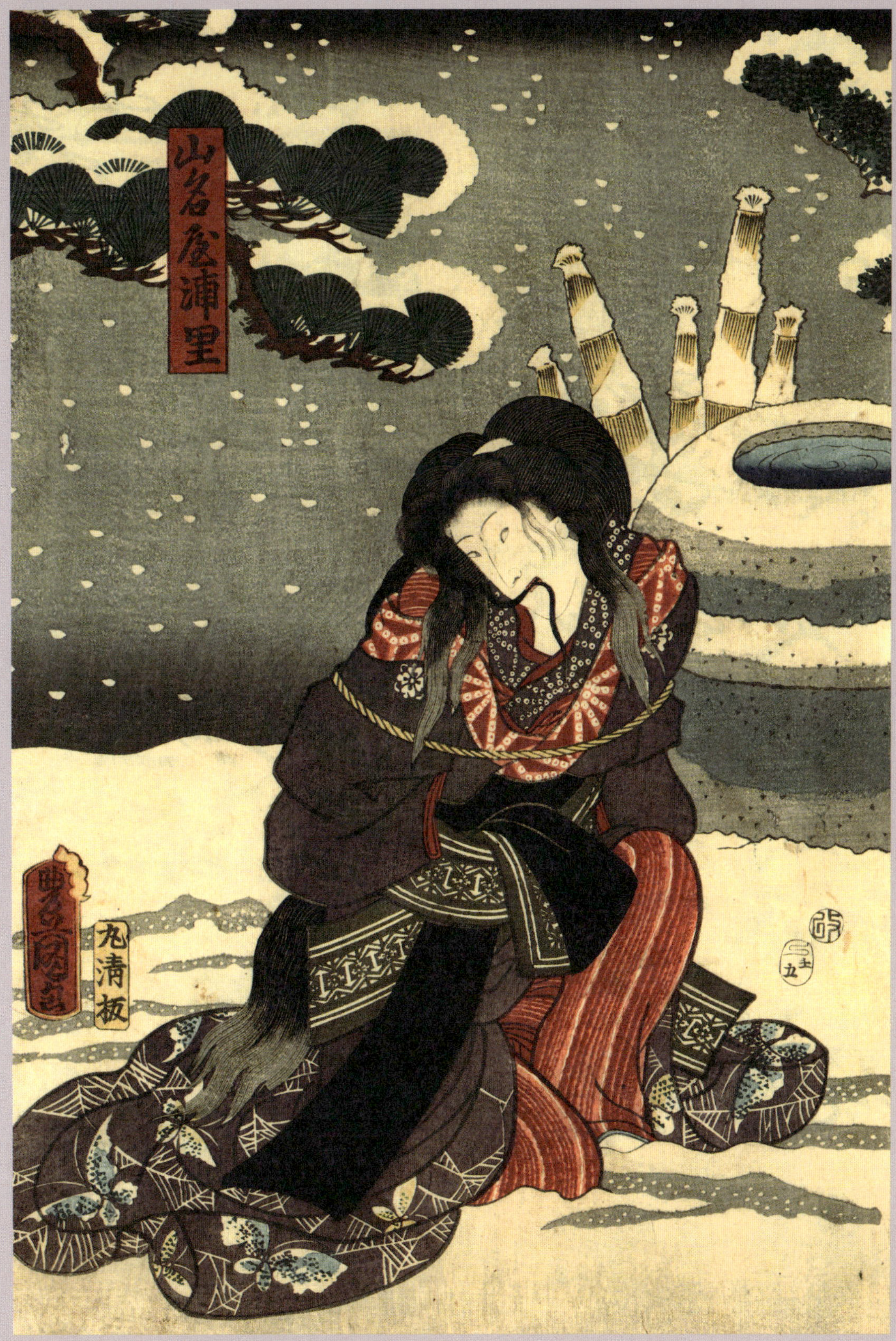

Seiu ITO (1882- 1961)

The hair in the mouth can also be seen in this much more recent print by **Seiu Ito**.

He is renowned as the father of kinbaku (the Japanese art of rope bondage), translated as 'the beauty of tight binding'.

Seiu Ito was a 20th century Tokyo artist best known for his sado-masochistic and bondage erotica. He produced prints, paintings and photographs and is revered among kinbaku enthusiasts. Many of his works were lost in the firebombing of Tokyo in 1944 and as a result, his prints are rare and highly sought after.

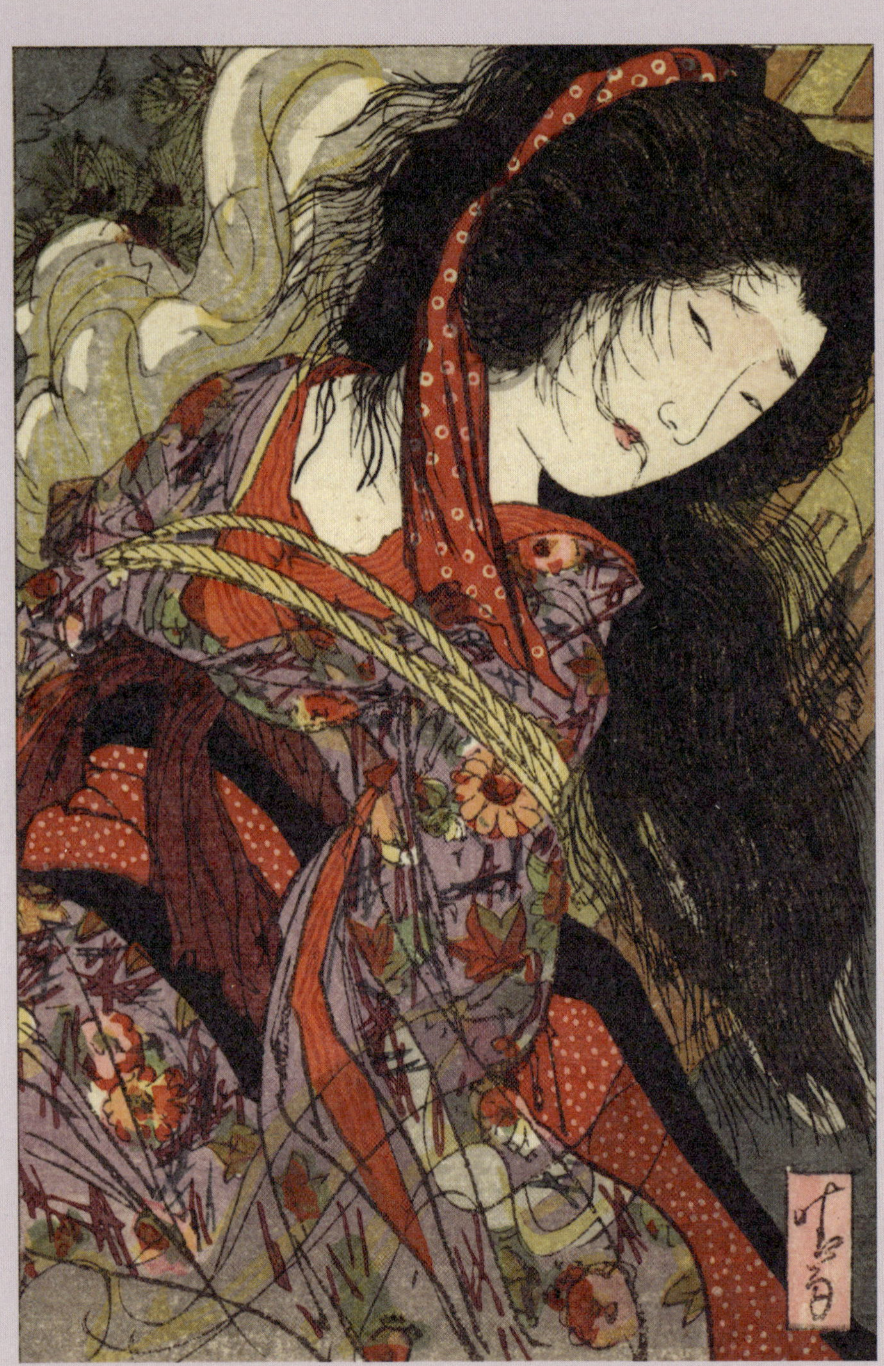

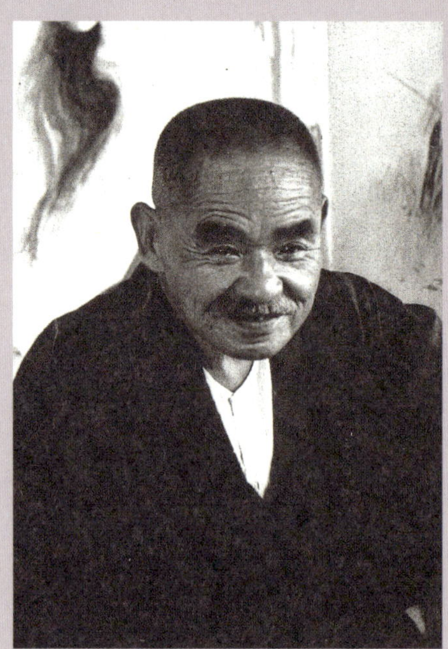

Taking inspiration from long gone predecessors is common in Japanese prints, with ideas, narratives and images constantly recycled as is the case here.

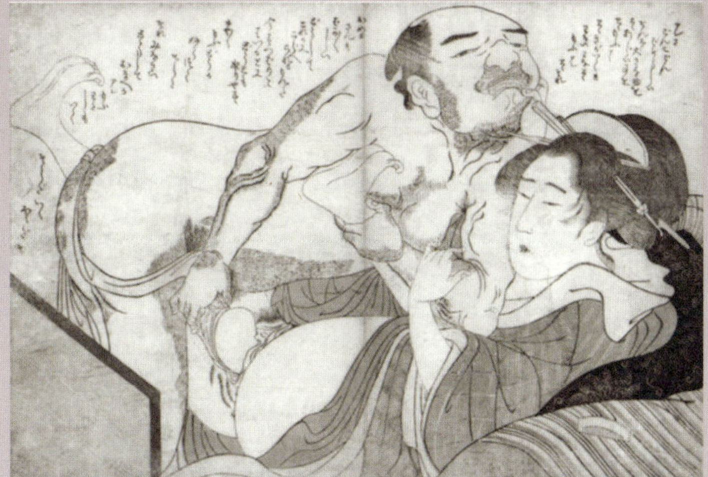

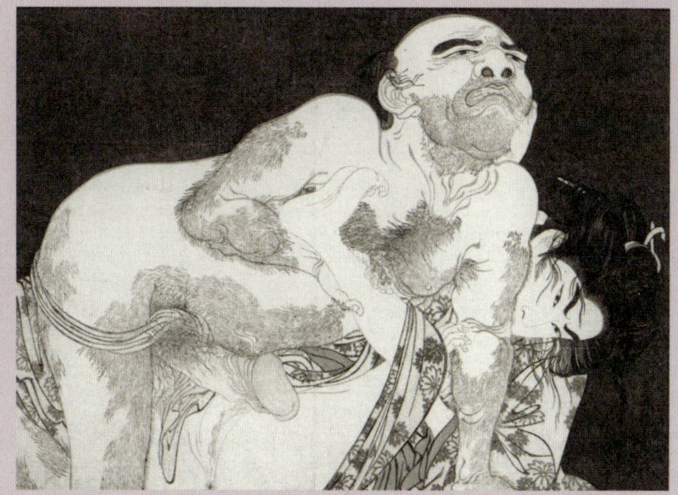

This rape scene by **Ikeda Terukata** (1900) is based on a famous print by **Eiri** in the series *Models of Calligraphy* (1801) which is very similar to an image by **Utamaro**, from *Poem of the Pillow* (1788) - in which the woman appears to bite the man's arm.

There is a fascination with sexual violence expressed in some shunga and bijin-ga which is almost a tradition. It filters down the generations and from artist to artist. It is a little puzzling why this should be. Is the **Ikeda** a homage to **Eiri**? Not quite copying but updating in the modern style. What does this say about the male artist's view of women as we enter into the 20th century?

More about **Ikeda Terukata** in chapter 4.

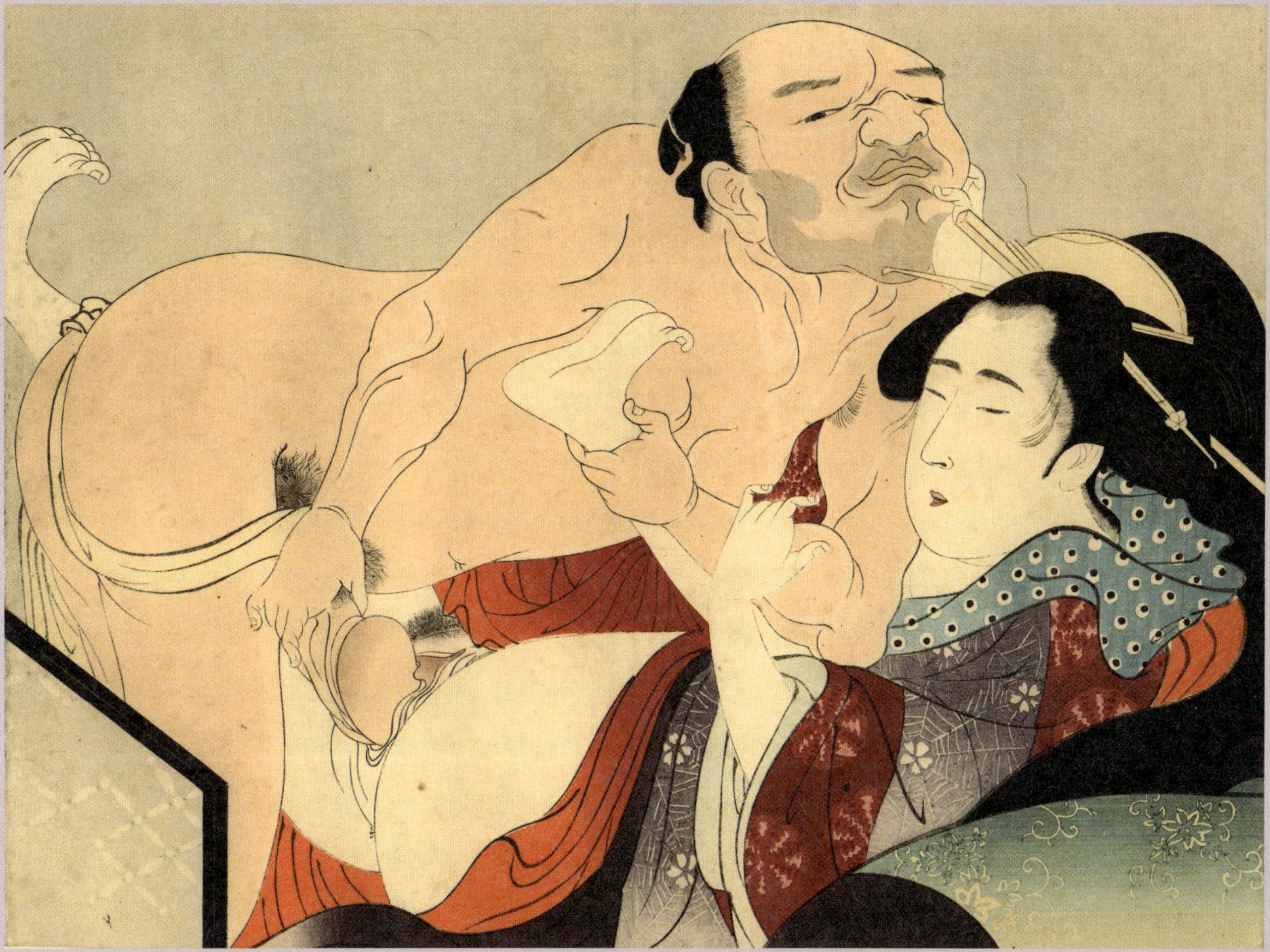

Chapter 4

A NEW BEGINNING

the turn of the century onwards - to the end!

WE WILL GO where so many writers on the subject fear to tread. By this I mean that many enthusiasts and collectors won't go near the work created in the early Mejji period, let alone anything just before or after 1900. It was a time when a new vision was required to keep the art of woodblock printing alive and various artists did just that at the turn of the century. I find some of the prints created then to be really wonderful and want to start showing examples from an artist we just left in RUMINATIONS.

Ikeda TERUKATA (1883- 1921)

We have just seen **Terukata**'s version of a rather challenging **Eiri** shunga. He must have liked doing this, or perhaps he was commissioned, because this is another (1900).

As before It is inspired by **Eiri**'s series *Models of Calligraphy* (1801) which was in turn 'borrowed' from **Utamaro**'s series *Poem of the Pillow* (1788).

Terukata was part of a shift in attitudes towards shunga during the westernisation of Japan at the end of the 19th century. Artists rejected the depictions of the pleasure quarters seen in earlier shunga and embraced the art-form as a representation of an exoticised 'Bohemian Parisian culture'. There is rarely any text within the images so backgrounds are sparse. The screens and trappings of bathhouses, tea parlours or private quarters are removed or minimised, leaving only the graphically drawn figures.

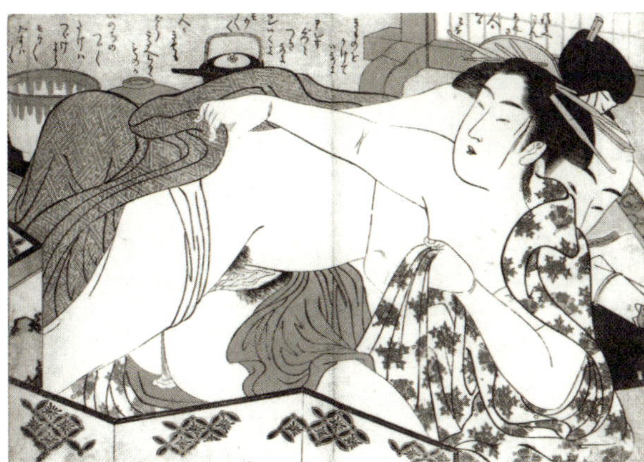

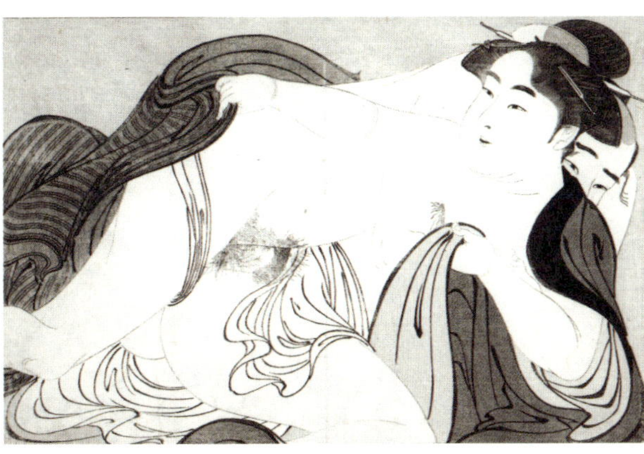

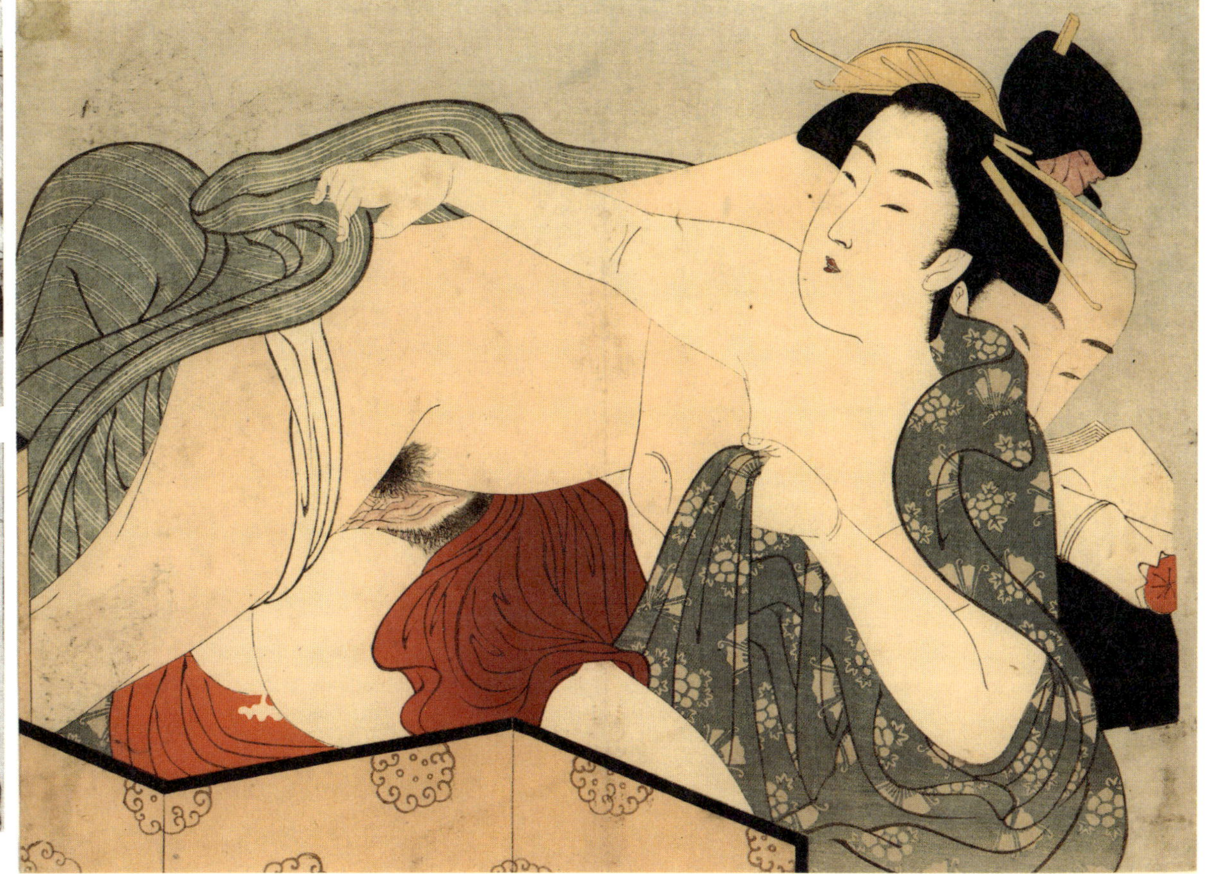

I have two prints that are, as far as I know, original concepts. The pictures tell the stories - but here are a few words anyway.

They are both about female gratification. In the first print the woman seems to be lost in attaining sexual pleasure, while the man is distracted and not engaging - except for giving attention by toe. I love the dramatic sweep of the bedcover.

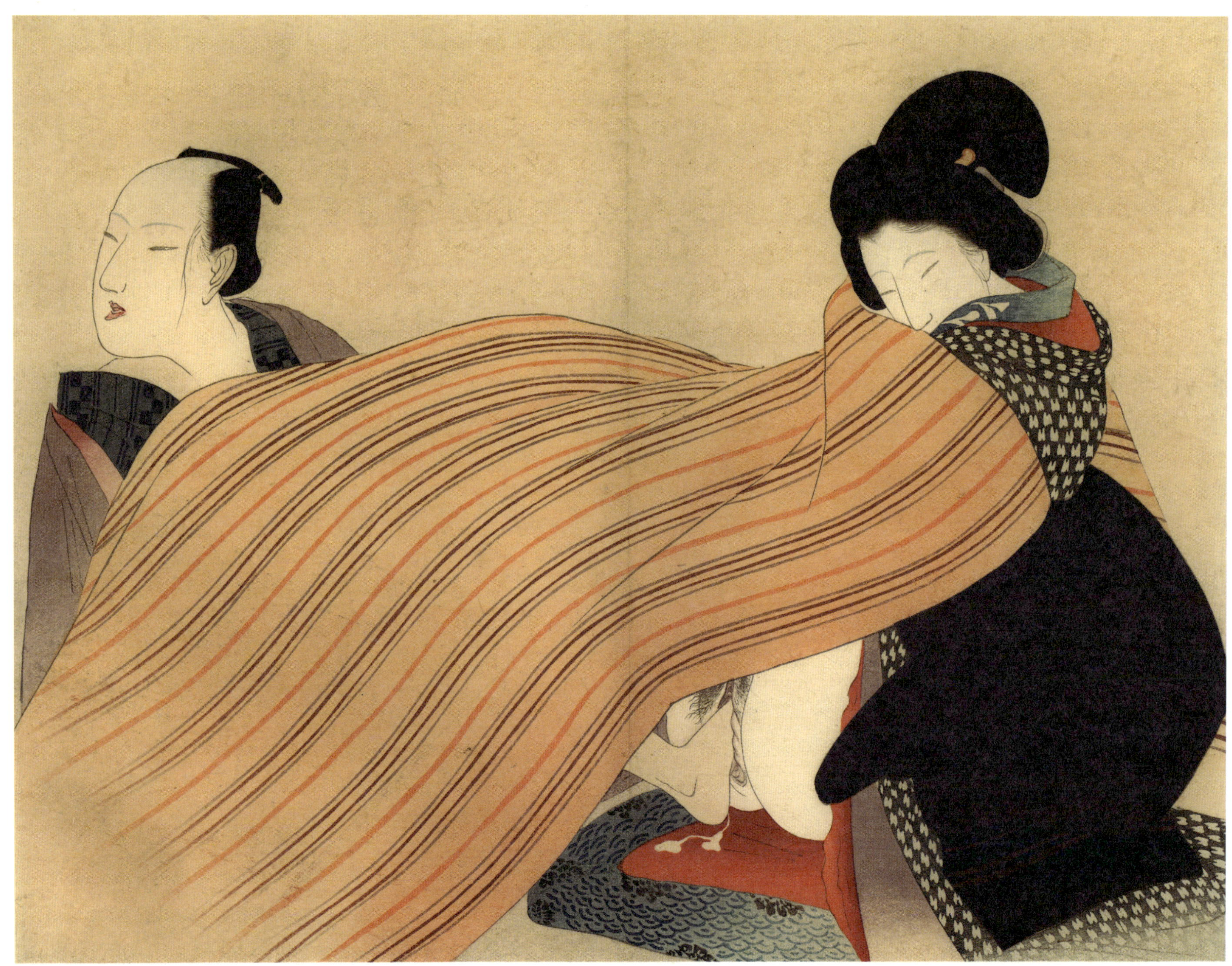

In the second print the woman is getting pleasure by arousing her man with an obscene image in a shunga publication (porn mag).

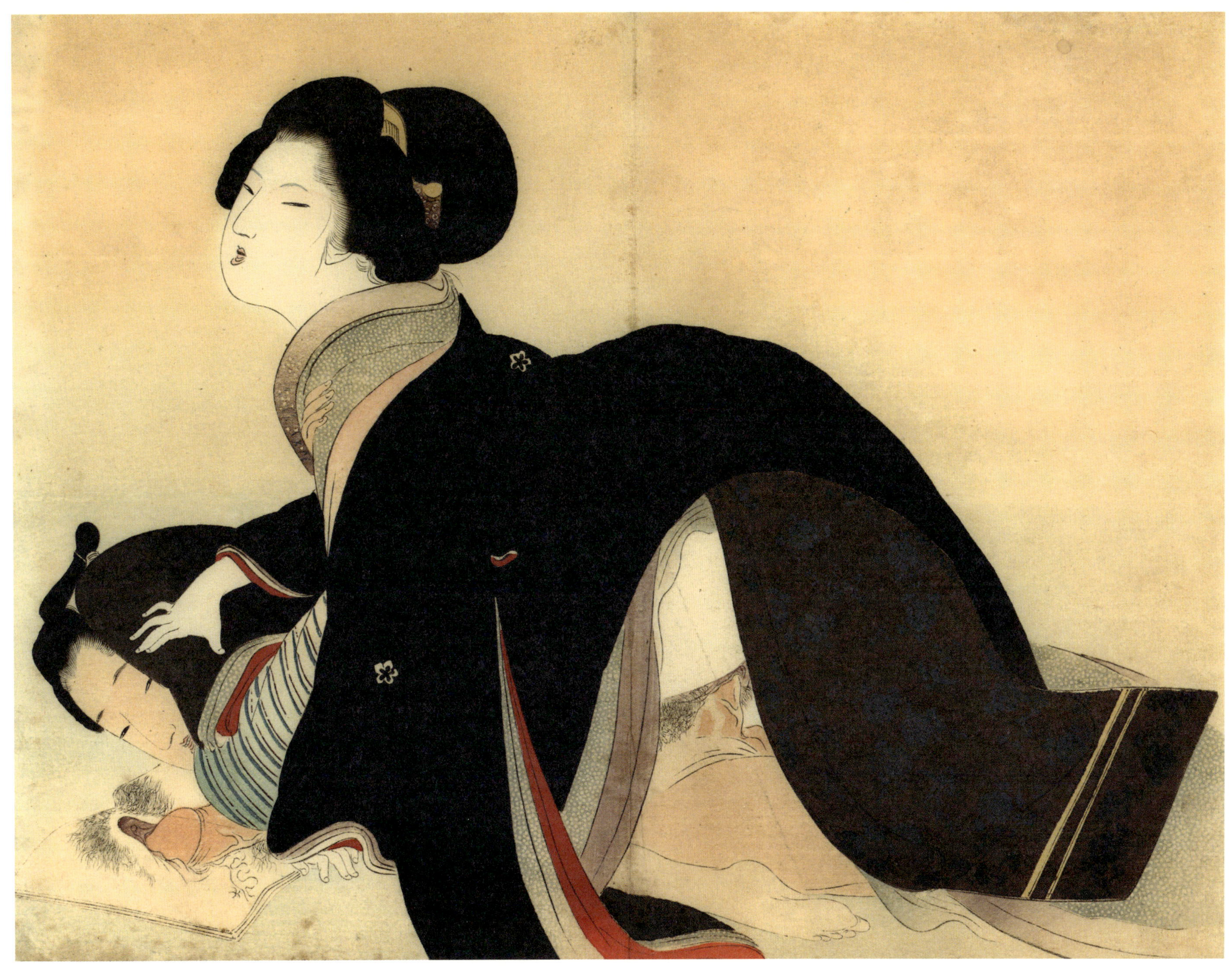

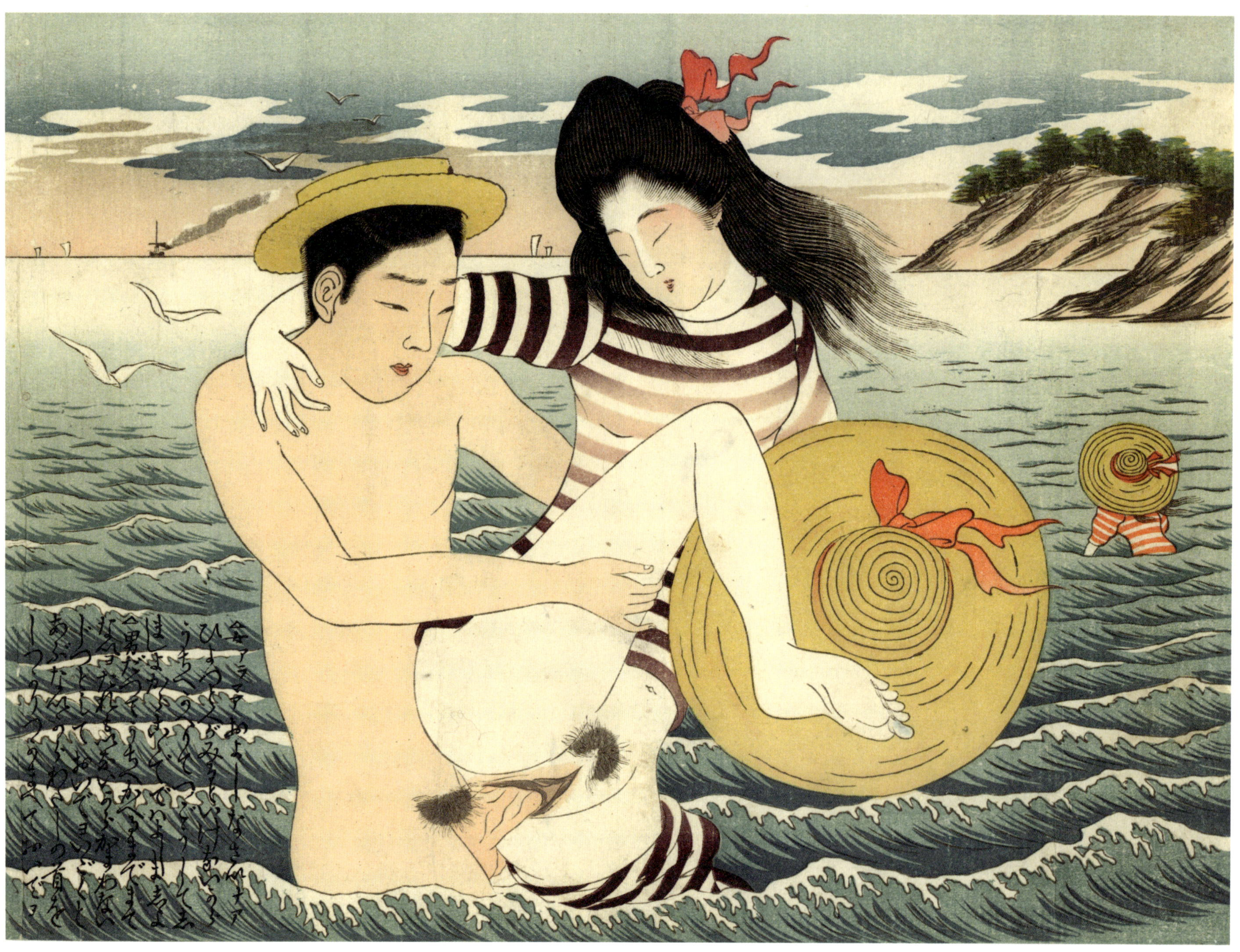

Terasaki KOGYO (1866-1919)

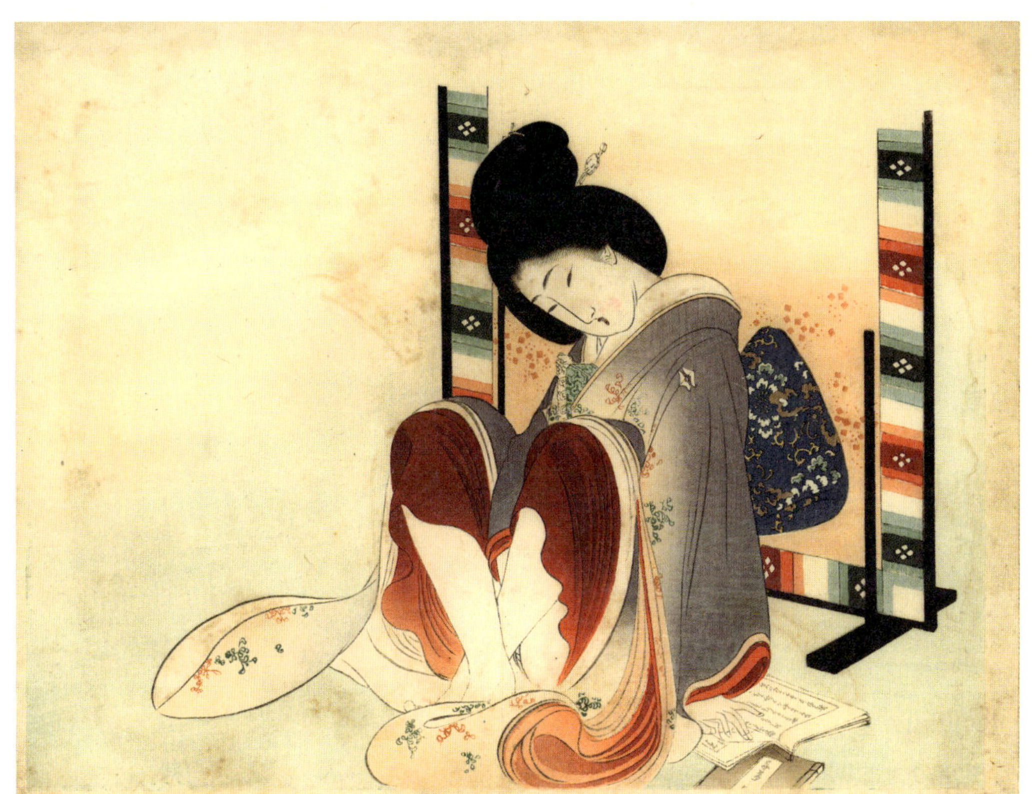

On the left is an iconic Meiji shunga from 1900, which expresses much about the changing culture at the turn of the century. Seaside bathing had only recently become accepted and was seen as an opportunity for women to socialise with men and show off their figures in fashionable bathing suits.

In this case the woman has inflamed her partner's passion as the text indicates. She says: 'Stop! Someone might see. We should go home'. He replies: 'I can't wait 'til we get home. There's no-one around, it's fine. But mind your footing, and hang on to my neck'. He presumably hasn't noticed the other bather.

I believe this to be a lithograph on crepe paper. It comes from a set of twelve and considered typical of late Meiji erotica - with it's bright colours, unusual scenario and characters.

Tomioka EISEN (1864 - 1905)

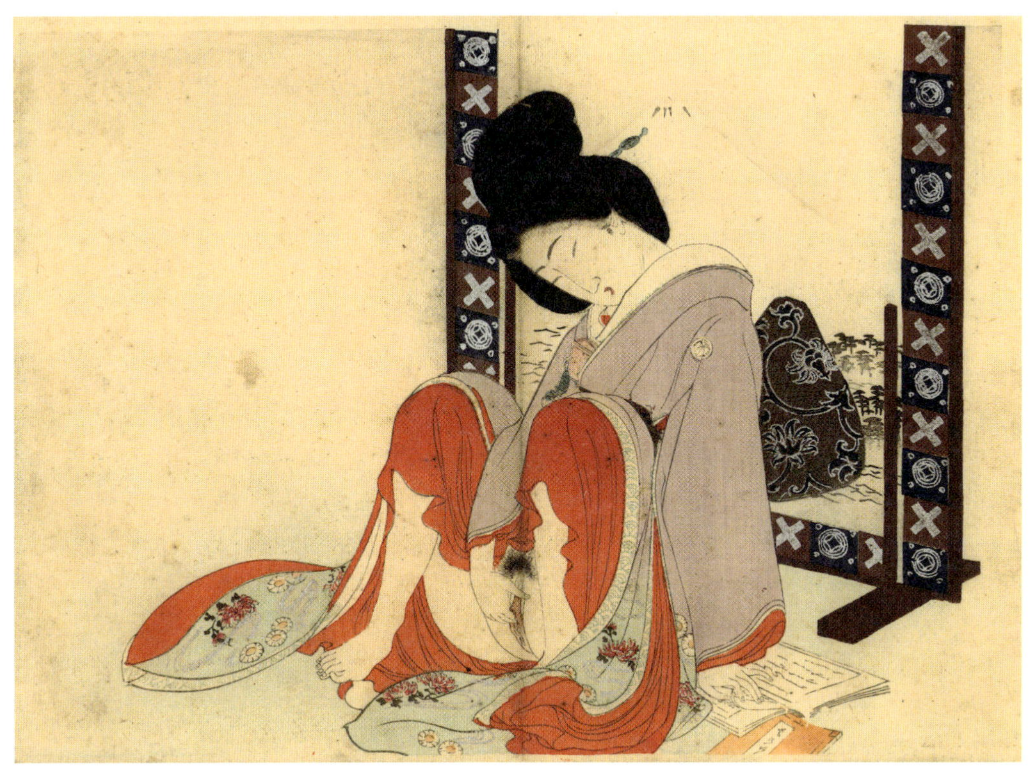

A contemporary of **Terukata** was **Eisen**, an interesting woodblock artist of the late Meiji era. On this page, the images are taken from two different sets of twelve, both named *Poetic Intercourse.*

They are about female gratification, using the idea of a women pleasuring herself - but one is more explicit than the other.

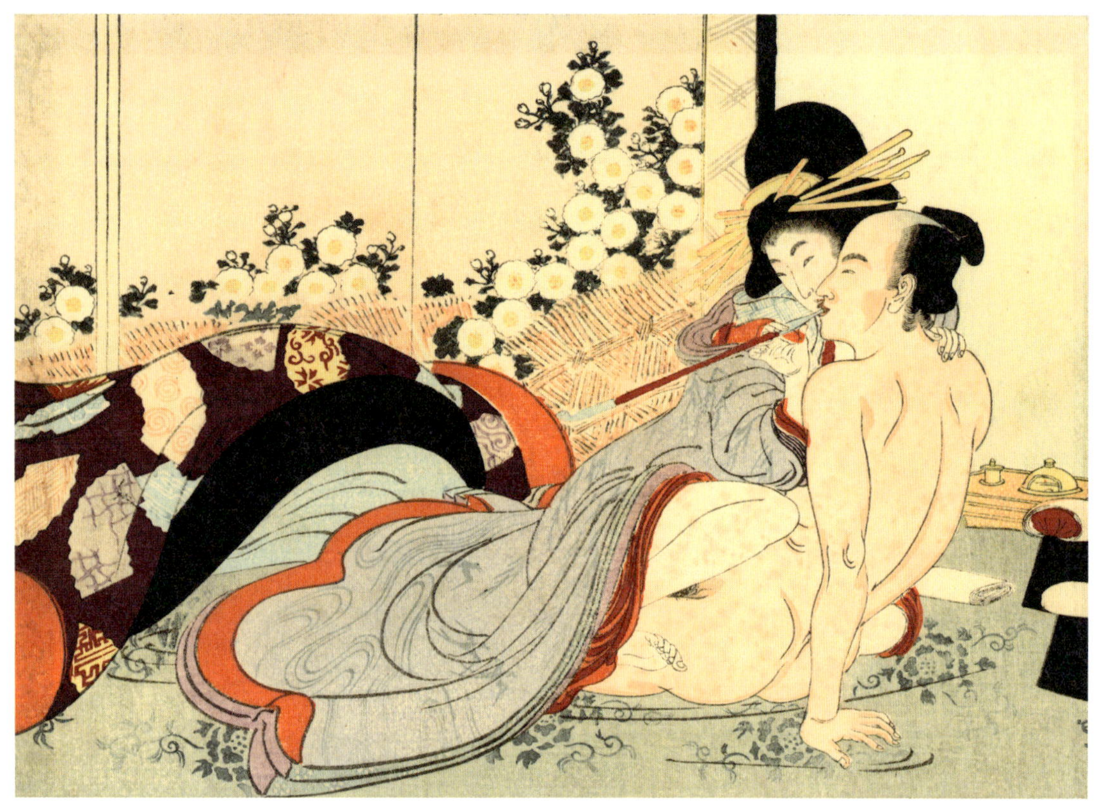

I don't know much about these two small shunga of about 1900. The one at the top is of a couple smoking after making love. Below is a couple being spied on by a rather excited voyeur!

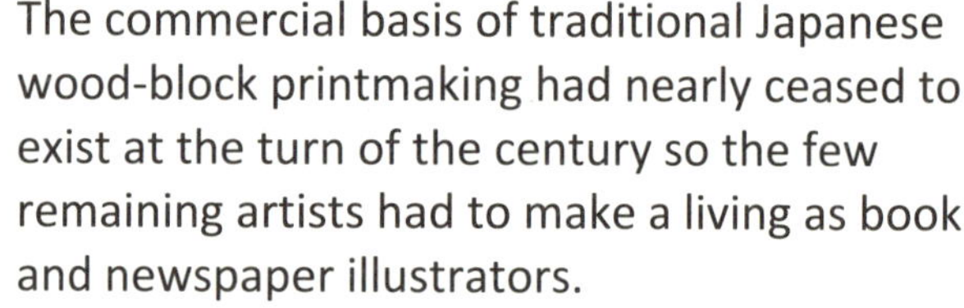

The commercial basis of traditional Japanese wood-block printmaking had nearly ceased to exist at the turn of the century so the few remaining artists had to make a living as book and newspaper illustrators.

On the facing page is a fine example of what was known as the kuchi-e print given the title *'Beauty with Umbrella'* (1902). The woman has a grey umbrella and pauses, as if to acknowledge someone passing in the other direction with a brown umbrella. I've seen this image reproduced on a greeting card.

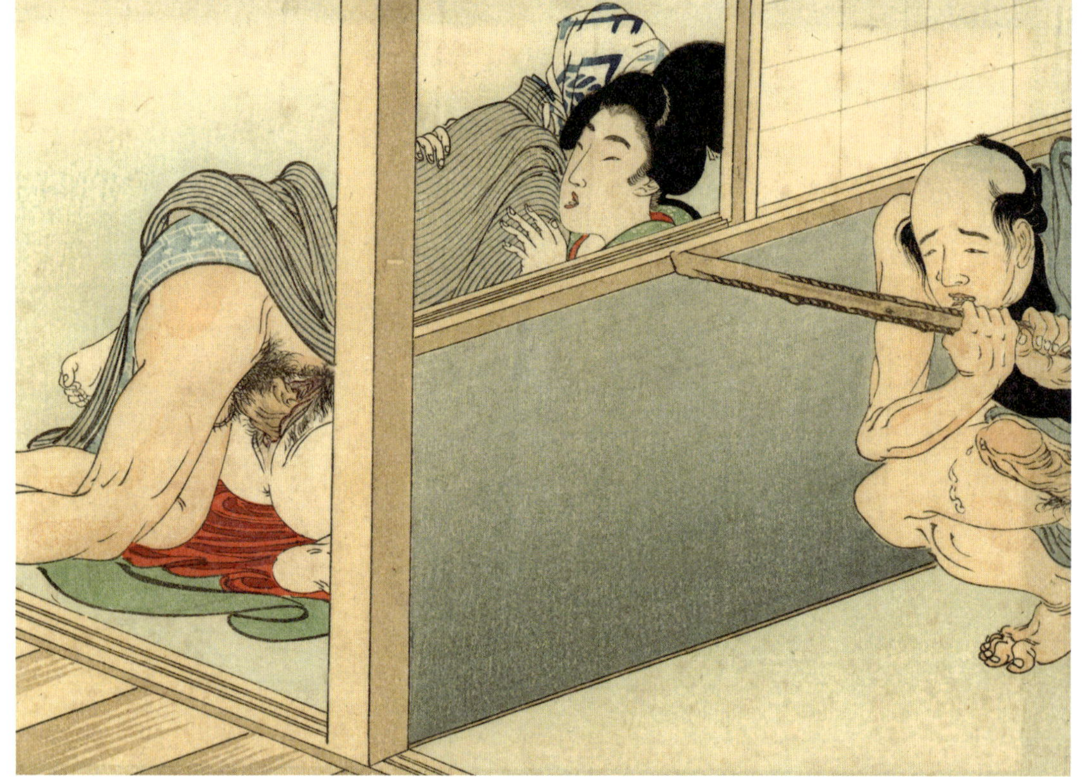

Kuchi-e prints were woodblock frontispiece pictures used in the publication of Japanese novels and magazines. Most were of women and continued the tradition of idealised 'beauties' whilst reflecting the artistic movement towards more western design.

They always have two folds, because of their insertion in a magazine or book as an illustrative print. As popular art they have been ignored by academics and collectors until relatively recently. Now they are taken more seriously - but nonetheless tend to be inexpensive.

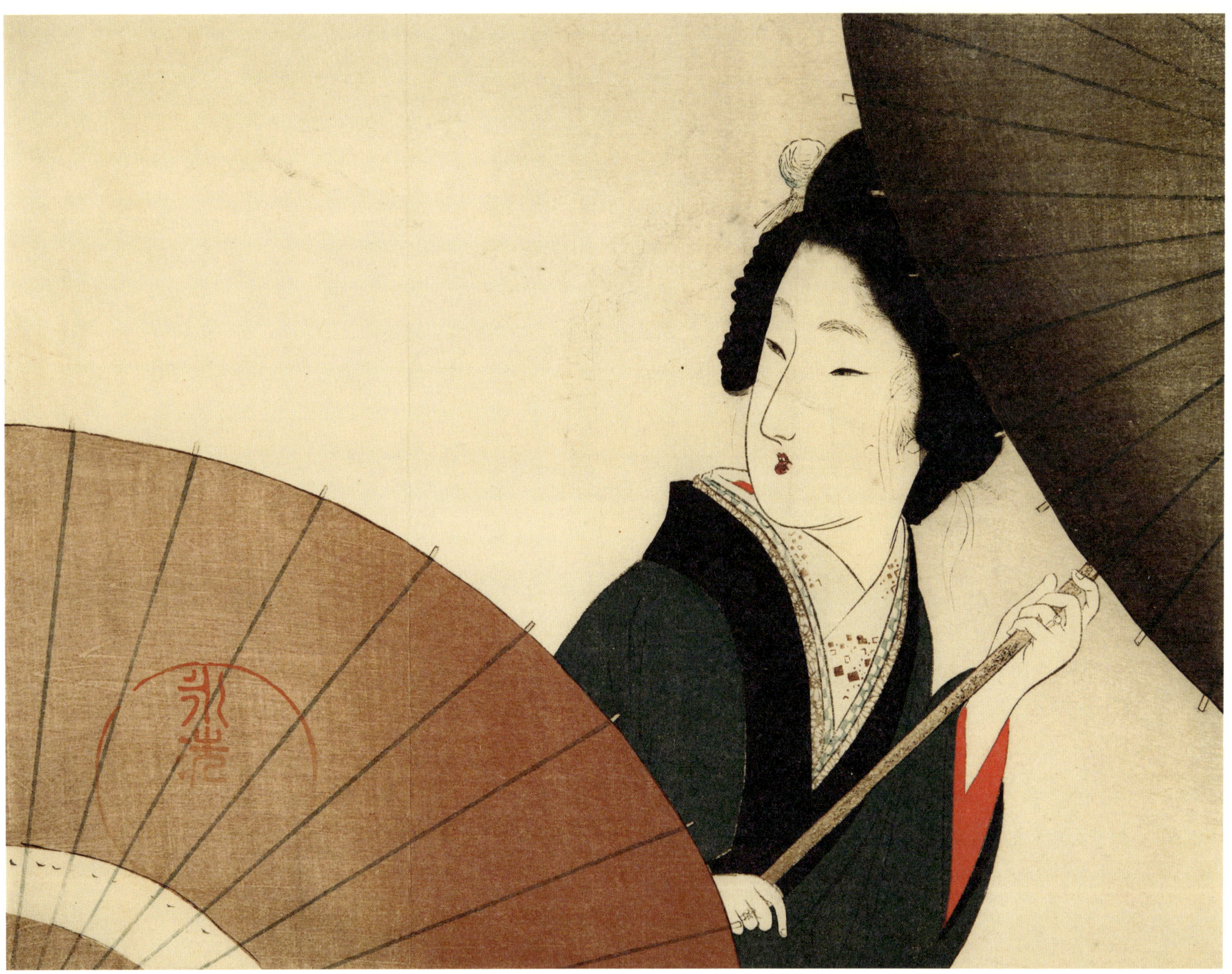

Another kuchi-e print is of two young girls (future beauties) carrying offering trays for the Doll Festival display during Girls' Day. The older girl holds a black lacquered bowl on a red and black tray, ready for placing on the display shelf covered with red cloth. She smiles over her shoulder at her younger companion, who offers a set of miniature dishes. Behind them the folding screen features a flowing stream and cherry blossoms.

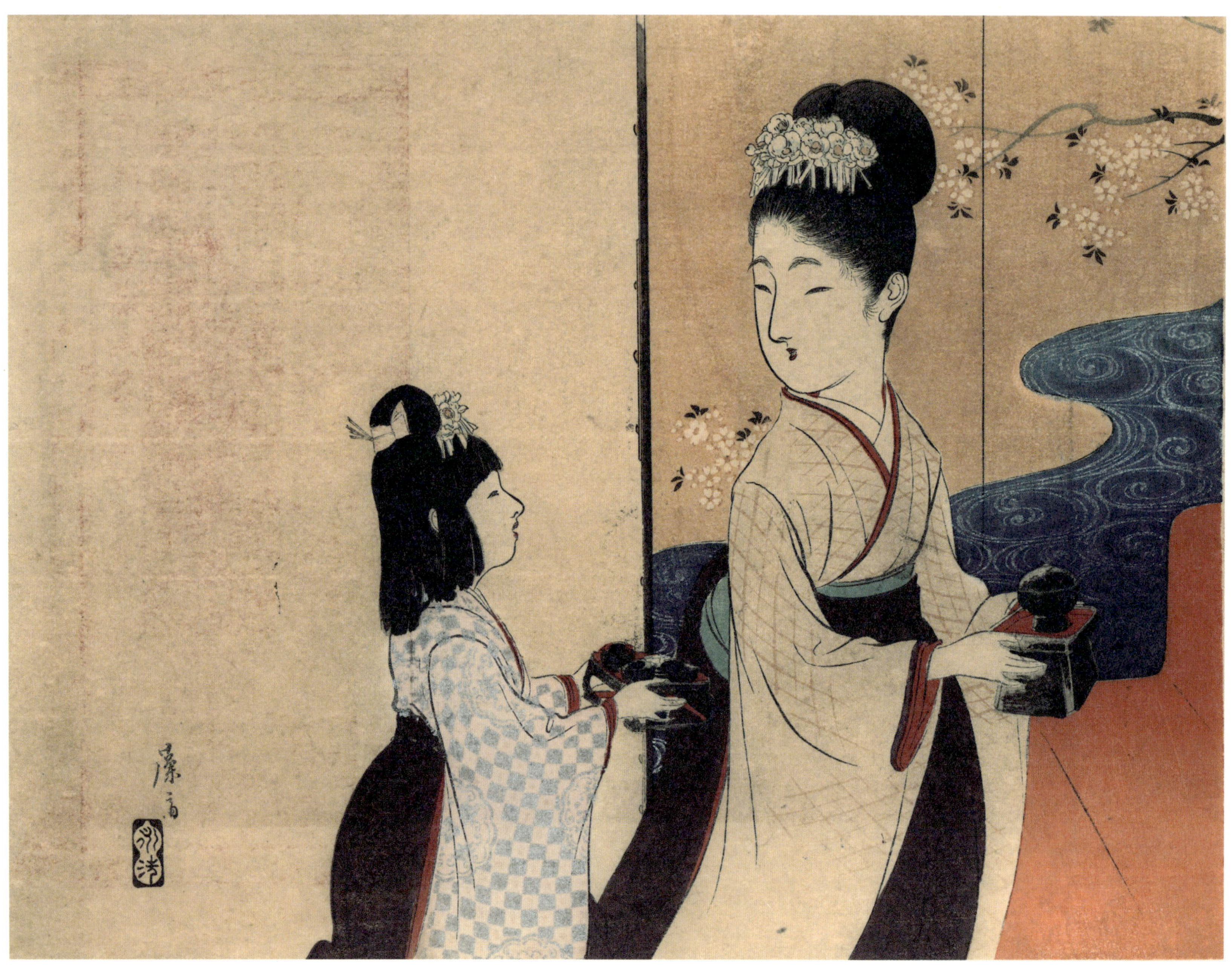

Mizuno TOSHIKATA (1866 - 1908)

Toshikata was a student of **Yoshitoshi** - seen in the previous chapter. He also taught his colleague **Terukata**. This kuchi-e print by him is an illustration for the novel *Jakko-in Temple* by Miyake Seiken. It is depicting the 12th century Empress Tokuko, who became a nun following the death of her five-year-old son. She is shown wearing formal court dress with layers of exquisite kimono, her long dark hair flowing over her shoulders. A finely drawn image in the background shows two nuns at the temple where she retreated from the world. The print is beautifully detailed with touches of silver mica in the kimono fabric and burnishing in the black hair.

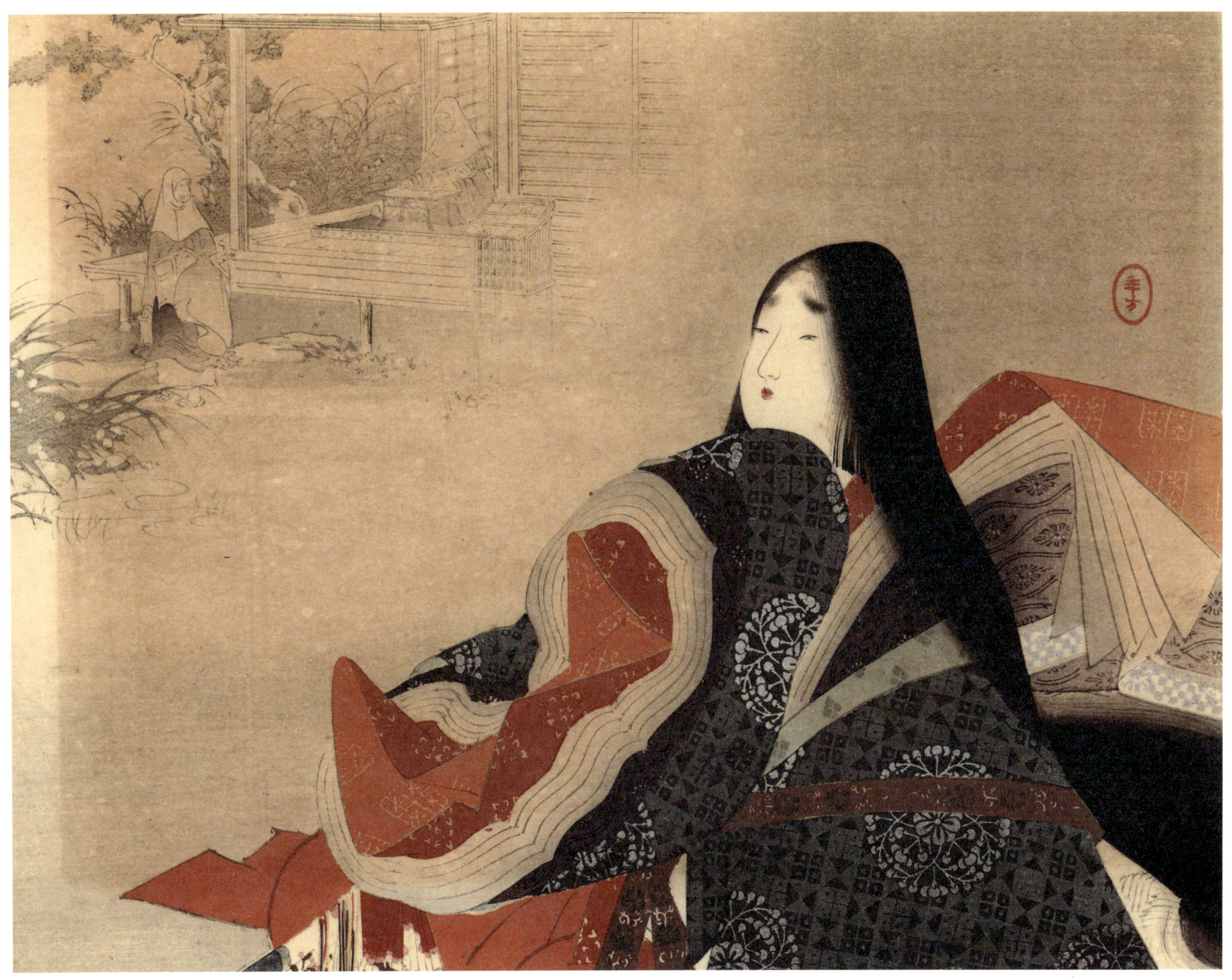

Another kuchi-e print by **Toshikata** uses the same idea we saw in the **Yoshitoshi** print- a 'beauty' swooning over the moon shadow of a pine sapling.

It is interesting to see the differences in composition, partly brought about by the required landscape format - and the brightness of what would have been a dark moonlit interior.

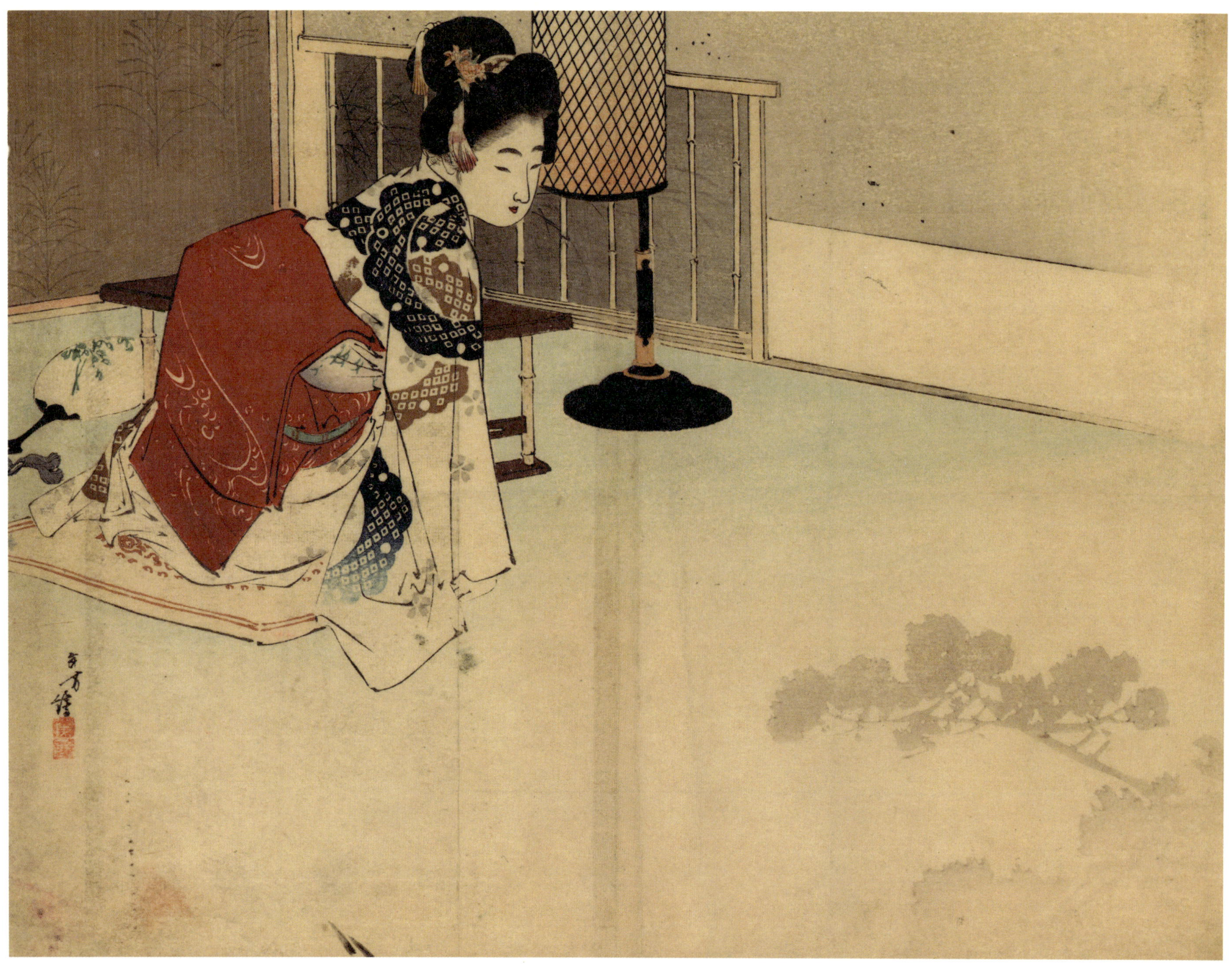

UNKNOWN ARTIST - 20th Century

The print here come from a couple of decades later - and I don't know the artist. It is a design from a series published in 1921, *The Loyal Ronin.* Based on the famous tale of the *47 Ronin*, it illustrates a scene from this classic story of honour and revenge *The Removal of Yosenin, Naganori's Widow, from the Mansion of Tepposu.* It has a wonderful 1920's vibe that breaks free from the look and style we have just seen. It belongs to a new movement known as **shin hanga.**

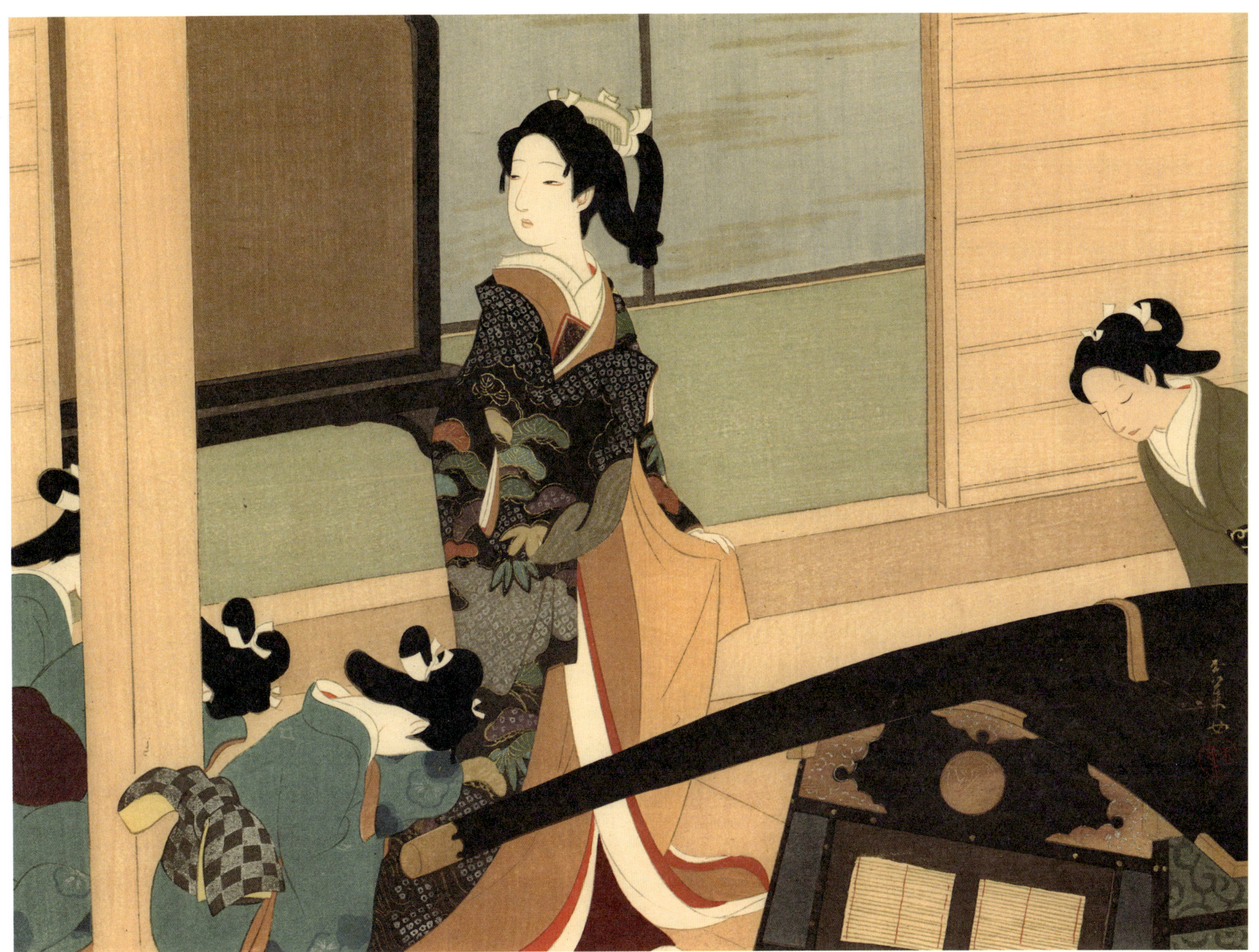

Shin hanga was an art movement in early 20th-century that revitalized traditional ukiyo-e art rooted in the Edo and Meiji periods. Influenced by western art it is hated by many purists, but loved by great numbers of other Japanese art enthusiasts.

I don't go for most of it myself but I do like the strangeness of these two prints from the series *The Complete Works of Chikamatsu Manzaemon.* He authored more than 100 plays, mainly for the bunraku puppet theatre, including historical romances and domestic tragedies, often based on true events.

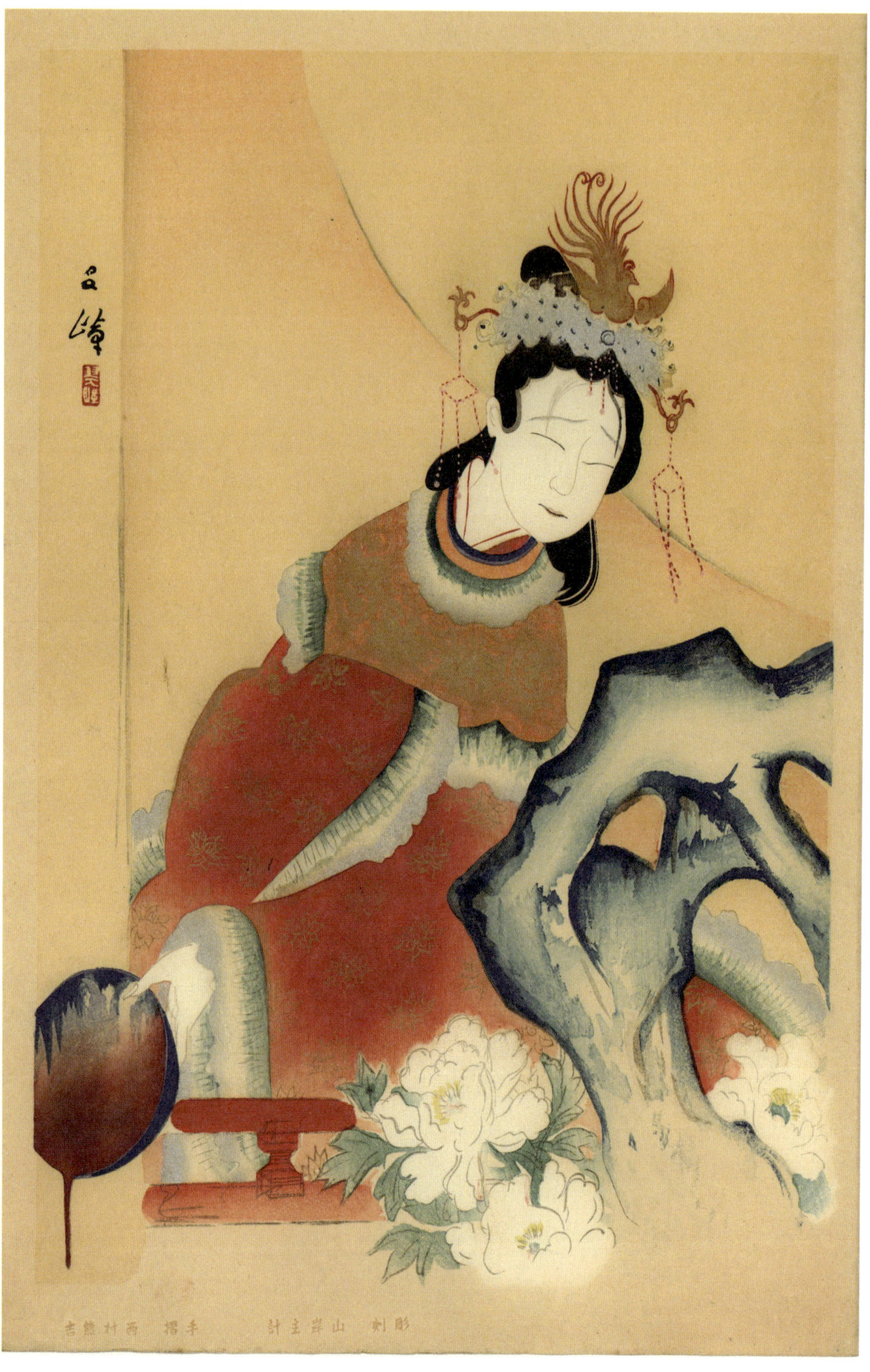

Suisho NISHIYAMA (1879 - 1958)

'Kokusen'ya Kassen - A Lady in Chinese Costume' (1923) is a portrait of the 'beauty' Kinshojo, pouring a cup of her own blood into the river in a scene from the play *Kokusen'ya Kassen.*

The warrior Watonai traveled to China to help restore the Ming Dynasty seeking the assistance of his half-sister, Kinshojo, who was married to the opposing general. To signal the results of a plea, Kinshojo was supposed to pour either white pigment for success, or red pigment for failure, into the river. As Watonai watched outside the castle, the anguished 'beauty' signaled defeat with her own blood, committing suicide. Dressed in exotic, elegant robes trimmed with ruffles, Kinshojo bows her head slightly, her eyes tightly closed.

The print is detailed with silver and gold mica in the robes and headdress, with embossing and hand-applied pigment. A beautiful but extremely dark and disturbing picture by an artist primarily known as a painter.

Shima SEIEN (1892 - 1970)

Shima Seien was one of two female artists who worked on the *Manzaemon* series. '*The Heroine Yugiri* ' (1923) is a fantastic image of the ghostly Yugiri from the play *Yugiri Awa no Naruto*.

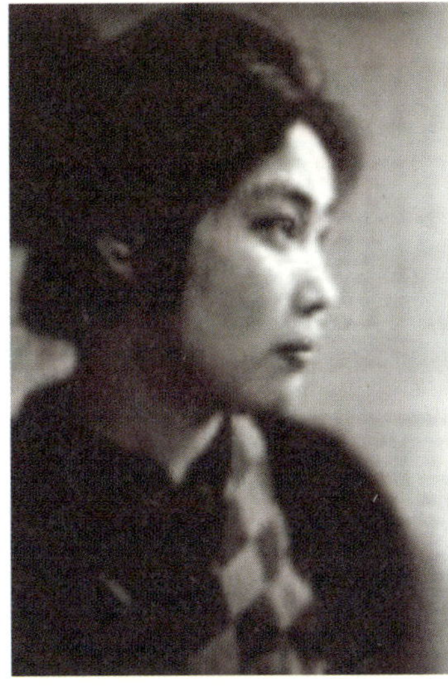

The beautiful young courtesan has returned as a spirit to haunt those responsible for her death. She glances over her shoulder, looking suspiciously out of the corners of her spooky red eyes.

It is printed with soft, watercolour-like tones and fine bokashi shading making it an eerie and unsettling portrait.

The image has the wonderful 1920's aesthetic that adapts accepted print making conventions while acknowledging the ukiyo-e portrait genre.

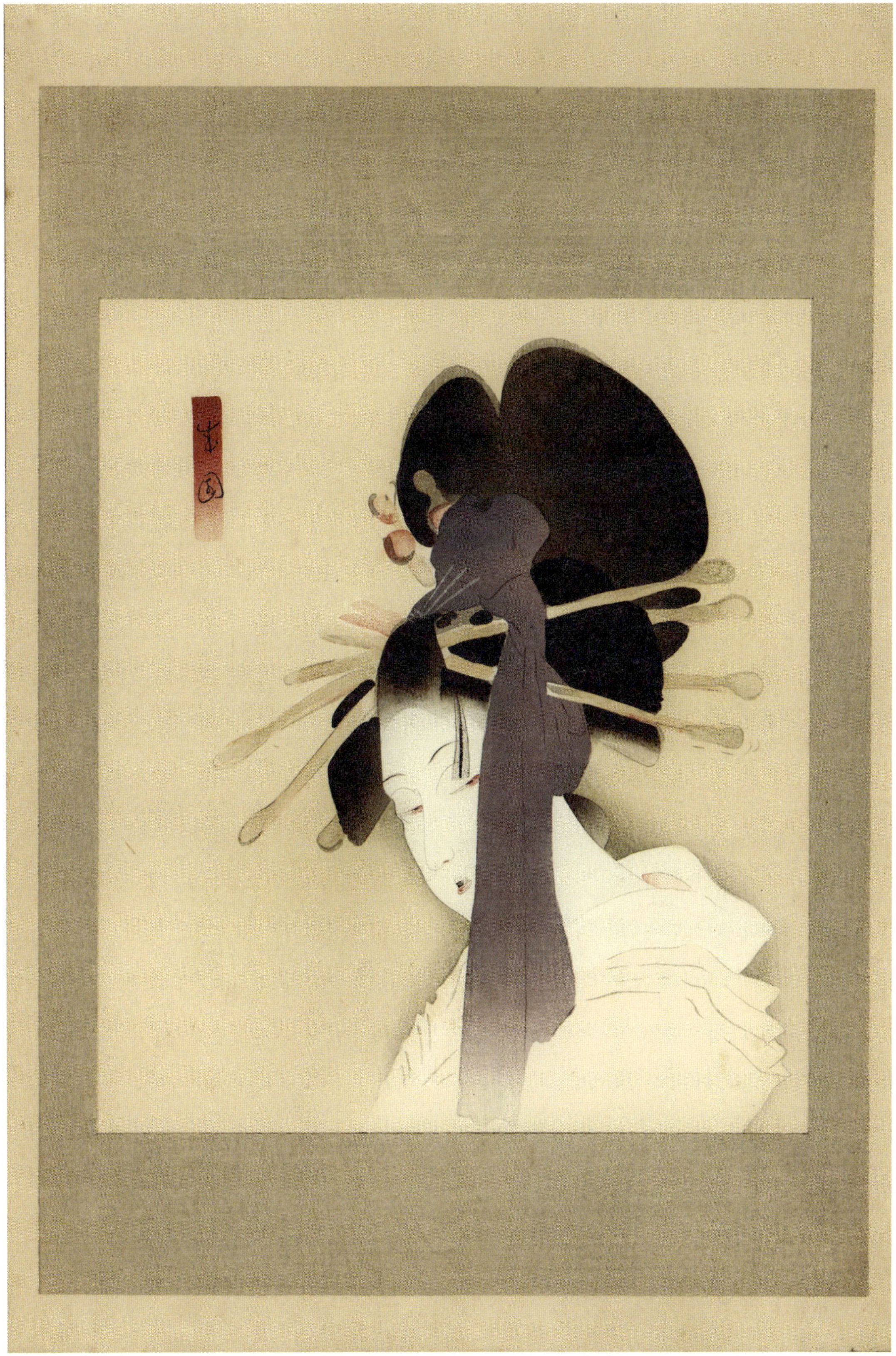

Maseo Ebina (1913 - 1980)

We have already touched on the other great classic story - *The Tale of Genji*. Now is the time to look in a bit more detail. It was written in 54 chapters and is one of the earliest and greatest works of Japanese literature. In fact it is the first example of the novel form.

Created during the Heian Period (early 11th century) by the female writer Murasaki Shikibu, *The Tale of Genji* explores trials of love, lust, patronage, and loyalty through the main character Prince Genji, a young man learned in speech, arts, manners and music. Led by his heart, Genji courts various 'beauties' and the story explores relationships of men and women of high and low status.

Print 26 - '*Perpetual Summer*'

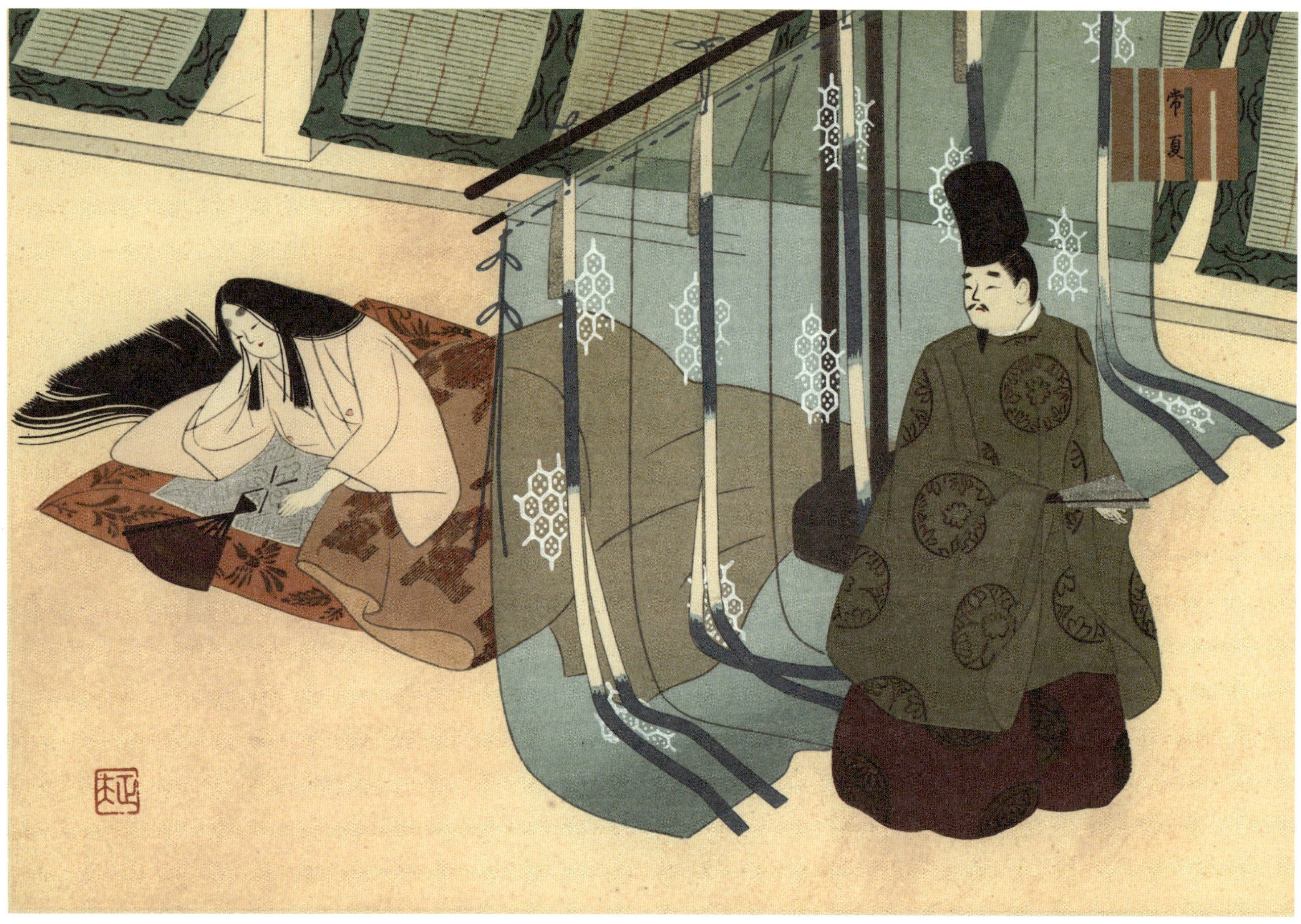

This *Tale of Genji* series was released in a limited deluxe edition of only 200 sets in 1953. Almost unbelievably in the box set notes it says that an average of fifty to sixty separate printing operations were performed to create each design, with some requiring up to one hundred. The prints have the Genji motif, but every one is slightly different, indicating the number of the chapter.

Ebina's imagery is based on the Kano School style of painting that originated in the 15th century. As we have already seen it is typified by elevated, flattened perspectives and simplified figures. The prints have a rich colour palette accented with metallic silver and/or gold. Most of the scenes are set in and around Genji's palace so we see blinds swaying in the breeze and the stream in the grounds.

Print 31 - *'Makibashira'*

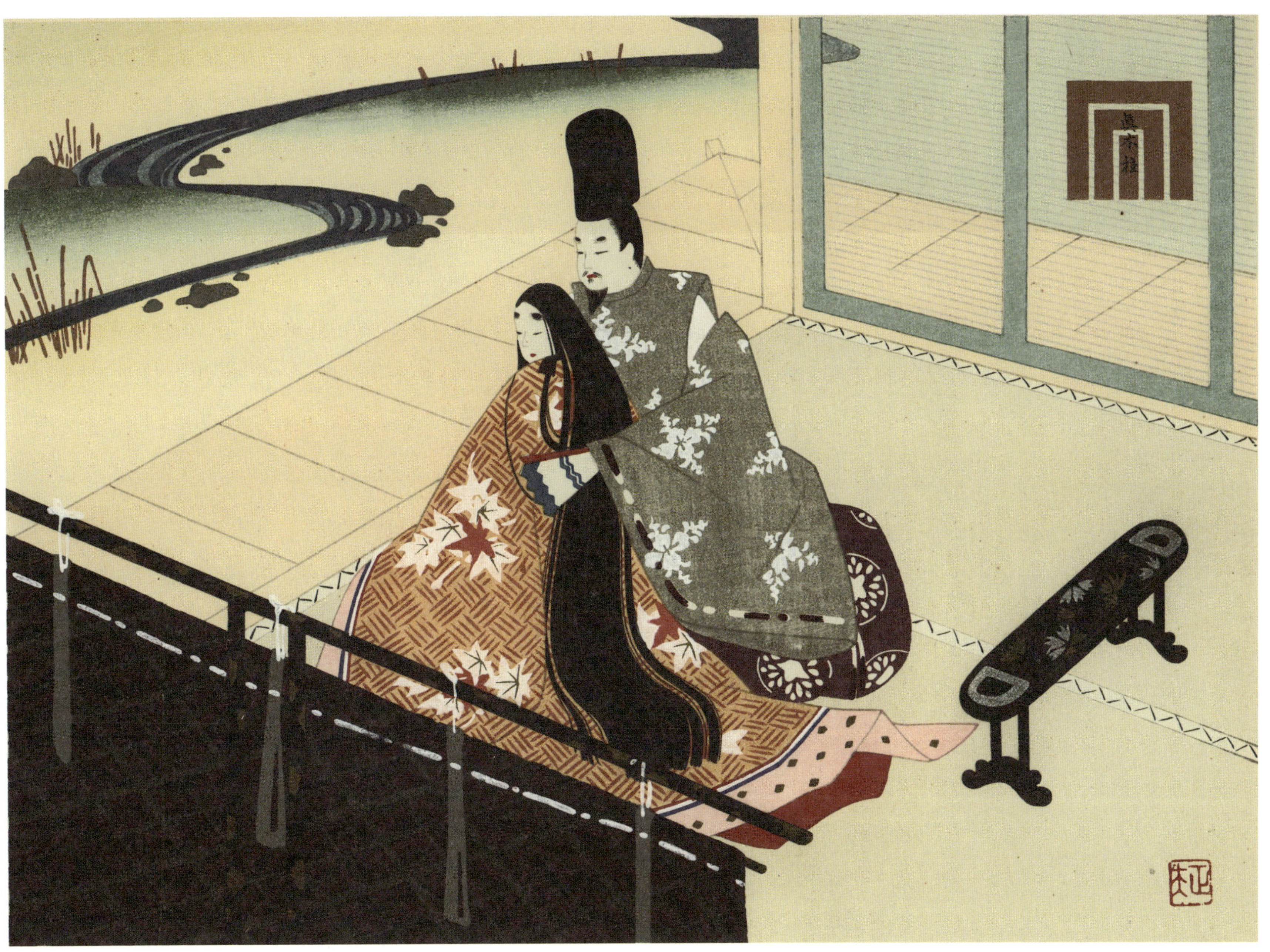

Print 36 - *'Kashiwagi'*

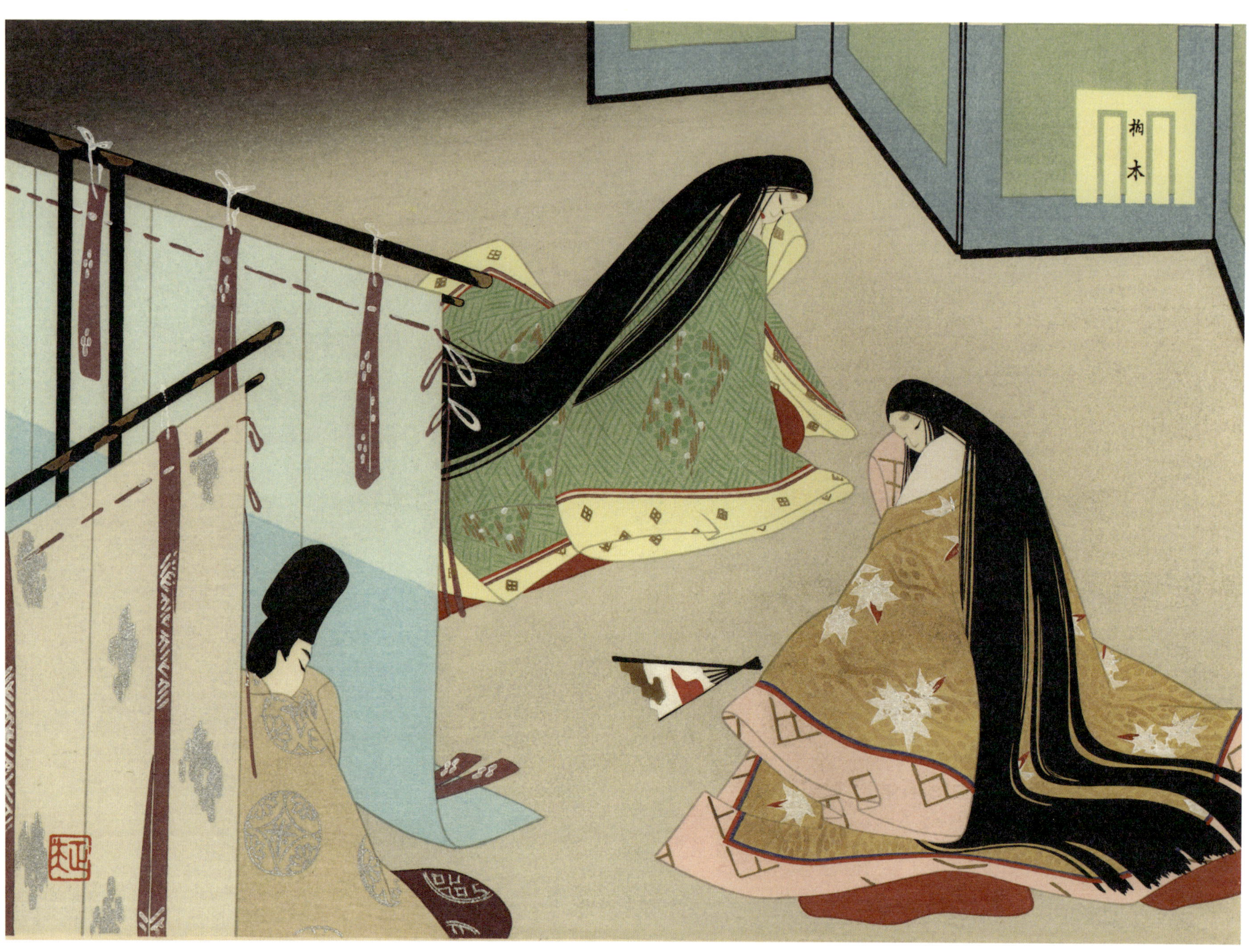

Print 8 - *'Hana-No-En'*

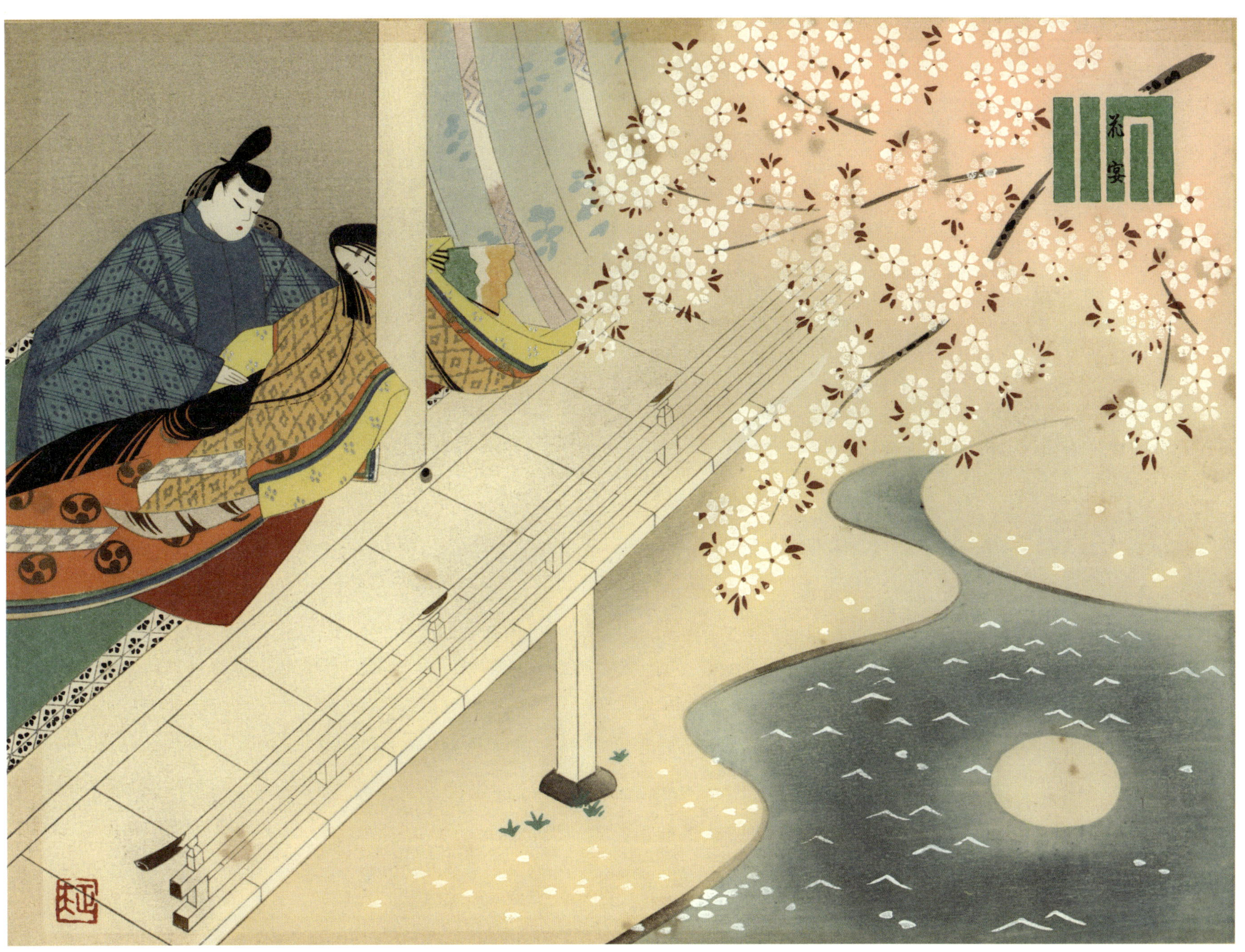

Print 25 - *'Hotaru (The Fireflies)'*

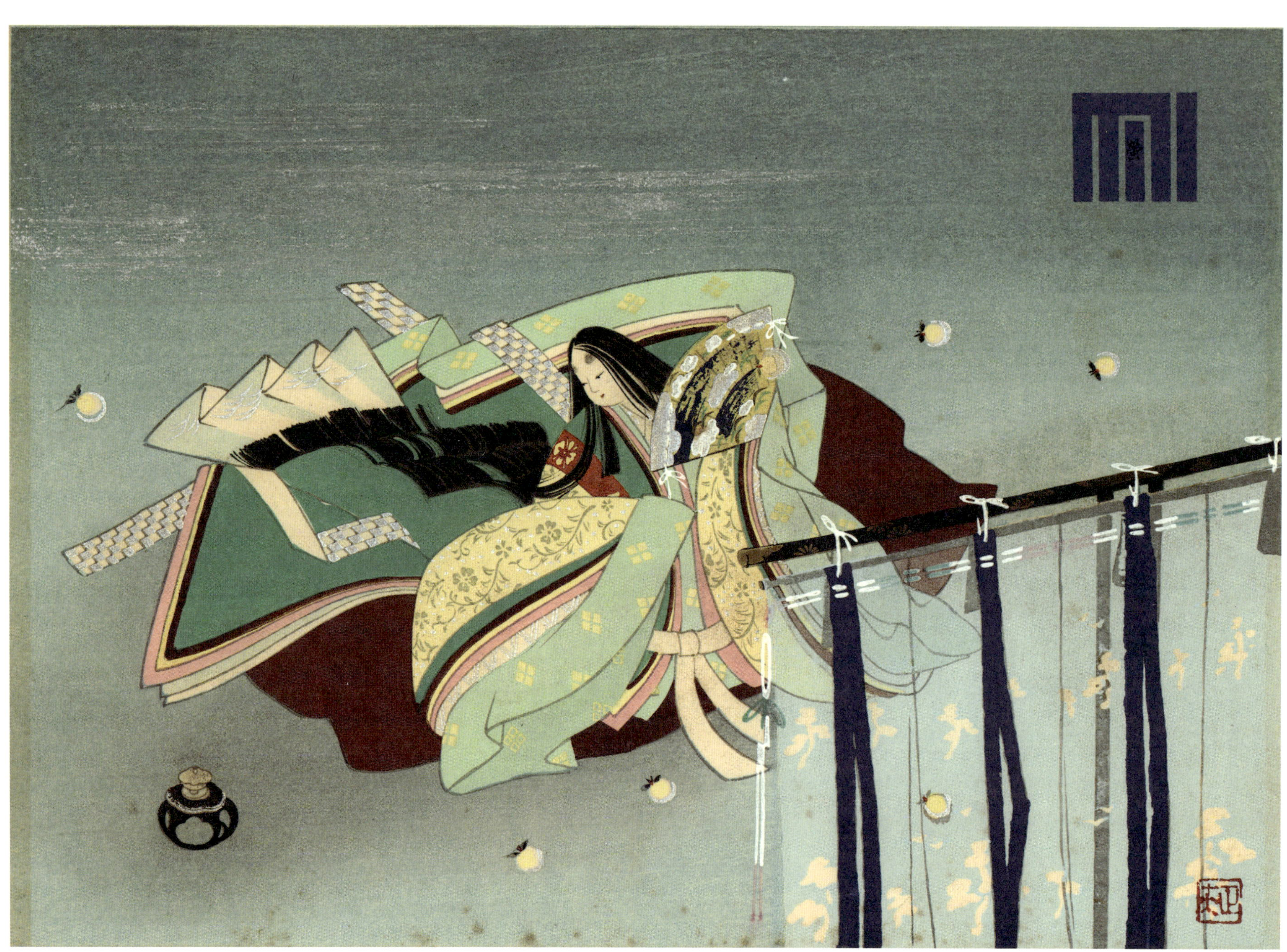

Print 21 - *'The Girls'*

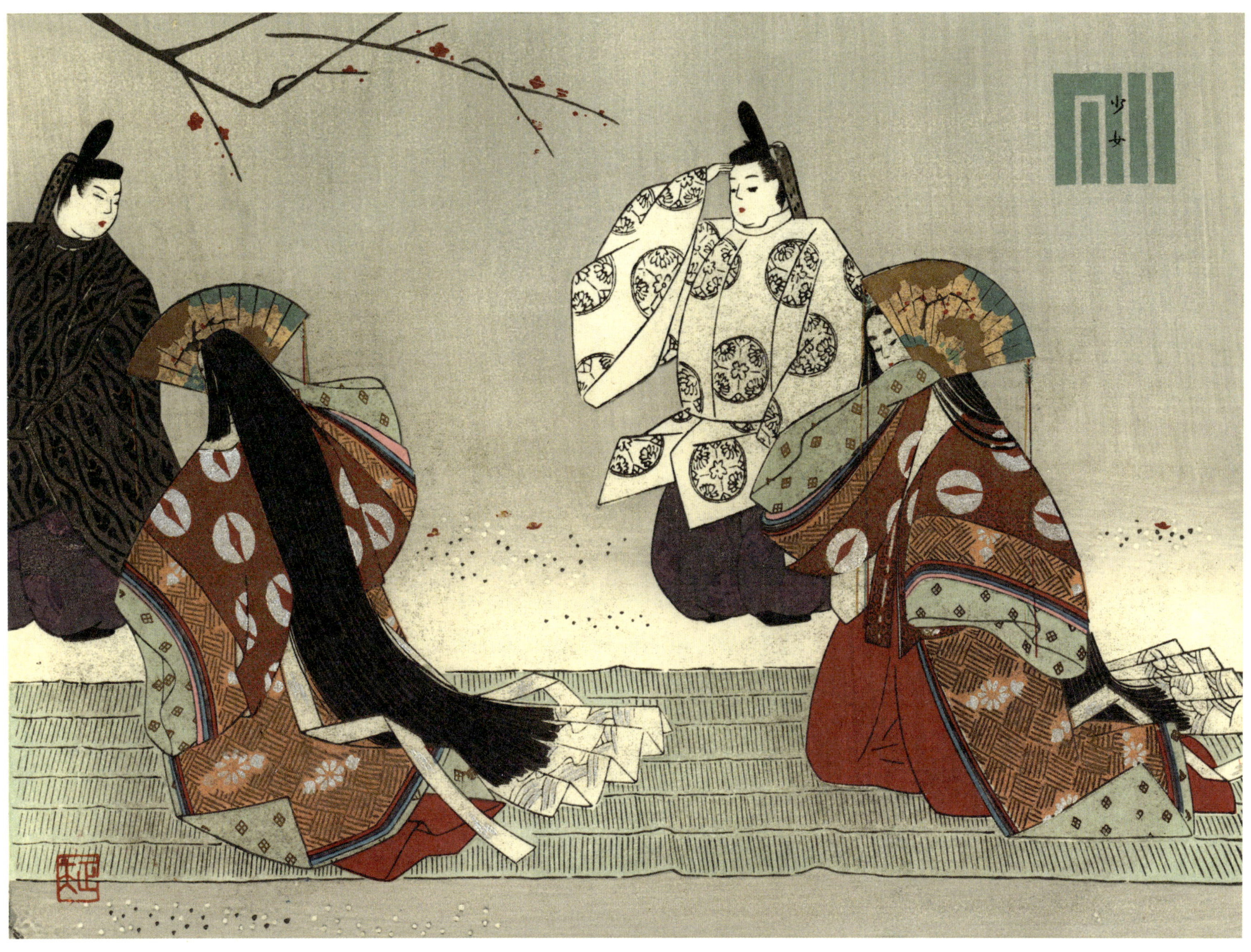

Print 34 - *'Wakana (Young Fresh Greens) Part 1'*

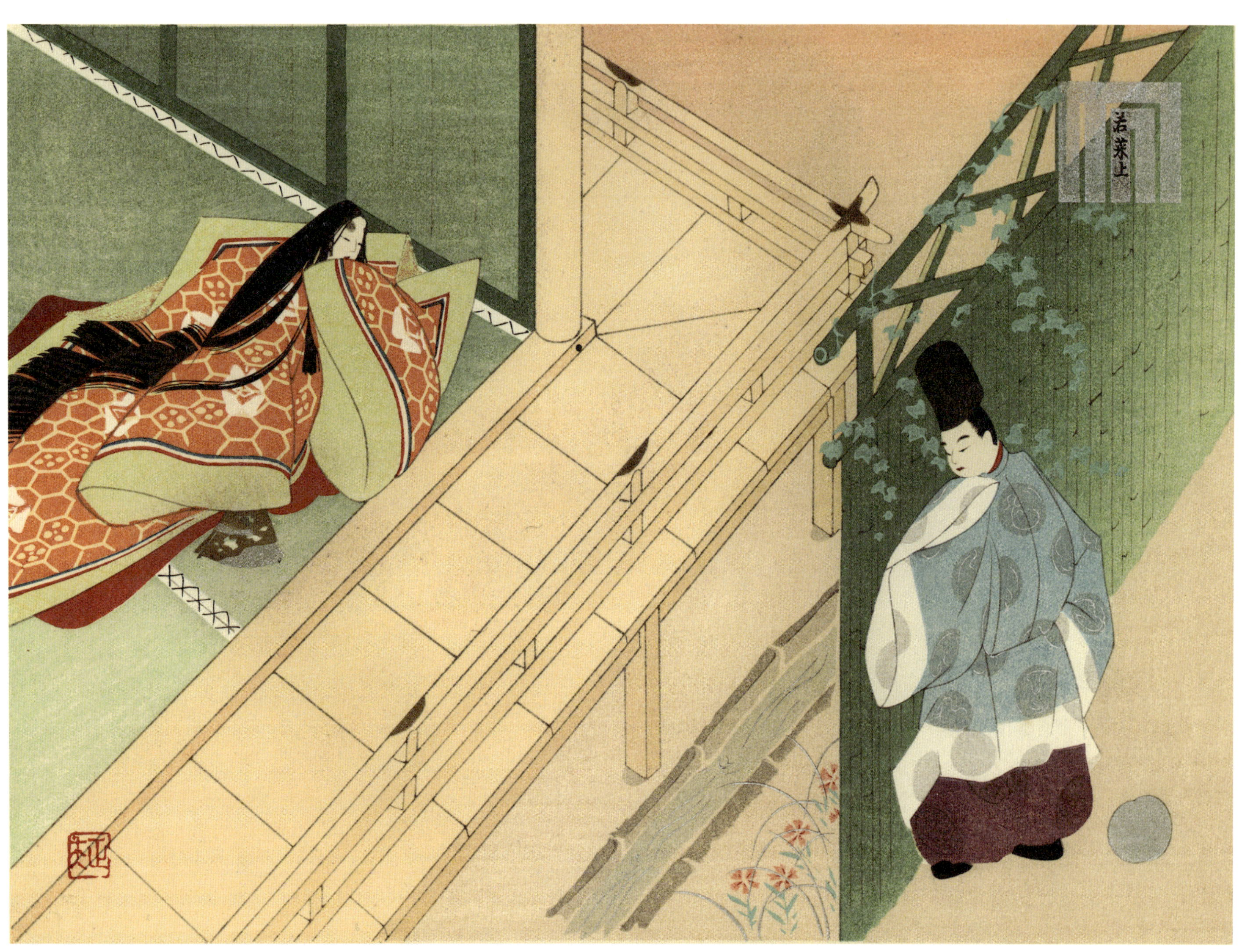

These prints were definitely designed with the foreign market in mind. If you acquire a print from the series it is likely that it will be in its original mount. This includes a description of the scene on a thin cover page printed in English as well as Japanese. This text here is for *'Wakana (Young Fresh Greens)'* to the left.

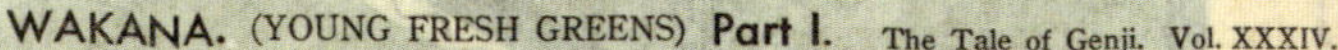

WAKANA. (YOUNG FRESH GREENS) **Part I.** The Tale of Genji. Vol. XXXIV.

From December of Prince Genji's 39th year to March of his 41st.
Shows Kashiwagi seeing Onna-Sanno-Miya with rapt admiration at a football game.

After his visit to Prince Genji's mansion at Rokujō, Sujakuin wanted to enter the priesthood since his chronic disease worsened. His only worry was about the future course of his favourite Onna-Sanno-Miya. Both Kashiwagi and Hotaru-hyōbukyō-no-Miya desired to win over her heart, but Sujakuin wished to place her under the care of Prince Genji.

Toward the end of this year, the womanhood ceremony of Onna-Sanno-Miya was solemnly observed. After this, Sujakuin suddenly renounced the world. The surprised Prince Genji made a rush to his home and was asked by him to take good care of Onna-Sanno-Miya.

On the twenty-third of the following January, a celebration of Genji's fortieth year took place at his mansion at Rokujō. As a gift, Tamakatsura presented him with young fresh greens.

About the tenth of February, Prince Genji invited Onna-Sanno-Miya to his mansion at Rokujō. Out of respect to Sujakuin, Prince Genji treated her with due courtesy. This naturally led to his frequent visits and stoppage for the night in her room.

Murasaki-no-Uye felt jealous of her, but the sight of innocent Onna-Sanno-Miya immediately melted her ill feelings toward her.

Oborozukiyo-no-Naishi who had attented on Sujakuin came back to her old home as Sujakuin confined himself to a temple. Prince Genji made a personal visit to her and made friends with her after a separation of more than ten years.

In the summer months, Akashi-no-Himegimi became conceived and returned to the mansion at Rokujō from the Imperial Palace. Murasaki-no-Uye took this occasion of inquiring after her, and seized a chance to see Onna-Sanno-Miya as well. The two women could easily throw off reserve.

After the tenth of March, next year, Akashi-no-Himegimi gave birth to a boy baby. Hearing of this, Akashi-Nyūdō thought that there no longer existed anything to worry about. Probably for this reason, he renounced the world by going God knows where.

This happened on a sunny March day. Kashiwagi, Hotaru-Hyōbukyō-no-Miya and others were playing foot-ball at Genji's mansion at Rokujō. Kashiwagi, who fondly loved Onna-Sanno-Miya, happened to be looking toward her room. A cat came running out of her room. The cord from the neck of the cat was stretched tight, and consequently the bamboo screen was pulled up. Her room was there fore to be seen. Onna-Sanno-Miya who was casting her eyes into the garden standing near the verandah was indeed beautiful. Kashiwagi stared at her with rapt admiration.

若菜上

蹴鞠の時、女三宮の美しさに見とれている柏木

源氏三十九才の十二月から四十一才の三月迄

朱雀院は、源氏の邸宅の六条院へ御幸の後、持病が重くなられたので、出家しようとされた。しかし、鍾愛の女三宮の身の振り方がきまらないのが、唯一の心残りだった。柏木も蛍兵部卿宮も、この宮を手に入れたく思っていたが、朱雀院は源氏に一任しようとされた。

その年の暮、女三宮の裳着の儀式が盛大に行なわれた後、突如、朱雀院は出家された。源氏が驚いてかけつけると、女三宮をよろしく頼むとのことだった。

翌年正月二十三日、源氏の四十賀が、六条院で賑やかに行なわれた。玉鬘は、みずみずしい若菜を源氏に献上した。

二月十日頃、源氏は女三宮を六条院へ迎えた。朱雀院への手前、女三宮を鄭重にもてなし、自然、その部屋に泊ることも多かった。紫上はそれをねたましく思ったが、無邪気な女三宮を見ては、心のもつれも解けるのだった。

朱雀院が寺にこもられたため、朧月夜内侍も里へ帰って来た。源氏はひそかに訪れ、十数年来の旧交を温めた。

夏の頃、明石姫君は懐妊され、六条院に下って来られた。紫上は姫君を見舞い、ついでに女三宮にも対面したが、二人は直ちにうち解けることができた。

翌年の三月十日すぎ、明石姫君は男の御子を安産された。その知らせを受けた明石入道は、今は何一つ思い残すこともなくなったので、山へ入り行方知れなくなった。

三月の空はうららかだった。柏木や蛍兵部卿宮などが、源氏の邸内で、蹴鞠の遊びをしていた。女三宮を恋慕する柏木が、宮の部屋の方を見ていると、飼い猫が部屋の中からとび出して来た。猫をくくった紐がぴんと張り、御簾が引き上げられたので、室内が見通された。縁がわ近く立って外を眺めていた女三宮の姿は美しかった。柏木は、その美しさに恍惚として見とれた。

源氏物語　第卅四帖

UNKNOWN ARTIST - 20th Century

These 20th century fan prints are also inspired by *The Tale of Genji* narrative - but not dated and the artist is unknown. As with **Ebina** there are silver and gold metallic applications but used in a much bolder and almost abstract way, with flecks overlaying the printed image.

On the first fan, 'beauties' are relaxing in the palace garden with a child, while another splashes around in the stream.

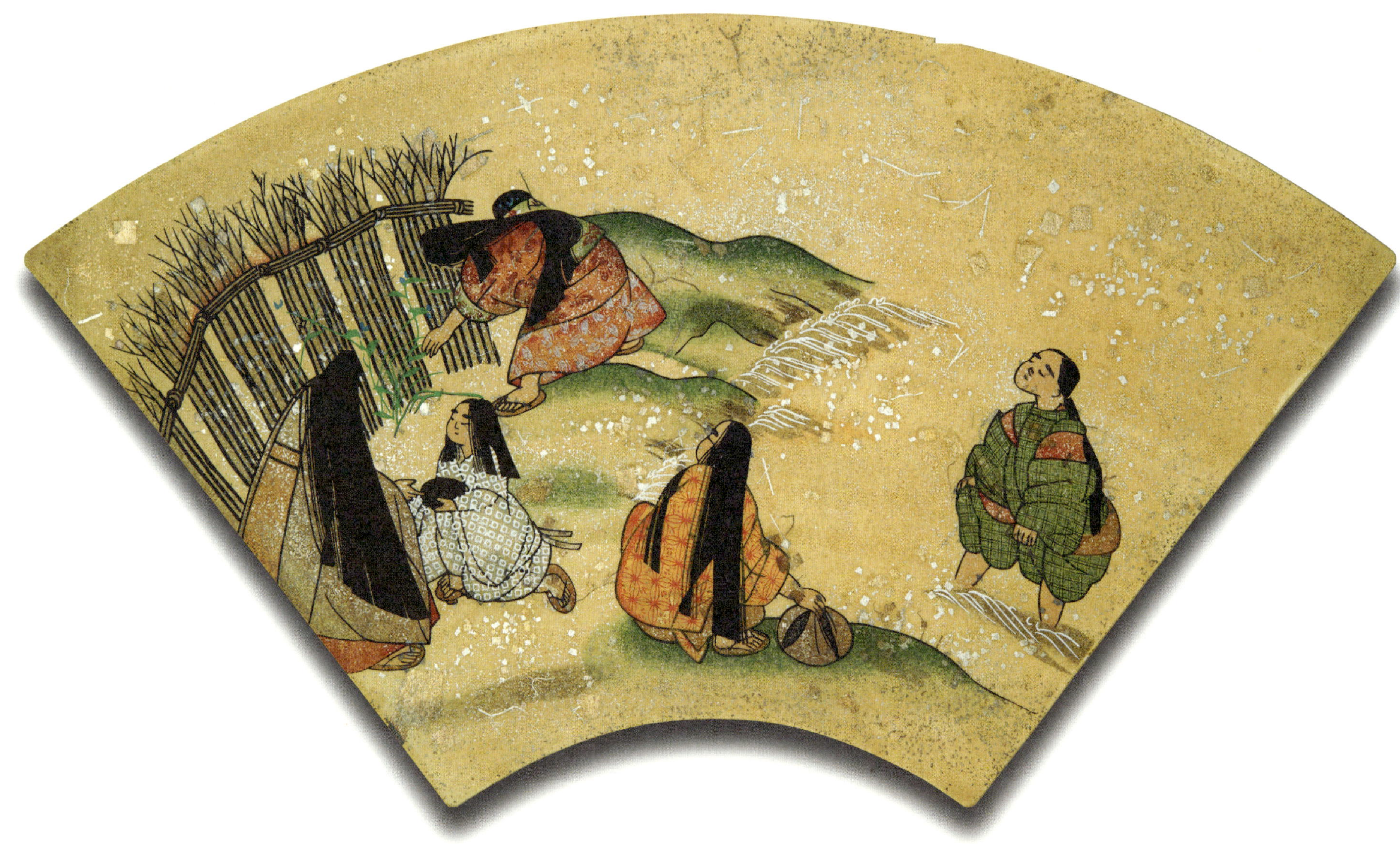

I don't know which individual stories they illustrate but the second seems a languid summery scene with 'beauties' under a tree near an out-house with Genji watching. The stream is hinted at in the background.

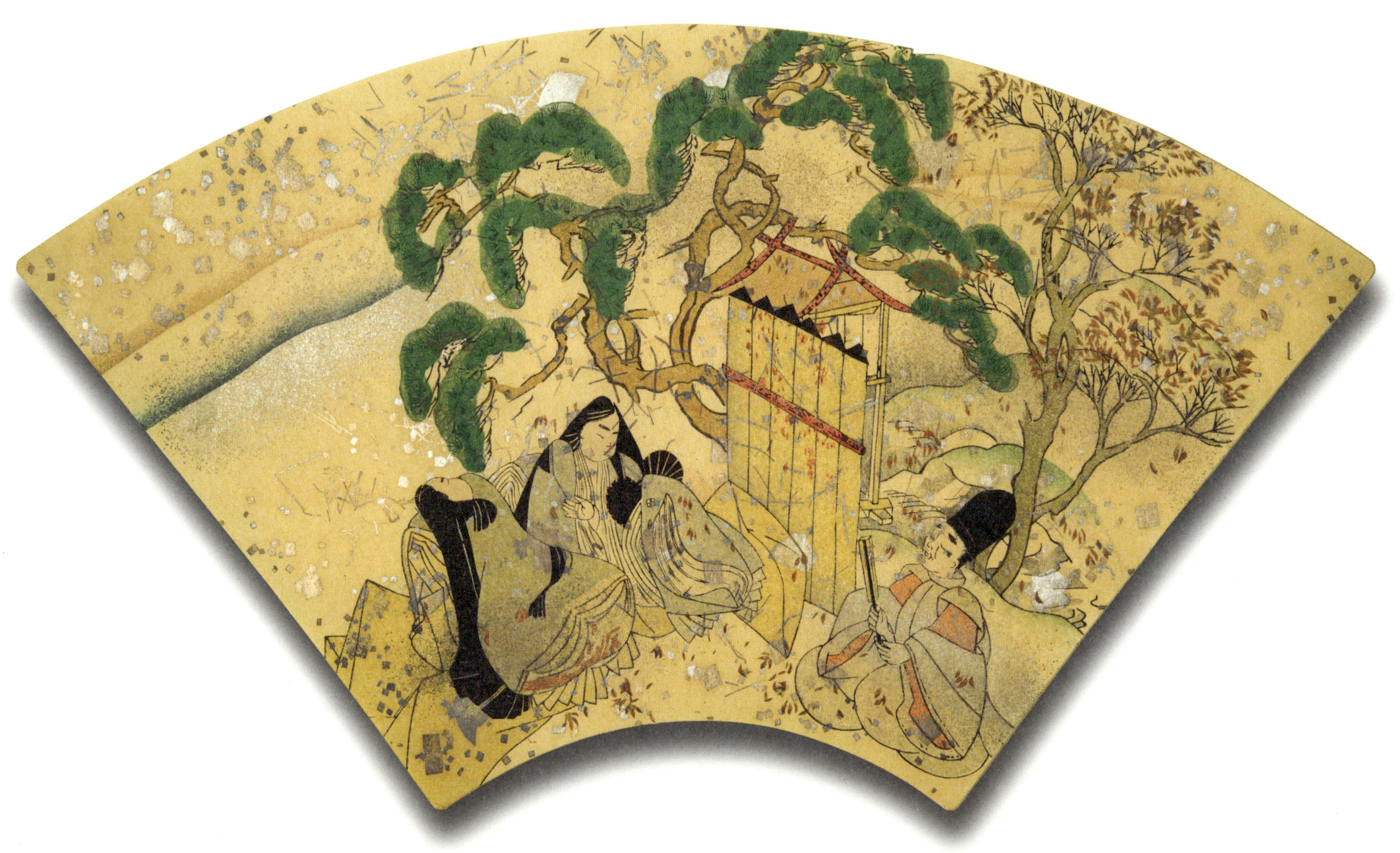

UNKNOWN ARTIST - 20th Century

I don't know the artist or the date of this set of four strange images. They appear to tell a tale, like in a storyboard showing two bizarre lovers coming together - consumed with passion.

They are ink drawings on thin paper, indicating that they could be sumi preparations that were never used to make woodblocks. What is odd about them is that they depict the worm damage that afflicts so many wonderful prints. The images appear eaten away at the edges and have holes (all drawn) at various random places, obscuring the action. I really like them.

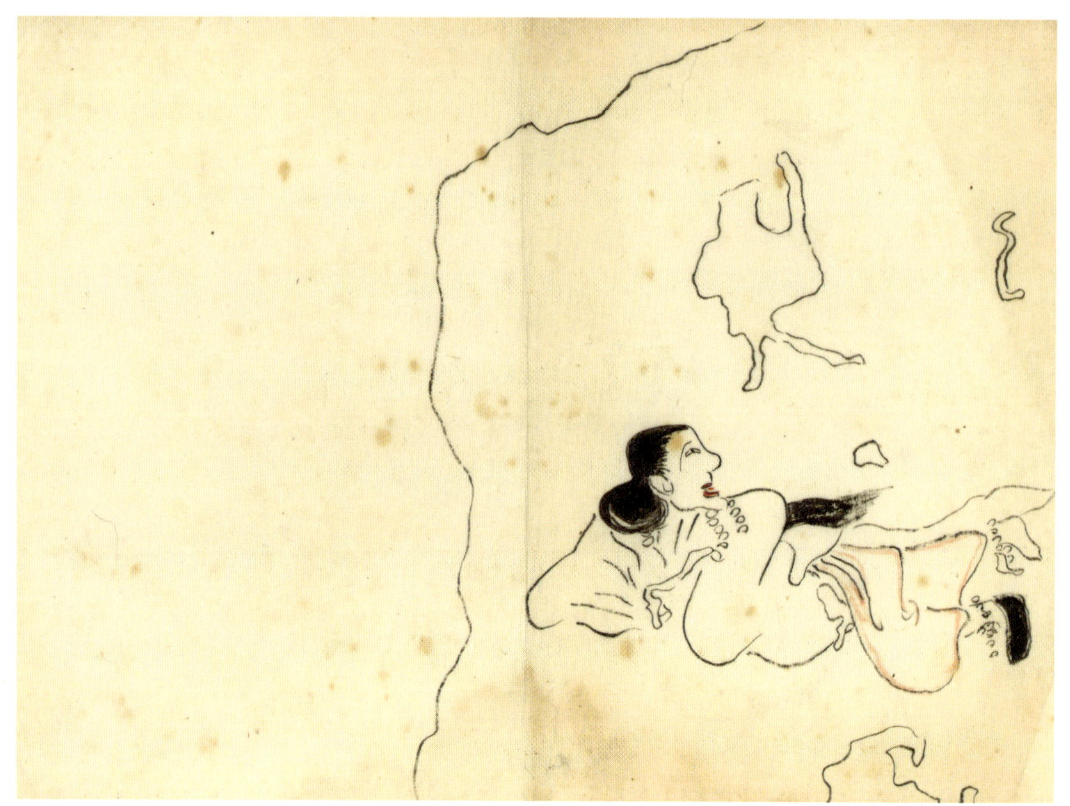

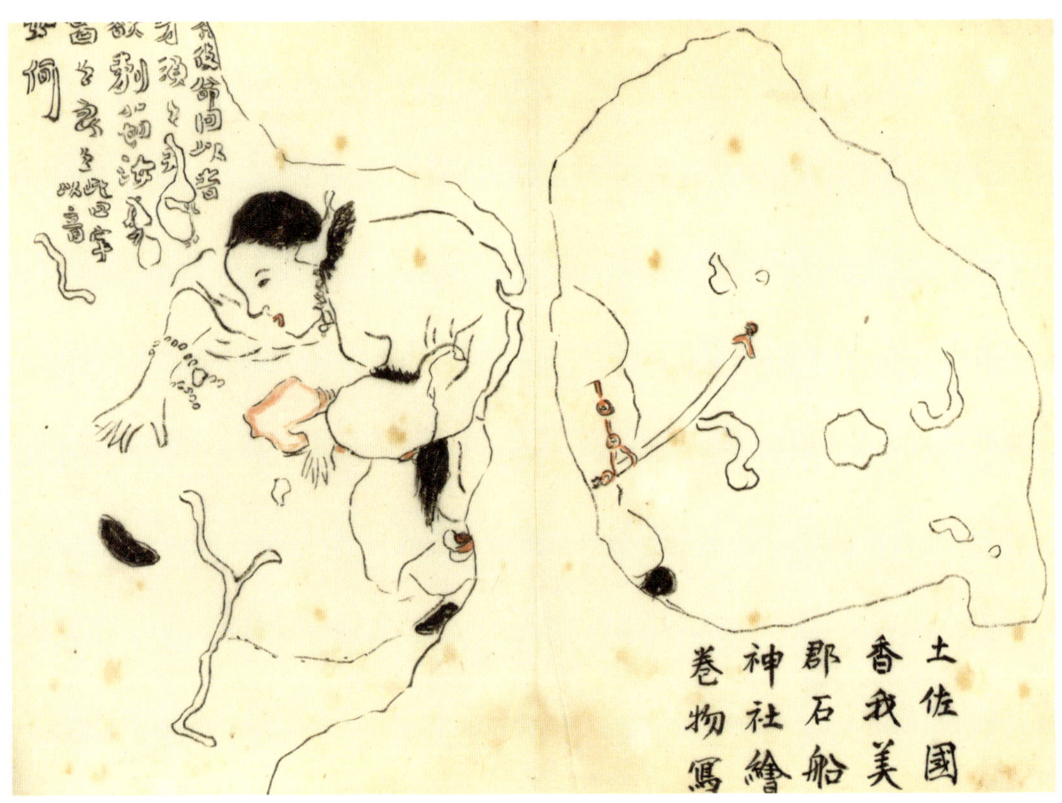

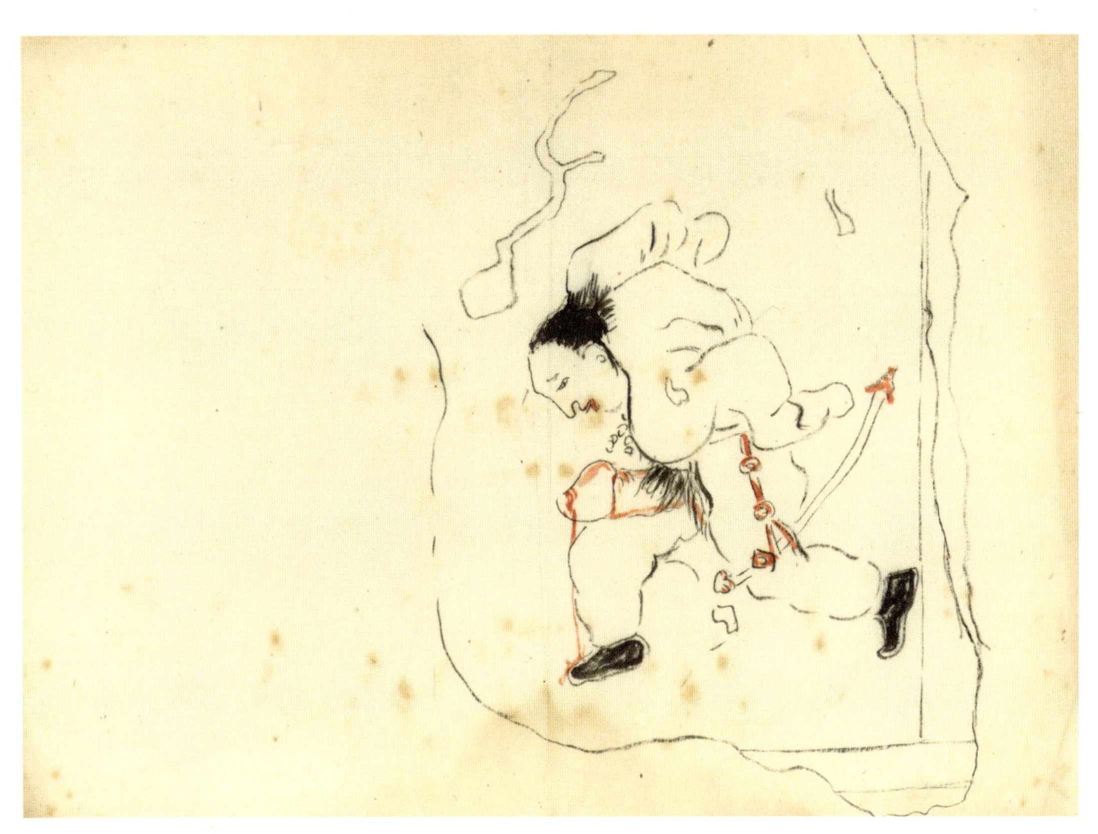

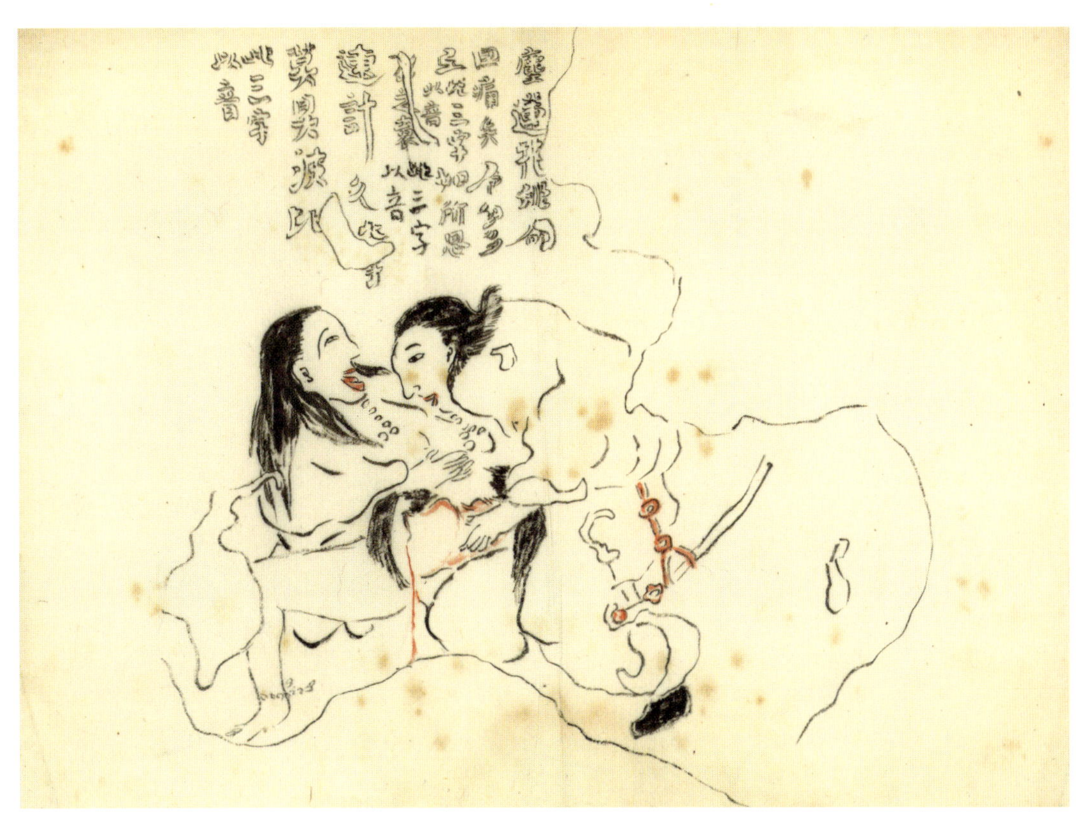

Two UNKNOWN ARTISTS - 20th Century

'A Woman Wearing a Hat' seems very Western influenced while being in the tradition of the Japanese portrait. I like the unapologetic directness and confidence.

It is though known to be from a creative print movement that began in the early part of the twentieth century called **Sosaku hanga**. Unlike the traditional collaborative woodblock printing process the movement emphasised artist involvement in all aspects of the creative process, to be the sole creator of the work. This gained popularity following World War II, earning international recognition.

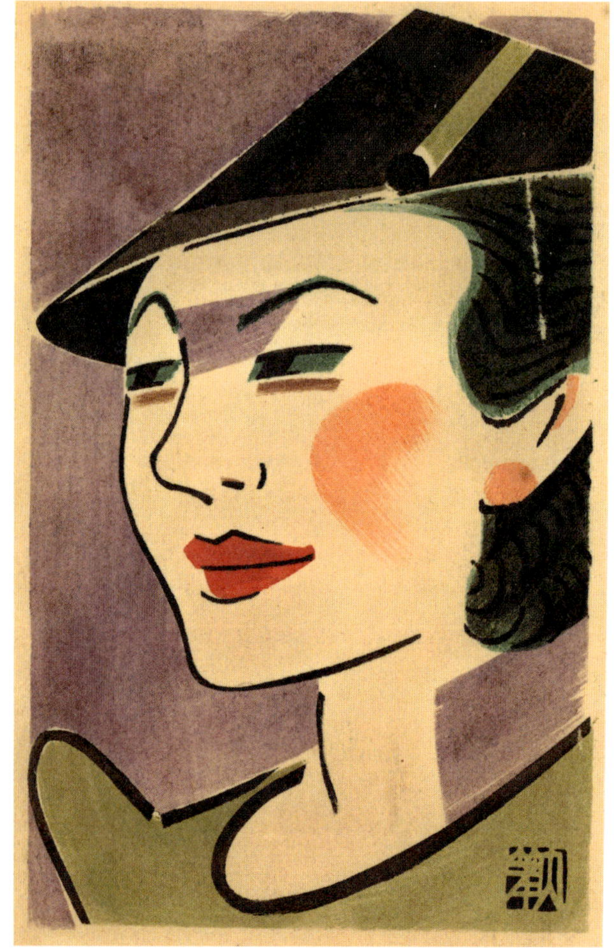

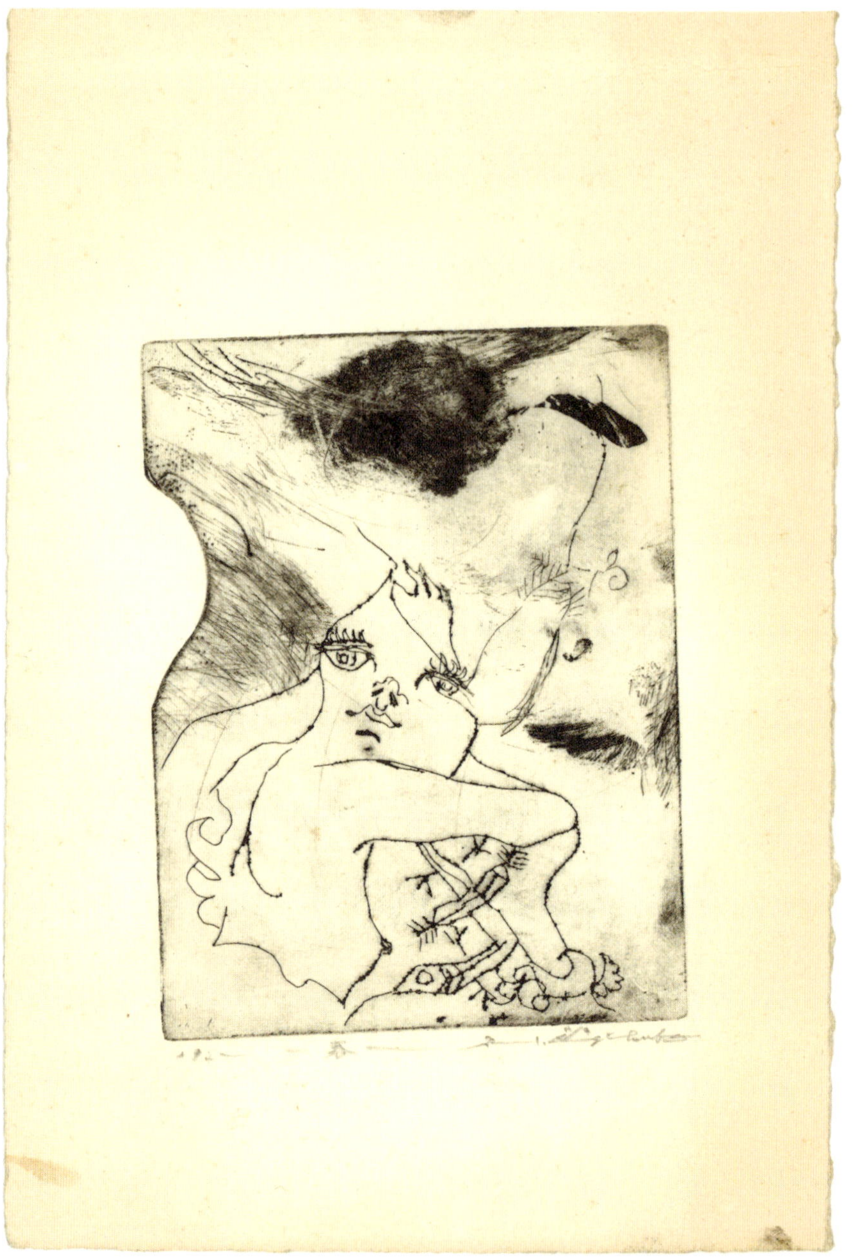

This is an etching but I can't quite make out who it is by, although the date is probably 1992. It is called a *'spring picture'* so the artist had shunga in mind.

I love the delicacy, the spontaneous nature of the artwork with its scratchy shading. I see the influence of Paul Klee - the fishy doodling and taking a line for a walk

I'm intrigued by the odd shape of the etching plate and the way in which it is printed in a rather wonky fashion - not very Japanese!

Hiroshi Nishikiori 1966 -

In the late 20th century cartoon books became popular. These manga had origins in The Floating World - **Hokusai** manga.

Anime is the animated version of manga, popular with adults as well as children. This painted animation cel for an individual frame is from a TV series *I'm Gonna be an Angel* (1999) authored by **Nishikiori** for Studio Pierrot.

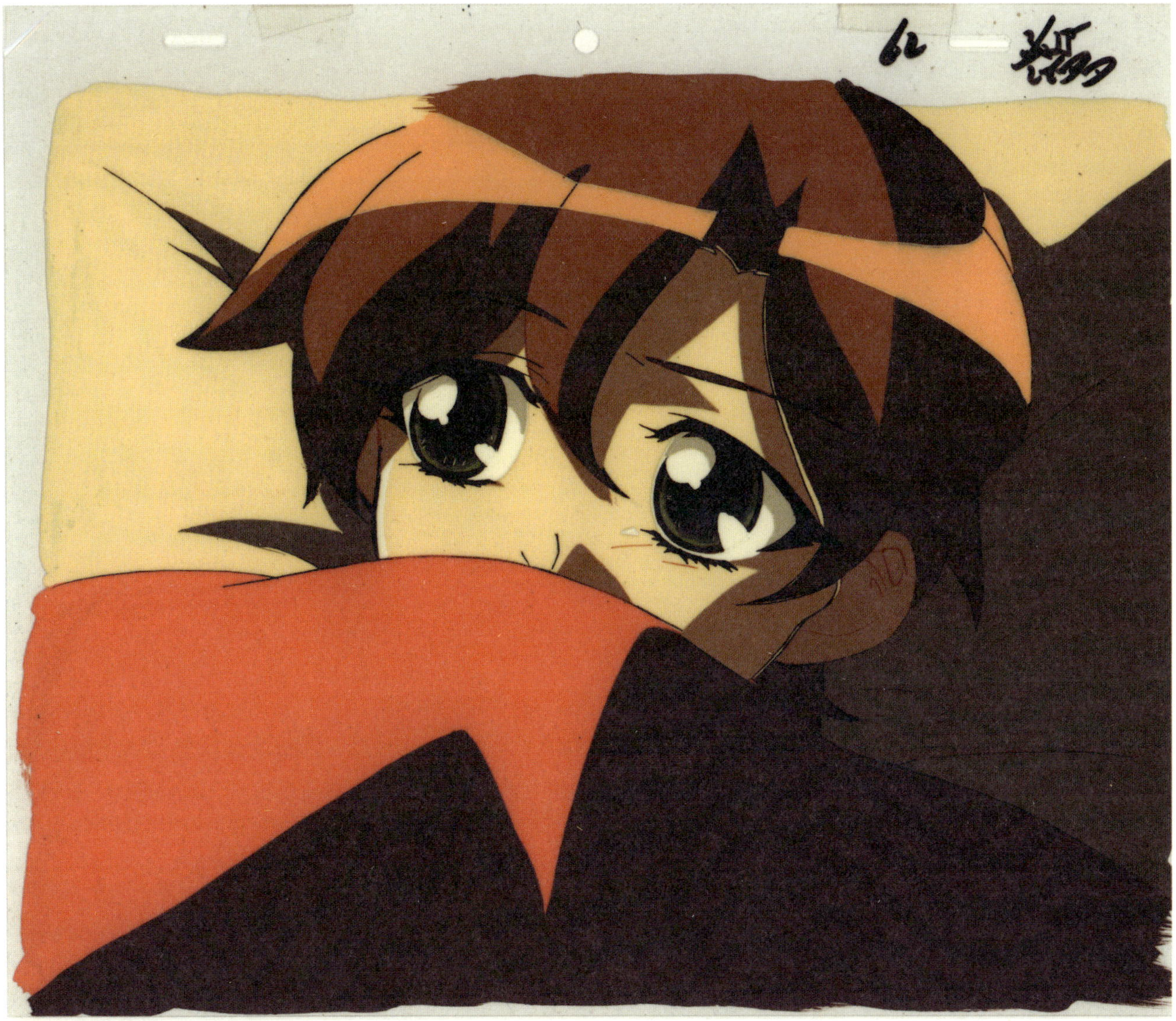

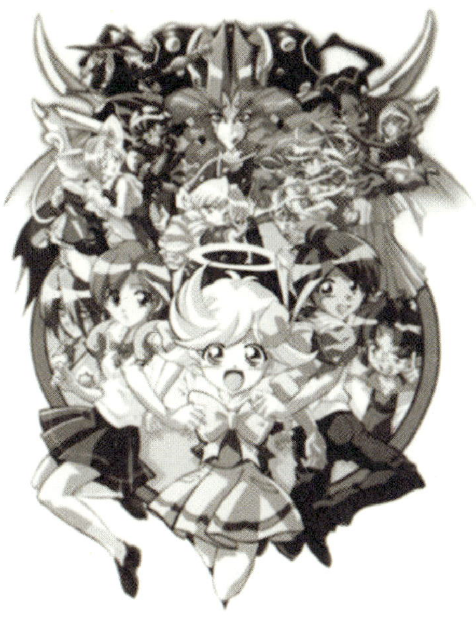

Cutesy childlike characters with big eyes are the thing with both manga and anime.

That's not the case with the work of **Shohei Otomo** (which I don't have). His ball-point-pen drawings subvert the genre, his women strong and defiant, their eyes hidden behind glasses - broken or not. Thoroughly modern bijin-ga!

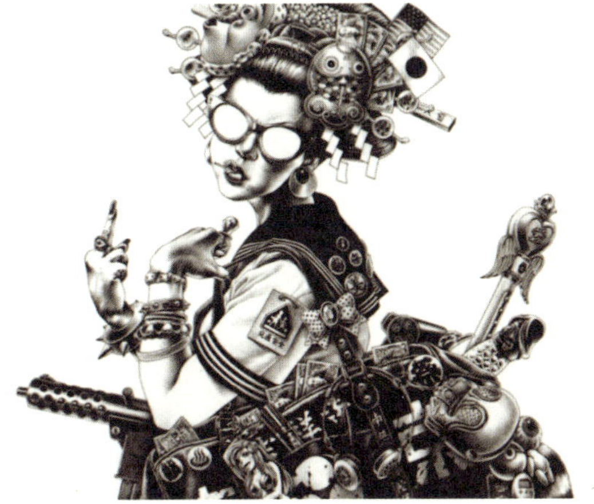

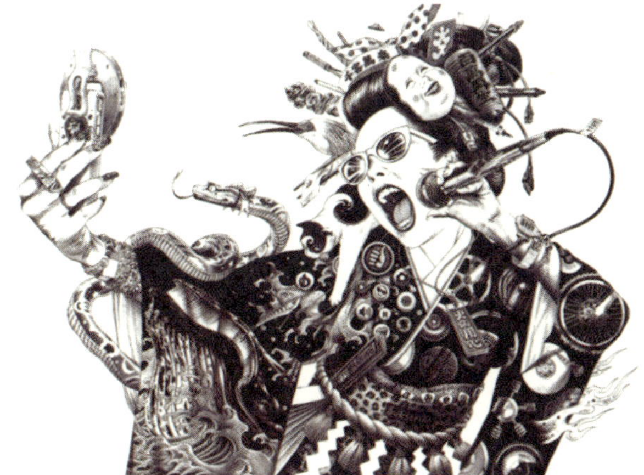

In coming to the end of the journey through my collection I began thinking 'Where is all this leading?' 'What's the ending?' It all seemed to be fizzling out, just as the art seemed to lack any real substance around the middle of the 20th century. The country so decimated by the 2nd World War had apparently, at least in the pictorial arts, lost it's aesthetic energy. All that was left was Shin hanga, Manga and erotic art that was prurient, not really reflecting the complexities of Japanese society.

Hashiguchi GOYO (1880-1921)

Then I was reminded of this extraordinary portrait by **Hashiguchi Goyo** considered perhaps one of the greatest 20th Century Japanese artists. **Goyo** died unexpectedly in 1921 at age forty-one so his output was limited and prints rare, particularly as he insisted on limited editions.

'Beauty Applying Powder' (1918) is clearly a homage to the works of the great **Utamaro**, with **Goyo** capturing the innocent allure of this young 'beauty' in a private moment applying powder to her neck using a small mirror (or perhaps a mobile phone!). The kimono slipping off her shoulder revealing a breast is inadvertantly showing us the beautiful and erotic in parallel.

The reference back to the greatest period of Japanese art would make it a tidy image to end with, but it is more than that - because of the man himself. He was a woodblock artist for only about five years and created just fourteen original prints. As his work was created before the Great Kanto Earthquake in 1923, many of his prints and all the wood blocks were destroyed. With the permission of **Goyo**'s heirs, a couple of small commemorative runs of his prints were produced.

This special large format print of **Goyo**'s great masterwork is a rare Yuyudo published print, created in exactly the same size and with the exquisite detail of the original. They give credibility to the humble re-print, particularly as **Goyo** had been the most authentic of artisans. It is no accident that he was often called the 'Taisho Utamaro'. He studied all the great masters and the love of this work compelled him to remake them in the most stunning detail in his own studio with a staff of the best carvers and printers. One such print is the **Koryusai** on page 22..

In many ways **Goyo** gives me 'permission' to collect fine reprints alongside old originals. It seems fitting that we end this final chapter with this lovely bijin-ga. Although I do have a few things to ruminate on.

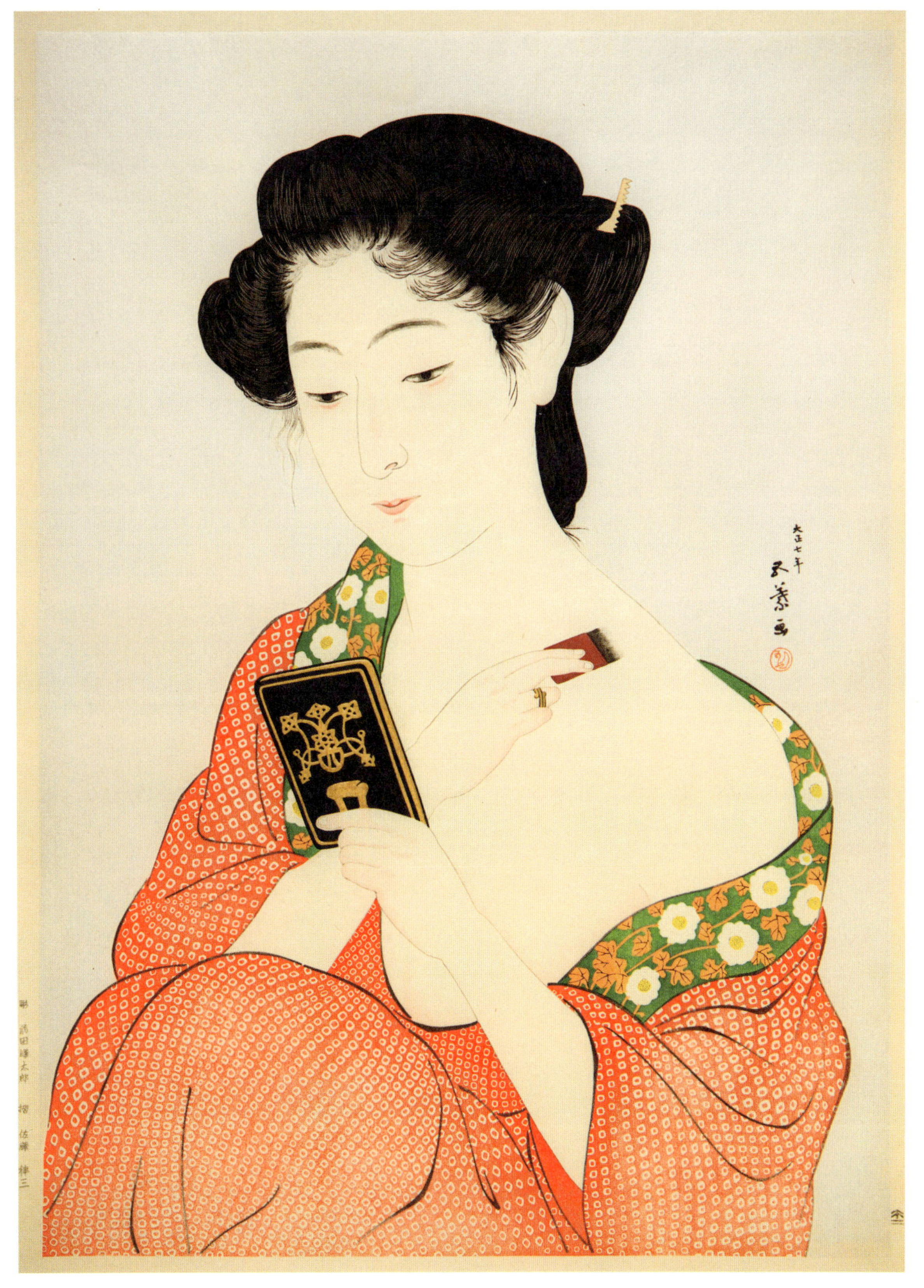
大正七年 五葉画

RUMINATIONS AFTER CHAPTER FOUR

No extras this time, just a few ruminations to wrap up.

It has been a real adventure putting together this journey through my collection of bijin-ga and shunga. I do have other wonderful prints from other sub-genres, but we can't do everything.

When I first started collecting I was drawn to the sheer beauty of the imagery, without fully understanding the social, sexual and artistic contexts. There is no point in being judgemental of the Japanese or their lifestyle any more than with my own but I'm aware many people will see the pictures in this book through the lens of 21st century Western vision.

In researching for this book I soon found myself to be an outsider looking in, to discover fascinating details about the images and culture - and some were quite disturbing.

Japanese culture is different enough now but two or three centuries ago it was even more exotic, which is why so many European artists were drawn to the extraordinary nature of the designs and the narratives they're often based on.

I love the visual exuberance of the art, the unpretentious confidence and obsessiveness of the artists. In a book that explores this it is unavoidable not to show the relationship between the predominately male artists and the female subjects. Some may see the 'objectivisation' of women, but if we go there we should consider all depictions of women in all cultures.

It is worth reiterating that the Japanese were not interested in the nude. Instead the eroticism is expressed in the use of fabric and design, posture and body language. Certainly the depiction of genitals is unavoidably ever present in shunga, but more often than not it is the male member that gets the treatment. Westerners were appalled when first confronted with such 'in your face' private parts but the problem was with the European - and the fig leaf sensibilities that are still with us today. Once over the shock of such abundance it is possible to see these images as they were by the people intended - both men and women.

I was surprised to find out the extent of the sexual activity in and around The Floating World period. The Yoshiwara was vast and it seems everyone was at it. Human nature doesn't change and no doubt such activities were enjoyed to a similar degree in other countries.

There certainly was considerable exploitation in the pleasure districts, but one should consider that the Japanese do tend to see things differently, with the concept of beautiful suffering built into the culture. Many of the more successful courtesans had high status with lives of luxury, completely at odds with the backgrounds they came from. Little can be said to justify the treatment of the women on the bottom rungs of the ladder - it is always the poorest that get the worst deal.

Nowadays the traditions that we see in the artwork have evolved into the contemporary activities we see in downtown Tokyo. In bars young women are adored by doting men of all ages - and with privacy often not an option the sex too is sometimes played out in public - as I witnessed when in Japan on another project and given privileged access not normally available for foreigners. Couples were having full-on intimacy in the bar of a club, with a play area for group activities. Mostly it was young people on a night out. All was so matter of fact that the idea of the 'buttoned up' Japanese went totally out of the window. The Floating World lives!

Many of the more liberal attitudes are now being eroded, and some for good reason. Child pornography has only recently been made illegal, although some of the restrictions are skirted around, particularly when it comes to hentai manga. Sex lives in the imagination and the Japanese have an abundance of that.

The collection this book is based on is not valuable - which is one of the reasons for doing it. Museums tend to have the best work although there are many affluent connoisseurs who have museum quality collections. Mine is a jumble of good, indifferent, startling and sumptuous - my choices, which probably reflect my eclectic nature.

I hope you have enjoyed me sharing it with you.

Bob Bentley

GLOSSARY

Anime: animated Film & TV interpretation of Manga
Beauty: another common term for bijin
Bijin: beautiful people (women)
Bijin-ga or **Bijinga**: pictures of beautiful people (women)
Bunraku: puppet theatre telling popular stories
Courtesan: woman working in the sex trade
Daiymo: Feudal lord
Edo: renamed Tokyo in 1869 when it became capital
Geisha: female entertainer - not normally in the sex trade
Kabuki: popular theatre with all male actors
Kuchi-e: frontispieces for books in Mejji period with 'beauties'
Kyoto: The Imperial capital until 1869
Manga: late 20th century comic magazines.
Nagasaki: Southern port with a Dutch trading station
Oiran: top ranking courtesan
Samurai: officer caste of military nobility
Shin hanga: early 20th century reinterpretation of woodblock art
Shogun: Military dictator (not ceremonial Emperor)
Shunga: erotic images 'spring pictures'
Sosaku hanga: as shin hanga but with the artist making the print
Takaido Road: main route between Edo and Kyoto
The Floating World: pleasure seeking life-style during Edo period
Ukiyo-e: pictures of The Floating World
Wakashu: adolescent male in kabuki and the sex trade.
Yoshiwara: the 'pleasure district' outside Edo

REFERENCES

IMAGES FROM THE FLOATING WORLD
Richard Lane - Alpine Fine Arts Collection

SHUNGA - SEX AND PLEASURE IN JAPANESE ART
Edited by Timothy Clark, C. Andrew Gerstle,
Aki Ishigami, Akiko Yano - The British Museum

SHUNGA - EROTIC ART IN JAPAN
Rosina Buckland - The British Museum

SEX AND THE FLOATING WORLD
Timon Screech - Reaktion Books

POEM OF THE PILLOW AND OTHER STORIES
Gian Carlo Calza - Phaidon

UKIYO-E
Gian Carlo Calza - Phaidon

CHATS ON JAPANESE PRINTS
A. Davison Ficke - T. Fisher Unwin Ltd

ACKNOWLEDGEMENTS

Philip Blakeley, Editor for Kahboom

Stephanie Howard

Rose Jones, Photographer

Fulmar Television and Film

Fuji Arts, Inc

BOB BENTLEY

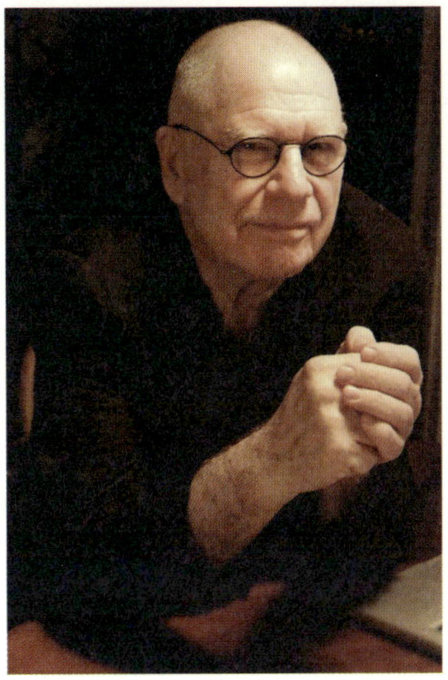

Bob Bentley is a film & Television director, as well as being the author of 'Shunga + Bijin-ga = Erotica'. This is his second book, the first being a companion piece to the feature documentary 'The Pleasure of Rope' about Kinbaku, the art of Japanese bondage (www.thepleasureofrope.com).

Bob is one of the UK's visionary directors. A BAFTA award winner with RECLUSE his work has been described as exquisite, intriguing, and beautifully crafted. His distinct style is evident across many genres and strands from his grand JESSYE NORMAN: SINGER, a definitive BBC portrait of this powerful Diva, to the elegant originality of his dance masterpiece TO A WOMAN'S HEART.

Bob entertains with eloquence, exploring subjects as diverse as Hokusai's Japan in THE GREAT WAVE to the killing fields of the American Civil War in the BATTLE OF SHILOH. Art and drama tantalise in New York with TIFFANY TOMB RAIDERS and in the very British AVAILABLE LIGHT.

As well as being a film & TV director and author, Bob Bentley is also a university lecturer and has recently returned to his first love of being a practicing artist.

www.bobbentley.co.uk

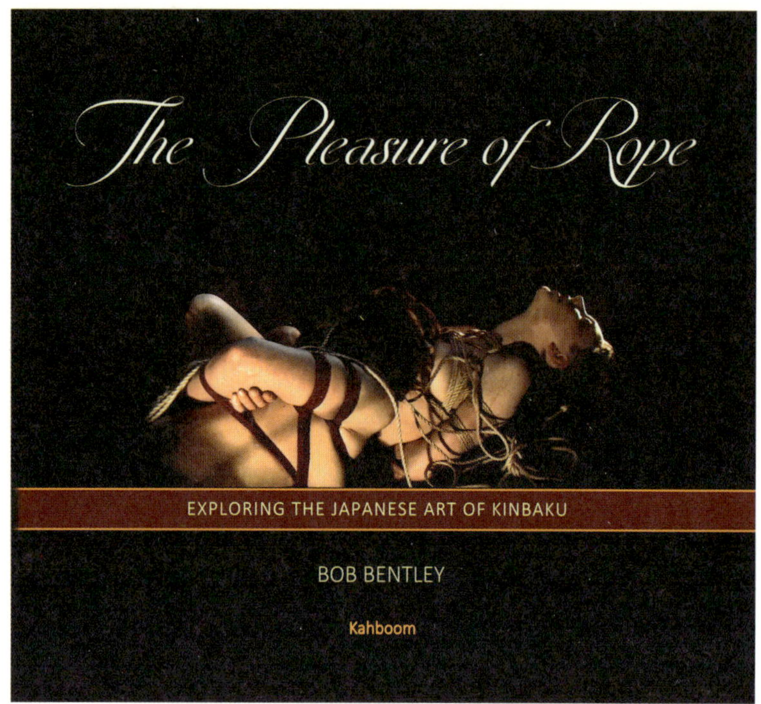

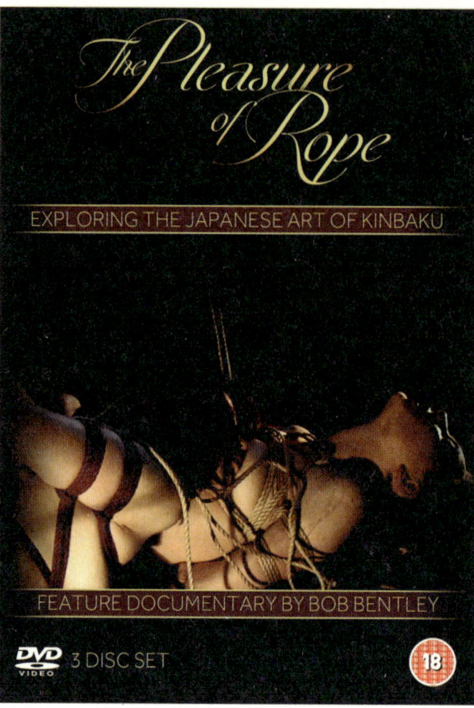

Also by Bob Bentley

The Pleasure of Rope

Exploring the Japanese Art of Kinbaku

www.thepleasureofrope.com

An amazing collection of real life bondage events which took place mostly in London and Tokyo. It features internationally famous performers including:

- Kinoko Hajime
- Akira Naka
- Midori
- Esinem
- Gestalta
- Miumi-U
- Kazami Ranki
- Osada Steve
- Nawashi Murakawa
- And many others

Hardback book ISBN 9780957627536 & 3 Disk DVD